Miracles and Prophecies
in Nineteenth-Century France

Thomas A. Kselman

Miracles &
Prophecies

in Nineteenth-Century France

RUTGERS UNIVERSITY PRESS

New Brunswick, New Jersey

Frontispiece illustration shows pilgrims at the
grotto of Lourdes, around 1900. Source:
Boissarie, *Les grandes guérisons*.

Library of Congress Cataloging in Publication Data

Kselman, Thomas Albert, 1948–
  Miracles and prophecies.

  Bibliography: p.
  Includes index.
    1. France—Religious life and customs.
  2. Catholic Church—France—History—19th
  century.   3. Miracles—History—19th century.
  4. Prophecies—History—19th century.
  I. Title.
  BX1530.K73   282'.44   82-3640
  ISBN 0-8135-0963-7   AACR2

For Claudia

Contents

Acknowledgments ix

Introduction 3

1. Folklore, Miracles, and the Church 12
   Religious Life During the French Revolution
   Healers and Healing Manuals
   Saints and Shrines

2. The Social Drama of a Miraculous Cure 37
   The Inadequacies of Secular Medicine
   The Social Drama of a Miraculous Cure
   Social Origins of the Miraculés

3. Prophecy and Public Order 60
   The Prophetic Tradition in the Ancien Régime
   Prophecy and Economic Crisis
   Prophecy and Politics in the Nineteenth Century

4. Miracles and Prophecies in Dogma and Devotion 84
   Miracles and Doctrines
   Miracles and Devotions
   Sentimentalism and Intimacy
   Suffering and Reparation
   Poverty, Simplicity, Humility

5. The Religious Revival of the Third Republic   113
   Apparitions, Pilgrimages, and Nationalism
   Religion and Royalism in the 1870s
   Prophecy and Ultramontanism

6. The Institutionalization of the Miraculous   141
   The Local Response to the Miraculous
   The Episcopal Investigation
   Development of the Cults
   Conflicts over Miracle Cults
   Church–State Conflict

7. Miracles and Modernity   189

Appendix   201

Notes   205

Bibliography   245

Index   277

Acknowledgments

I would like to thank those people who have read earlier versions of this work over the past few years, especially David Bien, William Christian, Jr., Susan Harding, John Kselman, Joseph Moody, Marvin O'Connell, Harry Paul, and Charles Tilly. The staffs at the libraries and archives where I did my research were all helpful, but I would like to single out Fr. Theodore Koehler and Brother William Fackovec of the University of Dayton's Marian Library for the personal attention they provided me. During one of my visits to Dayton I had the opportunity to talk with René Laurentin. Although we approach religious history from very different perspectives, Fr. Laurentin has been sympathetic and generous in his dealings with me. Anyone who looks through the notes of this book will quickly see how much I have relied on his compilations of documents on French Marian devotions.

This book started out as a doctoral dissertation at the University of Michigan. Since my first years in Ann Arbor Stephen Tonsor has always been a good friend and an able critic. Raymond Grew encouraged me from the time I began this project through its completion. Many of the ideas that follow emerged from our conversations together and from my reflection on his incisive comments on the early drafts of this work. I am indebted to him as well for his friendship.

My colleagues in the Department of History at the University of Notre Dame provided a congenial and stimulating environment while I made final revisions. I would also like to thank Raymond Schmandt, who first introduced me to the study of history when I was an undergraduate at St. Joseph's College in Philadelphia.

Thanks are also due to Janet Wright, Cheryl Reed, and Sandy Dewulf, who typed the manuscript, and to Michelle Burgoyne, who prepared the figures and illustrations.

Over the past ten years I have enjoyed the hospitality of Max and Marianne Scheck every summer; their generosity and kindness allowed me much valuable time to work on my manuscript. Although I do not share the beliefs of those people whom I write about, I have a great respect for the power and significance of religion. I am deeply grateful to my parents, Joseph and Rosemary Kselman, who taught me the meaning of religious belief and experience.

Claudia Kselman has always been able to convince me that she liked the previous versions of this work, even while she made innumerable suggestions for improving them. I am grateful for her tact and her knowledge, and for her love and support.

Miracles and Prophecies
in Nineteenth-Century France

For all religious phenomena, there are two traditional explanations. One— call it Voltairian, if you like—prefers to see the fact under study as the conscious work of an individual thought very sure of what it is doing. The other, on the contrary, looks rather for the expression of social forces of an obscure and profound nature; this might well be called the romantic approach. For has not one of the great services of Romanticism been its vigorous accentuation of the spontaneous in human affairs? These two kinds of interpretations are only apparently in contradiction. If an institution marked out for particular ends chosen by an individual will is to take hold upon an entire nation, it must also be borne along by the deeper currents of the collective consciousness. The reverse is perhaps also true: for a rather vague belief to become crystallized in a regular rite, it is of some importance that clearly expressed personal wills should help it to take shape.

Marc Bloch, *The Royal Touch*

Introduction

Miracles and prophecies have always been among the most controversial of religious events, for they raise in the clearest fashion the issue of the way the supernatural world impinges on human existence. Several historians have attempted to use miraculous events as a way to explore the relationship of individual and social anxieties to religious experience and the institutional Church. Most of these studies, however, have been concentrated in the medieval and early modern periods; miracles and prophecies in the modern era have received little serious attention except by those who have an apologetic stake in the matter. Professional historians seem to find it easier to deal with forms of religious belief and behavior foreign to their own experience only when these have receded into the distant past.[1] The reasons for this are complex and probably stem from the secular attitudes characteristic of most contemporary intellectuals. Belief in supernatural intervention in the world can cause puzzlement and discomfort in those who have adopted a secular view of the world. Nevertheless, as this study will show, belief in a personal and active God who intervenes miraculously in the lives of individuals and nations was central to religious life in nineteenth-century France.

The importance of belief in supernatural intervention is immediately evident if one considers the influence Lourdes has had on France and on the Catholic world in general during the past century. Pierre-Jakez Hélias, recalling his Breton childhood, testifies that the fame of Lourdes reached even his isolated village in the 1920s. In the 1960s three-fourths of the inhabitants of Chanzeaux, a village in Anjou, had made the pilgrimage to Lourdes, which today averages over three million visitors a year.[2] Novelists and theologians alike have used the devotion to Our Lady of Lourdes and the cures attributed to her as evidence for their claims about religion, whether favorable or hostile. The stories of Mary's appearances before Bernadette Soubirous and the cures at the fountain she discovered have been popularized in movies and literature.[3] Popular treatments stress the dramatic and marvelous elements of Lourdes and sentimentalize the facts to the point of outright distortion. Although some Catholic historians have done outstanding work in collecting, annotating, and publishing the documents related to the cult at Lourdes, their work still bears traces of an apologetical approach.[4] Some Catholics might disagree with me, but it seems fair to say that no professional historian has ever attempted to analyze the historical preconditions that might account for the nature and success of the Lourdes phenomenon.

While historians have paid scant attention to Lourdes and similar cults, they have by no means ignored the history of religion in modern France. Political, intellectual, and social historians have produced numerous surveys, *thèses*, monographs, and articles, which describe and analyze the patterns of religious continuity and change in French history.[5] A brief summary of their varied approaches shows, however, that specialization and methodological constraints operate even within a field as narrow as French religious history. To use Joachim Wach's model of religion as composed of doctrine, ritual, and institution, it can be said that political historians have focused on religion in its institutional form, intellectual historians have concentrated on doctrine, and social historians have studied ritual behavior.[6] Although the best work in each of these fields has always transcended these limits, it remains true that historical studies of French religion have often failed to integrate the various components of religious life into a coherent whole.

The role of Church-State relations in the political history of modern France was the first area to be studied thoroughly, and much work is still produced on this topic. The conflicts and compromises between Church and State have rightfully been acknowledged as central issues in the formation of political attitudes throughout the nineteenth century.[7] Without denying the importance of the relations between these two institutions, the political approach, taken by itself, distorts our understanding of religion's social significance. Two of the foremost historians of French religion have acknowledged the problem of a narrowly political focus: "In effect, in the traditional perspective of political history, religious facts are reduced to 'religious forces' which themselves are only variables permitting explanation of political behavior, defined as votes in various elections."[8] Religious belief and behavior continued to fulfill vital social functions outside the sphere of politics throughout the nineteenth century.

Those writers who have struggled with the problem of defining religion, whatever their particular formulation, have stressed its role in providing answers to questions about ultimate meaning.[9] A purely political approach, by ignoring such questions, misses a crucial aspect of religious life. A corollary to this point is that the emphasis of political historians on conflicts between Church and State is somewhat misleading. While religion was a divisive factor in French society it was also capable of working to integrate both local and national communities. Miraculous healings and pilgrimages in nineteenth-century France drew people together especially in times of crisis, when individual and collective existence were severely threatened.

The history of religious ideas in France suffers from limitations similar to those of political history. Intellectual historians, while concentrating on the development of doctrine and apologetics, have ignored religious beliefs that were formulated unsystematically.[10] But although such thought may have limited value from an intellectual perspective, it does reflect a great deal of real religious experience. Furthermore, there is some evidence that a study of the relations between popular religion and the intellectual fashions of "high" culture would show the two to have been involved in a dialogue that altered religious belief at both levels. Richard Griffiths, for example, has described the importance of the apparition of Notre-Dame de La Salette in Catholic conservative thought during the Third Republic. He pays scant attention, however, to the significance of this cult for religious life in general or to the relations between the popular cult and its intellectual adherents.[11] Harry Paul, in *The Edge of Contingency*, refers briefly to the importance of the Lourdes miracles for those intellectuals who criticized a mechanistic philosophy of science at the turn of the twentieth century. But Paul also states parenthetically that "the orthodox establishment and the apologists have always been sceptical of the popular religious tendency to resort unduly to miracles and supernatural acts."[12] This assertion of a fixed relationship between popular and elite religion could be questioned on the basis of Paul's own evidence, which suggests an increase in popular religion's influence on intellectuals in the nineteenth century. This criticism, it should be stressed, is not directed at the intrinsic value of past research, but at the limitations of traditional approaches for comprehending the nature and extent of religious influences on society and politics.

The current generation of social historians, in reaction to the failure of political and intellectual history to deal with the average Frenchman, has sought ways to describe and analyze the religious life of the masses. Led by Gabriel Le Bras, social historians have developed measures for assessing religious vitality and have begun exploring the world of popular belief and behavior. Following Le Bras' sociological program such writers as Fernand Boulard and Gérard Cholvy have attempted to go beyond intellectual and political conflict by means of the quantitative analysis of religious practice. Levels of attendance at Sunday Mass, reception of Communion, and the amount of time elapsed before baptism of infants have been evaluated against a background of social, economic, and demographic variables.[13] These historians have demonstrated the relationship between social, economic, and political factors and orthodox religious behavior; their work has resulted in a more precise understanding of the dechristianization of France. As René Rémond has pointed out, however, dechristianization is a problematic term; it implies a prior process of Christianization, which has yet to be clearly defined. Rémond's criticism raises the question of what constitutes "religious" behavior.[14] Is religion limited to orthodox practice, and does a decline in practice really indicate a decline in religious vitality? The analyses made by the sociological historians are based on the questionable assumption that religious faith is reflected in some form of attachment to the institutional Church. This position is based on a juridical view of religion, which fails to capture its larger social significance. The sociologists break down society into a set of variables and then trace the effect of these on religious practice, or the procedure is reversed and religion is the independent variable used to predict political affiliation or some other dependent variable.[15] In either case it is as if religion and everything else in life existed in isolation, related to each other only through some kind of mechanistic process. In a sense, this sociological approach is similar to the conflict model adopted by those historians who focus on the battles of the Church against the State and the secular intellectual community. In both cases religion is analyzed as a factor apart from and opposed to the political and social forces at work in the modern world.

An alternative approach used by social historians has been to study the internal development of the Catholic Church. Clerical recruitment, episcopal administration, and the Church's responsiveness to an urban environment are problems that have led to deeper understanding of the Church's successes and failures as it adjusted its pastoral mission to the conditions of postrevolutionary France. The best of these studies, such as those of Christianne Marcilharcy, Claude Langlois, and Yves Hilaire, relate institutional developments to both the political climate and the levels of religious behavior.[16]

Historians interested in exploring what French scholars have termed the "histoire des mentalités" have begun to provide an important complement to the sociological and institutional studies of religion and the Church. By studying religious belief and behavior unsanctioned and even condemned by the Church, the practitioners of this approach avoid the juridical and institutional bias that generally restricts appreciation of the richness of popular religious experience. Most studies in this area, however, have focused on the early modern period, and historians are only just beginning to study the religious culture of the nineteenth century.[17]

Studies of popular religion or of the institutional Church, while expanding the findings of the political historians and the sociologists, can also be limiting. Popular belief and behavior, for all their spontaneity, did occur within a political and institutional context; in fact they helped to shape that context and were in turn affected by it. A study of "mentalité" that neglects the political, institutional, and intellectual environment risks a distortion that is the mirror image of the one presented by the traditional historians.

The perspective I will adopt in this study is that religion—understood as a set of attitudes, beliefs, and behaviors, which provide answers to questions of ultimate meaning—exists in a dynamic relationship with religious and political institutions. The Catholic Church in France was intimately involved with the expression of fundamental religious concerns, but it did not have absolute control over them. Popular religious traditions, invoked to deal with crises faced by individuals and communities, were monitored and to some extent absorbed by the Church. Although it is sometimes difficult in practice to distinguish "popular" from "institutional" religion, the Church did respond and adjust to demands that religion fulfill its traditional tasks of providing meaning and order.

Miracles and prophecies helped serve the social functions of religion while at the same time attracting the attention of Church and State. Thus they provide ample material for examining the relationships between popular religion and these institutions.[18] In dealing with the social functions of religion I have used concepts drawn from the sociology and anthropology of religion. While these have, I hope, illuminated some of my evidence, my essential concern has been to observe and understand the ways in which popular religion and the Church adjusted to the conditions of a particular historical era.

Regardless of the period under consideration the study of miracles poses some difficult methodological problems for the historian. The major issue is the relationship that exists between the pristine "fact" and the testimony that describes it. Charles Guignebert focuses on the problem in his study, *Jesus*:

> It must be remembered that the miracles of the past, or for that matter of the present, were observed, or rather discovered, and reported only by believers. Moreover, very often, in fact for the most part, those who have reported the events were not those who actually witnessed them. Hence, in a great number of cases, the historian is confronted by the material impossibility of getting back to the exact fact which is described as miraculous, and which the inevitable interpretation begins to distort even in the minds of the eyewitness.[19]

Guignebert solves this dilemma by dissolving the boundary that separates the miracle from its evidence, and by concentrating on the belief system that "discovered" and transcribed the miraculous event. The attitudes of the witness and the chronicler become the significant fact; the miracle becomes a natural occurrence distinguished from others by its interpretation. The historian of nineteenth-century religion is in a better position with respect to evidence than was Guignebert, who was forced to rely on relatively few texts whose meaning is frequently obscure. The context of miraculous cures, for example, the kinds of people subjected to them, and the ritual behavior that called forth divine intervention can be documented for the modern era more readily than for the ancient period. But the focus of the historian of religion should, I believe, continue to be the fact of belief rather than the miracles themselves. As even the author of the Gospel of John acknowledged, what are miracles for believers can also be seen as natural events. At the conclusion of his public ministry Jesus was addressing a crowd when "a voice came from heaven. 'I have glorified my name, and I will glorify it again.' The crowd standing by heard it and said that it had thundered. Others said 'An angel has spoken to him'" (John 12:28–29). Whether it was thunder or the voice of an angel that was heard is a theological question. The circumstances and attitudes that led some people to believe and others to disbelieve are the proper subject matter of the historian.

Modern France offers an abundance of material that reflects contemporary understanding of the possibility, occurrence, and meaning of miraculous events. Folklorists, anthropologists, and local historians have left a large supply of observations regarding peasant superstitions, healing rituals, and communal cults. The descriptions and analysis of folklore and popular religion in the first chapter rely heavily on their work.

Documents produced by officials of both Church and State have provided additional materials on popular belief and behavior. But the official response to miracles and prophecies is most important for what it reveals about how popular religion was perceived and dealt with by religious and political institutions. Popular belief and behavior created administrative problems for both Church and State, which felt responsible for certain aspects of the new cults. The State's concern for social order and the Church's for doctrinal orthodoxy brought miracles and prophecies into the domain of the ecclesiastical and political authorities. The agitated response of the secular and ecclesiastical bureaucracies to the miraculous reveals the appeal of popular religion and a feeling of vulnerability within these powerful institutions.

The response of the Church to contemporary miracles is not, however, an issue that can be studied only by examining documents produced within the ecclesiastical hierarchy. In addition to official documents important evidence on the formulation of the Church's position can be found in the Catholic press. The publicity given to miracles in daily and periodical publications was an important force in the development of the religious authorities' attitudes. By exciting public opinion beyond the immediate locale of the miracle, the press increased the pressures on the Church to react in its official capacity as arbiter of the supernatural.

In relating the Catholic press to public opinion I have assumed that it is possible to use printed material as evidence of popular religious belief. Miracles and prophecies were the subjects of an enormous quantity of popular literature in nineteenth-century France. A sample of such literature is listed in the bibliography. Following Geneviève Bollème and Robert Mandrou, I believe that this literature does reflect popular mentality, but I am also sensitive to the criticism that such materials can be overinterpreted, and that one must exercise caution in drawing inferences on "mentalité" on the basis of this literature.[20] The pastoral, doctrinal, and political interests of the Church, for example, had an important impact on some of the devotional and prophetic tracts I use as evidence. The influence of romanticism can also be discerned in some of this material. But rather than regard such influence as contamination I see it as an advantage, for it reflects the interrelatedness of popular religion and the institutional Church which is the central theme of this book.

The book is organized thematically rather than chronologically. Such an organization reflects my belief that the relationship between popular religion and the Church can best be understood by looking for patterns of belief and behavior typical of the century as a whole. Within this thematic framework, however, I do point out how these patterns vary in the course of the century. The first chapter describes the religious crisis that accompanied the French Revolution, and provides an overview of the Church's attitudes toward folkloric belief and behavior. Catholicism's ambivalence toward popular religion is seen to result from its suspicion of supernatural graces obtained outside the sacramental system, and its simultaneous realization of the importance of such graces in the religious life of the ordinary believer.

The sources of the popularity of miracles and prophecies are explored in the second and third chapters. Chapter 2 focuses on the social function and expressive power of the healing rituals. In chapter 3 an eschatological perspective on current events is related to the need, satisfied in part by prophecies, to see meaning and order in the political and social disorders of contemporary France. The fourth and fifth chapters show the important role played by miracles and prophecies in the Church and in French political life. The impact of popular religion on the doctrinal and devotional life of the Church is treated in chapter 4. Miraculous devotions and prophetic cults assisted the Catholic Church in constructing defenses against ideas and values believed to be characteristically modern. At the same time popular religious belief was affected by the ideological posture of the Church and the sentimental romanticism that was intellectually fashionable. The eschatological attitudes characteristic of nineteenth-century Catholicism received a major impetus following the French defeat by Prussia in 1870. The fifth chapter treats the heightened interest in royalist prophecies and the series of mass pilgrimages to miraculous shrines that were a prominent part of the religious life of the early 1870s. The religious revival of this period had both political and religious significance, as Frenchmen looked for national salvation through supernatural intervention.

After treating the relations between popular religion, the Church, and the political order thematically in the first five chapters, chapter 6 offers a narrative of how, concretely, the Church reacted to miracles and the popular cults they inspired. The investigation and approval by the clergy of several major miracle cults confirms and refines the argument of the previous chapters. Popular belief, aided by the rapid and widespread diffusion through the press of miracle stories and prophecies, created substantial pressure within the Church for the approval of miracles and miracle cults. In the context of pastoral anxieties, Church-State conflict, and a sympathetic intellectual mood, miracles and prophecies were integrated into the life of the Church.

Chapter 1
Folklore, Miracles, and the Church

Despite serious attacks during the French Revolution and an altered relationship with the State, the Catholic Church in nineteenth-century France maintained its position as a fundamental national institution. The Church survived mainly because it continued to provide an authoritative framework for the expression of important individual and social needs. The responsiveness of the Church to these needs was conditioned by memories of the French Revolution. While historians of French religion argue about many things, all are agreed that the Revolution was a traumatic event for the Church.[1] Beginning with the appropriation of Church property and the suppression of religious orders in 1789, a series of laws was passed that attempted first to control and ultimately to eliminate the Catholic Church from French life. Religious practice was driven underground while revolutionary enthusiasts embraced and tried to impose on others surrogate religions dedicated to Reason, Humanity, and the Supreme Being. The conflict between Church and State and its effect on the religious life of the French people form the background against which one can better see and understand the pastoral and political initiatives undertaken by the Church in the nineteenth century.

Religious Life During the French Revolution

The crisis faced by the institutional Church as a result of the Revolution is most easily grasped by considering the plight of the clergy. Of the approximately 115,000 priests active before the Revolution as many as twenty thousand are believed to have abandoned their ministry in the 1790s, while another thirty thousand either emigrated or were deported.[2]

Throughout the 1790s, when the Church experienced intermittent persecution, clerical recruitment was negligible. Abdications, emigration, deaths, and the lack of recruitment led to severe shortages, the effects of which were felt into the nineteenth century. In the diocese of Isère, for example, the number of clergy fell from 1,897 in 1790 to 567 in 1804. There were over five hundred priests in the *pays creusois* in 1790, but by 1805 the number had dropped to 356, and by 1821 to 210. Bishop Pancemont of Morbihan described the situation in his diocese as a "famine," and wrote in 1806 that "if Providence doesn't come to our aid, we will have scarcely one priest for every four to five thousand souls." The decline in numbers of clergy meant that many communities were deprived of a priest, and thus did not regularly practice their religion or receive official religious instruction for much of the revolutionary period.[3]

The records kept by and about the clergy have allowed historians to observe their behavior during the Revolution, and to argue about its significance. It is more difficult to see how the religious life of the laity was affected by the Revolution, but on the basis of the available evidence it appears that not since the Reformation had French people been forced to confront so directly the issue of their religion's significance and utility.

For a number of Frenchmen, concentrated mostly in the cities, religion as it was administered by the Catholic Church was nothing more than a bundle of superstitions imposed on an ignorant populace by an avaricious and authoritarian clergy.[4] Moreover, the Church was condemned for its association with the ancien régime and feared for its potential as an agent of the Counterrevolution. The rejection of superstition and the fear of betrayal help account for the violent and destructive side of revolutionary dechristianization. Churches were sacked, statues destroyed, and the refractory clergy expelled and in some cases executed. The consequences for those who continued to practice Catholicism were at times severe. In a village in Morbihan the revolutionary emissary Le Batteux had eight Catholics shot in front of their local church after they had attended High Mass. Although this is an extreme case, less violent confrontations were common. The murders in Morbihan suggest the seriousness of the choices ordinary people were being forced to make about religion during the Revolution, when dechristianizing armies, composed for the most part of urban artisans, confronted a predominantly Catholic peasantry.[5]

The religious crisis was heightened by the fact that the Church was internally divided in its response to the Revolution. Many clergymen

refused to take the oath of loyalty required by the revolutionary government. Battles between these refractory priests and the constitutional
clergy were frequently bitter and sometimes led to violence. In southern
Anjou, where support of the nonjuring clergy was widespread, the village
of La Plaine communicated its intention to reject any priest who had taken
the oath in support of the revolutionary regime.

> The municipal officers of the parish of La Plaine and all the other
> inhabitants of the parish have the honor to tell you that . . . not
> only our parish but all the neighboring ones have decided never to
> recognize any other *curé* or vicar but those who are now in our
> parishes or their legitimate successors, and that as for anyone who
> comes to us from elsewhere (who would doubtless have taken the
> oath) we will not follow him in our parish.[6]

It was not uncommon for people like those of La Plaine to greet the
constitutional clergy sent to them with stones and jeers.[7]

The consequences of this internal conflict can be appreciated by considering the issue of sacramental validity. During the Revolution both of
the opposing clerical factions claimed an exclusive right to administer the
sacraments, forcing the laity to choose between them. Debates over the
validity of sacraments administered by the constitutional clergy continued
into the nineteenth century and constituted a serious problem for the
ecclesiastical hierarchy established by the Napoleonic Concordat of 1801.[8]
The sacraments of Baptism, First Communion, Marriage, and Extreme
Unction were (and still are) an essential part of religious practice in France,
as rites of passage that celebrate and sanctify the various stages in an
individual's life. Conflict over the sacraments would thus touch people at
critical moments. Mutually hostile exchanges about the inefficacy of the
other party's sacraments may thus have "relativized" the sacred and done
more to dechristianize the masses than some of the more active measures
taken by the revolutionary regime and by the officials sent from Paris.[9]

Revolutionaries shared a distrust or even hatred for Catholicism, but
only a few desired a society that totally excluded religion. As Albert
Mathiez demonstrated in his monumental work on the revolutionary
cults, most of the revolutionary elite sought to provide the Republic with
a religion whose forms mimicked those of Catholicism. They believed
that only a public cult with the attendant ceremonies and feast days could
commit the French people to the ideals of liberty, equality, and fraternity

espoused by the Revolution.[10] The Committee of Public Safety testified to this desire to create a surrogate religion in a circular sent to revolutionary societies in 1794.

> Popular societies, if you want to destroy fanaticism, to legendary miracles oppose the prodigies of liberty; to the victims of blindness, the martyrs of reason; to the mummeries of hypocrisy, the sublime conduct of Marat, Le Pelletier, and Chalier; to the masquerades of the church, the pomp of our national feasts; to the lugubrious songs of the priests, the hymns of liberty; to insignificant prayers, the love of work, noble deeds, and acts of charity.[11]

The first of the revolutionary cults, in which Reason was the central deity, was greeted with popular suspicion, and the denial by some extremists of an afterlife was also disturbing. Michel Vovelle has suggested, on the basis of changes in testamentary religious bequests during the eighteenth century, that there was a lessening of concern for the afterlife in the period prior to the Revolution. But although people may have asked for fewer masses for the sake of their departed souls, there was still a widespread conviction that the spirit lived on after death.[12] Both the Cult of the Supreme Being, instituted by Robespierre, and the Cult of Theophilanthropy, initiated by the Directory, affirmed the existence of God and the immortality of the soul. The Convention decreed on May 7, 1794, that "the French people recognizes the Supreme Being and the immortality of the soul"; the same two beliefs were affirmed as fundamental doctrines in the *Manuel des théophilanthropes*.[13]

The doctrinal spareness of the revolutionary religions, however, was insufficient for a laity accustomed to venerating a pantheon of saints. Popular cults based on Rousseau and the revolutionary martyrs Marat, Le Pelletier, and Chalier helped fill in the religious space that had been cleared by attacks on the saints, their statues, and their shrines. The revolutionary heroes, like the saints, were personal figures capable of serving as intermediaries between ordinary believers and the supreme deity. The frequent comparisons of Marat to Christ suggest both the continuing appeal of the figure of the suffering Christ, and the ability of the revolutionary cults to tap that appeal with their own heroes.[14]

The extent to which revolutionary cults relied on Catholic forms sometimes makes it difficult to term them revolutionary in any simple sense of the word. The extensive borrowing by the new religions led Bernard

Plongeron to ask "if it is a question of anything other than a pure and simple transfer."[15] The cult of Perrine Dugué illustrates how much a revolutionary cult could derive from an older religious tradition. Perrine was murdered by Chouans loyal to the Bourbons in 1796 while trying to assist her brothers, who were fighting for the Republic. Stories soon circulated that she was observed flying to heaven on "tricolored wings," and her grave was converted into a shrine that drew thousands of pilgrims in a single day. Thaumaturgic powers were attributed to the dirt and grass at the site of the shrine.[16]

The attempts to find satisfactory substitutes for Catholicism and the syncretism evident in the new cults suggest that the power of religious modes of thought and feeling was sustained in the revolutionary era. Some of the clearest evidence for the strength of religion in revolutionary France is found in reports of adherence to the Catholic cult in the face of dechristianization. In the regions around Paris, at the height of the Terror, many villages pressured their unwilling and frightened clergy into celebrating midnight Mass on Christmas Eve. Richard Cobb has suggested that anxieties raised by the Terror may even have led to an increase in the attachment to this traditional devotion. When priests were not available, magistrates, schoolmasters, gravediggers, and others donned vestments to administer sacraments and say Mass.[17]

The loyalty shown traditional religion extended beyond the Mass to include devotion to church bells, crosses, shrine images, and statues. In the Yonne, not noted for its counterrevolutionary activity, the women of one parish resisted the attempt to remove their parish bells by occupying the church for nine days.[18] The peasants of La Ferté-Gaucher also took direct action. They forced their municipal officers to replace the statues removed from their parish church and sacked the local Jacobin club to the cries of "Vive la religion catholique! à bas les Jacobins! Nous aurons nos curés. Nous voulons la messe les dimanches et fêtes." One of the rioters of La Ferté-Gaucher was reported as saying that the Jacobins "étoient la cause de ce que la Vierge et tous les saints pleuraient dans les églises."[19] The belief that statues wept over the Revolution was by no means an isolated phenomenon. Such tales circulated about many statues and became part of the folklore of French shrines in the nineteenth century.[20]

In assessing the position of the Catholic Church following the Revolution, emphasis has usually been placed on the difficulties that had to be overcome. New clergy had to be recruited, churches rebuilt, and discipline established on the basis of the controversial new Concordat. In its relationship to the laity the Church had to reestablish its claim as the sole dispenser of supernatural grace and instruct a generation that had been deprived of religious education. Finally, the Church had to work toward a closer relationship and a common vocabulary with its lay members, for during the eighteenth century there had been a tendency for religious elites to lose touch with the faith of ordinary believers.[21] In its pastoral work, one of the Church's main tools was the parish mission. Several days of emotional sermons and dramatic ceremonies under the direction of specially recruited missionaries were intended to impel the French to recall the essentials of their faith. There were aspects of the mission movement, however, that made it less than an ideal vehicle for creating a new sense of cooperation between priests and people. Parish missions occurred at most once every few years. Furthermore, mission preachers emphasized the themes of sin, reparation, and death. The punitive atmosphere characteristic of missions led at times to profound reactions in the lay audiences. But a religious appeal so limited in its emotional range was an insufficient basis for reconstructing religious bonds between the Church and the people.[22]

Religious leaders did not fail to observe the devotion to saints and shrines that continued throughout the Revolution. The attempt to find replacements for the saints and iconoclasm itself also testified to the survival of respect for supernatural intermediaries. Saints, shrines, and related cultic objects were needed for the spiritual and physical services they promised, and which many people believed they delivered. Such cults had been treated with skepticism in the eighteenth century, both inside and outside the Church, and this attitude may have been partly responsible for the gap that had formed between the clergy and ordinary believers.[23] In the nineteenth century the Catholic Church actively embraced the cult of saints and shrines, which became an integral part of a pastoral program designed to establish a closer relationship between popular religious belief and the institutional Church. In formulating this program the Church borrowed heavily from a tradition in which healers, magical prayers, sacred fountains, and miraculous cures were a familiar part of the religious landscape. But the Church did not simply adopt these manifestations of popular religion uncritically. The clergy were suspicious of individual healers, for example, and were more likely to support miracle cults when associated with a shrine. The diversity of popular religion in nineteenth-century France can be dealt with by organizing the various miracle cults within a hierarchy based on the relationship of the cults to the institutional Church. The interplay of folklore and institutional religion observed at the various levels of this hierarchy reveals a new and more intimate relationship between popular religion and Catholicism which is characteristic of the nineteenth century.

Healers and Healing Manuals

At the lowest level of the hierarchy of the miraculous were those healers whose powers were not attributed to a religious object or formula, but who cured through their own inherent powers, a family secret passed from generation to generation, or some herbal concoction.[24] Even at this level, however, there were traces of religious influences. Herbs, for example, were potent only if picked on the eve of certain saints' feast days, and many healers claimed they could only help baptized Christians or animals who belonged to Christians.[25] From the perspective of the sick who consulted a lay healer, there was probably no great difference between the nonreligious practitioners and those who included a prayer in their formula. In both cases the sick person was relying on mysterious forces beyond his control, which the healer had the power to coerce. As Keith Thomas has suggested in describing similar practices in seventeenth-century England, the theological distinction between magic and religion is not generally understood by people as they seek help during a personal crisis.[26]

Religion entered explicitly into the healing process when the healer invoked a saint by means of a prayer or pilgrimage, or performed some ritual associated with the Christian religion. Individuals who had traveled to the shrine of St. Hubert in the Ardennes could cure rabies, or ward it off, by applying a key obtained there and having their client perform a series of rituals.[27] A peasant woman from Eure-et-Loir treated rheumatism by boiling live cats and applying them to the affected areas while saying Paters and Aves. In the 1892 *L'ami du clergé* (a professional journal that dealt extensively with the concerns of the parish priest), a clergyman described the practices of healers who "in order to help out, as they say, treat sprains, burns, etc. without medicines . . . by saying, for example, *Ante, ante te, super ante te,* while making several signs of the cross."[28] Professional pilgrims agreed, for a fee, to make the required trip and perform the ritual at the shrine selected for those sick who lacked the time or energy to make their own pilgrimage. Peddlers sometimes combined trade in religious medals, pictures, and books with an ostentatious religiosity that encouraged people to hire them as professional pilgrims. A local scholar from Chartres, writing in 1876, has left a vivid description of these pilgrim-merchants.

> In our period, until around 1830, there were frequent reports of these wandering individuals in our streets and markets, their heads covered with large hats whose brim was pushed back to show a small figurine of St. Jacques de Compostello accompanied by two shells; these individuals, their faces decorated with long beards and dressed in robes garnished with capes on which were hung rows of little shells (called *de St. Jacques*) carried boxes which contained their merchandise. They presented themselves barefoot or with sandals; they held in one hand a long pilgrim's staff at the top of which hung a gourd, and with the other hand rung a small bell. These nineteenth-century pilgrim-merchants sang songs and offered to passersby pious pamphlets, medals, or blessed rosaries. They had as their goal to save our modern Christians from the embarrassment of making a long trip. It is to similar intermediaries, that is to say those women who make a profession of going to different shrines for asking the relief of the sick or the consolation of the afflicted, that we see in our period simple villagers confide the task of fulfilling pilgrimage vows.[29]

Some healers did not rely on pilgrimages but instead used a rich assortment of prayers and rituals. The manuals of these healers, some of which have recently been discovered, provide concrete evidence on the intermingling of magic and religion in healing rituals. The notebook of a Languedoc healer active early in the twentieth century contains, among other things, information about medicinal plants, conjurations, prayers designed to heal both men and animals, and a method for divining the weather.[30] Two similar notebooks, dating from 1800 and 1850, have been discovered in Seine-et-Marne. Like the manual from Languedoc, they contain prescriptions for the sick in which religious and medical elements are inextricably linked.[31]

The prayers written down in the manuscript notebooks were not secrets monopolized by healers. As early as the sixteenth century medical remedies had appeared in printed form; by the nineteenth century healing prayers were a familiar part of the *colportage* literature distributed by peddlers throughout France.[32] Charles Nisard, who served as a censor for the Second Empire, discussed these works in his analytical anthology of popular literature where he catalogued them under the heading "Religion and Morality."

> You would hardly expect to find a medical book among religious books; but you would be wrong. Hardly any of the common ailments are omitted, and for the cures you have no need of a doctor or a pharmacist. The same treatment is applicable to men, to animals, and to the fruits of the earth.[33]

Many of the prayers found in the manuscript notebooks of the healers also appeared in the *colportage* pamphlets, which suggests that by the nineteenth century healing prayers were an integral part of popular culture. It may be that by the nineteenth century the rise in literacy and the plethora of printed material had fixed the forms of prayers that had formerly been passed on through oral traditions.[34]

The most popular of the prayer collections was *Le médecin des pauvres*, which was still being reprinted in the twentieth century.[35] The cover of an 1851 edition of *Le médecin* preserved at the Bibliothèque Nationale immediately evokes a religious mood. It depicts Mary in the midst of the sun, her arms outstretched. Beneath her are three invocations: "Christus Regnat, Jésus Christ Regne. Christus Imperat, Jésus Christ Commande. Christus Vincet, Jésus Christ est vainqueur." This series is followed by a final "En Dieu la confiance." Following the cover page are prayers, usually directed toward particular saints, for the relief of a variety of ailments and mishaps such as fever, rheumatism, ringworm, colic, and burns. The prayer to St. Apolline, one of the most frequently printed, serves to illustrate the form.

> One day Saint Apolline was sitting on a marble stone. Our Lord, passing by, said to her, Apolline, what are you doing there? She answered, I am here for my master, for my blood, and for my toothache. [Jesus said to her] Apolline, return home; if it is a drop of blood [causing your toothache] it will fall; if it is a worm it will die.
>
> Say five Paters and five Aves in honor of the five wounds of our Lord Jesus Christ, and make the sign of the cross with your finger

over your jaw where you feel the pain, saying God has cured you, and in a very short time you will be cured.[36]

As is frequently the case the association between Apolline and toothache derived from the personal history of the saint. Appolline was an Early Church martyr who died when her teeth were forcibly extracted. She is usually represented in medieval art with a set of pincers, the instrument of her martyrdom.

Not just the saints, but also Christ and the Virgin were invoked in *Le médecin des pauvres*. An illustration of a trapezoid described as "the measure of the wound in the side of Our Lord Jesus Christ" is followed by a passage that details its miraculous properties.

> This was brought to the Emperor Charlemagne from Constantinople in a coffer of gold as a very precious relic. It has so much virtue that the one who carries it on him, with respect and devotion, will brave all danger, and will not perish in fire, nor in water, nor in battle, and will be happy and victorious over all his enemies: and the one who always carries it will not die a bad death.
>
> God be praised in all places. Amen.[37]

A prayer in the same edition of the pamphlet was supposedly found on the tomb of the Virgin, "and has so many virtues and properties that the one who reads it or has it read once each day, or carries it with him devoutly and in good intention, cannot perish by fire, or by water, or in battle."[38] The prayers to St. Apolline and the Virgin and the illustration of Christ's wound are presented as easily applicable remedies or conjurations, but they all make some effort to tie themselves to orthodox religious belief and practice. The prayer to St. Apolline requires Paters and Aves in honor of the wounds of Christ, while the others mention the necessity of devotion and piety if they are to be effective.

During the Second Empire there were attempts to refine this kind of literature according to a more orthodox concept of prayer in which God would be given more freedom of choice in his response. The Troyes edition of *Le médecin* is an example of this effort.[39] Referring to prior editions of the pamphlet which included conjurations to ward off evil spirits, it opens with an attack on the belief in ghosts and sorcery as irreligious. The new edition eliminated the illustration of the wound of Christ and all suggestions that simply by possessing or repeating a prayer one could avoid accident and disease. Most of the prayers aimed at specific medical problems added the phrase "pour demander" to the title to make them petitionary rather than manipulative. The prayer for toothache remained the same, but after the tale of Christ's meeting with St. Apolline it concluded by asking only for the five Paters and Aves, and left out the sign of the cross over the jaw and the final conjuration.

The Troyes pamphlet asked for a cure, while the prior editions were more self-confident. Nevertheless, the fundamental assumption was the same for all: prayers to God and the saints lead directly to physical relief. The call for a devout attitude was intended to encourage a belief that the relationship between the sick individual and the sacred being he invoked was not simply coercive but rested on some form of personal commitment. The Catholic Church had, since the Counterreformation, struggled against the belief that such prayers were automatically efficacious. Although it is impossible to know the frame of mind of those who actually used the prayers in *Le médecin* one doubts, as does Keith Thomas, the ability of the peasant to discriminate between coercion and petition.

Priests and nuns form a separate category of healers by virtue of their explicit association with the institutional Church. During the Second Empire at least ten departments reported convictions of priests for the illegal practice of medicine.[40] Their crime was frequently to sell "secret remedies," and it can be assumed that these were considered successful because of their religious provenance. In the same period medical dispensaries staffed by nuns increased dramatically and contributed to the association of religion and healing.[41] During the Third Republic *L'ami du clergé* regularly published medical advice that the clergy were expected to use in dealings with their parishioners.[42] As late as 1935 a French physician wrote of "the encroachment by nuns or parish priests into the medical world."[43] The healing reputation of the clergy was sometimes manifested at the tombs of popular and pious *curés*.[44] These tombs became popular shrines, falling into a pattern known in the eighteenth century, the most famous instance of which was the tomb of the deacon François de Pâris at St. Médard in Paris. Bishops also had reputations as healers[45] and the pope himself, not surprisingly, was the object of superstitious beliefs. During Pius VII's trip north in 1804 to crown Bonaparte, the pope passed through the village of Cosne in southern France. A woman of Cosne troubled by her sterility decided that she could remedy her problem by sleeping in the same bed as the pope after he had left it. She succeeded in getting into the bed but was discovered and ejected after several hours. The woman from

Cosne was still not pregnant, but she always maintained that she had not had sufficient time for the miraculous powers to work on her.[46] A less spectacular but more widespread belief in the miraculous powers attributed to Pius VII was reported by Collin de Plancy, writing in 1821.

> Few pious persons in our departments do not have a piece of bread blessed by the Pope when he traveled to France for the consecration of Napoleon. Some carry this preservative in a locket hung from the neck, to avoid thieves, while traveling. Others keep it on their chest as a remedy against diverse maladies.[47]

The bread blessed by Pius VII could ward off sickness and mishap, but there were other cases of individuals closely associated with the Church whose powers were more than prophylactic. Two of these individuals were not directly sponsored by the ecclesiastical hierarchy, but their cults did have the tacit consent of the institutional Church. Alexandre-Léopold-François-Emeric, Prince de Hohenlohe-Waldembourg-Schillingfurst, was ordained a priest in 1815 and quickly gained a reputation for his piety and preaching. The turning point in his career came in 1821 when he linked forces with a peasant from Baden, Martin-Michel, who was curing people by the laying on of hands and by exhorting the sick to have faith. A controversy was soon raging in Baden over the cures worked by the Prince and the peasant, but this did not prevent the rapid diffusion of the cult in France during the early 1820s.[48] It was propagated by the publication of pamphlets on a local level, but also by the reporting of the cures and supporting testimony in *L'ami de la religion*, the most widely distributed religious journal of the Restoration, which had close ties with the French hierarchy. While Hohenlohe started out by associating himself with the traditional practices of a lay healer, he soon added the requirement of a novena that included Mass and Communion.

Hohenlohe's cult provides an example of the absorption and adaptation of traditional ritual by orthodox religion, a process characteristic of the nineteenth century. His powers were publicized and approved by the Church because he was a clergyman who, in addition to the healing practices of his associate Martin-Michel, used the orthodox rituals of Mass and Communion. In 1824, however, *L'ami de la religion* stopped its coverage of the cures because of skepticism about the testimony in favor of the miracles, and because the stories themselves were becoming repetitious.[49] Hohenlohe's cult declined, but never disappeared entirely. Some miracles were again reported in 1833; in the 1830s editions of his prayers for the sick were still being published in Paris. As late as 1844 a woman who was eventually healed by Notre-Dame de La Salette sought and received Hohenlohe's help.[50]

Léon Dupont, the Holy Man of Tours, was another nineteenth-century healer who gained a national reputation for a period of time, exploited orthodox ritual in his practice, and benefited from the tacit support of the Church. Working from his home in Tours during the 1850s and 1860s, Dupont cured thousands of individuals, many of whom visited him on the advice of their local *curé*. After his death the diocesan authorities converted his home to an official shrine, and the cult he established still exists in France.[51]

The most prominent instance of a thaumaturge who was associated with the institutional Church was Jean Vianney, the *curé* of Ars. During his lifetime thousands of pilgrims and correspondents sought medical advice from him. After his death his popularity continued to increase, and his tomb remains a popular shrine today.[52] Of the three thaumaturges, the *curé* of Ars was the one by far the most closely associated with the Catholic Church. Prince Hohenlohe, while a clergyman, was also a nobleman with an independent reputation and a figure of controversy. Dupont, although he gained the tacit approval of his bishop, did experience some difficulty with the hierarchy because of his lay status; the cult he founded dedicated to the Holy Face was officially approved only after Dupont's death.[53] Jean Vianney was a model of obedience and devotion to the Church; the cures attributed to him redounded to its benefit as well as his own. Jean Vianney's piety, simplicity, humility, and obedience ingratiated him with his superiors, and his life at Ars was thought by them to exemplify the ideal relationship between a *curé* and his parish.[54]

Two individuals who never obtained Church sponsorship for their healing provide evidence that confirms the Church's suspicion of such healers. Bernadette Soubirous, during and just after the apparitions at Lourdes, became a cultic object whose touch was sought either directly or through her handling of rosaries, medals, and other pious objects.[55] Within weeks, however, the cult at Lourdes came to center on the grotto and the fountain rather than on Bernadette.[56] After her death in a convent at Nevers, Bernadette's tomb became a shrine and she was eventually canonized on the basis of miracles attributed to her, but she played no significant thaumaturgic role while she was alive. She was accorded an important place in the popular accounts of the Lourdes story as a pious visionary and not as a miracle worker.[57]

Eugène Vintras, the founder of a sect that aspired to the position of national church during the July Monarchy, was able to claim a following in part as a result of his healing gifts which proved the divine origin of his mission. The Church acted to suppress the cult and the State cooperated by prosecuting the prophet-thaumaturge for fraud.[58] The case of Vintras illuminates what the Church feared from individual miracle workers: any assertion of supernatural powers independent of the Church was a threat to its monopolistic claim that only its mediation between God and man could result in miraculous cures. The distinction between superstitious and religious healers was based on their association with the institutional Church. A similar distinction was made regarding rituals that did not require the participation of a healer. When questioned about the practice of swallowing holy images when sick in order to obtain a cure the editors of *L'ami du clergé* responded that such an act could be licit and beneficial, but only if it had the approval of the clergy.[59]

Individual healers and healing prayers and rituals had various and complex relationships with religion and the Church in nineteenth-century France. The Church at best tolerated such beliefs and practices and was in general suspicious of them. Only in rare cases did the Church promote cults associated with individuals, and such promotion depended on the extent to which the thaumaturge was attached to institutional Catholicism.

Saints and Shrines

The healers in France did not claim that their powers derived solely from personal charisma. Many of their activities were tied to shrines dedicated to individual saints, which were the central institutions in the dense network of the miraculous. Developments at these shrines constitute major evidence of the new relationship between folkloric beliefs and the Catholic Church which was characteristic of the period. Like the healers and their rituals, shrines and their related cults can be categorized according to their ties with the Church. Small shrines dedicated to local saints with little or no clerical involvement contrasted with those regional and national sites which were the subject of a major initiative by the Church.

Historians and anthropologists have consistently demonstrated the prevalence of *saints guérisseurs* (healing saints) and their shrines in nineteenth-century France.[60] The belief in saints' healing power still survives in France; surveys conducted in the 1950s and 1960s in both rural and industrial areas show that large numbers of French people still appeal to saints for relief when they are ill.[61] The saints to whom the sick looked for cures in the last century varied from area to area, with local saints remaining popular throughout the nineteenth century. As was seen in the discussion of healing manuals, prayers were frequently directed at individual saints for particular illnesses. Certain diseases were even named for the saint with whom they were associated.[62] In other cases the association with a disease was based on a pun that related the name of the saint to the nature of the ailment. St. Claire, for example, was applied to for diseases of the eye.[63] As was the case in the prayer to St. Apolline, a mythic event in a saint's life could also explain his or her power over a certain disease.[64]

The most common method for invoking a saint's aid was to make a pilgrimage to his or her shrine. The sick person could make the journey himself, or a family member, friend, or professional pilgrim could serve as a surrogate. The diagnosis, where difficult, could be made with the help of an expert consultant who could discern which saint ought to be approached for help. The rituals varied, but followed a general pattern. A stick of charcoal might be burned, or an earthworm trisected while the litany of the saints was read. The saint named as the fire went out or the worm stopped its movements was the one to whom a pilgrimage should be made.[65]

The focal point of the shrine itself was most frequently a fountain or statue. Statistics for Seine-et-Marne confirm the judgments made by descriptive anthropologists about the popularity of these objects. Of all rituals at shrines in that department 10 percent involved relics, 10 percent stones or other objects, 30 percent statues, and 50 percent fountains.[66] The particular rituals varied from shrine to shrine. Fountain water could be bathed in or drunk; statues could be rubbed, ex-voto ribbons hung from them, or a splinter taken from them. At a fountain in Haut-Limousin the pilgrims would walk around the fountain six, nine, or twelve times, then make a sign of the cross and drink the water from the palm of their hand three times, after which they would bathe the afflicted parts of their bodies.[67]

The pilgrimage to the shrine was frequently made to coincide with a novena to the saint for the intention of the sick person. The ritual would

Ex-voto depicting miraculous cure of a child by Mary, in Chapel of Notre-Dame du Beausset-Vieux (Var). Painted by the joiner Eusèbe Nicolas of Le Beausset (1855–1895). Collection of the Musées Nationaux, Paris.

also generally call for an ex-voto of some sort, ribbons, pins, sometimes money, and sometimes a painting depicting a miraculous cure.[68] Fountains, statues, pilgrimages, and ex-voto are the elements of a cultic pattern at the local level that influenced the miraculous institutions that developed at regional and national shrines under the guidance of the Catholic clergy.

Clerical involvement with local shrines was not uniform. Indeed, it has been suggested that in some areas priestly opposition to the shrines contributed to popular anticlericalism.[69] Conflicts over shrines and practices related to them have a long history within Christianity. During the

Counterreformation the Church began a major effort to "purify" popular religion, an effort that led in the eighteenth century to what Timothy Tackett has called a "confrontation between two religious cultures: between the religion of the *curé*—and thus the religion of the seminary, the religion of the city—on the one hand, and the religion of the rural parishioners on the other."[70] Clerical opposition to what were believed to be superstitious practices continued throughout the nineteenth century, but the mood of outright confrontation was replaced by a heightened interest in reconciling the faith of the people with orthodox belief. The editors of *L'ami du clergé*, in response to questions from the parish clergy, were critical of superstitions; but they also encouraged leniency on the part of the clergy for those who acted in good faith.[71]

The involvement of clergy with local shrines can be observed in their willingness to reconstruct chapels, revive pilgrimages, or participate in major processions. Although data on such activity are inevitably incomplete, the compilation of Marian pilgrimages published by Abbé Drochon in 1890 gives some indication of the extent of such clerical initiatives. During the July Monarchy there were at least 52 such events at local shrines (2.9 per year); this figure rose to 134 for the Second Empire (6.1 per year), and declined to 72 for the first two decades of the Third Republic (3.6 per year). These figures are only suggestive, but the recent study of Yves Hilaire on the diocese of Arras confirms this pattern of development. Hilaire sees a major revival of interest in pilgrimages encouraged by the Church starting with the cholera epidemic of 1849, and continuing into the 1860s.[72]

Another revealing instance of clerical sympathy with formerly suspect forms of popular piety concerns the practice of ringing church bells to stop a thunderstorm. During the ancien régime priests were sometimes forced to perform this ritual against their will and were held responsible for its failure. Mgr Pie, while a vicar-general at Chartres in 1846 (later he became bishop of Poitiers and an acknowledged leader of Catholic opinion), published a manual of *Prières et cérémonies pour la bénédiction des cloches* in which he admitted the potential danger of the ritual, since the bells drew lightning. Pie went on to argue that the ringing of the bells was nevertheless beneficial, since it was God's purpose to violate natural law and show his power by protecting the bellringer and stopping the storm.[73]

The participation of the clergy at local shrines involved a variety of rituals. Common practices included the reading of a gospel over the sick person or his representative while part of the stole rested on his head, the application of a relic to the sick, and the blessing of objects that took on healing properties. Of one hundred rituals that took place inside churches and chapels in Seine-et-Marne which required the presence of a priest, twenty involved relics, sixteen the reading of a gospel, ten the blessing of children, and sixteen the blessing of diverse objects. Some local shrines also stressed confession and communion, but this does not seem typical.[74]

Healing rituals were not invoked by individuals only. People also sought to restore or ensure communal health by means of Rogation Day processions, the blessing of crops, and bonfires lit on the eve of the feast of St. John the Baptist. Of these, the clergy were more likely to participate in the processions and the blessings of the fields than in the *feux St. Jean*. The latter provide a good example of clerical ambivalence toward folkloric practices that claimed to summon supernatural relief apart from the institutional Church. The bonfires lit in celebration of the feast of St. John were common in villages throughout the century in all but the eastern departments of France.[75] Despite a battle against this practice, in which the Church had been engaged since the Counterreformation, there were still cases of clerical participation in the nineteenth century. In the twentieth century the *feux St. Jean* formerly proscribed by the Church survived in some cases because of clerical support.[76] With or without a clerical blessing, there were ritual uses to be made of the fire. In some cases tradition allowed that those young men who could leap across the cinders safely would have good health for a year. More common was the use of ashes from the fire to protect homes against thunder and lightning. Within this folk custom many of the previously described elements reoccur: the belief in the magical power of objects when sanctified by religious ritual, the integration of religious with folk ritual to insure physical well-being, and in some cases the active role of the parish clergy in such ritual. The *feux St. Jean* illustrate, as do the shrines and their healing rituals, that religion, health, and healing were closely integrated in the consciousness of the nineteenth-century French peasant.

The role of the clergy during natural catastrophes was even more significant than their participation in rituals designed to cure individuals or in the annual *feux St. Jean*. In times of drought, flood, and epidemic it was the *curé*'s duty to lead the community in procession to the local shrine. Throughout the nineteenth century natural catastrophes were able to draw even the indifferent into the performance of religious ritual. Belief in the protective power of saints could be coupled with ignorance of orthodox doctrine; it could be divorced from reception of the sacraments and Mass attendance, and could even be accompanied by anticlericalism.[77]

The Church seems to have had fewer ambivalent feelings about communal cults than about those intended primarily for individual cures. Communal observances in a crisis could officially be interpreted as a general acknowledgment of God's power, and involved the priest in his public and official rather than his personal role. In the countryside *curés* might occasionally object to such traditional practices as dipping the processional cross into a sacred fountain to produce rain, but the procession to insure collective health was in general an acceptable practice. In urban as well as rural settings public prayers and processions during natural catastrophes were able to gain the approval of both civil and religious officials. In 1849, for example, during an outbreak of cholera, the mayor of Aix authorized a solemn procession of the statue of Notre-Dame de la Seds and the city's consecration to the Holy Mother. In 1884, during another cholera epidemic, the mayor suspended a prohibition of processions in order to permit the statue to be carried again through the streets of Aix. The republican journal of Marseille, *Liberté*, in describing a similar ceremony, noted a general revival of shrines as a result of the cholera epidemic of 1884.

> The cities threatened by cholera recall ancient customs, and pray to God as our fathers prayed to Him in the days of their trials. The ceremony celebrated this week at Notre-Dame de la Garde [in Marseille] has made an exceptional impression. Several years ago a radical majority of the city council broke with habit dear to the populace in suppressing the annual procession. The Chamber of Commerce has decided to honor the word of the aldermen who initiated the procession, and every year have a Mass celebrated to which the present circumstances have given a character even more important.[78]

It was not unusual for the Church, in proclaiming public prayer and ritual, to attribute the crisis to negligence in faith and religious practice. The bishop of Verdun addressed a circular to his clergy during the drought of 1870 which illustrates the point.

> Dryness desolates our countryside; it threatens our fruits and harvests. It is time to add to private prayer the powerful cry of public

prayer. Therefore call your dear parishioners to the foot of the altar, that they may storm heaven [*fassent violence au Ciel*] with unanimous supplications. Only let us not forget that the efficacy of our prayers is related to the ardor of our faith. In proclaiming the domain of God over our person, let us not hesitate to tell him that we await only from him the fecundity of our fields, since He controls the rain, the dew, the air, the warmth and light, that is to say all of those agents which make our work productive.

Let us no longer forget our iniquities, *in particular the profanation of the holy day of Sunday*, which unleashed on the earth storms, sterility, sickness, and plagues of all kinds. Let us join to prayer the serious observation of the law of God, in order that the Father of Mercy might deign to spread over our countryside a blessed and beautiful rain.

To this end:

1. Starting next Thursday, the feast of the ascension, a *Triduum* of prayers will be celebrated in all the chapels and churches of the diocese for the intention of rain.

2. In the evening a Benediction will be held for the same purpose.

3. We authorize those churches which possess authentic relics to expose them during the *Triduum*. In this case a prayer to the saint whose relics are exposed will be added to the Benediction prayers.

4. Until the drought ends all priests will say at the Collect, the Secret, and the Post-communion, *Ad petendam pluviam.*[79]

The exposition of relics and the public prayers called for in the bishop's circular were part of an attempt to associate the thaumaturgic aspect of religion with the orthodox pastoral goals of the Church. The Church was taking advantage of a crisis in which it hoped popular belief in the efficacy of prayer and ritual would bring about an increase in regular attendance at Sunday Mass. Recent scholars have frequently focused on attendance at Sunday Mass, or some other index of attachment to the institutional Church, as a measure of religious vitality.[80] The Church itself, however, at times acknowledged the existence of another type of religious belief, which tapped needs more fundamental than—or at least different from—those satisfied by the observation of Sunday worship.

Clerical involvement in local shrines and their role in maintaining the health and prosperity of the community were traditions inherited from the

Church of the ancien régime. In addition to these practices the nineteenth-century Church operated a vast network of regional shrines, which provide quantitative confirmation of the episcopal sanction of the thaumaturgic powers attributed to religious ritual and to the institutional Church. Regional shrines usually drew pilgrims from a larger area than parish shrines and were distinguished from these by a higher degree of formal institutionalization, defined as the permanent establishment of a chaplain or an order at the shrine. While local shrines depended on the parish clergy whose duties were not restricted to serving the pilgrims, a regional shrine existed outside the parish network and was served by priests whose full attention was directed at pilgrims. The permanent presence of the clergy led to an increased emphasis on orthodox ritual at these shrines; confession and communion were encouraged alongside the more traditional thaumaturgic rituals. The clergy also stressed the necessity for morality on the part of the pilgrims, in reaction to some of the abuses that characterized local pilgrimages. At the same time they continued to encourage the kinds of rituals described for local shrines. The miraculous fountains and statues were still the main attraction for pilgrims; the presence of the clergy at these shrines provided an orthodox and moral environment for the invocation and veneration of the miraculous.

Diocesan authorities were responsible for determining which shrines would be given special attention.[81] There were several ways in which this could be done. The simplest method was to appoint a permanent chaplain to serve the pilgrimage; in some cases a shrine chapel was made into a parish. Most important, however, were those shrines staffed by a group of diocesan missionaries or a religious order. Such shrines became an important part of the episcopal program for re-evangelicizing the diocese. The role of missions and missionary orders in this task has frequently been noted. Missions and a revived catechetical program were, in fact, the major innovations in pastoral work in the nineteenth century.[82] The fact that missionaries were frequently stationed at miraculous shrines adds another element to an understanding of this mission movement. Miracles at the shrines could serve to draw pilgrims and provide the missionaries with an opportunity to bring them inside the orthodox Church. The miraculous, as it established itself at these diocesan shrines, can be seen to play a role in the general movement to convert post-revolutionary French society.

Among the regional shrines that received prominent attention from the nineteenth-century Church were those dedicated to St. Jean-François Régis at Louvesc in Languedoc, to St. Martin of Tours, whose tomb was miraculously rediscovered in 1860, to St. Anne d'Auray, a shrine that drew pilgrims from throughout Brittany, and to St. Radegonde of Poitiers, whose statue was crowned in 1887.[83] Of these shrines only St. Anne d'Auray's recovered immediately after the Revolution; but by the end of the century they had all developed into major shrines staffed by diocesan clergy or a missionary order.

Of all the regional shrines, those dedicated to the Virgin Mary were the most numerous and important. Devotion to Mary was not, of course, a novelty, but commentators noted a substantial increase in Marian piety during the nineteenth century. Abbé Hamon expressed a common sentiment in the introduction to *Notre-Dame de France*, his seven-volume compilation of Marian shrines published in the 1860s:

> For the past thirty years a singularly remarkable religious fact has been evident in France; it is the unaccustomed élan of souls for the cult and the love of the Holy Virgin; the children of the faith love to dress in her livery, to wear her medals, to decorate her altars, to raise statues in her honor, to celebrate her feasts with pomp, and to devote the entire month of May to a series of solemnities in her honor.[84]

The most important innovation at regional Marian shrines was a "crowning," a ceremony that required Papal approval of an episcopal request based in part on proof of miracles at the shrine. Crownings were impressive rituals; they drew bishops from the surrounding dioceses and were celebrated with huge processions, illuminations, and fiery sermons in which the miraculous history of the shrine was eulogized. Crowds at these ceremonies ranged from fifteen to a hundred thousand. There were at least sixty-six such crownings between 1853 and 1890, covering most of the dioceses of France. At least twenty-eight of those shrines marked by a crowning were staffed by missionaries, with the Oblates of Mary being the most popular order. Some crownings did take place in parish churches, but it was common to assign extra clergy to these, whose responsibility would be to serve the pilgrimage rather than the parish.[85]

The history of Notre-Dame du Sacré-Coeur at Issoudon can be taken as an example of how a Marian shrine became, with episcopal support, an important part of the religious life of the diocese. A small shrine dedicated

to Our Lady of the Sacred Heart was first built in 1855 under the direction
of two priests from the diocese of Bourges. Their intention was to make
the shrine the center for a new congregation, the Missionaries of the
Sacred Heart. The archbishop of Bourges, Cardinal Dupont, approved
the new order in 1861, and this decision was renewed by Mgr de la Tour
d'Auvergne in 1864. That same year Mgr Guibert, the archbishop of
Tours, consecrated a basilica at the site of the old shrine, built with the
support of a public subscription. Soon after a diocesan confraternity was
established at the basilica, which later became an archconfraternity capable
of founding chapters throughout France. Popes Pius IX and Leo XIII
granted numerous indulgences to its pilgrims. Concurrent with the
growth of this shrine were, of course, miracles. During the 1860s requests
for assistance numbered between ninety and one hundred thousand
annually, and the missionaries claimed that ten thousand "favors" were
obtained each year as a result of the intercession of Notre-Dame du
Sacré-Coeur. The new cult culminated with a crowning of September 8,
1869, the feast of the Nativity of the Virgin. Thirteen archibishops and
bishops, seven hundred priests, and twenty thousand faithful attended the
services and Mgr Pie, a frequent orator at these crownings, preached a
sermon. In 1870 the Prussian decision not to occupy Bourges was attributed by some to the intercession of Notre-Dame du Sacré-Coeur. During
the great pilgrimage years of 1872 and 1873 crowds of twenty-five
thousand were reported at the shrine.[86]

Beyond the network of regional shrines was a final group of miracle
cults that, while including shrines as part of their repertoire, also stressed
practices that allowed the devotees to honor Mary apart from attending
the shrine itself. The cults of the Miraculous Medal, Notre-Dame des

Victoires, Notre-Dame de La Salette, Notre-Dame de Lourdes, and
Notre-Dame de Pontmain became generalized devotions in the nineteenth
century.[87] Images and pious literature from these cults were distributed
throughout France by religious orders and confraternities organized at the
parish level. These pious organizations met regularly for prayers and
sermons, usually under the guidance of the local clergy, and communicated with each other by means of periodical publications. The development and significance of these national cults will be discussed in chapter 6.
For now it is sufficient to point out that they offered miracles restoring or
ensuring individual health similar to those available at lower levels in the
supernatural hierarchy. But national cults are distinguished by a higher

level of commitment, both material and spiritual, on the part of the institutional Church. The development of generalized devotions, the most prominent of which was dedicated to Notre-Dame de Lourdes, is clear evidence of the seriousness with which the Church treated popular devotions and of the success it achieved in controlling and channeling popular piety.

Regional shrines, which became important pastoral tools as a result of episcopal support, and generalized devotions, which were a major innovation in nineteenth-century religious life, can be distinguished from local shrines and the array of folkloric practices and beliefs about healing by the extent of their identification with the institutional Church. National and even international miracle cults had existed since the Middle Ages, when Notre-Dame de Chartres and St. Jacques de Compostello drew pilgrims from throughout Europe. The pilgrims to a distant shrine, however, had generally been viewed with suspicion by the Church; their behavior, as Chaucer documented, was not always directed at spiritual progress.[88] The nineteenth-century cults, after some preliminary skirmishes had been resolved, were embraced by the Church. At regional shrines religious orders attempted to relate miraculous healings to orthodox religious practice. Generalized devotions sponsored by the clergy became and remain a familiar part of popular religious belief. The miraculous practices associated with regional shrines and generalized devotions were promoted by the Church because clerical supervision had been established over them. As one moves up the hierarchy from local to regional shrine to national cult the Church's control over the miraculous increases, and its suspicions recede. This is true, however, primarily for shrines and cults dedicated to saints. The healers and professional pilgrims who were an important part of the miraculous network at the local level were at best tolerated, and the Church countenanced folkloric practices and individual thaumaturges only when they could be tied to its own rituals and beliefs. Folkloric beliefs in the healing powers of individuals could not be absorbed or controlled by the Church as easily as those which attributed miracles to shrines and their saints.

An examination of the relations between folklore and institutional religion reveals that the Church was not at all systematically opposed to folklore as such, but in fact tolerated both individual healing rituals and communal processions when they were observed by or included the parish clergy. The Church actively promoted folkloric beliefs when the context was a diocesan shrine staffed by episcopal appointees, or a national cult whose diffusion was controlled by the clergy. The Church could simply have tolerated folkloric practices and made no attempt to control them, viewing them as marginal to its religious and spiritual concerns. Likewise it could have made a concerted effort to eliminate such superstitious practices, as seems to have been the policy of some eighteenth-century bishops. Given the variety of temperaments and intellectual positions of the nineteenth-century clergy, it is not surprising that both of these options were followed at different times and in different places.[89]

Beyond the varied responses to local superstitions, however, there was a general movement to promote folkloric behavior provided it was supervised by responsible clergy. Such activity resulted in a new wave of devotions, which absorbed numerous elements of folkloric belief about miraculous healings. The following chapter will place these requests for miraculous healings in a social and psychological context in order to understand why individuals were driven to seek supernatural help for their medical problems.

Chapter 2

The Social Drama

of a Miraculous Cure

The commitment of the Church to miraculous shrines in nineteenth-century France reflected a new tolerance of folkloric practices when these were formally associated with institutional religion. In making this commitment, the Church strove to integrate traditional healing rites with orthodox symbols and rituals. It was a source of pride for the clergy and of frustration for their opponents that this effort achieved substantial success. The figures for Lourdes show that the number of pilgrims rose constantly and rapidly from the time the shrine was founded; by the last decade of the nineteenth century it was estimated that over five hundred thousand visitors a year came to the grotto. Of these, seventy thousand (fifty thousand women and twenty thousand men) actually bathed in the fountain waters.[1] In analyzing this phenomenon some critics stressed the aggressive commercialism of the Church as an explanation for the success of the cult. According to this view, contemporary miracle cults such as Lourdes were the result of callous exploitation of the sick and the ignorant.[2] Émile Zola, in his novel *Lourdes*, developed a subtler position. Zola believed that the popularity of miracle cults resulted from the need of the sick and their familes to hope for a cure after normal medical remedies had failed.[3] Zola's recognition of the need for hope suggests that any attempt to understand the appeal of the miraculous must give a sympathetic hearing to those who sought cures. This chapter will describe and analyze the rituals through which nineteenth-century miracle cults united the sick and the healthy within a community of belief when illness or accident threatened to dissolve their mutual attachment.

The Inadequacies of Secular Medicine

The sick in nineteenth-century France, in turning to sacred symbols and rituals when ill, were not only responding to a set of religious beliefs; they were choosing a supplement to professional medicine. Such a choice should not be regarded as due to the power of archaic traditions alone, although these undoubtedly played a role in the decision. The proliferation of faith healers in the twentieth century suggests, however, that an assumed contrast between traditional and modern societies does not adequately explain why people seek miracles.[4]

The state of the medical profession in the nineteenth century was one important factor in the choice of a supernatural therapy. Doctors were scarce, especially in the countryside, and their methods were often of little or no value to their patients. The number of doctors declined in the second half of the century, dropping from 18,099 in 1847 to 14,538 in 1896. In the 1840s, just before this decline began, there was some concern that France had too many doctors; but this problem was restricted to the larger cities. Paris, with 3 percent of France's total population, had 13 percent of the doctors; rural France was poorly served by the medical profession.[5] The scarcity of doctors led one *curé* from the Haute-Loire to issue the following complaint in 1891:

> My parish is ravaged by smallpox. . . . There is little faith in the vaccine and the doctors are twenty kilometers away. . . . Why isn't there a law to make young doctors spend a period in an abandoned canton before settling with all the others in a city such as Le Puy where there is one doctor for every thousand persons?[6]

Even when doctors were available they were called only in desperate circumstances, for peasants begrudged the payment of a professional when folk healers and religious remedies were available.[7] In this context the healing role of the clergy discussed in the first chapter is relevant, for while doctors were not always available, the *curé* generally was. A priest from an Alpine department was prosecuted in the 1880s for performing a cesarean section, an operation illegal for nonprofessionals. The defense proposed by the local bishop was the unavailability of a doctor and the urgency of the patient's condition.[8] Under such circumstances the traditional belief in the healing role of the clergy was a necessary substitute for professional medicine.

When doctors were available they were often unable to help their patients. The leading medical theorists of the first half of the century have been labeled by one historian as "nihilists," and although their debunking role was important in clearing the way for future advances, it must have been of little comfort to the sick.[9] Later in the century and into the twentieth "there was no one medical science, and the rivalry between the different theories was as merciless and disruptive as the cutthroat competition of commerce."[10] Despite theoretical advances at Paris, the practices of bleeding and leeching were still common for much of the century, and could be carried to an extreme. Mlle Dumortier, before turning to Notre-Dame des Victoires for a cure, described the treatment she received in 1843, after suffering for two years from migraine headaches, gastritis, constipation, nausea, fever, and insomnia.

> At different times they applied 156 leeches; they also used baths which, like the leeches, gave me temporary relief; I took 140 of them. It is easy to see that these remedies, along with the restricted diet and intense pain, put me in a great state of weakness.[11]

Perhaps some of Mlle Dumortier's symptons were iatrogenic, but at any rate the medical remedies applied were ineffective and probably inappropriate. François Lebrun's judgment about the medical profession and the alternatives to it in the late eighteenth century seems equally true for the nineteenth: "Finally, it is the impotence of medicine, even among its most qualified representatives, that explains why the sick attempted to find means of cures elsewhere."[12] When the recourse to the miraculous is placed in such a context, the decision becomes more comprehensible, even from a secular perspective.

The choice of a religious remedy was not only due to practical calculations about the availability and effectiveness of doctors. Superstitious and religious theories about the causes of illness and accident remained common in nineteenth-century France, especially in the countryside; such beliefs were another factor in the choice of a supernatural therapy. Sorcerers were still widely suspected as the cause of sickness or other misfortune; those who believed themselves victims sought to ward off spells by using religious formulas and the advice of lay healers. A peasant from the Languedoc born in 1885 described his view of sickness to Daniel Fabre: "We weren't sick then as you are now; we worked until we couldn't. If you could move at all, you had to work. It was either the sorcerer or the dead who made us sick, and we were afraid of them."[13]

Such superstitions existed alongside a set of beliefs in which sickness was seen as chastisement sent by God. From the Counterreformation through the eighteenth century the Church had advocated prayer and penitence as the proper response to illness, and it was believed that Christians were especially susceptible to *les vérités du salut* (the truths about salvation) when they were ill.[14] The association between a feeling of personal guilt and sickness sometimes received explicit statement. In a devotional manual published in 1855 for Notre-Dame de Fourvières, a regional shrine in Lyons, the prayer for a cure included the following confession:

> I recognize, alas, that my body is afflicted to procure the health of my soul; forgetfulness of your name and the transgressions of the commandments of your dear Son are the cause of my sickness. . . . You help the sick either in rendering them healthy or in making them pass to a better life through the holy death you grant them.[15]

The emotional state of the sick and of those around them, and the ways in which religious ritual worked to resolve both guilt and illness, will be treated subsequently. For now it is enough to realize that the sick in nineteenth-century France, for both objective and subjective reasons, had cause to turn to religion for a cure.

The Social Drama of a Miraculous Cure

After the decision was made to seek a miraculous remedy, the sick were provided with a number of choices. As we have seen, they had recourse to a wide range of religious therapies, from the incantation of a prayer to St. Apolline to the pilgrimage to Notre-Dame de Lourdes. Those who turned to religion were not necessarily disappointed. Anthropologists have shown how symbols and rituals similar to those used by nineteenth-century French cults can be effective. By creating a dramatic setting through the manipulation of religious symbols, miracles were able to restore the sick to a sense of physical as well as spiritual well-being.[16] Victor Turner's concept of a "social drama" describes a four-stage process that illuminates the way the sick decided on a miraculous remedy, and the way this remedy was applied.[17]

The first stage of the social drama is the breach "between persons or groups within the same system of social relations." According to Turner's original usage, this would usually be a public act by an individual in violation of some crucial norm. For my purposes the breach is equivalent to the inception of the ailment. While a sick person did not willfully choose to violate the social cohesiveness of his family and community, there is a sense in which sickness put an individual into a subtle form of opposition to those closest to him.

A crisis occurs if the breach is not successfully closed, constituting the second stage of the social drama. In the case of miraculous cures, this period accompanied and followed the repeated failures of secular therapeutic techniques. Miraculous help frequently followed a judgment by the medical profession that the patient was incurable. The sick person was threatened by despair, and his family and members of his community felt repelled and alienated by the intractable malady.

During the third phase of the drama, "redressive action" is taken, through which "adjustive and redressive mechanisms . . . are swiftly brought into operation by leading or structurally representative members of the disturbed social system." As applied to miraculous cures, this action was a novena, a pilgrimage, or both, suggested by a *curé*, a nun, or a pious layman. By participation in such a ritual, and by focusing on a central religious symbol, the sick person and his community reasserted their solidarity and the crisis was resolved.

Finally, the fourth stage is the "reintegration" of the individual into the disturbed social group. This describes the period following the cure, when the *malade* had become a *miraculé*, with a new sense of religious responsibility; the community now regarded him as a cultic object, a living symbol of the omnipotence and mercy of God.

The onset of illness or the occurrence of an accident did not lead immediately to the request for a miracle. In the early stages of the drama folk therapy and doctors' remedies were relied on. Bleedings, leechings, and sedatives, for example, were prescribed for Victorine Pétiard, of St. Clare (diocese of Constances), for eight years following an accident in which she was kicked by a cow. She experienced intermittent relief, but in 1824 her symptoms—vomiting blood and convulsions—grew worse and the techniques of secular medicine no longer provided any relief. Similarly, for Sister St. Agatha bleedings and blisterings were used for five months in an attempt to cure her loss of speech in 1824.[18] Of the fifty-one reports of Prince Hohenlohe's cures in *L'ami de la religion*, twenty-seven include a reference to the care of a doctor whose repertoire of techniques was applied, usually for years, with little or no success.[19]

Toward the end of the century, at Lourdes, treatment by a doctor was a rigorously applied prerequisite for those wishing to verify a miracle. The national pilgrimage in August of each year, which brought over a thousand sick to the grotto, required of each sick pilgrim a certificate from a local doctor attesting to the ailment and specifying the treatment that had been given. All of the sixty-five cures reported by Dr. Boissarie in *Les grandes guérisons de Lourdes* occurred after recourse to the medical profession, which was given an important role at Lourdes in testifying to its own helplessness.[20]

As a consequence of secular medicine's repeated failures a crisis was reached, a state in which the sick and his family were forced to face a future in which a cure was not only unlikely, but seemingly impossible. The period prior to the crisis varied, but some idea of how long it was before the miraculous was invoked can be determined by calculating the average length of time between the onset of illness and recourse to religious therapy. Of twenty-nine cures by Prince Hohenlohe for which the information is available, an average of 7.6 years elapsed between the inception of the ailment and the consultation of Hohenlohe. For the second half of the century Boissarie's account of the miracles performed at Lourdes yields similar results. For the fifty-one cases on which Boissarie provides relevant information there was an average of 7.3 years from the time secular medical treatment began to the point at which Notre-Dame de Lourdes was invoked. The crisis stage of the social drama was reached when the illness had established itself as chronic and the treatment of the medical profession had proved to be of limited value.

The psychological state of the sick during the crisis can be discerned from their statements made after the cure. During this stage the sick, repelled by their own condition and conscious of the burden they imposed on others, felt alienated from their fellows and despaired of a cure. Mme Perron of Paris described her condition prior to the visit of a Daughter of Charity, who gave her a Miraculous Medal that eventually cured her:

> I had been sick for eight years and had lost a great deal of blood; I was in great pain almost constantly. I had no strength, I couldn't eat, and the little I did take made me sicker. . . . I don't remember during these eight years more than eight days of relief; the rest of the time I spent mostly in bed, unable to do the work necessary to help my poor husband feed his family; at one point I spent eighteen consecutive months in bed. I consulted many doctors who prescribed the ordinary remedies for this type of illness, without ex-

periencing any notable relief. My husband, unable to afford such expenses and seeing no end to my sickness, lost courage and was almost to the point of despair.[21]

Mme Perron felt acutely the effect of her condition on the household; her inability to work and the medical expenses added feelings of guilt to her physical problems. The miraculous, when invoked, addressed a spiritual and psychological ailment as well as the physical symptoms.

Similar fears of being an economic burden can be observed in the statements of those cured at Lourdes. Catherine Latapie-Chouat of Loubajac "could not use her left hand, either to spin or knit, or even for housework," after she broke her arm when falling from a tree where she was collecting nuts.[22] Mme Vendôme of Lourdes had been in and out of bed for seven weeks suffering from "pains in all her limbs, but especially in her legs and her knees, which were extremely swollen." At the suggestion of some passers-by on their way to the grotto, Mme Vendôme made the trip to the grotto and was cured. "Upon returning home she took care of the housework, which she had had to renounce for seven weeks."[23] Finally, Jeanne Crassus (Mme Crozat) of Lourdes, had suffered from paralyzed fingers for ten years before her cure at Lourdes. Her testimony stressed once again the concern over the inability to perform ordinary household tasks. "It was impossible for her to spin, to sew, to take any object in her fingers, nor could she take care of her house, except by directing her oldest daughter."[24]

Domestic incapacities were a source of hardship. Visible wounds, when serious, could lead to feelings of profound alienation. Mme Rouchel, whose face was disfigured by a tubercular growth, had contemplated suicide after five years of unsuccessful treatment by doctors. She was cured at Lourdes in 1903, but her prayers at the grotto reveal her anguish and sense of social isolation prior to the miracle.

> I placed myself on my knees. I asked the Virgin to take away this hideous bandage; I said to her that if I had to be punished for my sins, would she place the disease on my leg, but please would she not leave such hideous wounds on my face, which horrified everyone.[25]

A similar attitude toward illness was expressed by Joachime Dehant, also cured at Lourdes. Mlle Dehant, who had come on a train during the national pilgrimage, described the reaction to the purulent infection on her arm: "My traveling companions got back into the compartment, but were so nauseated by the unbearable odor that they themselves became sick and began to vomit. As for me, I was supremely humiliated and didn't dare raise my eyes."[26]

The feeling of alienation was more than an imagined sense of persecution on the part of the sick. The manual of the stretcher-carriers of Lourdes, while it stressed the sense of charity which the volunteers must bring to their work, also made it clear that they would have to exercise enormous self-control to remain calm in face of the miserable and repulsive sick confined to their care. Bertrin, an early historian of the Lourdes pilgrimages, was overwhelmed by the charity that could lead normal, healthy men and women to face the ill at Lourdes.

> This disinterested eagerness, this renunciation of habitual behavior, these delicate and considerate attentions for those unhappy individuals whose illnesses are repulsive, profoundly touch the heart and bring tears of admiration to your eyes. Lourdes is without doubt the greatest practical school of charity ever seen by any people.[27]

Even allowing for the usual emotional inflation that enters all apologetical works on Lourdes, Bertrin's point is well made. It was the religious atmosphere of Lourdes that allowed the healthy to confront the sick without manifesting their own disgust. In the crisis period of the illness, such feelings of horror or disgust must have been difficult to control, and the sick would have been insensitive not to realize their ostracization. Whether the symptoms were repulsive, incapacitating, or inconvenient, the sick experienced a sense of separation from the world of the healthy. This alienation may at times have been compounded by feelings of guilt; and it was likely to be reflected in the behavior of those closest to the sick, the families who were deprived of one of their members.

The redressive action for such a crisis was the third and climactic phase of the social drama. The parish *curé* was frequently the key figure in initiating this phase. Of the forty-two cures of lay people worked by Prince Hohenlohe and reported in *L'ami de la religion*, at least twenty-seven involved the local priest, who either wrote to the prince on behalf of the sick person or attested to the cure after it had occurred.[28] This pattern of involvement of the local *curé* can also be observed at regional shrines, for frequently he was the one to recommend and verify the cures worked at these centers.[29]

Religious confraternities also frequently initiated redressive action. Miraculous cures achieved through the prayers of local chapters of the Archconfraternity of Notre-Dame des Victoires were reported in the *Annales de l'archconfrérie*. Other confraternities associated with cures were the *pénitents blancs* and the *enfants de Marie*.[30] The activity of such groups within the social drama demonstrates that the source of hope in supernatural intervention was frequently a lay organization of highly committed religious virtuosi under the guidance of the local priest.

The network of Catholic charitable associations established in the nineteenth century could also initiate this third phase of the social drama. It was, for example, the association of Notre-Dame du Salut that recruited indigent sick from Paris, who were an important segment of the annual national pilgrimage at Lourdes.[31] The pious literature produced in such large quantities offered another source of information to the sick. All of the miracle cults benefited from the distribution of publications. Hohenlohe's popularity stemmed in part from the diffusion of pamphlets on his cures and the reports published in *L'ami de la religion*, a journal widely read by clergy during the Restoration. During the July Monarchy the Miraculous Medal and Notre-Dame des Victoires were popularized by manuals that described the history of these devotions and ascribed miraculous powers to them.[32] There were several cases in which the consultation of pious literature about Lourdes was interpreted as part of a larger providential plan which led to a miraculous cure.[33]

Literature promoting miracle cults was not new to the nineteenth century, for during the Counterreformation and throughout the ancien régime similar tracts had appeared. But with the expansion of literacy in the nineteenth century the impact of such material increased in significance. Moreover, the Church, which had always sought to control printed references to the supernatural, took advantage of the growth in literacy with a massive number of publications devoted in whole or in part to miracles.

Whatever the origin of the idea that a miracle was possible, the advice to the sick usually took the specific form of recommending a novena or a pilgrimage which would invoke the intercession of a particular saint or one of the various cults of Mary or Jesus. A novena required a series of prayers or readings for nine days, with confession required at some point during the period, and mass and communion either daily or on the last day. The novena literature typically began with a brief history of the cult, including references to its thaumaturgic powers, and concluded with a set of readings that focused attention on the cultic object or image, which was interpreted as a condensed symbol for all of Catholic doctrine. Pilgrimages to miraculous shrines were the second major technique for obtaining a cure. Often novenas would be performed during a pilgrimage, and in other cases a pilgrimage would be made after a successful novena, in thanksgiving for a miracle. Whatever the framework of a particular healing, it was necessary that some rite of passage prepare the sick for the reception of supernatural grace.[34]

It was during the stage of redressive action that the miracle actually occurred. The patient's physical condition was transformed by participation in a ritual that engaged his total self. The medical problem was transmuted into spiritual terms and the result could be miraculously therapeutic. The dynamics of this process can be illuminated with the help of another concept borrowed from contemporary anthropology. In an important essay on pilgrimages, Victor Turner posits that the pilgrim, during his voyage to the shrine, leaves behind the social structure that characterizes his secular life. He enters into a state of *communitas*, which is "a means of binding diversities together and overcoming cleavages." A pilgrimage is "a participation in a sacred existence, with the aim of achieving a step toward wholeness in oneself, both of body and soul; it is a forgiveness of sins, where differences are accepted or tolerated rather than aggravated into grounds of aggressive opposition."[35] Observers of nineteenth-century pilgrimages report an atmosphere that conforms to Turner's thesis. Abbé Boisnard, whose book describes several pilgrimages he made, related his trip to Notre-Dame de Verdelais in these terms:

> A pilgrimage, in effect, is a good fortune for a country. . . . They greet you on the highway and at your arrival with feelings of being related; and with a familiarity which does you good, all the faces smile at you . . . and seem to say: And there is another who is part of the family.[36]

Although Turner's concept of *communitas* was derived from the observation of pilgrimages, it applies equally well to the novenas used in the miraculous process. Both rituals separated the sick and a community of believers from the secular world of work and structured social relations. Through the mutual contemplation of sacred symbols during pilgrimages and novenas, the social bond that tied the sick to the world was renewed, and within this state of *communitas* a cure was achieved.

The Eucharist was one of the most potent symbols used by the Church in its miraculous rituals. The interaction of Eucharistic symbolism and the pressure of the community can be observed in the cure of Marie Gourmy of Laigné-en-Belin (Sarthe). Mme Gourmy had fallen from a roof in 1816 and had since suffered from paralysis of her right side and the loss of her voice. In 1824, when gangrene attacked her right arm, the local doctor advised amputation. Under these dire circumstances Prince Hohenlohe was contacted; he proposed to begin a novena for Mme Gourmy on July 1. On that day, while attending Mass, Mme Gourmy recovered her mobility and speech at the moment of the consecration of the host. Fifty people from the parish were present and witnessed the partial cure. Word spread to the area and on July 10, the final day of the novena, seven hundred attended Mass and sixty communicated. The cure was completed on that day, with the disappearance of the gangrene attested to by four doctors, the *curé*, and the local notables. The social support by the parish, the belief in the Real Presence of Christ in the Eucharist, and the knowledge of Hohenlohe's successful prayers as reported by the local *curé*, created an atmosphere of *communitas* in which the cure was effected.[37] It is a significant feature of Hohenlohe's cures that even as they involved the parish community they used the most universal of all Christian rituals, the Mass, and a devotion to the name of Christ. Local saints were still invoked in the last century, but the national publicity attached to Hohenlohe's miracles gave them a special prominence not shared by any single local cult. The tendency of the Church to promote universal rituals and symbols can thus be established in the first of the new miracle cults to achieve recognition.[38]

A fundamental element in the experience of *communitas* was the association between the sick individual and his family. Regardless of the cure's larger social context, the sick were generally described as engaged with their families in the quest for a miracle. Evidence from the cures of Hohenlohe and Lourdes indicates that the family played a role in nineteenth-century miracles at the parish, regional, and national levels. Not only the local *curé* but also family members were known to have initiated contact with Hohenlohe. At Lourdes, before the grotto had been officially approved by the episcopal authorities, the statements of those cured at the shrine generally included at least one family member as a witness.[39] At shrines that became the focus of official Church attention the family continued to play a role; but at regional and national shrines the quality and significance of family participation was altered. The significant relationship in a local cure was between the sick person, his family, and his parish. At regional and national shrines the relationship was more complex, with the sick and his family set in a context that included diocese, nation, and the ideological goals of the Church. The family remained an important support for the sick, but the atmosphere had been expanded, with the parish community as the mediating agent replaced by a crowd whose attention was no longer focused on the individual patient. Boissarie's description of the national pilgrimage of 1891 suggests how family and friends shared in the ritual of the Lourdes cures:

> It is time for the procession of the Holy Sacrament. The sick take their places, grouped on the path that they will follow. At the front, the stretchers, where the very sick lie, several small wheelchairs, scattered here and there.
>
> Behind the stretchers, seated, on their knees, leaning on their crutches, paralytics, the invalids, the whole range of wounds and white tumors. Finally, the immobile and anxious relatives and friends forming an impenetrable barrier, which extended from the grotto to the arcades of the Rosary, and from the [River] Gave to the boulders.
>
> This moment of waiting is imposing, grandiose. When the Holy Sacrament appeared all uncovered their foreheads, and bent their knees, and the heavens seemed to communicate with the earth.[40]

The sick were surrounded on one side by the Eucharist being carried in candlelight procession to the grotto of the apparitions and cures, and on the other by their expectant families and friends. Those cured during the procession (which was a daily occurrence during the pilgrimage season at Lourdes) rose from their sickbeds to follow the Eucharist to the grotto, to the acclamations of the crowd massed behind them.[41]

The use of the Eucharist as a thaumaturgic symbol in the cure of Mme Gourmy at her parish church and as part of the massive ceremony at Lourdes suggests its importance in the cults encouraged by the Church. The Eucharist was frequently combined with other symbols in a ritual pattern that reveals the Church's attempt to associate with and thereby benefit from the cures. The miraculous fountain discovered by Bernadette was and is a central element in the Lourdes ritual, but during the last fifteen years of the nineteenth century it was the Eucharist that proved most efficacious for the sick. In 1888, of forty-two cures verified by the Bureau of Medical Confirmation at Lourdes, six (14 percent) occurred during processions of the Blessed Sacrament, while the rest took place at the baths. By 1894 more than half of the verified cures came at the moment that the Eucharist passed by the gathered sick, and for the last decade of the century an average of 60 percent of the attested miracles were attributed to the Eucharistic procession.[42] This shift from fountain to Eucharist is significant, and a brief analysis will suggest why the Church encouraged the new ritual, thus altering the content of a popular cult.

Fountains are pre-Christian and cross-cultural symbols of healing and regeneration.[43] After the official acknowledgment of the veracity of the apparitions and early cures at Lourdes in 1862, the Church was in the awkward position of sanctioning a cult that placed a non-Christian symbol in a central position at the country's most popular shrine. The role of the Catholic sacraments as a channel of supernatural graces was, in a sense, compromised by the fountain at Lourdes. Transubstantiation is perhaps the most miraculous and most important single doctrine of the Catholic faith. How was it possible that Christ Himself, present in the consecrated host, was not as miraculously potent as the fountain at Lourdes, even given its supernatural origins? The elevation of the Eucharist to a central position in the miraculous ritual at Lourdes brought the cult there under the control of the traditional sacramental system, and resolved the Church's difficulty. The Eucharist served to legitimize the miracles at Lourdes, and at the same time was legitimized by them.

Other images and symbols instrumental in the redressive action of the miraculous cure become more comprehensible when they are placed inside this context of the social drama. The Miraculous Medal, representations of Notre-Dame de La Salette, the Holy Face of Christ, Notre-Dame de Lourdes, and others were not intended to be aesthetic objects, but symbols capable of evoking an immediate affective response that could be easily shared by all observers. The subtlety of serious art, which leads to criticism and varying interpretations, would not have served the purposes of a sick person and his community. These images sometimes stated a doctrinal point but, more important to the sick, they were simple representations of supernatural concern. The Miraculous Medal, for example, shows the Virgin crushing the head of the serpent-devil, her arms extended to bestow graces on France, surrounded by a prayer that invoked the Immaculate Conception. But a sick person was justified in seeing Mary's arms extended to him, her victory over the serpent a symbol of her conquest of the evil that afflicted him. The weeping Virgin of La Salette and the weeping Christ of the Holy Face were seen by the Church as mourning the blasphemy and materialism of the modern age. For the sick person who invoked these cults, however, it must have seemed that Christ and Mary were personally moved by his plight. Of course, the Church never tried to restrict the significance of these images; they were intended to be multivalent symbols lending themselves to both doctrinal and thaumaturgic uses. The Church was thus able to associate those who saw the symbols as essentially thaumaturgic with a set of institutional goals without having to engage in the complexities of theological or political discourse.[44]

An extended example demonstrates the range of miraculous symbols available in nineteenth-century France and shows how they were activated in the course of the social drama. The story of the newspaper worker Louis X's cure appeared in *Le Pèlerin*, a popular weekly magazine published by the Assumptionists, and as a pamphlet in 1883. Louis, after a pious upbringing, had deserted his faith and was employed by a socialist newspaper hostile to the Church. The author of the pamphlet, Abbé Dumax of Notre-Dame des Victoires, describes some of the pressure that worked on Louis through a variety of miracle cults.

> During this period of impiety, without asking himself why he did something so inconsequential, Louis continued to carry a small medal of the Virgin, the Miraculous Medal. . . . His grandmother had given it to him, and the *curé* of Ars had blessed it and placed it on him when he was nine years old. There is more. In his first walks through Paris he had occasion to enter Notre-Dame des Victoires. . . .
>
> Holy medal! Precious sanctuary of Our Lady! Pious meetings of the Archconfraternity! They formed the mysterious bond which, without his knowledge, restored this poor soul to God. The test of illness would soon strike him; but for him, as for many others, sickness was an undoubted expression of God's divine mercy, the first stage in his conversion.[45]

Prior to his illness, then, Louis was already under the influence of three potent nineteenth-century cults, those centered on the Miraculous Medal, the *curé* of Ars, and the Archconfraternity of Notre-Dame des Victoires. But after contracting tuberculosis of the lungs it was Notre-Dame de Lourdes that actually cured him, albeit in close cooperation with the other cults. Louis had been confined to a hospital staffed by the Daughters of Charity when a notice of the national pilgrimage "providentially" fell into his hands. Before leaving on the "white train," Louis made one last visit to Notre-Dame des Victoires, where he prayed for his cure and for the conversion of an atheist friend. The reception of the Eucharist and the contemplation of a statue of Mary combined to force a crisis in his physical and spiritual life.

> When the moment of communion came . . . pushed by an irresis-
> tible force, he raised his eyes toward the image of Mary and made a
> promise to consecrate himself to God in a monastery as penitence
> for his past life if she would cure him and convert his friend. After
> receiving communion he felt ill and a cold sweat swept over him.
> This crisis was followed by a great calm.[46]

At Lourdes, a few days later, the circumstances of the cure itself were less dramatic. Louis drank at the fountain the day of his arrival, and felt himself cured immediately afterwards. The crisis had been reached at Notre-Dame des Victoires before his departure. Upon his return to Paris, Louis' friend was converted on the basis of the cure as incontrovertible evidence of the reality of the supernatural. Louis himself entered a monas-tery as he had promised.

The details in this case are important because of the complex tangle of cults and symbols they reveal. Louis was first led to Notre-Dame des Victoires as a result of the Miraculous Medal blessed by the *curé* of Ars; he was cured at the grotto of Lourdes, but only after a crisis that resulted from the reception of communion and a heartfelt prayer before a statue in Notre-Dame des Victoires. Louis was engulfed by the miraculous, con-stantly mediated by a set of rituals and symbols that included medals, statues, publications, pilgrimages, the Mass, and the Eucharist. One is tempted to wonder how Louis could possibly have avoided a cure and conversion, given the battery of miraculous agents arrayed about him.

Furthermore, the miracle took place in the context of alienation I have described as the crisis that precedes the redressive action. In the hospital for ten months, Louis' condition had deteriorated to the point that it was openly acknowledged he had no hope for recovery. "A word that had escaped from one of the doctors in the presence of the young medical

students who accompanied him, convinced him that his days were henceforth numbered." At the moment that the notice of the pilgrimage to
Lourdes came to his attention, the nun who gave the pamphlet to him
remarked, "No. 17, you must go to Lourdes. The Holy Virgin, in curing
you, will do a beautiful thing."[47] Finally, it should be recalled that Louis'
sense of physical alienation was compounded by his spiritual condition.
The medal he wore, given to him by his grandmother, was a constant
reminder of his apostasy from the family faith in which he had been raised.
His cure and conversion illustrate how the redressive action of a pilgrimage, in connection with a personal devotion to the supernatural as represented in sacred symbols, was miraculously effective.

Critics of the shrines and miracle cults, with Zola a notable exception,
did not understand or appreciate the power of the healing rituals. They
stressed instead the political and financial benefits that the Church gained
by organizing miracle cults. According to the liberal newspaper *Le siècle*,
shrines like Lourdes were "a vast conspiracy . . . organized by the clerical
party against the development of the human spirit. . . . Miracles have no
other purpose but to come to the aid of the temporal power of the
Church."[48] As evidence for this position skeptics pointed to the emphasis
some cults placed on the gift of money the sick were asked to contribute to
the shrine. Indeed, some cults made the contribution the climactic moment of the healing ritual. A publication of the shrine of Notre-Dame du
Chêne, in describing the cure of a young girl, reported that "she was
suddenly cured at the moment that she leaned forward to place her coin in
the box. No more tumor!"[49] The shrine of Notre-Dame du Séez was
especially notorious for encouraging the sick to believe that their contribution could be instrumental in obtaining a cure. Even major shrines such as
St. Anne d'Auray and Notre-Dame de Lourdes called attention to the
relationship between gift and miracle. The bishop of Vannes claimed that
"in making your offering [to St. Anne d'Auray] you can ask with confidence the mother of the Holy Virgin, whom one never invokes in vain,
some particular grace: a conversion, health, or a success in business."[50] At
Lourdes the fifth article of the 1862 decree approving the cult called for
contributions and asserted that: "There is no doubt . . . that persons who
contribute by their generosity to the construction of this monument will
receive in exchange some important favor, either in the spiritual or temporal order."[51] This was not an outright promise of a miracle, but it did
imply an equivalence between the spiritual and material benefits that

might result from devotion to Notre-Dame de Lourdes; and it did directly relate these benefits to a financial contribution by the devotee.

The importance of money in the social drama did not, however, necessarily negate the spirit of *communitas* that formed the context of the cure. Although some cults at times emphasized the importance of a monetary gift, this was generally only one element of the ritual. Furthermore, the presentation of gifts at shrines was not due only to the venality of the institutional Church. In the days immediately after the apparitions at Lourdes, while the Church was still suspicious of the new shrine, people were already lighting candles and placing coins in a box at the grotto as part of the pilgrimage ritual.[52] In addition to money pilgrims also left other gifts; at Lourdes the grotto gradually became lined with the crutches of those who were healed. Gifts, whether money, crutches, candles, or some other object, were a symbol of commitment and gratitude to the shrine and to its patron saint. Those who emphasized the material element in the gift and ignored the sense of spiritual devotion it implied were perhaps justifiably critical of the institutional Church. But in the world of popular religion matter and spirit were not clearly distinguished, and religion was relied on for physical and material relief as well as for spiritual reassurance.

The fourth and final phase of the social drama of a miraculous cure was the reintegration of the sick person into his community. There were particular rituals for this part of the process, as for the others. Following the cure the *miraculé* was formally received by the community that had provided the support throughout the redressive action, usually by a public celebration that included the singing of the *Magnificat* or the *Te Deum*. It was not uncommon for a religious revival to follow a miracle, with increased church attendance, during which time the *miraculé* became a symbol to the community of God's omnipotence and mercy. The most famous *miraculé* of all, Pierre de Rudder, whose case still figures in controversies over the veracity of the Lourdes miracles, made himself constantly available for inspection and offered his prayers for the intention of those who sought his help. Between the time of his cure in 1875 at Notre-Dame de Lourdes in Oostacker (Belgium), until his death in 1897, he made over four hundred pilgrimages to the shrine for the sake of others who sought miracles. The operation of a miracle, then, did not conclude with a simple return to the status quo. The sick who were healed experienced an increased religious commitment, which was capable of affecting the entire community.[53]

Not all the rituals of reintegration were major community events. Often this phase of the social drama would be marked by a simple act in which the *miraculé*'s active participation in the community was affirmed. Statements of the first *miraculés* of Lourdes show that the renewal of ordinary domestic behavior such as cooking, sewing, and housekeeping could have a ritual significance for family and friends. The case of Marie Lanou, a widow of Borderies, near Lourdes, illustrates the point. Eighty years old, the widow Lanou had been paralyzed for two years and suffered from "confused ideas." After drinking some water from the grotto, she was cured. Her friends and relatives who accompanied her to the commission investigating Lourdes described the events following the cure. "The change was so astounding that when she returned to the fields, at harvest season, she asked for a pitchfork and began to work energetically."[54] It is doubtful that at age eighty Marie was really expected to do much productive work at the harvest following her cure; her activity was significant as a symbol of her reentry into the life of the community. As such, it concluded the social drama of her miraculous cure.

Social Origins of the *Miraculés*

The social drama, which led in some cases to miraculous cures, joined the sick and the healthy through its ability to create a spirit of *communitas*. Data on the age, sex, and marital status of *miraculés* drawn from the cures of Hohenlohe, La Salette, and Lourdes allow us to form an impression of what categories of people sought miraculous help. The results of this inquiry, shown in the following table, suggest that the sick who participated in such dramas were already isolated from the community, thus heightening their need for the support that flowed from these rituals.

The figures presented show that the highest percentage of *miraculés* were widowed or single adult women. One possible explanation for the disproportionate share of women *miraculés* is, of course, that women tended to be more religious than men. In addition to this factor, however, the examples cited in describing the crisis stage of the social drama indicate that the sick and their communities were concerned with the problems of isolation and dependency. When they were ill, these women must have created special problems for their families and communities. Sickness and accident would necessarily increase the dependence of the sick on their

TABLE. *Distribution of* miraculés *by age, sex, and marital status*

	Hohenlohe	La Salette	Lourdes (prior to Church approval)	Lourdes (after Church approval)	Totals
AGE					
0–10	1	0	8	4	13 (8%)
11–17	5	2	4	8	19 (12%)
18–30	11	16	6	14	47 (29%)
31–80	15	19	12	37	83 (50%)
SEX AND MARITAL STATUS					
Single/widowed males	1	1	3	5	10 (8%)
Married males	0	1	2	1	4 (3%)
Single/widowed females	21	29	9	31	90 (76%)
Married females	4	3	4	4	15 (13%)

Sources: Hohenlohe—*L'ami de la religion*, 1822–1825; La Salette—Giray, *Les miracles de La Salette*; Lourdes, prior to Church approval—*LDA*, 5; after Church approval—Boissarie, *Les grandes guérisons de Lourdes.*

relatives and neighbors, and it should be recalled that many of those treated were incapable of any work. Without a husband or children to serve as a buffer between themselves and the parish, these women must have felt especially vulnerable. Their neighbors, friends, and relatives were in the uncomfortable position of having to care for the sick, perhaps at the expense of their own immediate families. Christian charity demanded such assistance, but it is likely that such dependence generated ill-will and guilt about these selfish feelings. The situation of the sick seems to resemble that described by Keith Thomas and Alan MacFarlane in their works on witchcraft. According to their findings, witches in sixteenth- and seventeenth-century England tended to be single or widowed women whose requests for community support created feelings of animosity and guilt in the community, which partially account for the witchcraft accusations of the period.[55] In both situations it is a sense of social alienation that partially accounts for the manifest problems of illness or witchcraft. The social drama of the miracle provided an effective mechanism for overcoming this tension between single women and their communities.

Emile Durkheim, in *Suicide* and *Elementary Forms of the Religious Life*, continually returns to the point that religion and religious ritual play a central role in social integration.[56] The statistics in *Suicide* show that it was single men and women who were most likely to commit suicide in nineteenth-century France, and within this group it was single men who accounted for the preponderance of deaths. According to Durkheim, single women were less likely to commit suicide in part because they were able to find solace in religious devotions. Suicide results from a loosening of the social bonds that tie people to each other, and participation in family life and religious devotions are factors that protect people from the social isolation that encourages suicidal tendencies. Similarly, I propose that sickness tended to isolate afflicted individuals and that family life and religious devotions were forces that provided the support needed for recovery. When a sick individual had no immediate family, the burden fell more heavily on religious ritual as the means to provide him or her with the assurance that was needed. Miraculous ritual, then, was an expression of social solidarity that had therapeutic results. A passage from *Suicide*, which describes the effects of social integration, could easily be applied to the dynamics of the miraculous process.

> The bond that unites individuals with the common cause attaches them to life and the lofty goal they envisage prevents their feeling personal troubles so deeply. There is, in short, in a cohesive and animated society a constant inter-change of ideas and feelings from all to each and each to all, something like a mutual moral support, which, instead of throwing the individual on his own resources, leads him to share in the collective energy and supports his own when exhausted.[57]

Only a few of the reports and statements on miraculous cures make reference to the social or economic status of the *miraculés*, but what information is available suggests that the use of a miraculous remedy was not restricted to a superstitious peasant class. At least five of the *miraculés* treated by Hohenlohe had respected social positions. Four were from noble families, and one was the sister of a deputy from the Estates General of 1789. The other scattered references in *L'ami de la religion* reveal that two *miraculés* were injured while doing farm work, one was the wife of a vintner, and one was characterized as a "poor girl."

Somewhat better data are available from the episcopal subcommission that investigated Lourdes in 1858. Of thirty *miraculés*, only nine were able to sign statements attesting to their cures. The other twenty-one could simply swear to the fact, and were unable to sign the *procès-verbaux* transcribed by the commission. Of those who signed the statements, additional information shows that one was a stonecutter, one was a laborer, one a cafe manager, and one a student in a convent school at Bordeaux. Two of the illiterate *miraculés* were day-laborers, one a pastry-maker who described herself as "young and poor." This evidence from the *procès-verbaux* indicating that the sick in the early days of the Lourdes pilgrimage were mostly from the poorer and less educated classes is confirmed by the report of the police commissioner to the prefect on the status of the pilgrims. According to Commissioner Jacomet,

> The sick come for the most part from the countryside, and the rest belong to the working classes. The most important offerings are contributed by this category of visitors, who are the most miserable and poor. We have had only one coin left in the basket which was gold.[58]

The case of Mlle Moreau, the student from the convent school at Bordeaux, is of special interest because her parents, who wrote lengthy and articulate letters of testimony about their daughter's cure, were the only bourgeois involved with the Lourdes cult who claimed a cure during this early period of the shrine. The Moreau family, which resided in Tartas (Landes), learned of the grotto by means of a miracle story in the *Messager Catholique* of Bordeaux, while all the other *miraculés* investigated by the subcommission were informed of the miracles at the fountain by word of mouth.[59] Mlle Moreau was the only *miraculé* investigated who came from beyond the local area. This pattern is repeated in the later stages of the Lourdes cult. After the shrine had developed into a national center, the *miraculés* were more likely to be from outside the department of the Hautes-Pyrénées, to have heard of the cult through the printed word, and to be of the middle classes. A distinction can be drawn between local shrines, which drew their clientele from local peasants and tradesmen, and regional and national shrines, which drew from more varied social groups and a wider geographic area, and relied on publications to disseminate information about their miracles.

Evidence from Boissarie's work on *Les grandes guérisons* can be used to support this point. Of the twenty-three *miraculés* he describes on whom relevant information is available, five were members of doctors' families, two were successful businessmen, one was a popular journalist, one was a hotel manager, and one was the daughter of a deputy. If it is permissable to label these ten *miraculés* members of the "middle classes," the thirteen remaining cases can be characterized as part of the "working classes." Four of these were domestic servants, two were day-laborers, one was an itinerant singer, one was a soldier, one was an employee of a printing works, and four were simply labeled "poor women." Since Boissarie was defending the Lourdes cures, he had a natural interest in selecting those *miraculés* who would impress the reader with their social position: hence the large number of cures from doctors' families. But the fact that such examples were available for Boissarie's exploitation does indicate that the cult at the grotto had expanded its clientele since its early stages.

The geographical distribution of 2,002 *miraculés* of Lourdes, based on a list compiled by Georges Bertrin, is a final piece of evidence that yields an important point about the clients of this national cult. The distribution of *miraculés* in absolute numbers and as a proportion of departmental population shows the ability of Lourdes to draw from a national clientele (see Appendix). The Seine and the Rhone lead the list of departments that provided *miraculés* for Lourdes, and Bertrin's information indicates that Paris and Lyons accounted for most of these. It appears that the cult of Lourdes did not rely exclusively on Catholic rural areas for its followers, although the numbers do indicate that the traditionally pious north and west produced more cures than the areas east and south of Paris, which are usually classified as "indifferent."[60] The large number of religious orders and the organization of Catholic charity is one factor that may partially account for the numerous *miraculés* of Paris and Lyons. The strong desire of the Lourdes organization and its apologists to demonstrate the national extension of the cult must also be taken into account. It is likely that local pilgrims still came to Lourdes for treatment, but it was the important organized pilgrimages that drew the attention of the Bureau of Medical Confirmation and of Bertrin. Nevertheless, many *miraculés* did come from major urban centers. The sick who did not have recourse to a local fountain or shrine were able instead to turn to Notre-Dame de Lourdes.

The evidence presented here suggests that the regional and national shrines that were developed in the nineteenth century drew from a broader social base and from a wider geographic area than traditional cults. Qualitative evidence from other sources supports this position. Biographers of the *curé* of Ars cite evidence that as the pilgrimage to Ars gained a national audience, people from the middle and upper levels of society began to consult the *curé*.[61] Mlle des Brulais' description of the early days of the pilgrimage to La Salette makes a clear, though unconscious, distinction between the local peasants and artisans who came in procession with their parishes and the bourgeois like herself who came alone or with a few friends, from great distances, to participate in the pilgrimage. Mlle des Brulais and others like her were granted private interviews with the bishop of Grenoble and the shepherd children who had seen the apparition; they stayed in the local convents and in the guest hotel on the holy mountain. La Salette, like Lourdes, was a shrine that served the interests of both the local population and the pious middle classes.[62] I have shown in the first chapter that in the nineteenth century the Church made a substantial effort to develop regional and national miracle cults. This institutional initiative was accompanied by an expansion of the miraculous to include literate and middle-class Catholics. People like Henri Lasserre and Mlle des Brulais felt comfortable with miracle-working rituals at an officially sanctioned shrine staffed by missionaries who related the particular cult to some aspect of Catholic dogma; they might have been embarrassed to attend a local fountain or shrine, the use of which could be construed as superstitious.

The role of the Church was undoubtedly a crucial factor in the popularity of nineteenth-century miracle cults, but those opponents of the cults who dismissed them as a consequence of superstitious clericalism failed to appreciate the social needs fulfilled by recourse to the miraculous. The use of supernatural remedies is not, after all, peculiar to societies in which the Catholic clergy have a widespread influence.[63] If miracle cults were popular, it was in part because they helped the sick, their families, and their communities to deal with feelings of alienation that resulted from, or in some cases caused, the physical symptoms. That the social drama through which these feelings were resolved sometimes resulted in a cure confirms what anthropologists and psychologists have discovered about the effectiveness of nonscientific medical techniques. The popular need for miracles is thus as important as the institutional initiative in accounting for the flourishing of miracle cults in nineteenth-century France.

Chapter 3
Prophecy and Public Order

The hope for a miraculous cure touched people at moments of severe personal crisis and related that crisis to religious faith and the Church. The other category of miracles traditionally important in the world of popular religion was prophecy. Prophecies dealt with collective rather than personal crises; their warnings about the present and their predictions of the future were responsive to social and political circumstances believed to threaten the survival of the community.

Prophecies in nineteenth-century France built on a tradition that had flourished in the ancien régime. Prophets were among the leaders of the Protestant rebellion in the Cévennes mountains and were equally important in the Jansenist sects of Paris. Prophecies circulated in printed form and the single most important form of *colportage* literature, the almanac, featured predictions of Nostradamus or other prophet-astrologers on problems of the weather, epidemics, and social and political conditions.[1] Although a detailed understanding of these prophetic manifestations is unnecessary, a review of some of the attributes of this tradition will provide a context within which the prophetic movements of the nineteenth century can be presented and evaluated.

The Prophetic Tradition in the Ancien Régime

Whatever specific social or political concerns may have been addressed by prophecies, they must first of all be considered as religious phenomena. A concern for a living God's activity in the world was common to all prophecies and established their religious dimension. In Max Weber's analysis the divine calling was the fundamental characteristic of the prophet as a religious type.[2] This personal vocation served as tangible proof of God's existence, of his immediate concern with the world and with the group addressed by the prophet. In the Protestant rebellion in the Cévennes that began in the late seventeenth century, and in the Jansenist sects of Paris a generation later, prophetic communications and instructions were the essential evidence for the participants that these movements were a precise reflection of God's will. The more orderly prophecies of the almanacs similarly interpreted the world of present and future as being under the immediate supervision of Providence. These eighteenth-century prophecies were not part of a reasoned argument intended to refute Enlightenment deism or atheism. Rather, they spoke directly to the emotions and satisfied the spiritual needs of people who required not simply that God exist, but that He exist as a personality who could directly communicate His desires and plans to His followers.

The prophecies of the ancien régime not only gave assurances of God's presence in the world but also provided a key to the proper understanding of past, present, and future events. To the uninitiated, the pope might appear to be the successor of Peter, but the Protestant rebels of Languedoc knew he was in fact the Antichrist, whose appearance presaged the Second Coming of Christ. The Jansenists who listened to and read the revelations of their prophets found similar eschatological and spiritual significance where others might see only the ramblings of religious fanatics. The prophecies of the almanacs tended to be more mundane, but these astrological predictions for the coming year also claimed to provide a special knowledge not otherwise available to the common man. Students of popular culture in the ancien régime have noted that much of the literature from the period reflects a "taste for the marvelous."[3] Prophecies were one important means of satisfying this desire to experience a reality that was deeper and more significant than that of everyday existence by providing it with an historical and eschatological context.

A third characteristic of prophecy in the ancien régime was its political orientation. The prophetic responsibility for judging the political establishment on the basis of a religious standard was of major importance in the history of Israel, and the Christian West inherited this function as part of the prophetic tradition.[4] It was this political aspect of prophecies which allowed them to serve as a major ideological weapon for radical opposition to established regimes prior to the emergence of socialism in the nineteenth century. Scholars have stressed the role of prophecy in millen-

nial movements of oppressed peoples, but it was also possible for prophecy to offer support for a political regime.[5] The apparitions of Christ to
Margaret Mary Alacoque in the seventeenth century called on Louis XIV
to dedicate France to the Sacred Heart, and promised the monarch great
victories.[6] Whether the prophecy called forth opposition to the regime or
attempted to support it, the function remained the same: prophecies
insisted that the political order align itself with the supernatural order, and
strive for the creation of a godly kingdom on earth.

Finally, prophecies in the ancien régime were anti-institutional. Neither
the political nor the religious establishment, despite attempts to appropriate the prophetic tradition, ever abandoned its suspicion of those who
claimed an immediate knowledge of God's will. From the point of view of
the Church, contemporary prophecies were inherently dangerous, for
they made available an extrasacramental access to the sacred and thus were
in direct competition with the institutional Church and the priests who
served it.[7] The State saw prophecy as a powerful means to challenge
political authority and the social order in general. Prophecies were used to
attack established institutions because they were one of the few means
through which unrepresented, neglected, or ignored groups could establish some form of legitimacy for their positions on political, social, and
religious issues.

The prophetic tradition was both dangerous and attractive for defenders
of Church and State. Prophecies were feared because they could serve as
vehicles of social protest and millennial expectation, but were admired for
their ability to capture and direct popular interpretations of current events.
In the nineteenth century prophecies continued to express the concerns of
common people for political and social order. The vitality of the prophetic
tradition made it useful for ideologues, and in particular for supporters of
the monarchy, who used prophecies to demonstrate the supernatural
legitimacy of the Bourbon kings.

Prophecy and Economic Crisis

The economic crisis of the late 1840s is familiar to all social historians. The
crop failures of 1846 reached the southeast of France with the predictable
results of food shortages and high prices.[8] People responded to this catastrophe with prayers and pilgrimages to saints who controlled the weather
and the harvest. In the midst of the crisis, on September 19, 1846, the

Virgin Mary appeared to two shepherd children on the mountain of La Salette, criticized the religious behavior of the people of the area, and predicted further catastrophes if they did not reform. A shrine was immediately built at the site of the apparition and began drawing crowds of pilgrims. Pamphlets on the apparition were soon circulating throughout France and drew the attention of civil officials. The apparition and prophecy of Notre-Dame de La Salette, and the belief they engendered, exemplify the ways in which prophecies responded to and dealt with economic and social crises in the nineteenth century.[9]

There were two messages presented to the children, Mélanie and Maximin, who witnessed the apparition at La Salette. The public part of the prophecy offered a simple explanation for the crisis and a way of ending it. The crops had failed because of the irreligion of the people, and more disasters would follow if they did not reform. Specifically, Mary promised that if people would stop blaspheming, attend Sunday Mass, and abstain from meat on the appropriate days, the famine would end and further catastrophes would be prevented.

If my people do not want to submit I will be forced to let go of my Son's hand, it is so heavy, so leaden, that I can no longer restrain it.

If the potatoes rot, it is your fault. I made you see it would happen a year ago, and you did nothing about it.

If you have wheat, do not sow it, the animals will eat all that you sow, and anything that ripens will turn into dust.

There will be a great famine.

Before the famine the tiny children under seven will get a trembling fever, they will die in the hands of the people who hold them, and the others will repent by hunger.

The hazelnuts will spoil and the grapes perish.

If they convert, the stones and rocks will become mounds of wheat, the potatoes will be fertilized by the earth.

You must pray, my little ones, morning and night; when you can do it no longer, say a Pater and an Ave Maria, and if you have time say more.

Only a few aged women go to Mass and the others work all summer; on winter Sundays, when they do not know what to do, they go to Mass to mock religion and during Lent, they go like dogs to the butcher's.

So, my children, tell all my people.[10]

Popular illustration of Marian apparition to shepherd children at La Salette, distributed by the *Société de Saint-Victor pour la propagation des bons livres et arts Catholiques* in the 1850s.

Mary's message was immediately assimilated into an older tradition of calamitous predictions and heavenly communications; it was first published as a letter from heaven, such letters being a familiar part of popular religion.[11] The prophecy soon spread throughout France and caused considerable official concern, for the government feared that such predictions might lead to social disturbances. The story of the rapid diffusion of the prophecy and of the unsuccessful attempts by the State to suppress it can be followed in reports sent to the Minister of Justice by French prosecutors. The prosecutor of Angers, for example, reported large sales of three different versions of the prophecy. His comments reveal a fear that the apparition might lead to some form of public demonstration which might degenerate into a riot:

> Similar tales are the sort that make an impression on the religious and unenlightened class of the inhabitants of this region, and even if they escape penal law they are nevertheless dangerous, especially when they are diffused so rapidly that the booksellers declare they cannot satisfy all the demand for them. The threat and the predictions placed in the mouth of the Virgin alarm people, lead them astray, impassion public opinion, and lead the humble people to demonstrations that are all the more fearsome because guided by the exaltation of fanaticism.[12]

The prosecutor at Amiens wrote that the prophecy of La Salette "seeks to inspire terror about the coming harvest. . . . In current circumstances it is not without danger." Similar reports were also received from Lille, Rouen, and Lyons. The Minister of Justice responded with a note that expressed special concern about the predictions of famine and childhood mortality, and the warning that it would be futile to plant wheat for the coming year.

> Such passages can produce and have in fact already produced bad effects on ignorant people; they might, in a time of famine, even compromise public tranquility; but we have not found in the penal code or the press laws any grounds for prosecution.[13]

A decision finally was made to seize the pamphlets on the grounds that they violated the press law. This measure was ineffective, for by the time it had been communicated to the provinces most of the literature had already been distributed.

The evidence from the files of the Ministry of Justice establishes the widespread popularity of the pamphlet literature on La Salette. The official fears about the impact of the message are harder to assess. Social historians have shown that the revolution of 1848 encompassed traditional rural conflicts on the issues of food supply and the right to use forest and common lands.[14] Given the economic crisis, it is not unreasonable to believe that a penitential procession or pilgrimage inspired by the apparition and designed to end the crop failures might have turned into some type of social protest. This, at least, seems to have been the fear of the public prosecutors. In fact, there is no evidence of such demonstrations, although the forecasts of famine may have contributed to the general anxieties that fed rural conflict.

The significance of this prophecy's popularity does not lie in its contribution to rural social unrest. Mary's explanation of the famine and plague and the solution she proposed did not deal with the inequities of the social structure, the need for collective action, or the nature of traditional conflicts that divided the rural community. The causes of the economic crisis were clearly identified as common sins of the people: the nonobservance of Sunday, blasphemy, and the violation of laws of abstinence.

One of the many pamphlets of La Salette preserved in the Bibliothèque Municipale of Grenoble closes with an illustration that summarized the causes of the famine and presented the remedy in graphic terms. At the top of the page are four heavenly figures: an angel sheathing his sword, another dropping grain to earth, and Mary kneeling before Christ in supplication. For the literate, a caption explains: "Mary presenting the prayers of humble and repentant hearts to the Master."[15] That this type of explanation was still possible—as is implied by the popularity of the pamphlets—confirms what anthropologists and, more recently, historians have proposed about nineteenth-century France: traditional beliefs, including those which attributed natural events to a Providence that could be angered and mollified by human actions, survived long after the Revolution had inaugurated the modern age.[16]

Notre-Dame de La Salette proposed an explanation and a solution of the 1846 crisis using traditional religious and moral categories which had wide appeal. This appeal can be explained in part by considering the psychological satisfactions that Mary's message and similar prophecies offered. In a period of social, economic, or political crisis the proposal that catastrophic events were the result of sin and could be brought to an end by conversion allowed believers to gain control over their circumstances. Prophecies not only warned of chastisements; they promised fertility and peace. The prophetic tradition could rise to the occasion during nineteenth-century crises and offer people a way to bridge the gap between social catastrophe and personal action. The harvest that was threatened could be saved, the revolution that seemed inevitable could be delayed or prevented, if only one were more devout, more regular in religious practice.

The public message of Notre-Dame de La Salette was first interpreted as a warning of further economic and social catastrophes. Following the revolution of 1848 a political interpretation became fashionable. The overthrow of the Orléanist monarchy and the violent social conflict of the June days were easily assimilated into Mary's predictions of further catastrophes if France did not convert. The episcopal decree announcing the construction of a church at the site of the apparition explicitly related the public message of La Salette to the subsequent political revolution.

This apparition of September 19, 1846, was it not the presage of great events? Observe the popular agitation, the overturned thrones, Europe in upheaval, society tending toward ruin. Who has preserved us and will preserve us from even greater events, if not the One who came from on high to our mountains, to plant there a sign of hope and salvation, a luminous beacon toward which pious souls have raised their eyes to forestall heavenly anger and heal our incurable wounds.[17]

As will be seen, a political interpretation of prophecies was common in the nineteenth century.

There were two prophecies delivered at La Salette, the public message that dealt with the economic crisis and private messages for both Maximin and Mélanie. In addition to the general and rather orthodox application of the public prophecy to political conditions, there was also an attempt to link the private message of Maximin to one of the false claimants to the Bourbon throne. In 1851 followers of Henri de Richemont, who claimed to be Louis XVII, almost succeeded in persuading Maximin to reveal his secret, believing that it predicted the imminent restoration of their leader.[18] Of the two secrets, however, Mélanie's was the one that came to play an important political role in the prophetic movement of the nineteenth century.

Of all the prophecies of nineteenth-century France none was to have a longer or stranger career than the secret of Mélanie. With the end of the economic crisis of the 1840s the public message of La Salette became a standard devotional tract accepted by the Church and no longer feared by the State. Mélanie's secret began to draw attention when it circulated in manuscript in the 1860s. By the time it was published in 1870 it had become a full-fledged political and religious tract.[19] Unlike the public message, Mélanie's secret discussed religious policies of the French State, called for closer relations between Paris and Rome, and was critical of the French clergy. The immediate popularity of the shorter public prophecy resulted from its ability to explain the economic crisis of the 1840s. The secret flourished because it repeated and elaborated those political themes that constituted the permanent core of the nineteenth-century prophetic movement.

Prophecy and Politics in the Nineteenth Century

The quarter-century that concluded in 1815 with the Restoration of the Bourbons to the French throne was one of unparalleled political and social turmoil. Ever since this period historians have been trying to make sense of the revolutionary process; but the problem has not been confined to the historical profession. During the period immediately following the fall of Napoleon there was a need on the part of both political leaders and the French people to subject recent events to historical law. The almanacs that were so important a part of French popular literature testify to this need. Their calendrical predictions for a particular year were generally set inside a larger historical context defined by the major events in the history of the Christian religion and the French nation.[20] Prophetic imagery and Christian eschatology were a familiar element of popular religious belief.[21] During the Restoration a large quantity of prophetic literature appeared which placed past, present, and future in a comprehensible relationship. These prophecies imbued the Enlightenment, the Revolution, and the Restoration with eschatological significance by seeing recent events as part of a providential plan for the salvation of France and the world.

Most of the prophecies published during the Restoration followed a similar pattern that lasted throughout the century, with details added as required by later events. The pattern was described by Abbé Lecanu in his *Dictionnaire des prophéties et des miracles*:

In general [Restoration prophecies] promised the king of France sovereignty over the entire world and universal peace; to the Church they promised the conversion of the infidels, the restoration of the holy places, and a pope of renowned sanctity, who would be followed by the end of things.[22]

A prophecy attributed first to St. César and later to Jean Prêcheguerre, who was identified by some as Savonarola, typifies the tone and content of Restoration prophecy. Prêcheguerre described events that would purportedly occur between 1499 and 1525.[23] This period was depicted as plague-ridden and filled with political conspiracies. The flight of the French monarch was foreseen, and the rise of an "eagle" who would dominate for a time all the countries of Europe. These political changes were to be accompanied by social revolution and the slaughter of the nobility.

Most of the nobility will die, they will be brutally pursued, excluded from honors and positions by a populace which knows no other rules but its own caprices, and nothing will move the people, nothing will quench its thirst for the blood of kings, of princes and nobles. . . . The populace will be master, there will be nothing but it in the world. Unhappy France, it is your destiny to be the most lamentable victim.

The Church of France would share in the desolation, according to the prophecy, but State and Church would eventually be saved by the return of a French king and the election of an angelic pope. These rulers would join forces and create a universal Christian empire.

[The pope] will be powerfully supported by a pious monarch from the most holy race of French kings, who will work with him for the reform of the universe, and the universe will allow itself to be reformed, for the anger of God will be appeased. Henceforth there will be only one law, one faith, one baptism, and even one manner of living. All men will have only one heart and one soul; the most profound peace will last long years.

For the readers of Prêcheguerre's prophecy during the Restoration, the significance of the sixteenth-century oracle was clear: the events described were exact predictions of the Terror, Napoleon, and the restoration of the Bourbons. In some editions of the prophecy little was left to the readers' imagination; the correspondence between the predictions and current events was made explicit by footnotes and marginal comments. By reading current events as the fulfillment of the prophecy, this interpretation implied that the period of universal peace in which the great king and the angelic pope would rule over a world empire had either arrived or was imminent.[24]

Jean Prêcheguerre was the most prominent of the prophets revived during the Restoration. Other sixteenth- and seventeenth-century figures, such as Nostradamus, Richard Roussat, Pierre Turrel, Pierre d'Ailly, and Abbé Holzhauser were also reexamined and found to have foreseen the dramatic events of 1789, 1793, and 1814.[25] In 1815, for example, a work based on Holzhauser's seventeenth-century commentary on the book of the Apocalypse was published in Paris. Holzhauser divided history into seven periods, with the last three described as times of affliction, consolation, and desolation. Abbé Viguier, the editor of the Restoration version of Holzhauser, believed that the sixth age had begun with the return of the Bourbons.[26] The title of a new edition of the prophecies of Nostradamus clearly asserted their relevance for the contemporary period: *Véritables prophéties de Michel Nostradamus en concordance avec les événements de la révolution pendant les anneés 1789, 1790, et suivantes, jusques et y compris le retour de S. M. Louis XVIII.*[27]

Prophets active in the eighteenth and nineteenth centuries repeated the warnings of their predecessors and brought them up to date by blaming the Enlightenment and its pride in human reason for the Revolution. Jeanne Leroyer (1730–1798), who took the religious name of Soeur Nativité, spent her life as a Franciscan nun in the diocese of Rennes. Her career as a prophet was not an unmitigated success, for throughout most of her life her visions and revelations were treated with suspicion by her spiritual advisors. As a result of the Revolution, however, she began to receive support from her superiors. In 1790 Abbé Genet became chaplain of Soeur Nativité's convent at Fougères and began a series of interviews which he edited while an *émigré* in England during the 1790s. His manuscript was published in 1818 and became widely known during the Restoration.[28]

Soeur Nativité claimed, on the basis of her visions, that the *philosophes* were agents of the devil who were working for the reign on earth of the Antichrist.

God has made me see the malice of Lucifer and the diabolical, perverse intentions of his henchmen against the Holy Church of Jesus

Christ. On the order of their chief, these wicked ones have tra-
versed the earth like madmen, in order to prepare the roads and
paths for the Antichrist whose reign is approaching. These emissar-
ies of the devil, these precursors of the Antichrist, as I have been
made to understand, are the impious writers, who by their licen-
tious and seductive systems have for a long time cast the foun-
dations of irreligion. . . . The matter infects, the contagion is
communicated everywhere, it is nothing else but this impure composition of impiety . . . libertinage wins everywhere and causes all
evil, under the specious name of *philosophe*, which it never has
merited.[29]

Readers of Soeur Nativité during the Restoration had no trouble identifying the Revolution with the reign of Antichrist; this interpretation demonstrated the veracity of the prophecy and implied that the return of the
Bourbons marked the defeat of the Antichrist and the start of the
millennium.[30]

Pride and the feeling that humanity had liberated itself from dependence
on God were blamed by all the prophecies as the major source of God's
anger with France. An attack from within the ranks of the *philosophes*
themselves stressed the wisdom and foresight of those who relied on God
rather than on human reason. At a dinner party in 1788, which included
Condorcet as a guest, Jacques Cazotte predicted the deaths of most of the
company present, as well as that of the king, during a revolution that was
about to occur. The prophecy occurred in the context of a conversation on
the "révolution qu'avait fait Voltaire" in which the intellectual changes
brought by the Enlightenment were praised and a reign of reason foreseen. Jean-François de la Harpe, a *philosophe* who converted to Catholicism shortly before his death in 1803, claimed to have witnessed the
prophecy, and was responsible for transcribing it. As with the warnings of
Soeur Nativité, the prophecy of Cazotte was not published until the
Restoration, when its critique of rationalism had become intellectually
fashionable.[31]

The interest in prophecies that foresaw events that had already occurred
was not, obviously, based on their predictive power. The publication and
circulation of this material during the Restoration reflected the desire to
impose order on the recent historical crisis, which was seen as repeating a
familiar paradigm based on the history of Israel found in the Old Testament. God's chosen people sinned by pride, by turning to false gods, and

were punished. In a sermon delivered at Notre-Dame de Paris in 1776, Père Beauregard predicted the worship of pagan gods in the cathedral, and compared Israel's worship of the golden calf to France's apostasy in the eighteenth century. During the Restoration this kind of parallel was satisfying both as a causal explanation for the Revolution and as a rationalization for confidence in the future when France, the new Israel, would be restored to its position of honor among nations.[32]

The Restoration itself produced several prophets, the most important of whom were Mlle Le Normand and Thomas Martin. Mlle Le Normand made her living by means of her supernatural powers. From her apartment on the rue de Tournon in Paris she gave individual consultations using a repertoire of divinatory techniques that included palmistry, cartomancy, and gazing into a crystal ball. Balzac used Mlle Le Normand as a model for the character of Mme Fontaine in *Cousin Pons*. According to Balzac, the consultation of fortune-tellers was common among the shopkeepers, domestic servants, and tradespeople of Paris in the first half of the nineteenth century.[33] In addition to her consulting work Mlle Le Normand claimed a political mission had been given to her by the spirit world, which bore vague resemblance to the idea of a Christian heaven and included the prophet Cazotte, Henri IV, and Louis XVI in its population. Most of Mlle Le Normand's work lacked permanent appeal and her popularity seems to have declined after 1830. She did, however, succeed in making one significant contribution to the prophetic literature of the nineteenth century. In 1827, as part of her popular *Mémoires de l'impératrice*, Mlle Le Normand published the prophecy of Philippe-Dieu-Donné-Noël Olivarius, reputedly based on a sixteenth-century Benedictine manuscript. This prophecy foretold the birth of a "supernatural being" in "Gaule-Italie" and proceeded to trace Napoleon's career in suitably oracular language.

In his youth this man will arise from the sea, learn the language and the mores of the *Celtes-Gaulois*, open up a path to the soldiers against all obstacles, and become their chief. . . . He will give laws to the Germans, and will pacify the troubles and terrors of the *Gaulois-Celtes*, and will hence be named not king, but emperor, by great popular enthusiasm.[34]

Until the second Restoration the events depicted remain clear, but following the final defeat of Napoleon the prophecy turned to vague warnings of war and predicted the triumph of a young warrior from the line of Capetian kings who would defeat the other European nations in a great war. Victory would be followed by the declaration that France is the "great mother nation," and the young king would then "rule the destinies of the world, giving sovereign counsel to every nation and people." Mlle Le Normand was clearly drawing on the older prophetic tradition that equated the millennium with the coming of "le grand monarque" to France. But in her rendition this prophecy is given specificity and relevance by means of explicit references to the Napoleonic era. The prophecy is characterized by enormous pride in Napoleon's achievements; in fact the Bourbon millennium foreseen by Mlle Le Normand amounts to a permanent version of the Empire, for it is based on the military victories of a French sovereign and a peace that is the result of acknowledged French hegemony.

Thomas Martin was a peasant from Gallardon (Eure-et-Loir) whose prophetic career was based on visits with the Archangel Raphael that began just after the Restoration of Louis XVIII. Martin's followers later became part of the heretical Vintras sect and through this association the prophet was able to influence late nineteenth-century occultism.[35] The original message delivered by Raphael included information designed to discredit Louis XVIII's liberal minister Decazes. From the outset of his career Martin was involved with the Ultra party of the Restoration which believed that Decazes' opportunism was compromising the principles of legitimacy. It is evidence of the seriousness with which prophets were treated that Martin, on the basis of his revelations, obtained interviews with Decazes and the king himself. Martin's visions were vigorously supported by his *curé* in Gallardon and by members of the royal chaplain's corps, including the Abbé Frayssinous, who later served the Bourbons as Grand Master of the University and Minister of Ecclesiastical Affairs. A pamphlet describing Martin's visions and giving them a legitimist interpretation circulated in his home department of Eure-et-Loir, and was known as far away as Albi, Nancy, Versailles, Montauban, Anjou, Aveyron, and Dauphiné. Martin's *curé* was in correspondence with people throughout France who were interested in the prophet's message; it is likely that he was the one primarily responsible for the publication of the pamphlet.[36] Later in the Restoration Martin became associated with one of the first sects that believed Louis XVII had survived the Revolution. At the time of the revolution of 1830 Martin was consulted by Charles X on his flight from France, and also influenced the actions of important members of the French episcopacy.[37] Apparently Martin believed that the revolution would culminate in the restoration of Louis XVII. A letter of Bishop Mazenod of Marseille written just after the revolution testifies to the credence given to Martin's prophecies.

> I shall not be seeing the Bishop of Nancy or the old Bishop of Strasbourg; both of them are up to their necks in prophecy. Cardinal de Rohan is also quite steeped in it, as is Father Perrin, secretary of the Cardinal Rohan-Chabot, also some of the chaplain's corps and Heaven only knows how many laymen. . . . Whenever anyone talks with them, they discuss these prophecies very calmly as if they were sure of their facts. The archangel told it to Martin. What more do you want? Meanwhile one must put up with this nonsense and, what is worse, endure the frightful calumnies which range Louis XVIII, Charles, the Dauphin, etc., alongside scoundrels of the worst sort. No matter! Martin said it and so there is no doubt about it.[38]

The prophecies of Martin serve as the starting point for the only recent discussion of the prophetic movement in nineteenth-century France. In his ambitious study *The Occult Underground*, James Webb portrays Martin and succeeding prophets as offering a solution of "true legitimacy" for the political and social anxieties that date from the time of the Revolution.[39] Webb is right to see the prophetic movement as a response to the problem of political legitimacy, but in restricting himself to Martin in considering Restoration prophecy he provides too limited a view of prophecy for that era. Prophecies were not relegated to the margins of Restoration culture, as Webb implies; they were a familiar element in the attempt to integrate contemporary history into the traditional framework of Christian eschatology.

One of the most influential of Restoration thinkers, Comte Joseph de Maistre, included a vigorous defense of prophecy in his critique of Enlightenment thought. The eleventh dialogue of his *Les soirées de Saint-Petersburg*, published in 1821, criticized the neglect of prophecies during the eighteenth century. According to Maistre, for those who had ears to hear, there had been ample warning of the Revolution. "There are never any worldly events that have not been predicted in some fashion. . . . You have a recent example in the French Revolution, predicted on all sides and in an incontestable way."[40] Maistre believed that all evil, natural and political, individual and collective, was providentially determined chastisement for sin. The Revolution in particular was God's punishment of France for the blasphemous pride of the Enlightenment. Maistre did not restrict himself to a defense of past prophecies; assuming the role of prophet for himself, he invoked the need for public and private prayer and called for the conversion of mankind to the fundamental Christian truth of man's total reliance on the mercy of God. Only such a conversion could prevent God from inflicting the punishment that men rightfully deserve. Maistre combined his call for repentance with apocalyptic warnings:

> We must be prepared for an immense event in the Divine order, toward which we march with an accelerated speed which must strike every observer. There is no longer any religion on earth: the human species cannot remain in this state. Fearsome oracles announce everywhere that *the time has come.*[41]

The immense event was neither explicitly described nor precisely dated, and here again Maistre followed the prophetic conventions. But he did indicate that the new age to come would see the unification of Christianity, the conversion of all Moslems, and the realization that science supports rather than contradicts Christian doctrine. This view of a unified world was commonplace in prophetic literature; that such a world would include harmonious relations between science and religion was the addendum of an intellectual sensitive to the conflicts of the modern age.

Prophecies circulated during the Restoration in a variety of forms. The works of Jean Prêcheguerre and Mlle Le Normand were issued as cheap pamplets that were aimed at a mass audience. But the support given prophecies by Maistre suggests a more widespread intellectual and social credibility. Like Mesmerism, which had been in vogue since the late eighteenth century, the prophetic movement was able to draw support from both the educated and the popular classes.[42]

The prophetic interpretation of history also received strong support from the Church. Missionaries charged with bringing the French nation back to God constantly stressed the themes of national sin, divine chastisement, and the need for reparation.[43] Abbé Frayssinous, in addition to his support of the peasant visionary Thomas Martin, argued in a series of sermons preached at Notre-Dame that God, in immediate control of history, had punished France by allowing the Revolution to occur. "The

Revolution is at the same time a punishment and a lesson: a punishment inflicted on the revolt of minds against religion and its precepts: a lesson given to kings and people alike, to keep them wary of evil doctrines."[44]

Church support for the prophetic movement was given spectacular encouragement by the apparition of a cross in the sky over Migné (diocese of Poitiers) in 1827. The apparition occurred at the conclusion of a sermon preached during a mission, and caused a violent emotional reaction in the crowd, which was reported to fall on its knees and beg for mercy. The miracle was soon given a prophetic reading by the Church in which the themes of the sin, chastisement, and redemption of France were clearly portrayed. Within a few months of its occurrence the bishop of Poitiers issued a decree that sanctioned belief in the apparition and attached prophetic significance to it.

> O divine Providence: it is in France, which the devil regards as his conquest, that the sign of human redemption has suddenly appeared. . . . It is the cross that has conquered hell, redeemed the world, and subdued the universe. . . . Why should we not see in the cross of Migné a protective sign which promises to this king-dom better days after so many tempests?[45]

In a defense of the miracle published in 1830 Abbé Vrindts confirmed the official interpretation of the miracle as a sign of the continuing concern of Providence for the French nation:

> For centuries France has been the country where the political and religious character of the most civilized quarter of the world has been formed, because it has been the seat of Catholicism. Provi-dence has always had vast designs for France; its destinies have been bound up with those of the imperishable Church of Jesus Christ; Providence has made France the object of its solicitude, even to the point of working miracles in her favor.[46]

By 1830 the prophetic tradition had renewed itself in a variety of forms: in the reappearance of prophecies of a "great king" and an "angelic pope," in the publication of eighteenth-century prophets critical of the Enlighten-ment and fearful of a revolution, in contemporary prophets who identified themselves explicitly with the principles of legitimacy, and in the pro-phetic miracle of Migné. Taken as a whole these prophecies placed the events of the recent past in a familiar and reassuring perspective. France had sinned in the Enlightenment, had been chastised by the Revolution, and was now able to reassume its role as the leader of the Christian world. In the future, France was destined to play a decisive role in the providential events that would culminate in the Christian millennium. This historical drama, in the context of which the prophecies espoused antirationalism, royalism, and nationalism, established itself as an important part of the ideological program defended by legitimists for the rest of the century.

Prophecies and prophetic movements have frequently been associated with millennial cults seeking radical social change. The prophetic movement as it existed during the French Restoration, however, never developed into a full-fledged millennial cult, if this is defined as a religious movement whose goal is collective, terrestial, imminent, and total salvation.[47] Nevertheless the functions attributed to millennialism by a recent scholar were in many ways served by the prophecies popular during the Restoration. Michael Barkun, drawing on the ideas of Anthony Wallace, sees millennialism as a program of "revitalization . . . to explain the previously inexplicable changes and to restore individual senses of meaning."[48] The prophetic movement, like the millennial sects described by Barkun, attempted to create a sense of order following a series of social disasters. The order described by the prophecies did not depend on the overthrow of the established regime, however, but on its survival. According to Restoration prophecies it was the past and not the present that was intolerable. It may be that the scholarly focus on millennial movements has given a slightly distorted view of prophecies, in which they serve only to express the desire for social change. In the 1870s the prophetic tradition was to play a role in the legitimist campaign to overthrow the republic and restore the monarchy following the loss of the Franco-Prussian War.[49] But during the Restoration prophecies supported the existing political and social order.

The revolution of 1830 and the series of political crises that marked the July Monarchy disillusioned those who believed that the Restoration had ushered in the golden age foreseen by Jean Prêcheguerre. Prophecies were again called on for an explanation and justification of what appeared to be the endless turmoil of French political history. The themes established during the Restoration continued to dominate the prophecies, with the important exception that none seems to have argued that Louis Philippe was the great king foreseen by Jean Prêcheguerre and others. Prophecies attacking the new regime were circulating in the Catholic west just after the revolution in July, and similar publications recurred throughout the July Monarchy.[50] Four months after the revolution of 1830, well before anxieties about the future of France had receded, Catherine Labouré, a novice of the Daughters of Charity living in Paris, had a vision in which Mary reassured her that France had a special place in the Virgin's affections. In November of 1830 a medal was revealed to Catherine, one side of which showed Mary standing on a globe and extending her arms. Beams of light flowed from her open arms to the earth; while seeing the medal Catherine heard the words: "These rays are the symbol of the graces Mary obtains for all men, and the point toward which they flow most abundantly is France."[51] During the 1830s millions of what came to be known as Miraculous Medals were distributed throughout France. A pamphlet describing the history and miracles attributed to the medal went through five editions between 1832 and 1836. The popularity of the Miraculous Medal helped keep alive the idea of France's special role in world history during the July Monarchy.[52]

In 1839 and 1840 a political crisis, which led to fears of international war and further domestic upheaval, provided the context for another addition to the prophetic literature. The prophecy of Orval was published for the first time in 1839 and subsequently appeared both as a separate brochure and as part of Henri Dujardin's anthology, *L'oracle pour 1840*.[53] The prophecy was supposedly based on a manuscript found at a Belgian abbey during the Revolution of 1789. For the rest of the century its defenders labored to prove that the manuscript had been known prior to the events it "predicted." In content and style the prophecy of Orval owed much to Mlle Le Normand's Olivarius. The reference to all events down to the Revolution of 1830 and the rise of Louis Philippe are unequivocal: "The Cock will wipe out the white lily and a great one called the king of the people [will reign]. A great commotion will be felt among people because the crown will be bestowed by the hands of the workers who fought in the great city."[54] The prophecy goes on to predict the fall of the weak "king of the people" and the reestablishment on the throne of the "offspring of Cap." Following an indeterminate period of peace, the legitimate monarch would again be overthrown, and the prophet concludes with the conventional prediction of a vague but ominous apocalyspe. The prophecy of Orval, like those of the Restoration, was an attempt to link legitimist principles and the Bourbons in particular with the popular belief that Providence was guiding France through a series of eschatological events.

The prophecy of Orval shows that the prophetic tradition was still active during the July Monarchy. But in contrast to the Restoration, when Church and State tolerated and at times encouraged legitimist prophecies, the July Monarchy gave them a more critical reception. While most of the clergy may have remained legitimist after the July Revolution, the Church sought an accommodation with the Orléanist regime, as it did later with the Second Republic and Second Empire. Consequently, legitimist prophecies that might formerly have been tolerated were now officially suspect. The prophecy of Orval was condemned by the bishop of Verdun in 1849, and the episcopal support given Martin seems not to have been repeated.[55] The State in turn actively prosecuted leaders of prophetic sects. James Webb's view of a prophetic underground may not be entirely accurate for the Restoration, but it does describe the situation after 1830, when belief in another legitimist Restoration survived as part of a larger occult counterculture. Several individuals claiming to be Louis XVII were able to gather small groups around them throughout this period. Eugène Vintras organized a heretical sect, the "Oeuvre de Miséricorde," which believed among other things that the third and final age of the world, the age of the Holy Spirit, was about to dawn.[56] Vintras associated the imminent millennium with a belief in the restoration of Naundorff, one of those claiming to be Louis XVII. Jean-Simon Ganneau, otherwise known as the Mapah, had a coterie of followers who combined a belief in the return of Louis XVII with Polish messianism and radical socialism.[57]

The belief that the restoration of Louis XVII would lead to a socialist utopia suggests a relationship between millennialism and the socialist ideologies that were emerging in the first half of the nineteenth century. In *The New Christianity* (1825), Saint-Simon called for a reorganization of society according to what he understood to be "the sublime principle which contains everything that is divine in the Christian religion . . . . *All men must behave as brothers towards one another.*" Saint-Simon's appeal for a new social order was infused with a sense of prophetic mission:

> Listen to the voice of God, which speaks to you through my lips; become good Christians once again, and stop looking upon armies, noblemen, heretical clergies and perverse judges as your principal

sources of sustenance. United under the banner of Christianity, you will be able to accomplish all the duties that this banner imposes upon the powerful; remember that it commands them to employ all their forces in advancing as rapidly as possible the social well-being of the poor![58]

Barthélemy-Prosper Enfantin, a disciple of Saint-Simon's, became the leader of a quasi-monastic order that awaited the arrival of a female messiah from the Middle East. Enfantin's followers believed that this messiah, *la Mère*, would marry their leader, who took the title *le Père*; this mystical union of East and West would initiate an era of brotherhood and happiness for mankind.[59] In the 1840s Alphonse Constant, who would later be known as the occultist Eliphas Levi, published apocalyptic visions in which the Virgin Mary announced the marriage of Christianity and socialism which would bring about the millennium.[60] During the same decade Étienne Cabet, the most prominent socialist leader in France, published *Le vrai christianisme* (1846) and called for the creation of a Christian-Communist utopian community in America.[61] Working-class poets of the 1830s and 1840s also combined their support for a socialist regime with Christianity.[62] Following the revolution of 1848 many socialist workers believed that the new republic would bring about an era of peace and prosperity that resembled the millennium of the legitimist prophets, but with the people replacing the Bourbons as the agent of regeneration. A "Profession of Faith of the Organized People," written by a tapestry weaver shortly after the February revolution, described the future that awaited France:

> Then the act of regeneration of the human race will begin, the gospel of the people, as pure as the first, will come to illuminate the universe; like that of Christ, it has given, and will give again, if it must, its martyrs, and then erect its grandeur by gentleness on the ruins of despotism.[63]

The accelerating pace of social and economic change in the nineteenth century threatened the status, income, and working conditions of French artisans. Socialist ideologies that sought an alternative to the social organization of capitalism were based on corporatist traditions inherited from the ancien régime.[64] But the language and some of the ideas of Saint-

Simon, Enfantin, Cabet, and their followers also borrowed from the same prophetic tradition that flowed into the legitimist prophecies of Thomas Martin and Comte Joseph de Maistre.

The appeal of the prophetic tradition for both socialists and legitimists was based on its ability "to fit what was new and unprecedented into categories that were old and familiar."[65] In adopting an eschatological and even millennial perspective, legitimists and socialists helped their adherents become accustomed to thinking in terms of rapid and fundamental political and social change. Such a perspective not only made it possible to grasp the meaning of successive revolutions, but also created the expectation of some apocalyptic event that would result in either a socialist utopia or a Bourbon restoration. Prophetic cults continued to hope for a restoration throughout the century, and a major revival of interest in legitimist prophecies occurred following the catastrophes of the early 1870s. Perhaps the belief of Georges Sorel and some French syndicalists that a general strike could lead immediately and spontaneously to a new social and political order also owes something to the prophetic tradition.[66] According to Clarke Garrett, "The language and imagery of millennialism may have served as medium for the reception of what we recognize today as the modern revolutionary consciousness."[67] In nineteenth-century France revolutionary consciousness was not the sole prerogative of the left. The expectation and affirmation of revolution were shared by ideologues of both right and left, who drew on the resources of the prophetic tradition and Christian eschatology.

The social changes that help explain the popularity of prophecies in nineteenth-century France had similar effects in England. Between 1780 and 1850 a number of millenarian sects committed to social change attempted to deal with the crisis of early industrialization. As in France, radicalism and millenarianism were closely related. According to J. F. C. Harrison, "Dig into the history of popular radicalism almost anywhere before 1850 and the chances are good that a millenarian reference will be unearthed."[68]

The emphasis of French legitimist prophecies on the providential role of France in world history also had parallels elsewhere.[69] The French prophecies were a call to the nation to lead the world to a new era of peace and prosperity. In Italy Abbé Vincenzo Gioberti believed that his nation, unified under the leadership of the pope, was destined to play a redemptive role in European history. The conclusion of Gioberti's *Del primato morale e civile degli Italiani* is a vision of a glorious future in which the nations of Europe pay homage to Italy.

> I see the eyes of Europe and the world fixed on this future Italy; I see the other nations at first astonished and then faithful and devout, receiving from her through a spontaneous motion the principles of truth, the form of beauty, the example and standard of good behavior and elevated sentiment. . . . I see religion positioned at the summit of all human works; and [I see] principles and peoples competing among themselves in reverence and love for the Roman pontiff, recognizing him and adoring him, not only as the successor of Peter, vicar of Christ and head of the universal Church, but as *doge* and *gonfalonier* of the Italian confederation, paternal arbiter and pacifier of Europe, teacher and civilizer of the world, spiritual father of humankind, heir and natural and pacific tool of the expansion of Latin greatness.[70]

Gioberti's vision was predicated on the religious primacy of Italy, but his feeling that Providence had singled Italy out was shared by the other great ideologue of the Risorgimento, Giuseppe Mazzini. While rejecting Gioberti's neo-Guelphism, the anticlerical Mazzini did base his ultimate expectations of a united Italy as the leader of the world of nations on a vaguely articulated theism.[71] Poland, like Italy, was viewed by nationlist prophets as a country whose persecutions and suffering were redemptive. Josef Marie Hoëné-Wroński, August Ciezowski, and Adam Mieckewicz believed that Poland, as leader of the Slavic peoples, would be instrumental in establishing the Kingdom of God on earth.[72]

Polish and Italian messianism, like the French variety, originated in the revolutionary era, when Napoleon raised the question of national existence in his reorganization of the European state system. A prophetic and nationalistic view of world history stemming in part from the Revolution was not, then, restricted to France. Neither was messianism peculiar to those nations whose quest for statehood was unsatisfied. In addition to the French example, the Slavophiles of Russia believed that Moscow was destined to become the Third Rome, the capital of a newly united and spiritually revivified Europe.[73] In the United States what Robert Bellah has called the "civil religion" postulated that America, like Israel, was chosen by God as the promised land. In his inaugural address Washington described the role of Providence in American history. "Every step by which we have advanced to the character of an independent nation seems to have been distinguished by some token of providential agency."[74]

Italian, Polish, Russian, and American messianic nationalism share certain characteristics with the French prophetic revival. The political aspect of romanticism, which stressed the affective ties that bound a people to their nation, is crucial to all of these ideologies. A view of history in which distinct stages are separated by apocalyptic events, and a belief in providential guidance are other elements relating these national prophecies to each other. French prophecies seen in this context are examples of a Europe-wide movement. The sources for the movement vary from nation to nation, but the fact that it appeared simultaneously in several places in the early nineteenth century suggests that some cross-national explanation might be possible.

Perhaps the key issue confronting the European prophetic movement was political legitimacy. The French Revolution had shown that both geographic boundaries and political constitutions were mutable, thus raising the question of what should serve as the basis of the state. Romanticism proposed racial and linguistic solidarity and a sense of a common past as the constitutive principles. At the same time romanticism looked favorably on mystical intuition and religious faith as ways of knowing superior to rational inquiry and analysis. Popular belief in prophecies, suspect during the Enlightenment, was therefore regarded favorably by nineteenth-century intellectuals. The prophetic tradition was able to serve as a link between the intellectual elite and the common people in shaping attitudes toward existing and emerging states.

Chapter 4
Miracles and Prophecies
in Dogma and Devotion

Prophecies and apparitions expressed the political and social anxieties confronted by the French in the nineteenth century. Miracles, however, did more than satisfy needs defined by the political and social systems. Devotions inspired by miracles were a common feature of popular piety in the nineteenth century. The prayers, practices, and images of these devotions, and the religious models they presented, helped set the psychological tone of nineteenth-century Catholicism.

The basic doctrines of Catholicism have changed much more slowly than has devotional life. But in the nineteenth century the Church added significantly to the doctrines it required Catholics to believe when it claimed that Mary had been conceived without original sin, and that the pope was infallible when he spoke on matters of faith and morals. Miracles and prophecies were used to defend and interpret the doctrines of the Immaculate Conception, papal infallibility, and other doctrines threatened by skepticism and rationalism. Together the doctrinal and devotional aspects of miracles and miracle cults provide an approach to the religious history of nineteenth-century France from the point of view of what people believed and how they felt about God, the saints, and the Church, which claimed to be their agent.

Miracles and Doctrines

Official Catholicism has always been distinguished by a core of dogmas defined by the authority of the Church. To be a member of the Church meant that one had to believe in these dogmas and surrender personal judgment based on a reading of scripture or independent rational inquiry in favor of the definitions and arguments propounded by the religious authorities. The body of dogma received by the nineteenth century had been defined and codified by the Council of Trent, acting in response to the crisis of the Reformation. The corpus of Tridentine dogmas and reforms served the Church well in the sixteenth and seventeenth centuries. They ended much of the confusion surrounding such major issues as the nature of the sacraments, of the Church, and of grace, and established clear boundaries within which Catholicism could be defended.[1] During the eighteenth century, however, Catholic doctrine became a target for the rationalistic barbs of the *philosophes*. How could God be both Trinity and Unity? How was it possible that bread, while remaining bread, could become the body of Christ? Miracles were used by eighteenth-century apologists, but Enlightenment theologians generally relied on the eyewitness accounts of the Gospel miracles and not on contemporary supernatural phenomena.[2] In the nineteenth century, in addition to the standard theological arguments in defense of Catholicism, a series of miraculous visions served to verify both the events of scripture and the major dogmas of the Catholic Church.

The first nineteenth-century visionary to gain prominence in France was the German Anne-Catherine Emmerich (1774–1824), a woman who spent her adult life praying and fasting as a follower of the Third Order of Augustine. During the Restoration pamphlets circulated in France telling of her miraculous visions and her personal experience of Christ's Passion through the stigmata.[3] Catherine Emmerich's reputation as a visionary was firmly established by the German romantic Clemens Brentano; in 1818 Brentano began daily conversations with the mystic, which he then transcribed and published. The results of this work were two "histories" of Christ and the Virgin, which were translated into French and enjoyed a sustained popularity throughout the nineteenth century.[4] In these works Catherine Emmerich claimed to have witnessed all of the major events of Christ's life, from his birth to his Resurrection. Details were added which, as will be seen later, conformed to popular taste; but for now the essential point is that Catherine Emmerich's miraculous visions were interpreted as independent confirmation of sacred scripture, including the miracles on which Christianity was founded.

The miraculous facts of Christ's life confirmed by Catherine Emmer-

ich's visions were probably the least controversial of all miracles, for even
liberal Protestants were willing to grant the occurrence of miracles in the
Apostolic age. But Catholic theologians claimed that miracles continued
throughout history as confirmation of Christ's continuing presence
within the Church.[5] The teaching authority of the Church, which allowed
it to define and elaborate dogmas not explicitly contained in scripture,
required supernatural support. In nineteenth-century France healings at
miraculous shrines helped establish the power and truth of the Catholic
religion. In some cases healings were part of a cult associated with a
specific doctrine; this was the case with the Lourdes cult and the Immaculate Conception. But it was the visions and revelations of these cults,
not their healings, that explicitly defended the fundamental beliefs of
Catholicism.

The mystery of the Trinity and the miracle of the Eucharist, fundamental doctrines long subject to broad rationalist attack, were both
confirmed by nineteenth-century miracles. The visions of Soeur Nativité
and Marie Lataste, though separated by fifty years, offer parallels that
show how these dogmas were defended in miraculous visions. Both of
their multivolume works began with lengthy revelations on the doctrines
of the Trinity and the Incarnation. The concept of a triune God was open
to rationalistic criticism as both self-contradictory and unfounded in scripture. Christ's message to Soeur Nativité asserted that the very irrationality
of the concept was a virtue, and the fact that Christ himself announced the
dogma to the visionary obviated the need for historical evidence. Christ
instructed Soeur Nativité in this way:

> The Trinity is the mystery of faith which is the basis of our reli-
> gion, and which we must believe and adore, although it infinitely
> surpasses the limits of our intelligence, as well as the arguments by
> which they try in vain to explain and attack it. . . . O, adorable
> mystery which cannot be understood and which has never been
> understood by any creature![6]

Christ's defense of the Trinity in this passage is directed explicitly at
doubters, at those of "our religion" who had attempted to explain the
doctrine rationally. An early message of Christ to Marie Lataste included a
similar warning against the temptation of rationalism in the comprehension of mysterious doctrine: "What odious pride in these men, what
senseless arrogance, what mad pretensions. . . . True knowledge has fled

from them to find a refuge among simple men who adore without seeing and believe without understanding.'"[7] The history of Catholic theology is filled with discussions of the relationship between faith and reason in the attainment of knowledge of God. With few exceptions the primacy of faith has been asserted, but reason has generally been given a crucial supporting rule.[8] The defense of the Trinity and the Incarnation presented by Christ to both Soeur Nativité and Marie Lataste is, on the contrary, couched in language that amounts to a rejection of reason's role in the discussion of doctrine. Such a position was compatible with the traditionalist theology inaugurated by Maistre and Bonald, which dominated French Catholicism until the scholastic revival late in the century. Visionaries may not have relied on the "common sense" of the traditionalists, who believed that the universality of belief throughout history was an argument in favor of Christianity; but they did share with them a distrust of applying logic and reason to theological questions.[9]

Christ's revelations about the Trinity and the Incarnation to Soeur Nativité and Marie Lataste took the form of pious meditations and contained a repetition of the miraculous facts of his conception and birth. The dogma of the Real Presence was affirmed more dramatically. Of all the doctrines in the Catholic canon none has been more controversial and miraculous in implication than the concept that the consecrated host transubstantiates into the body and blood of Christ. Nocturnal Adoration societies and Eucharistic Congresses in nineteenth-century France asserted and defended this quintessential Catholic dogma.[10] Not surprisingly, the Real Presence also figured in revelations. A typical pattern was for Christ to appear at the Elevation just after the priest had pronounced the miraculous formula: *Hoc est enim corpus meum.* Between 1840 and 1842 Marie Lataste saw Christ at the Elevation of every Mass she attended, and her description was designed to impress the reader with the magnificance hidden within the host.

At the moment of the Elevation, when the priest made his genuflection, after having pronounced the words of consecration, I used to see an exceeding brightness filling the sanctuary, and beheld Jesus appear upon the altar, where he remained until the Communion. His countenance was usually full of benignity and sweetness, but sometimes He looked grave, and seemed to be displeased. His splendor surpassed that of the sun; His majesty was such that on earth there is nothing comparable to it: His throne was of the most

refulgent gold; His robe was not formed of any [material], not even
of the finest, or, if it was of [material], I have never seen the like; it
looked as though it were transparent and sparkled with light like a
diamond or a precious stone. He was seated on His throne; His left
hand rested on His Heart, and the right hand reposed gently on His
knees. His eyes were generally fixed on the people, and at certain
moments—for example, during the Pater and the Agnus Dei—
always on the priest.[11]

In this detailed and vivid description, it is almost as if the popular images
of Christ had come to life through her visions. Soeur Nativité's vision of
Christ was on a smaller scale, and reveals another avatar of Christ prevalent in the world of popular piety. At the moment of the Elevation at the
Christmas Eve Mass, Christ appeared as a radiant child in the hands of the
priest.[12] Soeur Nativité's vision amounted to an assertion that Christ's
presence in the host was no less real than if he were visible in human form.

The irony of visions that confirmed the Real Presence is that in attempting to verify the dogma they also verified the reality of doubt in even the
most pious Catholic. Both Soeur Nativité and Marie Lataste prided themselves on their piety and orthodoxy, but they seem to have been unfamiliar
with Christ's dictum to Thomas, "Blessed are those who have not seen yet
believe" (John 20:29). The visionaries and those clergy who supported
them may have believed in transubstantiation, but they also felt the need
for new, concrete, and miraculous evidence on the matter.

In the cases of the Trinity, the Incarnation, and the Real Presence the
visionaries in general followed the orthodox teachings of the Church.[13]
Neither the visions of Soeur Nativité nor Marie Lataste were declared true
by any episcopal investigation, and there is even some evidence of official
suspicion. Mgr Ladoue, vicar-general of Auch, treated Lataste's discussions of doctrine as unexceptional and uninspired in a report addressed to
the bishop of Aire following the publication of her writings in 1863. Her
prophecies were described by Ladoue as either false or unverifiable; despite this report Marie Lataste's works were republished in 1866, with
Mgr Epivent's imprimatur. Church officials were willing to allow reports
of visions not regarded as indubitable to be read as edifying texts.[14] As long
as visionaries were willing to commit themselves to the fundamental
Catholic dogmas and the authority of the Church, they were able to obtain
a hearing. Orthodox dogma was defended by Catholic apologetics in the
nineteenth century, but visions and revelations were undoubtedly more

convincing for some, and the Church was not inclined to reject such supernatural confirmation of its own positions.

Miracles affirmed established doctrines, but they assumed an even more important role in the popularization and promulgation of a dogma defined in the nineteenth century: the Immaculate Conception of the Virgin.[15] The doctrine of the Immaculate Conception holds that Mary was conceived without original sin in honor of her future role as the mother of Jesus. The consequences of the doctrine are of major significance for both theology and devotional life. By setting Mary apart from the rest of humanity, including the saints, the doctrine places Mary in a special position, one which can easily become that of a demigod.

The veneration of Mary has, since the Reformation, been a point of division between Catholics and Protestants, and within the Church Mariolatry has also been a controversial issue. In the eighteenth century a movement within the institutional Church discouraged the theological emphasis on Mary's role in Christian history.[16] During the nineteenth century, however, the Church encouraged Marian piety. Well before its final promulgation in 1854 the doctrine of the Immaculate Conception had become the object of popular devotions. By 1847 even the Dominicans, who had opposed honoring Mary under this title since their dispute with Franciscans in the Middle Ages, dropped their objections. In 1849 Pius IX requested Catholic bishops to report on the sentiments in their dioceses regarding an official definition. Of the 603 respondents, only fifty-six indicated dissent. The promulgation in 1854 was greeted with enthusiasm throughout the Catholic world. *L'Univers* reported processions and illuminations throughout France in celebration of the event, and twenty-five years later Mgr Pie recalled the hopes excited by the papal definition.

None of those who were men or even adolescents in the year of grace 1854 has forgotten the immense and profound emotion which seized the entire Church, when Pius IX, using his prerogative and fulfilling his ministry as supreme and universal doctor, proclaimed the doctrine of the Immaculate Conception. . . . Most of us remember that great hopes accompanied the joy. They said it was Mary's destiny to be a divine dawn. In the terrestial and historical order she was the dawn of the sun of truth, justice, and peace, of Jesus. This new glorification of the mother must thus be the sign and prelude of a new glorification of the Son: that is, of a manifest expansion of his reign, of a more abundant harvest of saints, of greater liberty for the Church, or an increase in power and honor for the papacy, of a period, finally, both glorious and prosperous for the human family of God.[17]

The doctrine of the Immaculate Conception can be viewed, from the perspective of the history of the Church, as another move designed to counter the rationalism and irreligion believed to be the characteristic defects of the modern world. As such, it was part of a series of events that dates at least to the pope's refusal to cooperate in the formation of the Italian nation-state, and continued with the "Syllabus of Errors" and the declaration of papal infallibility at Vatican I.[18] Such an interpretation has some merit, for the Immaculate Conception is a doctrine that did encourage the insular mentality of nineteenth-century Catholicism. Mgr Pie's sentiments, however, reveal that the Church did not view the Immaculate Conception simply as a gauntlet thrown down to the modern world. At the time of its proclamation it seemed to offer a promise of the Church's triumph, a hope that was especially intense in France. The reasons for such optimism can be understood by placing the doctrine in the context of a tradition of prophecy dating back to the early eighteenth century. According to this tradition the second coming of Christ would be preceded by an age of Mary. As a result of this association the nineteenth-century renewal of Marian piety and the declaration of the Immaculate Conception took on eschatological significance.

The prophecies of Grignon de Montfort, whose missionary activity in the early eighteenth century made extensive use of Marian devotions, form the basis of the prophetic expectations Mary aroused in nineteenth-century France. In 1842 a manuscript of Montfort's was discoverd in a field at St. Laurent-sur-Seine, and according to the preface of the third edition (1846), "by a sort of Providence, although all the pages of the manuscript were separated from each other, nevertheless all of them were in the right order, and well preserved." The manuscript, published as *Traité de la vraie dévotion à la sainte vierge*, became one of the most popular devotional works of the century.[19]

Much of Montfort's *Traité* is devoted to pious meditations on aspects of Mary's life and her power in heaven. But integrated with these are straightforward claims that the Second Coming of Christ and his reign on earth would be preceded by an age of Mary.

If then, as is certain, the reign of Jesus Christ will arrive on earth, it will necessarily follow the knowledge and reign of the very holy

The Miraculous Medal, inspired by apparitions of Mary to St. Catherine Labouré in Paris, November 1830. Laurentin collection, all rights reserved.

saint Virgin Mary, who gave him to the world for the first time and who will make him burst forth the second.

Mary has produced with the Holy Spirit the greatest thing that has ever been and will ever be, which is a God-Man, and consequently she will produce the greatest things at the end of time. The formation and education of great saints who will come at the end of time will be her task, because only this excellent and miraculous Virgin can produce, together with the Holy Spirit, great and extraordinary things.[20]

The prophecies of Grignon de Montfort were repeated by others, including St. Léonard de Port-Maurice and Marie Lataste.[21] The plethora of Marian apparitions and cults in nineteenth-century France was evidence that the age of Mary had dawned. Most of these have already been introduced in the context of miraculous cures. The thaumaturgic component of Marian devotions was, in fact, related to their doctrinal implications, for the healings verified the apparitions and, implicitly, their dogmatic revelations. In her apparition to Catherine Labouré in 1830,

Mary gave an important impetus to the doctrine of the Immaculate Conception by revealing the prayer, "O Mary conceived without sin, pray for us who have recourse to thee," as part of the Miraculous Medal. The rapid diffusion of the medal throughout France helped develop grassroots support for the dogma. Similarly, the official title of the confraternity established at Notre-Dame des Victoires in Paris was "Archconfrérie du très saint et immaculé coeur de Marie." The Miraculous Medal devotion and the Confraternity of Notre-Dame des Victoires associated the doctrine of the Immaculate Conception with thaumaturgic powers, but also with eschatological events.[22] The depiction of Mary on the Miraculous Medal, crushing the head of a serpent and wearing a crown of stars, evoked the woman of the Apocalypse, "clothed with the sun, with the moon under her feet, and on her head a crown of twelve stars" (Revelation 12:1).[23] The popularity of these devotions, the flourishing of new religious congregations dedicated to Mary, the miraculous apparitions at La Salette and to Alphonse Ratisbonne at Rome all were proof that the Marian age foreseen by Grignon de Montfort had dawned, and that the Second Coming of Christ could be expected to follow.[24]

The diffusion of belief in the Marian age was so great that it went beyond the boundaries of orthodox Catholicism and penetrated even into political radicalism. The work of Alphonse Constant published in 1844, *La mère de Dieu, épopée religieuse et humanitaire*, was condemend by the Church for its vision of a socialist utopia ushered in by Mary. The orthodox hoped that the Marian age would culminate in the triumph of the Church in cooperation with the State. Beyond these differences, however, was a shared vision of rapid and fundamental change based on the intervention of Mary in history. The work of Constant, by its very extremism, serves to highlight the millennialism that was implicit in the belief that the era of Mary had arrived, with its locus in France.[25]

By the time of its promulgation in 1854, the Immaculate Conception was a popular doctrine whose cause had been aided by prophecies, miraculous apparitions and cures, devotional cults, and pious literature ranging from the orthodox to the heretical. It was only after the decree of 1854, however, that the single most important miracle of doctrinal significance occurred. On March 25—the feast of the Annunciation commemorating Christ's conception—in 1858, Mary announced to Bernadette at Lourdes, "I am the Immaculate Conception." Almost immediately this revelation became a focal point of Church concern. How could an illiterate shepherd-girl have learned of such a sophisticated doctrine? The fact that Bernadette was familiar with the Miraculous Medal and its prayer seems not to have been considered, and the conclusion reached was that the statement amounted to proof of the supernatural nature of the apparition. Then, using a logic that was almost disarmingly circular, Catholic apologists asserted that the apparition confirmed the Church's proclamation of the doctrine.[26]

The apparitions and cures at Lourdes were affirmed and supported by the Church, and the shrine at the grotto where Mary announced her title to the world became the most important pilgrimage center in France by the end of the century. The cult at Lourdes was further evidence that the age of Mary had arrived. French Catholics were quick to note that it was within France that Mary worked most actively to establish and confirm her Immaculate Conception. The theme of the Marian age was thus integrated into the nationalism that was characteristic of the nineteenth-century prophetic tradition. Prophets and prophecies predicted that France was destined to play the central role in the imminent eschatological events. The prophecies and proofs of the Marian age were further evidence of the providential role of France, as argued by Père Aladel in the standard devotional work on the Miraculous Medal.

Since the definition of the Immaculate Conception, as well as before it, France continues to be the privileged country of Mary; nowhere are miracles so numerous, or graces so abundant. Whence arises this glorious prerogative? So far as we are permitted to penetrate the secrets of God, it appears thus to our understanding: France, who has wrought so much evil by disseminating philosophical and revolutionary doctrines, is to repair the past by propagating the truth, and Mary desires to prepare her for this mission: Everyone knows, moreover, that the French character possesses a force of expansion and a power of energy that render the French emminently qualified to maintain the interests of truth and justice. Then, again, is not France the eldest daughter of the Church, since she was baptized in the power of Clovis, the first of the Most Christian Kings; and in virtue of this title, is it not her duty to devote herself under the patronage of her Mother in heaven to the defense of her Mother on earth?[27]

In the period following the apparitions of Lourdes, the theme of the Marian age was reiterated in pious literature and repeated by other visionaries. In *Le rosier de Marie*, a magazine devoted to Mary and distributed nationally, letters appeared in which Lourdes was seen as evidence that "the reign of God which we pray for every day is on the point of arriving on earth by the reign of Mary."[28] In 1866 the *Mémorial Catholique* published the revelations of Madeline Porsat, a peasant girl to whom Christ had given the following message.

> We are at the end of time. Now evil ends and goodness begins. . . . It is a great epoch which is opening, the third.
>
> After the Father who created us in order to know, love, and serve Him; after the Son who has saved us, now the Father and the Son, to console us, send us Their triumphant Spirit, with His wife Mary. It is a great miracle.[29]

By the 1860s the theme of the Marian age, supported by the doctrine of the Immaculate Conception, had become a commonplace in Catholic piety. The Immaculate Conception, like the dogmas discussed earlier, had benefited from supernatural confirmation. The implications of this new dogma, however, had more contemporary relevance than those of the Trinity or the Real Presence. The declaration of the Immaculate Conception was an important part of the Church's attempt to encourage a universal cultic symbol capable of appealing to traditional religious needs and sentiments. In supporting the doctrine, however, and in its emphasis on Marian piety in general, the Church was also implicitly encouraging a set of eschatological expectations in which the triumph of the Church and the Second Coming of Christ were seen as following from Mary's conquest of France. The doctrine of the Immaculate Conception, along with the miracles and devotions which supported it, are thus of interest not only because of their impact on the evolution of Catholic doctrine, but because they suggest the eschatological frame of mind characteristic of French Catholicism.

Miracles and Devotions

The Church's official position on the doctrine of the Immaculate Conception was in part due to the popular support generated by the Marian apparitions. Other visions and revelations also had a widespread appeal, which was expressed in popular devotions that encouraged an attitude of reverence toward sacred figures. Any attempt to understand the religious life of the past century must take account of such devotions, for the Catholicism of everyday life was more likely to be influenced by devotions than by formal dogma. Dogmas can only tell people what to believe, while devotions translate beliefs into terms meaningful in a particular time and place.[30]

Popular piety in nineteenth-century France presents a bewildering array of devotions, most of which made some claim of possessing miraculous power.[31] In addition to those inspired by specific miracles, some devotions formed around contemporary saints and others focused on some particular detail from the lives of Christ and the saints. Beneath this multiplicity, however, certain themes recur which shaped the character of nineteenth-century piety. The first of these is the sentimentalization of Catholic piety, and in particular the emphasis on affective bonds between the devotee and the object of his or her devotion. The familial metaphor was frequently used to express this theme, which relates devotional life to larger questions of social and intellectual history. Second, Catholic devotions emphasize the guilt of the modern age and the need for redemptive suffering by a religious elite. Of course, such an idea is no novelty in Christianity, and it would be hard to find an age in which the clergy did not stress guilt and the need for redemption. In the nineteenth century, however, this theme achieved dramatic popular expression in several contemporary devotions. The interest in the stigmata exemplifies the concern for suffering and redemption; stigmatics became devotional objects in themselves while providing new impetus for a devotion to the suffering of Christ. Finally, poverty, simplicity, and humility were stressed as ideals in devotional life. Without making any claim for the novelty of these themes, they were used by the Church in the nineteenth century to criticize the growing wealth and sophistication of modern society, which threatened to destroy the "sacred canopy" of religious symbols and values.[32]

Sentimentalism and Intimacy

The pilgrimages and novenas that were a prominent part of devotional life were a source of hope for people when they were sick, and when drought, flood, or political catastrophe threatened their collective existence. But while thaumaturgy was an important part of popular piety, it did not totally define the relationship between believers and their devotions. The medals, holy cards, manuals, and pious biographies produced for devotees were not merely instrumental talismans. Most of the prayers and meditations in the devotional literature did not ask for physical or material assistance; they were expressions of belief and trust designed to help the reader establish emotional intimacy with God and the saints. This characteristic of nineteenth-century piety, like so many other facets of modern French religious life, has its precedent in the seventeenth century. The writings of the French school, including such figures as Bérulle and Olier, emphasized the physical maternity of Mary and the sense of obligation that Christ felt toward his mother. The French school, however, was interested in using their reflections on Christ and Mary to achieve a mystical rather than a sentimental experience, and they did not reach the kind of mass audience reached by nineteenth-century pious authors.[33] The ancien régime did not ignore sentiment in its religous literature, but in the nineteenth century affective and personal relations were elevated to a central position in popular devotions sanctioned by the Church.

The biographies of Christ and Mary transcribed by Clemens Brentano from the visions of Catherine Emmerich were an early influence in the formation of a devotional attitude toward the Holy Family. This attitude was one of empathetic identification with Jesus, Mary, and Joseph in which their human problems and relations were made a point of contact between the devotee and the Holy Family. Emmerich's "histories" of Mary and Jesus filled in missing periods of Christ's life, provided intimate descriptions of the relations between Christ and Mary, and sentimentalized the Gospels' account of Jesus.[34]

Ironically, Ernest Renan, the secular historian of Christ, took a view of Jesus' life that was in some ways similar to Emmerich's. Renan's biography was condemned by the Church because of its attack on the miraculous nature of Christ's life, but its commerical success was nevertheless unprecedented for a scholarly work.[35] In part this popularity was based on the public controversy surrounding the work; but Renan also provided details that satisfied the desire of nineteenth-century readers to know a more personal Christ than the one presented in the New Testament. In describing Christ's entry into an ordinary house, for example, Renan allowed his imagination some play:

His entering a house was considered a joy and a blessing. . . . In the East, the house into which a stranger enters becomes at once a public place. All the village assembles there, the children invade it, and though dispersed by the servants, always return. Jesus could not permit these simple auditors to be treated harshly; he caused them to be brought to him and embraced them. Women came to pour oil upon his head, and perfume his feet. His disciples sometimes repulsed them as troublesome, but Jesus, who loved the ancient usages and all that indicated simplicity of heart, repaired the ill done by his too zealous friends. . . . Thus women and children loved him. The reproach of alienating from their families these gentle creatures, always easily misled, was one of the most frequent charges of his enemies.[36]

Renan's purpose was to present Christ as a great moral teacher, but in carrying out his design he constructed a sentimental vision of Christ and the early Church. The similarity between the work of a visionary who claimed to have personally witnessed the events of Christ's life and a scholar who personified the "new criticism" suggests a unity in the nineteenth-century comprehension of Christ, which stressed the emotional ties between Christ and his followers. The contrast is equally striking, for the Virgin Birth, the miracles, and the Resurrection were all confirmed by Emmerich and explained away by Renan. But while the visionary and the scholar held diametrically opposed views on the occurrence of miracles, they shared an interest in the details of Christ's daily life which conformed to nineteenth-century sensibilities.

The inclusion of the devotee in the emotional intimacy attributed to Jesus, Mary, and Joseph was one of the most significant developments in the world of popular piety. Revealing evidence for this is the uniformity with which the familial metaphor occurs in describing the relationship between the devotee and the object of his devotion. The family relationship as idealized in the literature reflects what historians have found to be characteristic domestic ideals in the nineteenth century.[37] Marriage as a sentimental union and affectionate ties between parents and children were prevailing metaphors in devotional life. Christ was not just sovereign, but also husband and father; Joseph was addressed as father; and, most important, Mary became a symbol of modern attitudes about maternity and femininity.

The images of Christ as father and as husband were frequently conflated, sometimes in a manner that is ostensibly incestuous. In addressing Marie Lataste, Christ simultaneously assumed both roles:

My daughter, be happy; I choose you for my spouse. Let this title
be dearer to you than that of queen. I am your beloved. Never
share your heart, then, with any creature. Whom could you find
more beautiful, more loving, more wealthy, more powerful, more
perfect than Me?[38]

The theme of Christ as the ideal husband and lover was expressed in
various forms. A deck of playing cards designed for Catholic schoolgirls
presents a revealing picture of the devotional–marital relationship. There
were thirty-three cards in the deck, one for each year of Christ's life, and
each card bore a title, a secret, and a prayer. Theoretically, the girls would
choose a card each day and use it to help them meditate on their association
with Christ. Among the titles were some that described the romantic
stereotype of a modern wife: The Lover, The Conquest, The Ideal Com-
panion, The Wife, The Captive, The Privileged Happy One, The Well
Loved, The Victim. The messages on the cards reinforced the idea that
romantic intimacy should characterize a woman's feelings toward Christ:
"My loved one is all mine and I am all his"; "The imperious need of love is
to yearn for union with the object of love, to search for it and procure it by
every means"; "I am the only object really worthy of filling and satisfying
this heart, created for me alone."[39]

In Flaubert's *Madame Bovary*, Emma found solace in religious fantasies
after her abandonment by Rodolphe. The sentiments formerly associated
with her human lover were now transferred to God: "When she knelt on
her Gothic *prie-dieu*, she addressed to the Lord the same suave words that
she had murmured to her lover in the outpourings of adultery."[40] Thérèse
of Lisieux, who became one of the most popular saints of the twentieth
century, offers a final illustration of the theme of Christ the husband in her
autobiography, first published in 1898. Eight days after Thérèse entered
the convent at the age of fifteen, in 1888, her cousin Jeanne was married.
Thérèse wrote that her cousin "told me of all the care she lavished on her
husband. Her words struck me and I said to myself: It's not going to be
said that a woman will do more for her husband, a mere mortal, than I will
do for my beloved Jesus." Jeanne's tactlessness had obviously affected
Thérèse, who had so recently embraced a celibate life. She responded by
composing the following invitation, which was read for the amusement of
the novices to make them realize "how trifling are the pleasures of an
earthly union compared with the glory of being the bride of Christ."

ALMIGHTY GOD Creator of Heaven and Earth, Supreme Sovereign of the Universe and THE MOST GLORIOUS VIRGIN MARY Queen of the Court of Heaven

Announce to you the Spiritual Marriage of their august Son Jesus, King of Kings and Lord of Lords with Little Thérèse Martin now Princess and Lady of the Kingdoms of the Childhood of Jesus and His Passion, given to her as a dowry by her divine Spouse from which she holds her titles of nobility OF THE CHILD JESUS and OF THE HOLY FACE. It was not possible to invite you to the wedding held on the Mountain of Carmel, September 8, 1890, as only the heavenly court was admitted, but you are nevertheless invited to the At Home tomorrow, the Day of Eternity when Jesus, the Son of God, will come in the clouds of heaven to judge the living and the dead in the full splendour of His Majesty.

The Hour being uncertain, you are asked to hold yourself in readiness and to watch.[41]

Thérèse's choice of a wedding invitation to demonstrate the insignificance of an earthly union is an ironic instance of the extent to which devotion to Jesus was understood in terms of the marital metaphor.

Marriage to Christ was, of course, limited to women. There is some evidence that an analogous relationship of males to Mary as wife was also important, at least in the training of clergy. Mgr Duperray, in reflecting on his seminary education, wrote in his memoirs:

Mary played a major role in my vocation, because without her it would have been impossible for me to become a priest. My sensitive heart desired pure, sweet affection, which is feminine affection. But Jesus proposed that I abandon everything, including the affection of a wife, in order to follow him and become a priest. How fortunate that the Holy Virgin was there! Was she not able to furnish me with the feminine influence I needed so badly? Yes! She offered me even more than the affection of a wife. Because she is the ideal, the most womanly woman. . . . She is in Heaven, no doubt. But she is also a living reality in my heart of flesh.[42]

Christ portrayed as the ideal husband who was at once master and lover was thus complemented by Mary as the ideal wife, the epitome of sweetness and affection.

Metaphors of husband and wife were restricted in application by the sex of the devotee. The same was not true of the roles of father and mother. Devotions to St. Joseph as an ideal father and worker date from the nineteenth century, with several cults claiming him as their patron.[43] Even more important, however, was the devotion to Mary as the ideal mother. No theme is more common in the enormous literature spawned by the Marian revival than the universal maternity of Mary. The manual of the Confraternity of Notre-Dame des Victoires concluded with a hymn in which Mary's maternal love for Jesus is extended to all devotees.

What is happening? I feel my heart opening up to hope.
It finds peace again, it beats with love;
I did not implore her clemency in vain,
The mother of Jesus is my mother today. . . .[44]

Mary's love encompassed not just individuals, but all of France. Nationalistic pride in the contemporay apparitions and the new devotions was also expressed through the maternal metaphor. A manual dedicted to Notre-Dame de Lourdes compared Mary's concern for France to a mother's love of a favorite child.

In families the father and mother love all of their children; nevertheless there is always one whom they cherish in a special way. Among his twelve sons the patriarch Jacob preferred the chaste Joseph. Among the twelve apostles, Jesus seemed to love one better than the other.

It is the same among the great families that make up the Catholic Church. The queen of heaven and earth loves and protects all of them as a tender mother, but she has a well-known predilection for France.[45]

Devotion to Christ and Mary in which divine figures and devotees were assimilated into an ideal family are significant manifestations of a shift in religious mood. Christ and Mary remained figures of grandeur, the King and Queen of Heaven, and such royal metaphors have never been totally replaced.[46] But devotional life was responsive to the changed attitudes toward the family that accompanied the altered demographic and economic circumstances of the nineteenth century. Middle-class women in France were less likely to help their husbands in business, and increasingly became the standard bearers for culture. According to Simone de Beauvoir,

A function that man readily entrusts to woman is the weighing of values; she is a privileged judge. Man dreams an Other not only to possess her but also to be ratified by her; to be ratified by other men, his peers, demands a constant tension; hence he wishes consideration from outside to confer an absolute value upon his life, his enterprises, and himself. The consideration of God is hidden, alien, disquieting; even in times of faith only a few mystics longed for it. This divine role has most often devolved upon woman. Being the Other, she remains exterior to man's world and can view it objectively; and being close to man and dominated by him, she does not establish values foreign to his nature.[47]

Beauvoir's argument is based on her reading of Stendhal, Balzac, and Flaubert, but the descriptions of Mary in devotional literature conform to this image of women as divine figures who judge and console men. In a pamphlet of 1873 Gustave Mathevon claimed that Marian devotions were particularly suited to the mentality of the nineteenth century.

We need an ideal to allow our faculties to soar and rise. . . . The woman is at the same time the most eloquent and complete symbol of all of the conquering forces, and an ideal which can be loved. Let us render to woman her legitimate sovereignty, the crown of modesty, the scepter that is so sweet to submit to, of shining goodness. Give her respect and holy affection, the throne of purity from which she will let fall on us the unction that heals wounds. . . . Mary is feminine beauty with no mixture of accursed seductiveness. . . . She is beautiful with this real beauty which is on the foreheads of our sisters, who have remained pure, the reflection of the splendor of God. It is so good for the heart to escape the multitude of fallen women by contemplating the celestial virgin. . . . The dignity of our mothers, the virginal purity of the young girl gives an idea of the singular destination of women; only Mary has given us the complete manifestation of it. An exquisite perfume of innocence envelopes her as a garment of snow, and from her virginal hands rivers of an unparalleled purity descend on our heavy hearts.[48]

For Mathevon the nature of the feminine ideal is paradoxical; Mary represents both maternity and virginity. The tension between the two roles is rooted in ambivalent feelings about feminine sexuality that are characteristically romantic.[49] It may be that Marian devotions were an important mechanism for the dissemination of romantic attitudes about women in the world of popular culture. Mary's popularity was in part due to her unique ability to symbolize the contemporary feminine ideals of maternity and virginity. Thus the Marian revival, including the popularity of the Immaculate Conception in which her moral perfection and purity were emphasized, had psychological as well as doctrinal significance.

Suffering and Reparation

The role of woman as victim was an important element in the devotional understanding of femininity. Images stressing the suffering of Mary were part of all the Marian devotions. On the Miraculous Medal the heart of Mary appeared alongside Christ's, and both were pierced by the same sword. At La Salette Mary wept for the sins of France, and at Lourdes she sighed and called for "Pénitence, pénitence, pénitence." The sufferings of Mary were associated with those of Christ, and like his were assumed to have redemptive value. The victimization of Mary because of the sins of mankind is just one example of the theme of suffering and reparation which played such a significant role in nineteenth-century devotional life. An analysis of this theme reveals another set of religious concerns and their social and psychological implications.

New devotions designed to assist Catholics in making reparation appeared throughout the century; virtually all the cults that were based on contemporary miracles included practices whereby devotees could, by prayer and sacrifice, compensate for the sins of individuals and of France as a whole. The Confraternity of Notre-Dame des Victoires was specifically intended to be an association of prayers for the conversion of sinners. In 1845 a confraternity to combat blasphemy was formed at Poitiers. The work of this association was advanced by Soeur Saint-Pierre, a Carmelite of Tours, and Léon Dupont, the thaumaturge known as the "Holy Man of Tours." Soeur Saint-Pierre provided the new devotion with a suitable image when it was revealed to her in a vision that the face of Christ as depicted on Veronica's veil should serve as the confraternity's symbol.[50] In 1847 Mgr Parisis, the bishop of Poitiers, attempted to dissociate his organization from Soeur Saint-Pierre's visions, and from the Holy Face in particular. Consequently, Dupont formed an independent devotion which was eventually granted the status of an official confraternity.[51] The cult of the Holy Face, as popularized by Dupont, stressed the sinfulness of France in the modern world. Soeur Saint-Pierre's revelations included the unorthodox notion that Christ was suffering anew because of the irreligion and immorality of the nineteenth century. By cultivating a devotion to the face of the tortured Christ one could, however, compensate for sin and relieve Christ's pain.

> The divine Savior has made it known to me that the impious renew the outrages inflicted on His Holy Face by their blasphemies. . . . I have understood that all the blasphemies . . . fall like the spittle of the Jews on the Holy Face of Our Lord who has made himself the victim of sinners. I have also heard Our Lord say that in applying ourselves to the practice of the reparation of blasphemy, we render Him the same service as the pious Veronica, and that He looks on those who render him this service with the same satisfaction with which he regarded this holy woman during His Passion.[52]

The image of the Holy Face was, then, a devotional aid to assist the devotee in recalling and identifying with Christ's sufferings, and thereby partially alleviating them.[53]

Confraternities which could compensate for modern sinfulness were accompanied by other devotions in which the idea of vicarious suffering was more dramatically portrayed. The reappearance of individuals marked by the stigmata, and the devotional interest they aroused, suggest that the ideal of suffering with Christ had increased significance in nineteenth-century religious life. Catherine Emmerich's life was publicized during the Restoration, and stigmatics from Switzerland and Italy drew attention throughout the century. These individuals were religious virtuosi, but they were also devotional models whose identification with the sufferings of Christ was held up as an ideal for all Catholics.[54]

A devotion to the sufferings of Christ and a desire to make reparation for sin are not, of course, novelties. The doctrine that suffering is redemptive is, after all, the basis for the Christian religion. The devotions of the nineteenth century suggest, however, that this traditional theme was receiving new emphasis, which resulted at times in an abuse of the Christian ideal. The devotion to St. Philomena went beyond redemptive suffering or religious devotion. The remains of this supposed martyr were discovered in the catacombs early in the nineteenth century, but nothing was known of her life and death until the visions of an Italian nun provided biographical details. The Church never beatified St. Philomena on the basis of these visions, but it did actively promote devotion to her and publicized the martyr's life as it had been revealed. St. Philomena was, according to the devotional literature dedicated to her, an adolescent virgin who became an object of lust for the Emperor Diocletian. On refusing his offer of marriage Philomena was stripped and scourged in the presence of several men. She was then beheaded after the arrows which were to kill her turned and killed the archers instead.[55] The nun who received these visions prayed to Philomena especially when she was tempted by sins of "impurity"; Philomena was presented in the devotional literature as a model of Christian virginity.[56] The vision of Philomena's torture and martyrdom would bear psychological interpretation as a masochistic expression of sexual repression. Even without engaging in psychohistorical speculation, however, the martyrdom of Philomena does seem to focus on the sexual element in her story, as opposed to the redemptive implications that a more orthodox view of Christian suffering entails.[57]

The career of Mélanie, one of the visionaries of La Salette, provides more evidence of the extremes to which nineteenth-century devotional life was liable. In 1855, while a Carmelite novice, Mélanie concluded a letter to a priest who had written and asked for her prayers:

> I have a great desire to love Our Good Savior, Jesus Christ and to shroud myself in His sacred wounds, oh! when one sees this good Savior on the cross, who could not love Him, yes, love Him and give his blood for His Love. . . . It is through Mary that one obtains all, it is in Mary, this good and tender mother, that one must evaluate science and divine love, oh! Love Mary, Love Notre-Dame de La Salette, pray to her to make us love Jesus and the Cross of his life, the Cross of Our Salvation.
>
> > I am, Monseigneur
> > your very humble and unworthy
> > servant, Mary of the Cross,
> > Victim of Jesus, unworthy
> > Carmelite novice.[58]

Mélanie's letter expresses a love of suffering in the context of a sentimental relationship with Christ and Mary. The devotional themes distinguished here were in practice frequently combined. But with Mélanie it was suffering that assumed the central position in her devotions. In her auto-biography, edited by Léon Bloy and published after her death in 1904, Mélanie's love of suffering is a constant motif, and she severely castigates all those who refuse "to be crucified with Christ." Bloy goes so far as to compare the redemptive value of Mélanie's suffering with Mary's, a comparison that Mélanie doubtless would have appreciated.[59] Bloy's role in support of Mélanie was not at all exceptional. The concept of vicarious suffering was the focal point for an important group of Catholic writers during the Third Republic, and Mélanie was a model for these individuals. This intellectual movement derived strength from the world of popular piety; the image of the weeping Virgin of La Salette which had spread so quickly in France in 1846 and 1847 became for them an especially impor-tant symbol.[60] Writers like Bloy and Huysmans, in their emphasis on suffering, were operating within and expanding a devotional tradition that was already a familiar part of Catholic life.

Without attempting a comprehensive explanation of the theme of suf-fering, I believe that its appeal can be understood on at least two levels. From the psychological perspective, suffering as an ideal relates to psychic needs that are timeless. The appeal of the crucified Christ who suffers and dies that others might live suggests the permanence of this ideal in the Western world. Nineteenth-century devotions sometimes strayed from the central Christian symbol, substituting Mary for Christ as the victim. Such shifts are critical, but the need for a symbol which expressed and affirmed the value of sacrifice seems undeniable.

From an institutional perspective, suffering and reparation were emphasized because of the novel historical situation. The French Church was confronted in the nineteenth century with a society that no longer uniformly embraced Catholicism. Official tolerance of other religions, or of irreligion, made it possible for disbelief to be expressed publicly with-out even the threat of censorship. Religion had become a voluntary rather than a prescriptive affair. Even though the vast majority of Frenchmen still accepted nominal membership in the Church, there was a new aware-ness of a distinction between Church and society. The Church's response to this situation took many forms. The development of regional shrines designed to appeal to popular beliefs about sickness and health was one way to hold Catholics to their faith. Missions and pilgrimages may have been effective mechanisms for warming up the tepid faith of believers, but they did not deal with the problem of the indifferent and the hostile. Such individuals had to be taken into account, even if they remained outside the Church. By supporting devotions in which the prayers and sufferings of those who believed could compensate for those who did not, the Church partially resolved the dissonance it experienced in confronting unbelievers. Prayer and suffering might lead to their conversion, but even if they did not, such devotional practices would serve to counteract their sins and forestall God's anger.

The devotional interpretation of suffering and reparation in nineteenth-century France contrasts with that of previous centuries. Formerly, reparational devotions had concentrated on gaining indulgences and insuring the personal salvation of one's own soul, or of one's family and *confréres*.[61] Such devotions continued to be important in the nineteenth century, but they were combined with others whose purpose was not to merit the salvation of professed Christians, but to bring the unconverted into the Church, and to make public reparation for those who refused to believe. Moreover, devotions were no longer personal and local in their focus. Just as personal sinfulness was perceived in collective terms as the cause of the successive revolutions and natural catastrophes in France, personal prayer and suffering were seen as the means of national salvation.[62]

Poverty, Simplicity, Humility

The poverty, simplicity, and humility characteristic of nineteenth-century devotions can be grouped together, for they are consistently linked in the pious literature. The books and pamphlets produced for the Miraculous Medal, Notre-Dame de La Salette, Notre-Dame de Lourdes, Notre-Dame de Pontmain, and the devotion of the Holy Face featured the visionaries as models of these virtues. The themes were not fortuitous, but were responses to France's specific situation. Of course, religious reformers have always used these fundamental Christian virtues as standards by which contemporary society and frequently the Church itself should be measured. In the ancien régime Jansenists had effectively criticized the Church as corrupted by excessive luxury and obfuscating theology. But only with Benoit Labre, near the end of the eighteenth century, does a popular model emerge who exemplified these virtues and remained within the orthodox Church.[63] The massive publicity, approved by the

Church, given to popular prophets in the nineteenth century seems to have no analogue in the seventeenth and eighteenth centuries.

At the most general level of explanation, the revived popularity of these ideals can be seen as the result of a dialectical process in which the values denied by the secular establishment are affirmed by religion. The emergence and growth of the Franciscan and Dominican orders in the thirteenth century is a prime example of the process in which religion affirms spiritual values of poverty, chastity, and obedience currently unfashionable in an expanding economy and urbanizing society.[64] Any reader of Balzac is familiar with a social world in which professional success, conspicuous consumption, and power are the dominant values. An urban, affluent culture in which the daughters of Goriot could flourish required the balance of alternative models of behavior, and this was provided in part by the pastoral figures of Mélanie, Bernadette, and their colleagues.

Literary pastoralism, an element in the romanticism that pervaded nineteenth-century culture, bears some responsibility for the diffusion and appeal of such figures. The shepherd children Mélanie and Bernadette especially benefited from the vision of a countryside as a place free from the demoralizing struggles of urban France.[65] Literary fashion and popular taste are not enough of an explanation, however, for they fail to get at the substance of the virtues of poverty, simplicity, and humility. In defending poverty as an ideal, devotions emphasized an aspect of the Christian message that was perceived to be jeopardized by the relative affluence of the nineteenth century. The clergy's complaints of the desire of their parishioners for luxury were expressed by Abbé Desgenettes, who bemoaned the venality of the age and blamed it for the dissolution of affectionate relationships between classes: "Money! Money! There is the single universal cry; we descend into the abyss of shame and dishonor to get it." In another context Abbé Desgenettes unintentionally revealed the mood he was trying to combat. In the first story of a conversion presented in his *Manuel* for the Confraternity of Notre-Dame des Victoires, Desgenettes described the conversion of a dissipated young man who had formerly been unable to work for his living: "Today he has an administrative job in which he makes 1,800 francs a year!" For Desgenettes, at least in this case, spiritual and financial rebirth were closely related.[66]

Almost all of the visionaries of nineteenth-century France were poor. Evidence from Lourdes shows that poverty was part of the devotion in its earliest stages. Stories that circulated by word of mouth at the time of the Lourdes apparitions asserted that Bernadette's poverty was the source of God's favor. One such tale related how Bernadette and her flock, in a barren country, were teased by a rich man who offered her his meadow, which was out of reach across a river. As related by the local police commissioner, the story concluded, "the heavens wanted . . . to confound the evil rich man who humiliated the poor child. As soon as the peasant, after having spoken, turned his heels, the waters of the stream stopped and the herd passed into the prairie, crossing the river bed with dry feet."[67] This theme of God's concern for the poor in their struggle against the rich did not disappear in the official treatment of the Lourdes apparitions. The most famous single work on Lourdes, which was published with an approving letter from Pius IX, established the contrast between rich and poor, and God's preference for the latter, as its central message. Henri Lasserre criticized the patronizing attitude of the rich in these terms:

> Save a few rare Christians, none think of the poor person as a brother, as an equal. . . . Well, the poor one is loved by the universal Father. Since this world has been forever denounced by the infallible word of Christ, it is the poor, the suffering and the humble who are good company, the chosen society, for God, who conform to His heart. . . . Almost always, aside from some unimportant exceptions, apparitions, visions, revelations, and shining grace have been the privilege of these poor whom the world despises.[68]

Lasserre concludes the statement of his theme by recalling the example of Christ's life, and quoting the Gospel: "God has elected him who is weak according to the world to confound him who is powerful."

Lasserre's treatment of Bernadette as an example of divine predilection for the poor echoes the treatment given to other visionaries throughout the century.[69] This amounts to a social inversion in which the Church publicly acknowledged the moral superiority of the poor. With important exceptions, the Church responded slowly to the "social problem" in the nineteenth century, and the standard solution to questions of social justice and poverty was to advocate an increase in charity.[70] But while programmatic solutions developed slowly, the concept of the moral superiority of the poor, confirmed by their special graces of visions and revelations, can be seen as an attempt to respond to the social question on a symbolic plane. The willingness of priests and bishops to listen to and learn from the poor who were blessed with revelations must have proved satisfying both to Church and people. The Church could draw strength from its affirmation of this fundamental Christian virtue, while at the same time avoiding the practical consequences of either embracing or abolishing poverty. For the people, the visionaries could be seen as representatives who, because of their poverty, could gain a hearing with God and the world.

The ideals of simplicity and humility were, like poverty, a reaction to what were seen as the threats of the modern world. Simplicity was a reaction to the rationalism inherited from the Enlightenment and made fashionable by the positivists. In their discussion of doctrinal questions, visionaries made a virtue of irrationality; simplicity was designed to counter the claims of rationalism from a different angle.[71] Pious literature described visionaries as people capable of witnessing God and Mary because they had not been corrupted by excessive learning. Visitors were fond of noting how the "simplicity" of Mélanie and Maximin could confound the wisdom of those who tried to trick them into contradictions.[72] Special note was made of the fact that many of the visionaries were illiterate. This was in part an attempt to verify the apparitions, since it was argued that simple and illiterate people could never have imagined the sights and words they described. But simplicity and illiteracy were also presented as advantages, which allowed the soul to cultivate a pious and reverent attitude. Given the massive literature produced by the devotions themselves, it appears that the Church did understand that universal literacy was inevitable. The pious simplicity of religious models was not intended to discourage reading, but to encourage a credulous attitude toward the supernatural.[73]

Rationalism, criticized by the ideal of simplicity, led to a false pride in personal judgment. To counter the latter vice, the virtue of humility, in particular of humble obedience to the Catholic Church, was included in the religious model presented by the devotions. Humility has not always been a virtue associated with prophets and visionaries. Several scholars have observed that prophecy can serve as a form of social protest on the part of those ignored by institutional power structures. Women prophets during the English Revolution, for example, were able to speak publicly and gain attention for their positions because of their claims of divine inspiration.[74] The fact that so many nineteenth-century French visionaries were poor may in part be a reflection of social discontent. Humility, however, was an effective check on any social protest latent in the devotions, for this virtue insisted on willing submission to the constituted authorities. While the poor and the simple could gain credibility and symbolic status through their visions, in the process of reporting and spreading their message, their role as representatives of the people became subordinated to their role as representatives of the Church. One common pattern, followed by Soeur Nativité, Catherine Labouré, and Marie Lataste, was for the prophet or visionary to entrust herself completely to a clergyman who functioned as a spiritual advisor.[75] If the visionary was not already a nun, she usually joined an order within a few years of her vision. From within a religious order it was especially difficult for the visionary to avoid the co-option of her revelation by the Church. Only one visionary, Mélanie of La Salette, was able to resist the pressures put on her by the religious establishment, and even she relied on the support of dissident priests and bishops.[76]

Visionaries were effectively controlled by the Church, and freely acknowledged that their revelations would have to coincide with official dogma. They conceded to their advisors the right to determine whether the voices they heard or visions they saw were divine or diabolical. Yet at the same time the Church was encouraging the creation of spiritual models whose simplicity and poverty made them intimates of God. There is an ambivalence here that stemmed from the Church's desire to retain its prerogative as the only legitimate intermediary between God and man while at the same time granting the reality of direct revelations to the favored poor. The model of the poor but pious visionary was an affirmation of a Christian virtue rooted in the Gospel. The total obedience such individuals gave to the ecclesiastical hierarchy was an assertion of a fundamental tenet of institutional Catholicism which became all the more important as the Church became both more centralized and defensive in the nineteenth century. The image of a simple, humble, obedient visionary was designed to reach out to the poor and draw them to the Church, but only on the Church's own terms.

Miracles affected both what and how people believed in the nineteenth century. The Immaculate Conception as a doctrine received both popular and official support as a result of the Marian apparitions in France, while the devotions which spread news of these miracles helped define the psychological atmosphere of Catholic piety. I have suggested that the use

Bernadette Soubrious, the visionary of Lourdes, photographed by Paul Dufour, publisher and bookseller of Lourdes, in 1864. Laurentin collection, all rights reserved.

of contemporary miracles in support of doctrine is evidence of a defensive attitude within the nineteenth-century Church. If this is the case, the outbreak of the miraculous that was so widely commented on might not have been a sign of strength and hope, as the Church and its followers believed, but of doubt and even fear. Miracles and their devotions, interpreted in this way, were part of an attempt by the Church to shut out the rationalism, positivism, affluence, and urbanization that threatened orthodox belief.

Such an attempt could only be successful, however, if it could interpret the traditional Christian message in terms believers could understand. In order to castigate modernity, the Church had to use a modernized vocabulary. Evidence from the devotions has revealed just how much Catholic piety borrowed from the romantic culture of nineteenth-century France. This ambivalence toward modernity could, perhaps, be viewed as further evidence of weakness and doubt. I believe it would be fairer, however, to interpret it as a sign that, whatever its explicit ideological positions, the Church remained attuned to and a part of French cultural life. Religious beliefs and attitudes changed with the times and in response to them. Regardless of one's views about those beliefs and attitudes, such a response was an indication of religious vitality.

Chapter 5
The Religious Revival
of the Third Republic

I n the early 1870s large numbers of Frenchmen, shocked by the defeat of their nation in the Franco-Prussian war and by the violence of the Paris Commune, turned to their religious shrines for hope and consolation. In analyzing the pilgrimage movement most historians have stressed its nationalist and royalist aspects, but these cannot be understood apart from the eschatological mood of the period.[1] A major revival of the prophetic tradition accompanied the wave of pilgrimages in the 1870s. Throughout the century this tradition had viewed political history as an eschatological drama; now it was able to provide an interpretation for the loss of the war which offered hope that God would soon restore France to its position of world leadership. The pilgrimage movement and the prophetic revival of the 1870s were climactic expressions of religious and political themes that were an established part of nineteenth-century French Catholicism: a sense of guilt due to the belief that France was being punished for the unexpiated sins of the Revolution, and a hope that public prayer and ritual could serve as reparation. The miracles and prophecies of popular religion were a significant expression of the anxieties and hopes that formed the political climate of France in the 1870s.

Apparitions, Pilgrimages, and Nationalism

The political collapse of the Second Empire was sudden and unexpected. For the fifth time in forty years a regime had been overturned and replaced. The crisis of 1870–1871 was compounded by the invasion and occupation of the German armies. The National Assembly elected in February 1871 added to the confusion, for it was seen only as a transitional body whose purpose was to negotiate peace with the Germans and then replace itself with yet another regime, presumably a constitutional monarchy. In the face of such political instability many who sought a sense of national solidarity and common purpose resorted to religious symbols. In a series of new apparitions Mary served as an important symbol of national hope and salvation. Concurrently the pilgrimage movement, which brought Frenchmen to miraculous shrines throughout the nation, demonstrated and expressed sentiments at once religious and nationalistic. The movement culminated in a series of massive demonstrations in 1872 and 1873 at Lourdes, Auray, Chartres, and Paray-le-Monial.[2] There was, of course, opposition to the expression of religious nationalism by those who feared it was being exploited by the royalists. Pilgrims were, on a few occasions, subjected to harassment and counterdemonstrations.[3] But for many the miracles and pilgrimages were welcome evidence that France would not be abandoned by Providence.

The most important of the Marian miracles occurred at Pontmain in the diocese of Laval on January 17, 1871. The apparition was immediately seized on as a hopeful sign in an area that was threatened by the Prussian army. As at La Salette and Lourdes, Mary appeared to children, who were responsible for transmitting her message to the world. The apparition began in the evening; before its conclusion more than fifty parishioners, along with the *curé* and the nuns from the local elementary school, were praying and singing hymns behind the five visionaries. The central message of the apparition was printed on a scroll that appeared at Mary's feet and read: "Mais priez mes enfants, Dieu vous exaucera en peu de temps" ("But pray my children, God will answer your prayers in a little while"). In a letter of January 18 to her superior, Sister Timothy of Pontmain told of the confidence inspired by the apparition. "I am going to tell you some happy news, the only news which can support us in the midst of the dangers to which we are exposed." The *curé* of Pontmain, Abbé Michel Guérin, reported a dramatic shift in public mood immediately following the miracle. "Many sinners from different places have presented themselves to the tribunal of Penitence, prayers not normally heard have been said everywhere, confidence in Mary grows ever greater, and the excessive fear of the enemy diminishes day by day, courage is reborn."[4] Letters from laymen of the area to friends and relatives described the miracle and its impact in similar terms. One correspondent wrote from Fougerolles, a village near Pontmain, that "they think of nothing but it in our canton, they are full of hope after the inscription which was read by the children."[5]

The position adopted by the Church confirmed the popular judgment that Mary's apparition was an act of divine protection. Just three days after the miracle chaplains from the French forces in the area met at Pontmain to hear the story of the apparition and signed, along with *curés* from several villages, a statement certifying "our edification and conviction." In a letter to the clergy of Laval in April of 1871, the bishop of the diocese, Mgr Wicart, described the threat posed by Prussian forces at the time of the miracle.

> Already a first combat had taken place on the 18th, just three kilometers from Laval. The enemy was near, and the first victims had been brought within our walls. New attacks were expected from moment to moment. A general quarter was established before the city, and a battery of artillery and machine guns, and troops under arms, were posted near St. Michel. . . . The following day, as far as the French scouts could go along the river, they perceived innumerable Prussian soldiers on the left bank, whose movements were impossible to discover.[6]

In these circumstances, before knowing anything of the events at Pontmain, Mgr Wicart led a congregation of four thousand to Notre-Dame d'Avenières, where he publicly vowed "to restore the tower and the beautiful steeple of her church, if the powerful protection of the Immaculate Virgin deigned to preserve us from the fire and pillage which threatened us imminently." In his April letter, Wicart stopped short of asserting that Mary had definitely intervened at Pontmain to turn away the Prussian troops, but he concluded that

> We are not of the number of these poor spirits who suppose that God does not occupy himself with the things of this world, or who believe that miracles are difficult for the One who is Goodness itself and to whom all power belongs, on earth as in heaven.

An episcopal investigation was quickly mounted, and its conclusion confirmed the suggestions in Wicart's letter. In February of 1872 Mgr Wicart published a decree verifying that a miracle had truly occurred, and relating Mary's appearance to the delivery of Laval from the Prussians. "There is no one who has not been struck by the exact concordance of the words [Dieu vous exaucera en peu de temps] with the decisive circumstances which immediately followed the event itself."⁷ Laval was not the only diocese where Mary's intervention was invoked during the Prussian invasion. In Nevers thirty-two parishes vowed to rebuild the chapel of Notre-Dame de Pitié if preserved from enemy attack. A chapel dedicated to Notre-Dame de Délivrance was constructed at Langres in thanksgiving for Mary's protection in August of 1870, when counterorders prevented a Prussian attack on three different occasions.⁸ But although Mary's intercession was widely sought, it was at Pontmain that her concern for France was most clearly and miraculously revealed.

At Pontmain Mary had appeared to predict the delivery of Laval and to offer consolation to France. The prophetic tradition maintained that Providence would always make an appropriate response to the problems and prayers of Frenchmen. In the atmosphere of the Franco–Prussian War, the apparition at Pontmain seemed to be evidence that such supernatural intervention was in fact occurring.

The original interpretation of Notre-Dame de Pontmain, put forward by the local participants and the bishop of Laval, was elaborated as the cult began attracting national attention. The miracle inspired belief among army officers as well as the people and clergy of the area. On March 10 General Charette, commander of the *Légion de l'ouest*, his chaplains, and several officers, signed a statement affirming their belief following a visit to Pontmain.⁹ Commentators soon worked the apparition into an eschatological interpretation of current events. Abbé Curicque's view was typical; he believed that after Pontmain, "the battle is henceforth engaged between heaven and earth." The words on the scroll, interpreted by Wicart to refer to the preservation of Laval, took on larger meaning for Curicque. They were for him a prediction of "the era of prosperity after which all of humanity will sigh with relief; Mary's words foretell the sixth age of Christianity, which must precede the end of the world." As the crowd sang "Mère de l'Espérance," the visionaries reported that the apparition of Mary grew larger. This was also given an eschatological and nationalistic gloss by Curicque, who saw it as evidence that France would restore the pope to Rome, and thereby reassume a central position in world affairs.¹⁰

The apparition at Pontmain was the most prominent of a series of Marian miracles during the period 1871 to 1873. Apparitions in Alsace were reported in July of 1872 when four girls saw Mary in a forest near Neubois. Just prior to the first apparition the girls had agreed that they would refuse to convert to Protestantism, suggesting that the annexation of the province had stimulated anxieties about the toleration of Catholicism. Accompanied by their teacher, a Catholic nun, and their fellow students, the girls returned to the site of the miracle on several occasions. Mary again appeared and led them to the site of an ancient shrine, supposedly the place of Clovis' conversion. Pilgrims soon began to gather there; the German subprefect responded by having the chapel destroyed. The new pilgrimage established by Mary survived, however, as people congregated at a nearby stream. Soon pilgrims were reporting visions that included the pope as well as Mary, and others in which Mary threatened Germany with a sword. By early 1873 as many as fifteen hundred pilgrims were gathering in expectation of further apparitions, and as many as forty were reported having visions at the same time. The visions in Alsace received extensive and favorable coverage in the French Catholic press where, like the apparitions at Pontmain, they were judged to be a sign of Mary's protection of France and a promise of the future recovery of the lost provinces. Eventually, rather than risk a full-scale confrontation, the German authorities withdrew their opposition to the pilgrimage.[11]

Similar Marian miracles were reported in Lorraine. At a home for unwed mothers in Nancy run by the Sisters of St. Charles, the eyes of a statue of Mary opened three times. The miracle occurred in November of 1870 at the conclusion of a hymn in which the Virgin was asked to save France. In April of 1873 a series of apparitions followed a miracle at the village of Buising, where Mary showed herself to a girl of thirteen. At least six other villages soon reported similar apparitions, and German officials had to call in the army to disperse the pilgrims who flocked to the sites of the miracles. A pamphlet relating these apparitions to those at La Salette and Lourdes appeared, reporting that Mary had announced the liberation of the east from German oppression and had brandished a sword toward the Rhine.[12]

The apparitions and the response they evoked are clear evidence of Mary's ability to symbolize patriotic and religious yearnings in a period of crisis. The defeat of France and the annexation of Alsace and Lorraine threatened the social and political order in a nation in which religious traditions retained much of their vigor. The miracles of the 1870s indicate the existence of a religious movement through which individuals found comfort and relief in the contemplation of symbols which promised the restoration of order through divine intervention. A young woman from Metz, in her prayer before the miraculous statue of Nancy, suggests the power of such symbols.

> O my Savior, Jesus Christ, we are so unhappy at Metz, so unhappy to be no longer French. Can you not give us some small hope of being reunited with our country soon? I beg you to do it through the intercession of your Holy Mother. I am going once more to see the Virgin of the Hospital. . . . My God, I beg of you, give to these children [her nephews] a visible sign of the protection of Mary.[13]

There are other instances of visions and other forms of miracles from this period. A luminous cross was seen in the moon on December 8, 1870, in Calvados, and a serpent appeared over Lorraine with its tail facing Metz and its head toward Paris. It was also common to interpret natural catastrophes as prophetic warnings. The floods of 1872 were judged by Abbé Curicque as "a final warning of divine mercy, always desirous of saving the world, but only if it converts." Fires, earthquakes, volcanic eruptions, and epidemics were all given similar interpretations.[14] The Marian manifestations were, by way of contrast, hopeful and consoling in their implications for France's future.

The sites of the miracles at Pontmain and in the east quickly became shrines at which pilgrims could express their religious nationalism. The religious revival of the 1870s saw thousands gather at these and other shrines, and crowds at Lourdes, Auray, Chartres, and Paray-le-Monial drew national attention to the pilgrimage movement. The sentiments of the pilgrims, expressed in song and ceremony, reflected their need to demonstrate to themselves and to the nation a sense of solidarity in a period when France seemed irreversibly defeated and divided.

The pilgrimage to Lourdes in October of 1872, known as the "National Pilgrimage," was the first in a series of mass religious events that lasted through 1873.[15] The most telling ritual of the Lourdes pilgrimage was the procession of four hundred banners from other Marian shrines throughout France to the church of the grotto. This expression of national unity under Mary's protection was given added poignancy by having the procession led by banners draped in crepe from Metz and Strasbourg. Before beginning his sermon Mgr de Langalen ceremoniously kissed the banners and read the following dedication to the crowd of forty thousand.

O Mary, Virgin Immaculate, Our Lady of Lourdes, you see at your feet all your children. We are come, sent from all the departments of our France, to remind you that we are your people, and that obedient to your voice we wish to say anew that our faith and hope are in you.

We come to thank you for your miraculous apparitions; we come to ask you to lead us back to your dear Son, Our Lord; we come so that you may obtain for France pardon and mercy.

We promise to become Christians again, we wish to make public reparation for the outrages which have been done to the divinity of our well-loved Savior Jesus Christ; we attest the faith of our France, we have confidence in you.

Be charitable with us and we will live; take away the sorrows of our fatherland, remake France in returning to us our unhappy brothers. She is always the eldest daughter of the Church, she believes, she loves, she prays, and you are her queen! She is sure of her salvation and of becoming again through you the most powerful Catholic nation.[16]

M. F. de Champigny, writing in *Le Correspondant* of October 25, 1872, described his reaction to the Lourdes pilgrimage as one of renewed hope. At Lourdes one was able to overcome the sense of division and despair and believe once more in the permanence and unity of France.

We did not know each other; we arrived by different roads; in this community, generally so unsociable, of people who travel by train, we had begun to know and understand each other; by the time we got off, we were all brothers. . . .

What existed always, and what was ever-present in our minds, was our mother, France. We had come to pray for what was most dear to us; how could we not pray for our fatherland? We did not arrange ourselves around political standards which are always more or less the flag of a party; we arranged ourselves around these pious banners from our churches, our dioceses, our sanctuaries which came from all corners of France to share in common the prayers, adorations, requests, petitions of all of France.[17]

Sentiments similar to those of Champigny were expressed in the popular hymns sung by the crowds at Lourdes, one of which contained this assertion of patriotic fervor:

What favor, o my dear France!
To have received this pearl from the skies. . . .

She said to you: I am the Immaculate Conception!
I have come here to announce it to all human beings,
But it is France, where I am especially loved,
Which will receive my gifts from full hands.
O noble France, o daughter of Mary,
No, you know that you cannot perish!
No longer fear Satan or his fury!
The hour has come, the Heavens will bless you.[18]

The pilgrimage movement, like the Marian apparitions, succeeded in creating an atmosphere in which France, despite its immediate problems, could still look forward to the recovery of her vitality. Just two weeks after the pilgrimage to Lourdes, *L'Univers* gave expression to the hope inspired by the movement.

The pilgrimage movement, in its spontaneity and extension, is a manifest sign of God's work. The pilgrimages have nothing to do with politics. . . . What they do is greater: they remake a Christian France, the France of our ancestors, the true, unique French fatherland. The effects are evident, an abundance of graces are diffused; there is hope in the air. To hope is to be strong.[19]

In September of 1873 Cardinal Guibert, writing in support of the construction of the basilica of Sacré-Coeur, referred to the "truly miraculous religious movement which has occurred in our nation, and which must save it."[20] With the benefit of hindsight it is possible to see the attitudes of *L'Univers*, Guibert, and other observers as optimistic if not naive. As Abbé Brugerette has pointed out, the revival seems not to have had any lasting effect on religious behavior.[21] Such a position, however, should not lead to the conclusion that the miracles and pilgrimages of the 1870s were insignificant. The religious revival may not have saved France as Guibert had hoped it would, but it allowed Catholics to think that France would be saved. Miracles and pilgrimages were thus social-psychological phenomena which allowed people to master fears raised by the current domestic and international turmoil. Catholics may also have felt some relief that France as well as the Church appeared to be suffering. The association of France with the troubles of the Church could remove in part the anxiety that religion was out of step with the age. Instead, it appeared that both Church and State were being persecuted by the dark forces of the modern era prior to a joint redemptive dawn.

Religion and Royalism in the 1870s

The conservatives' attempt to restore the monarchy in the early 1870s received important support from the Catholic Church. Pilgrimages and prophecies which excited nationalist sentiments took on partisan significance because of the Church's promotion of the candidacy of the Bourbon pretender, the Comte de Chambord. Catholic support may have helped Chambord, but the anticlericalism that resulted from Church intervention in politics also served to compromise his chances and colored both republican and conservative attitudes toward the issue of Church–State relations throughout the Third Republic.[22]

The royalist revival in the Third Republic was closely tied to the Catholic Church for a number of reasons. Catholicism in France remained strong in rural areas where politics were traditionally royalist; this association helped convince the Church that religion would fare better under a monarchy than a republic. Royalist politicians and the majority of French bishops also shared a common ideology based on belief in a political and social order in which both revolution and peaceful change were seen as sacrilegious. Both Bourbon supporters and Church leaders favored an authoritarian and hierarchical social-political structure in which the Catholic Church would play a major role in establishing public policy.[23] Finally, the Roman question served to unite royalists and the Church; part of the reason for the royalist defense of the pope's temporal claims was a desire to draw in a large and coherent constituency to the cause of a Bourbon restoration. The support of Chambord for the pope and the belief on the part of churchmen that the pretender would somehow restore the papal territories seized by the Italian state was a critical factor leading Catholics to uphold the royalist cause.[24]

While Catholic leaders publicly expressed their support for a restoration, the alliance between religion and royalism was not limited to bishops and politicians. René Rémond has called attention to the relationship between popular piety and the political atmosphere of the Third Republic. Rémond's description of "Assumptionist Catholicism" after the order whose activity helped give expression to the popular mood stresses the prophetic expectations of the era.

> The formative factor in Assumptionist Catholicism was that it came into being just after a national disaster and a social tempest. To those familiar with scholastic analogy, practiced in deciphering the spiritual meaning of sacred texts, it seemed natural to look for the hidden meaning of every event beneath its visible causes. They were going, then, to scrutinize circumstances and make history speak. . . . In this apocalyptical light, mystical souls believed they were living in the days heralding Judgment. Catastrophism became millenarianism; Catholic opinion awaited, with a confidence which among some replaced political sense, the double miracle which would simultaneously return pope and king.[25]

Rémond is right to stress the role of prophecy in popular Catholicism, but his account neglects the earlier history of the prophetic tradition without which the outburst in the 1870s would have been impossible. By 1870 the expectation of apocalyptic political change was already a well-established element in French religious life; prophecy had been closely tied to royalism since the Restoration of 1815–1830. The crisis of 1870–1871 accentuated but did not create royalist prophetic expectations.

The popularity of prophecy in the early years of the Third Republic is evident in the increased attention given to it in the press and by the Church, and in the number of of prophetic works published. The production of prophetic books and pamphlets increased more than fivefold in the decade 1870–1879 as compared to the previous ten years.[26] Mgr Dupanloup, in a decree of 1874 critical of the literature, related the popular interest in prophecy to the same political crisis referred to by Rémond.

> Everywhere there is talk only of miracles and prophecies, and to our generation one can say what Our Lord said to his: "This generation looks for a sign, *Generatio ista signum quaerit*," (Mark, 8:12).
>
> This phenomenon does not surprise us. Troubled epochs such as ours are ordinarily both witnesses and causes of it. How could we, amidst our trials, not have need of this *signum in bonum* spoken of by the psalmist. When great political and social commotions have shaken our minds, when unaccustomed calamities have struck a people, when profound revolutions have shaken a nation to its depths, the imagination begins to work: it seeks to pierce the

obscurity of events, to glimpse the mysterious unknown which veils the future, to discover finally what salvation will be, who the savior is that is expected. Thus we leave the real, where we see nothing that reassures us, for the imaginary, where we can see everything, especially what we hope for; prophecies surge, and thaumaturges also; visions, oracles, prodigies multiply; and frauds are mixed in with the believers [*illuminés*] of good faith.[27]

The most politically significant themes evoked in the new wave of prophetic literature were the restoration of the Bourbons to France and the future of the papal territories and the Roman Catholic Church. Royalism and ultramontanism dominated political discussions in the early 1870s; the prophetic literature reveals an eschatological dimension in the popular understanding of these issues.

According to the prophetic tradition a "great king" would return in triumph to save France and create a new world empire after a crisis involving international war, foreign invasion, civil strife, and the destruction of Paris. Formerly the Revolution of 1789 and the restoration of 1815 had been fitted to this paradigm; the loss to Germany in 1870–1871, the subsequent occupation, and the Commune seemed to be another cycle of the events foreseen by the prophecies. The identification of the Comte de Chambord as the great king seemed especially suitable. Even his birth, which assured the Bourbons a male heir, was providential. In 1820 he had been celebrated as "l'enfant du miracle" because of his arrival seven and a half months after the murder of his father, the Duc de Berry. The papal nuncio at the time, Mgr Macchi, proclaimed: "This child . . . is the prediction and guaranty of the peace and repose which must follow so much agitation."[28] It was also reported that St. Michael the Archangel had revealed to Mère du Bourg in 1830 that "the royal child that is led into exile will someday return to govern France."[29] With such a history behind him, Chambord fitted easily into the role of the great king of the prophetic tradition.

The candidacy of the pretender was a central theme in the prophetic literature that was so prevalent in the postwar period. *Le grand roi et le grand pape*, which equated Chambord with the great king, went through at least ten editions in 1870 and 1871, and the two most prestigious compilations, Abbé Chabauty's *Lettres sur les prophéties modernes* and Abbé Curicque's *Voix prophétiques*, both advocated the restoration of "Henry V." Curicque's anthology was approved by five bishops, including Mgr Pie, all of whom congratulated the author for demonstrating the continuing prophetic role of the Church in the modern age.[30] The apparition of Mary at Pontmain was also interpreted as a prophecy that Chambord would soon return to France. In 1871 the royalist committee of the Mayenne collected money for a statue of Notre-Dame de Pontmain which was presented to Chambord. The message that accompanied the statue explicitly related the message delivered at Pontmain with the restoration of the Bourbon pretender.

> "Mon fils se laisse toucher." [My son lets himself be touched.] In a little while, Sire, we hope to see Your Majesty retake possession of the throne which belongs to him. . . . Everyone is praying for the reestablishment of the legitimate monarchy; even those who don't know anything about politics and ask God only for the triumph of the Church pray without knowing it for Your Majesty. No! France will not perish . . . and in order for her not to perish she must have the King chosen by God to be her savior![31]

The supporters of Chambord in the Mayenne, influenced by the apparitions at Pontmain and the prophetic literature of the day, believed that God was about to respond to the prayers of France by returning Chambord to the throne. But their acknowledgment that not all Catholics who prayed for the Church were also praying for a restoration reveals a problem that troubled royalist politicans and Church leaders during the 1870s. On the one hand pilgrimages and prophecies were encouraged because they evoked a mood of national unity based on a common religious yearning in a time of crisis. If, however, the religious revival was turned into an overtly royalist political campaign, republicans could attack the Church's partisan stance and thereby discredit its claim to stand for the French nation and not for a particular party.

Church leaders and the lower clergy were almost uniformly legitimist in the 1870s, but during the Second Empire they had begun to distinguish between the interests of the Church and of the Bourbons. Although they still saw royalism and Catholicism as related solutions to the social and political problems of France, to some extent the pope had supplanted the king as the object of primary loyalty.[32] This growing sense of the independence of religion and politics was reflected in the Church's attempt to divorce the pilgrimages of the 1870s from the royalist cause. Catholics and legitimists were still allies but the sermons preached at the major pilgrim-

ages of the 1870s avoided the overtly royalist rhetoric that had characterized those of the mission movement that followed the restoration of
1815.[33] The distance between royalism and Catholicism remained slight,
however, and was bridged by the prominent participation of royalist
deputies at several major pilgrimages, and by references to Chambord
that, although veiled, could easily be interpreted as royalist propaganda by
the audiences. Pilgrimages to Chartres, Auray, and Paray-le-Monial in
1872 and 1873 included delegations of royalist deputies, and the gathering
of Catholics at the shrines accompanied increased hope that the problems
forestalling a Restoration could be solved.[34] Royalism was certainly evident at the national pilgrimage to Chartres on May 27, 1873, just days after
the fall of Thiers. Mgr Pie, a major intellectual and political influence on
Chambord, provided the forty thousand pilgrims with an interpretation
of recent history in which the French people, repentant of their destruction
of the God-given monarchical constitution, called for the return of the
king, which would be affected by divine action.

> The thought of all these souls [of the pilgrims], in whom Christian
> society is personified, I find in the book of Esther, who prayed to
> the Lord God of Israel, saying: Lord, O God, who is our only King
> . . . come to our aid in our isolation. Such is the cry of the
> Church. . . . Such is the cry of France in distress, which awaits a
> leader, which calls a master, but which has none, and which, with-
> out foreign alliance, without internal strength and cohesion, hopes
> only in the King of heavens, or rather in the King Jesus who has
> been pleased to call Himself the King of France, and who has de-
> clared more than once his love and predilection for France.[35]

At the conclusion of his address, Pie invited the crowd to attend the next
major pilgrimage at Paray-le-Monial, on June 20, and the pilgrims dispersed singing the popular hymn of the period, "Sauvez Rome et la
France, au Nom du Sacré-Coeur." Pie had not mentioned Chambord's
name, but his words "France . . . awaits a leader," in the context of the
ministerial crisis suggested the possibility of a restoration.

The ties between the pilgrimage movement and the royalist cause were
confirmed at Paray-le-Monial, where 150 of the deputies who supported a
restoration, led by Gabriel de Belcastel, took part in the dedication of
France to the Sacred Heart. Such a vow had originally been requested of
Chambord's ancestor, Louis XIV, and the Sacred Heart had since become

a symbol of the counterrevolution in the Vendée. Chambord was known to be a fervent disciple of the cult.[36]

The pilgrimage movement and the prophecies of the great king helped create a public mood that would accept Chambord's restoration just as the royalist majority in the National Assembly was beginning to reach internal compromises on divisive issues of religious and political significance. The combination of a charged religious climate and the political situation in France can be observed in the history of the construction of Sacré-Coeur on Montmartre.

A Jesuit, Père de Boylesve, was the first to suggest the idea of a French basilica dedicated to the Sacred Heart in a sermon at Mans in October of 1870. Over two hundred thousand copies of the sermon were printed and distributed, and the support of Mgr Pie was soon obtained. The magazine *Le messager du Sacré-Coeur* began promoting the idea and in February of 1871 the project received papal approval. By March of 1873, when Cardinal Guibert, then archbishop of Paris, petitioned the government for its support of the basilica, over six hundred thousand francs had already been collected by public subscription. In the Assembly the issue created the expected political divisions, with republicans in opposition and royalists divided internally on the precise wording of the resolution. By July a compromise was reached, with the approval of Guibert, in which an. explicit reference to the Sacred Heart was removed from the measure. After an acrimonious debate during which the republicans tried to tie the issue to royalism and insisted on a concrete answer as to the utility of the project, the measure approving construction passed by a vote of 393 to 164.[37]

Although some effort was made to keep the issue of the basilica separate from the royalist cause, the passage of the resolution was a clear sign of royalist strength. Charles Chesnelong might protest that "C'est une pensée supérieure à nos divisions; c'est une pensée de patriotisme," but Chesnelong himself was one of the most important members working for a compromise on the flag issue in order that Chambord might be returned to the throne. The fact that the comte himself was a believer in the apparitions in which the Sacred Heart had been revealed to Margaret-Mary Alacoque, and publicly supported the construction of the basilica, was also well known. The passage of the resolution was a favorable sign for Chambord. The royalist majority had shown its ability to achieve internal compromise in agreeing to delete an explicit reference to the Sacred Heart from the resolution.[38]

The debate over the construction of Sacré-Coeur typifies the relationship between politics and religion during the early years of the Third Republic. Mass pilgrimages and an increase in religious devotion inspired popular pressure for a renewed political order. Even when such pressure did not result in explicit support for a Bourbon restoration Chambord still benefitted, for he was the clearest, most available alternative to the republican and imperial constitutions.

The fall of Thiers in May removed the most prestigious republican from power, and the vote on the construction of Sacré-Coeur in July had demonstrated legitimist strength and unity. These favorable signs were followed by the August 5 visit of the Orléanist pretender, the Comte de Paris, to the Comte de Chambord at his residence in Frohsdorf. Following the visit, which implied that Paris now acknowledged Chambord as the only legitimate successor, there was a wave of royalist anticipation in Paris; even the respectable *Figaro* shared in the mood which saw 1873 as a year of prophetic significance.[39] But throughout the summer of 1873 the issue of the flag continued to divide the legitimists. The *Chevau-légers* of the extreme right supported Chambord's insistence on retaining the white flag of the Bourbons, while the moderates pressured him to accept the *tricolor* as the only flag acceptable to the majority of the National Assembly. These competing symbols expressed an important substantive difference between the extremist and moderate legitimists. For the *Chevau-légers* a legitimist restoration could not depend on a vote of the National Assembly, for this would raise the possibility that some future assembly could revoke the decision and depose the king. The moderate right, which included men who had previously supported the Second Empire, saw the issue in practical terms. The only expedient way to bring back the monarchy was through the intervention of the National Assembly, and the assembly would vote for Chambord only if he accepted the flag that the nation had used for most of the nineteenth century.[40]

In late October Chambord, in a letter to Chesnelong that was published in the royalist journal *L'Union*, reasserted his commitment to the white flag and brought an end to the general expectation that a restoration was about to take place. Even though many extremists regretted Chambord's decision, they accepted his argument that the Assembly had no right to set conditions on his return to the throne.[41] Supporters of Chambord argued that a restoration would result from providential rather than political action. Mgr Saivet, the bishop of Mende and a correspondent of the prophetic publicist Abbé Chabauty, wrote to *L'Univers* following the October letter that he retained his confidence in Chambord and Providence, despite the refusal of the National Assembly to vote for his return.

> I have unlimited confidence . . . I am sure that God, through Henry V, will save us before long . . . [Chambord's] letter reassures rather than frightens me. It outlines the situation, clarifies ideas, and saves the truth from the muddle in which some had wished to compromise it.[42]

Such optimism, however, was difficult to maintain following the disappointment of October. The reaction of *L'Univers* in a front-page editorial on the eve of 1874 reveals how royalists reacted to the failure of their expectations.

> There was a universal presentiment that the year 1873 would see something end and something new begin. But now there is nothing, neither life nor death. Humanity seems a void. Asphyxiated, cadavers slide to the bottom of a moral abyss. History offers few examples of this absolute infecundity. Odorless and silent pestilences infiltrate everywhere, killing everything, and nothingness seems to have conquered being.[43]

The pessimism of *L'Univers* was relieved by a small glimmer of hope. "If the pope was not the Vicar of Christ, the only son of God, the last hour of the world would not be far away, because the world, limping on its way, has no principle of renewal in it." For *L'Univers* providential intervention could still salvage the future, although the prophecies of a new world order based on an alliance between the French king and the pope had been disappointed. This hope was expressed in a revealing phrase: "How will this miracle occur? Christian faith knows what will be the cause of it, humanity is ignorant of the means."

The strained belief of *L'Univers* that a miracle might yet save France and the pope was echoed in the post-1873 prophetic literature. Abbé Chabauty, whose concordance of prophecies had predicted a restoration for 1873 and a triumphant Franco–Roman alliance, published *Les prophéties modernes vengées* in 1874 to show that his earlier predictions were the result of a misinterpretation, and that the prophets had really indicated the summer of 1874 as the time for the "great event."[44] As the years passed and the possibility of a restoration receded, the hope that Providence would act in favor of the Bourbons survived. The Comte de Chambord, until his death in August of 1883, encouraged such hopes. Addressing a delegation of followers from the Vendée in September of 1882, Chambord spoke hopefully of the future: "Believe me, and repeat it loudly: events move quickly. We approach the hour of salvation. . . . Each instant increases my confidence in the success of the providential mission given to me."[45] *L'Univers* also continued to hope, as late as July 1882, that Providence would restore the Count to the throne.

> Fifty years of exile have not been able to make those who love the fatherland forget the prince who, by law, is the king of France, and they pray for him. They ask for a miracle. Yes, a miracle, and we do not doubt it, the miracle will happen.[46]

Immediately following the death of Chambord there were those who assigned the mantle of the "great king" to the Orléanist pretender, the Comte de Paris. In *La Croix* of September 8, 1883, the lead article dealt with a prophecy attributed to St. Valéry. The medieval thaumaturge had purportedly appeared to Hugh Capet and announced that there would be seven generations of French kings. According to *La Croix*'s interpretation, the fall of Louis Philippe had concluded the sixth age, and the seventh was still to come. While avoiding an explicit prediction of the restoration of the Comte de Paris, the article concluded: "It is not for us to judge; . . . but the friends of the Comte de Paris are no doubt pleased that we cite the celebrated prophecy of a saint whose pilgrimage is so near to the Comte's chateau of Eu."[47]

Even in the 1890s the Intransigents who opposed the *ralliement* of Catholics to the Third Republic did so in part because of "a futile belief in a future restoration." Legitimist deputy Henri Remy de Simony wrote in 1891 that "we are among those who believe that France is monarchist in temperament and that sooner or later—that is the secret of providence— she will return to those traditions the violation and abandonment of which are the cause of our present woes."[48] From a rational, secular point of view such a position was absurd. But for some legitimists it was the secular perspective which was fallacious, for it ignored the control that Providence exercised over history. The faith of the *Chevau-légers* and their supporters in the role of Providence, fed by prophetic expectations and the pilgrimage movement, was thus a critical factor in their unwillingness to negotiate a political settlement.

Prophecy and Ultramontanism

The disposition of the papal territories was a major concern, almost an obsession with French Catholics in the nineteenth century. Official Catholic opinion on Church–State relations was, to a large extent, determined by the attitude of the government toward the pope and his temporal domain.[49] The prophetic tradition had encouraged such a concern by depicting the Roman question as a pivotal issue in French history. The tradition maintained that France had a divine mission to protect the pope, which had been carried out in the eighth century when Charlemagne defended Leo III from a Roman conspiracy, and again in the fourteenth century when the popes found sanctuary from Italian intrigue in Avignon. The prophetic tradition associated these past actions with periods of French glory. Conversely, the persecution of Pius VI and Pius VII during the revolutionary era was associated with France's current difficulties. According to the prophecies, the king of France would restore a "great pope" to Rome. This alliance was a duty imposed on the nation by God, and thus not subject to political and diplomatic calculations. Miracles and prophecies recalled France to its mission whenever mundane circumstances threatened to lead the nation astray.

The shift in policy of 1859 in which French troops fought for Italian unification at the expense of the papal states had led directly to a miracle in which divine disapproval was clear. At Vrigné-aux-Bois (diocese of Rennes) a consecrated host bled from five points corresponding to the wounds of Christ. Abbé Morel, a journalist who wrote for *L'Univers*, published a pamphlet in which he argued that the bleeding host marked a renewal of Christ's sufferings as a result of France's desertion of the pope. Ten years later the miracle at Vrigné-aux-Bois was recalled as a warning to France, whose defeat at Sedan was interpreted as chastisement for abandoning the pope.[50]

Bishop Pie, one of the most ardent supporters of the pope among the French episcopacy, used a prophetic metaphor to express disapproval of French acquiescence in the annexation of the papal territories in 1860. In his address at the sixth centennial of Notre-Dame de Chartres' consecration in October 1860, Pie resorted to the prophetic mode in his analysis of current and future events.

> I have learned from Saint Augustine . . . to study the mysterious coincidences of numbers. I have thus searched the scriptures to see if the number 600 [is important]. Noah had just turned six hundred years old when the waters of the great abyss broke through their barriers and when the waters of the sky broke. . . . O you, sacred edifice . . . are you destined in this centenary year to see burst forth an even greater deluge of calamities, a more fearful cataclysm than those which you have already witnessed? . . . Surrounding us there are very sinister plots against Jesus Christ, against his Church, and against his Vicar . . . popes assailed by factions, exiled by the disquieted and discontented nature of the Romans, this is nothing new for this old basilica. But evil erected into good, shadows called lights, perfidious malice and hypocritical seduction of the Antichrist making their appearance on earth; but persecution taking on the mask of protection; in a word, isn't everything which occurs at this time a deluge of evil without precedent which signals this six hundredth year?[51]

The references to hypocrisy were clearly intended to apply to Napoleon III for his betrayal of the pope. For Pie the loss of the papal territories was bound to have world-historical and eschatological consequences. The events of 1870 and 1871 seemed to offer confirmation of these fears.

The prophetic literature of the Third Republic is virtually unanimous in attributing France's defeat to her position on the Roman question. Abbé Chabauty believed the two major "facts" of the Second Empire to have been "the physical and moral abasement of France and the persecution of the papacy." For Abbé Curicque the dates on which France withdrew from Rome coincided "mysteriously" with the defeat elsewhere of French forces. He wrote, for example, that the withdrawal of troops from Rome occurred on the day France lost its first battle to Prussia at Wissembourg, that the Empire's fall on September 4, 1870, marked the tenth anniversary of the alliance with Cavour designed to create a unified Italy, and that Italian troops entered Rome the same day Prussia occupied Paris. According to Curicque, just as scripture has established "an eye for an eye" as a standard for justice, God worked on the principle of "a day for a day."[52]

The purported relationship between the fall of Rome and the fall of France was a prelude to the second major theme of the prophetic tradition as it flourished in the 1870s. The restoration of the French monarchy would lead to a rejuvenated Church whose triumph would inevitably follow a period of chastisement and expiation. The key figure in prophetic hopes for the future of the Church was the pope. For Catholics the pope has always served as a potent symbol capable of relating past and future within a context of faith in the Church's continuity and ultimate triumph.

In the nineteenth century a combination of circumstances led to an increase in the authority of the pope and an exaggeration of his role as symbol of the continuity of the Church. The growing centralization of authority in the papacy, exemplified in the forced resignation of French bishops as a result of the Concordat of 1801, led to a greater emphasis on papal leadership within the Church. This leadership was actively exercised, as is evident in the successful pressures put on French bishops to replace local practices with the standard Roman liturgy.[53] A second factor in the increased importance of papal symbolism was the reign and character of Pius IX. The unprecedented length of his tenure (1846–1878), his patient and stubborn resistance to political pressures, and his personal piety made him a respresentative figure around whom support as well as resistance to papal policy could polarize.[54] Finally, the perception in the 1850s and 1860s that the Church as a whole was threatened by the loss of the temporal possessions of the pope helped to focus the issue: the Church was endangered, and the responsibility of all Catholics was to rally to the pope's support. The Roman question was not restricted to the problem of temporal possessions, but also involved issues of papal authority and the survival of the Church itself.[55]

The prophetic tradition, sensitive to the power of papal symbolism, responded to the fears of Catholics with predictions that fed eschatological expectations. The prophecy of St. Malachie, which listed all of the popes who would reign to the end of time, was the subject of much attention in the 1870s. Abbé Curicque proposed that Pius IX, because of his persecution, was *Crux des Cruces*, tenth from the last.[56] Other elements of the prophetic tradition could be more explicitly related to current history. The predictions that the Church, in a period of great persecution, would be saved by a "great council" and a "great pope" dates at least from the fifteenth century, when it was hoped that the conciliar movement in cooperation with a reformed papacy would succeed in reuniting the

Christian world. Subsequently the belief that the pope was infallible on questions of faith and morals came into conflict with the position that a general council represented the ultimate authority in the Church. In the nineteenth century the Vatican Council of 1870, which confirmed the doctrine of papal infallibility, seemed to reconcile these opposing traditions and, at the same time, fulfill the predictions for a great council.[57] The intense devotion to the figure of Pius IX and the Church's commitment to his infallibility suggested that he was the "great pope" who would oversee the miraculous conversion of the world to Catholicism. Abbé Firminhac, a canon of Bordeaux, stated the Catholic belief that the council, working under Pius IX, would usher in a new era of world history.

> The promised day approaches, the great day of the council;
> People clap your hands, unite your voices;
> Prelates, assemble from all ends of the universe;
> Angels of the skies, watch over them and the city . . .
> The infallible doctor will speak in [the name of the Holy Spirit] . . .
> With a docile ear listen to his oracle;
> Which dogmas, which secrets will he reveal to us? . . .
>
> The Church will dress itself in a new glory,
> Its passionate voice will appease the furor,
> Its divine clarities will make error recoil,
> At the contact of its hand the rocks will soften,
> Faith will be extended far and the deserts will flourish,
> The proud lion will lie down with the peaceful lamb
> And graces will pour down from Heaven . . .
> Astonished people will admire its splendors,
> And the kings, at its feet, will adore its grandeur.[58]

The expectation of a "great pope" was, as has been seen, integrally related to the theme of the "great king." In October of 1873 Chambord announced that "the two questions on which he could never yield were the question of the white flag and the restoration of the temporal power."[59] The fact that Chambord was publicly committed to the restoration of Rome to the pope consolidated his position as the prophesied king whose return would result in the glorification of both the French nation and the Roman Church. Prophetic publications were filled with discussions of the "mission providentielle" and "destinée divine de la France" in which

French soldiers marched triumphantly on Rome.[60] At Lourdes one of the most popular hymns among the pilgrims, "La France à Notre-Dame de Lourdes," concluded with what amounted to a call to arms.

> Yes God wants it, go deliver your father,
> He is captive, go, fly to his aid!
> Rome awaits you, she has hope in you alone;
> Defend her cause and you will always vanquish!

> Glory to Pius IX, our infallible father;
> Glory to Pius IX, the pious Pontiff!
> Glory to Pius IX, attacked by the earth;
> Glory to Pius IX, defended by the heavens.[61]

Abbé Firminhac's poem "Les grands jours" held out the promise of revenge on Germany, but this victory would come only after France had given Rome back to the Pope and assisted him in the extirpation of heresy.[62]

In fact, France was incapable of marching on Rome, much less Germany. Henry V was not restored, and Rome became the permanent capital of the Italian state, not the center of a universal Catholic empire. The prophetic movement was deluded in its predictions; its commitment to the cause of the pope frightened and divided a France that was still shocked by the German victory.[63] Nevertheless, the prophecies and pilgrimages of the 1870s did represent an important current of popular opinion. Bismarck's warning to the French ambassador at Berlin in January of 1874 reflected his fear of the political potential of extremist Catholic support for Rome. "Take care lest the masses become fanaticized in the name of the persecuted Catholic religion, for then the clerical party will seize control and will espouse all the quarrels of the Roman curia, and you will inevitably be drawn into war against us."[64]

While anxieties about the influence of the clerical party faded with the failure of Chambord to gain the French throne, the conviction that France was destined to ally itself with the Church and restore the temporal possessions to the pope died hard. As late as March 1902, in the midst of a crisis in Church–State relations, Leo XIII still expressed a belief that France would save the papacy.

> There are voices who tell me that it is France who will deliver me.
> What are these voices? Voices of history or voices from heaven . . .

I firmly believe in them. The Holy See is not free. The Vicar of Jesus Christ cannot fulfill his mission without being independent. France will give the Pope freedom. How? I have no idea. By arms or diplomacy? I do not know. But I rely upon her. And then these gentlemen of the Quirinal will realize that it does not do to be the enemy of France.[65]

Leo's remarks echoed the prophetic predictions that continued to search for the date of "le grand coup." Publicists such as Emil Combe, the author of *Le grand coup avec sa date probable*, were able to sustain at least some Catholics in their hopes for a Franco-papal alliance and a world empire. Prophecies were less explicit than they had been in the 1870s about the way the two powers would join forces, but ignorance about means did not eliminate hope that by some miracle a reconciliation could be achieved.[66]

Prophetic expectations survived among some Catholics, but even true believers were forced to admit that the failure of 1873 caused prophecies to lose much of their public support.[67] But although the direct impact of the prophetic tradition on political beliefs declined, prophetic imagery and language continued to influence the conservative politicians who succeeded the legitimists of the 1870s. Conservatives in the Third Republic suffered from internal divisions and an inability to formulate a clear alternative to republicanism that could replace their devotion to the monarchy.[68] But there were occasions when conservatives were able to mobilize voters by combining attacks against republican policies and corruption with vague appeals to God and nationalism. In the Chamber elections of 1885, the *Union des Droites* drew 44 percent of the popular vote by waging a campaign "against waste, against faraway expeditions, against violence, against infamy, against Republican turpitude! Vote for God, for Order, for *La Patrie!*"[69] In their attempt to build a constituency on the basis of such negative appeals, conservatives in the 1880s increasingly used Masons and Jews as symbols to focus popular discontent with the republican regime. It was through the anti-Masonic and anti-Semitic movements that the prophetic tradition helped shape the political attitudes of the Third Republic. In their view of history and their understanding of the process of change both of these movements repeated themes that had previously been expressed in prophetic literature. Anti-Masonism and anti-Semitism, like the prophetic revival that preceded them, focused on violent conflict between good and evil as the driving force in world history. According to the prophetic tradition, these forces were doomed to battle until one triumphed and destroyed the other. Related to this view was a search for scapegoats to account for political failures, and a belief that the political order was capable of renewal through a rapid and drastic change in leadership. The *Secret* of Mélanie, the visionary of La Salette, illustrates these themes. Published for the first time in 1870 it was among the most popular of the Third Republic prophecies and continued to exert influence on Catholic opinion into the twentieth century. The *Secret* depicts current events as the direct consequence of a battle between the legions of Christ and Satan, and concludes with a description of the vengeance Christ would enjoy following his victory.

> Then Jesus Christ, by an act of his great justice and mercy for the just, will command his angels that all his enemies be put to death. All at once the great persecutors of the Church of Jesus Christ and all men given to sin will perish, and the earth will be as desert. Then will come peace, the reconciliation of God with men; Jesus Christ will be served, adored, and glorified; charity will flourish everywhere. The new kings will be the right arms of the Holy Church. . . . The Gospel will be preached everywhere, and men will make great progress in faith, because there will be unity among the workers of Jesus Christ, and men will live in the fear of God. . . .
>
> Then water and fire will purify the earth and consume the works of the pride of man, and everything will be renewed: God will be worshipped and glorified.[70]

The sense of apocalyptic conflict conveyed by the *Secret* was common in the Catholic press of the Third Republic. *La Croix* believed that the laic legislation of the Republic was responsible for natural disasters and would result in even greater chastisements:

> Law is changed; the Revolution is complete. . . . Does not God respond to these tremors of hatred with earth tremors? Have they ever been so terrible and so unusual as in recent years? . . . France will be terribly chastised along with all the neighboring nations which have drawn back from God and his Church. The unwonted phenomena that are happening in the world are the harbingers of appalling desolations.[71]

The other and complementary aspect of the prophetic tradition, the hope that salvation could be attained in this world, also found expression in *La Croix*:

Humiliated from without, persecuted from within, prayers and tears are all that remain to you, O Well-beloved France. Who knows? By strength of prayer and suffering you may soon be the mother of some great Christian destined to enlighten and renew the whole West, like the converted Augustine. May this desired hero come![72]

The other major Catholic paper of the era, *L'Univers*, though less spectacular, shared the prophetic perspective which allowed no reconciliation with enemies of the Church. In January 1883, Eugène Veuillot depicted the conflict between Church and Republic as total and irremediable.

Between the Republic and religious France agreement has become impossible. It is impossible ever to expect Catholics to follow the party that has declared them its enemy, and who, when in power, turn the forces of *L'Univers* against their beliefs and consciences. . . . M. Gambetta has said that there are now two Frances: this is true. . . . But Catholic France will get the better of republican France.[73]

The implications of a prophetic and apocalyptic view of history help explain the intransigence typical of Third Republic politics. Victory was ultimately assured by God, but only if one held firmly to principles and refused the temptations of Satan. Political success would come not through negotiated settlements but through a battle to the limit at the conclusion of which total victory would be achieved, by divine intervention if necessary. Within this historical framework Catholics sought to identify those individuals and groups who were cooperating in the work of the devil. Prophetic literature taught that the real causes of events were not overt and tangible, but hidden within a mysterious providential design which at times allowed the devil temporary success. This attitude was useful in accounting for the persecution of the Church during the Third Republic. The prominent role taken by Freemasons in advocating secular legislation provided the Church with an easy target for this "devil" theory of history. Although there was a satanist movement in France at this time, there is no evidence that the Masons were part of it. The case of Leo Taxil demonstrates, however, how eager the Church was to identify its political opponents with the devil. After starting his literary career as an anticlerical polemicist, Taxil pretended to convert to Catholicism. His memoirs, *Confessions of an ex-Free Thinker*, were greeted enthusiastically by Catholics, and in an audience with Leo XIII Taxil was personally congratulated by the pope for confirming the satanic character of Masonism.[74] By identifying Masons with Satan, Catholics were able to explain their political failures and the subsequent persecution as the result of a diabolical conspiracy. Such an interpretation was comforting for two reasons. First of all Christian eschatology as presented in the prophetic literature taught that the victory of Satan could only be temporary and that the ultimate triumph of Christ and his Church was assured. Second, by identifying their political opposition with absolute evil, Catholics were able to avoid rethinking their positions on the relationship between Church and State. The reformulation of Catholic opinion on Church–State relations was long and painful, lasting well into the twentieth century. Catholics were neither intellectually nor psychologically prepared to confront the secularization of the State that began in the 1880s. The mystification of the political issue by identifying the proponents of a secular state with the devil was thus a useful device for putting off the task of political negotiation and compromise with the Republic.

Anti-Semitism, like anti-Masonism, was based on an assumption that French history was determined by the clash of two wholly incompatible groups. Like the Masons, the Jews were secret conspirators whose plots threatened to destroy Catholic France. The Jews, like the Masons, were associated with the devil, and their elimination was necessary before France could achieve international prominence and a stable social order. The eschatological tone of anti-Semitism was, in large part, derived from the prophetic movement that preceded it. In 1881 the first anti-Semitic newspaper appeared, published by Abbé Chabauty, the same *curé* of Poitiers who had spent the 1870s writing concordances and defenses of prophecies.[75] The leader of the anti-Semitic movement, Édouard Drumont, was a believer in prophecy, and Gaston Méry, an editor of *La Libre Parole*, was the leading advocate of Mlle Couédon, a clairvoyant and prophet popular within the anti-Semitic movement of the 1890s.[76] The Assumptionist paper *La Croix*, which replaced *L'Univers* as the most influential organ of Catholic opinion in the Third Republic, consistently integrated anti-Semitism into an eschatological frame of reference. When anti-Semitic riots swept France in 1898, editor Père Bailly interpreted them as a sign of the imminent salvation of the nation. Bailly believed that the era of anti-Semitism would immediately precede the conversion of Jews to Christianity, after which would come "the end of time."[77] The subscribers who sent money in support of the widow and child of Colonel Henry, who committed suicide after his forgery in the Dreyfus affair was discovered, frequently expressed themselves in eschatological terms.

> An eschatological terminology for advocating the expulsion or the extermination of Jews with the view of restoring a Christian order was common: for example "Christ! Help us, Lend us your whip to chase the Jewish peddlers from the temple of France"; or again "Cry Noel! Noel! over old France. For its rebirth through Our Lord Jesus Christ."[78]

The crisis in Church–State relations surrounding the separation law of 1905 offers a final illustration of the affinities between anti-Masonism, anti-Semitism, and the prophetic tradition. Throughout the period 1903 to 1905, the Parisian journal *La France chrétienne*, a weekly review of anti-Masonic and anti-Semitic news, gave extensive coverage to the prophecy of Mélanie of La Salette, relating it to the details of the current crisis. According to *La France chrétienne*, the struggles of the French Church and the power of Masons and Jews in government and society were chastisements predicted by Mélanie. After France had been purified through its suffering, "le grand coup" would fall and the Church would be restored to its rightful position.[79]

Both anti-Masonism and anti-Semitism reflected a desire for a society in which all conflict has been abolished. This society was both a mythic past and an eschatological future, and its profile had been presented in the prophetic literature. The crisis of the 1870s had led to a major revival in the prophetic tradition in which the restoration of the Comte de Chambord and the papal territories were dominant predictions. Following Chambord's failure, royalist prophecies lost their appeal, but the chiliastic desire for political legitimacy and social order survived and was reflected in anti-Masonism and anti-Semitism.[80] The prophetic movement not only contributed to the vision of order driving these movements, it also explained the process by which it would be achieved. France was a battleground on which hostile forces clashed violently prior to the restoration of peace and security. In a recent assessment of anti-Semites, Stephen Wilson has stressed the psychological compensation they derived from the violent rhetoric of the movement.[81] This gratification must have been enhanced by the certitude of ultimate victory. The eschatological aspect of anti-Masonism and anti-Semitism was a key element in their appeal, for without the conviction that triumph and vengeance were near at hand, they would have been unable to generate enthusiasm.

The relations of Church and State dominated much of the political life of the Third Republic. Secular education, the divorce law, the status of religious orders, and the abolition of the Concordat were key issues in the formation of party allegiances. Treatments of these issues generally stress differences in political and social assumptions as the basis of political conflict. Secular education was bound to corrupt the morals of youth, or it was destined to liberate men's minds; divorce would rupture the most fundamental social bond, or it would strengthen it by permitting remarriage. Such differences, however, do not explain the depth of feeling displayed by the Catholic right in the 1880s and 1890s. Underlying their position was a belief that current events mirrored some deeper clash between good and evil, Christian and Jew, Christ and Satan. The sense of fundamental conflict and the belief in ultimate triumph derived from the revived interest in prophecies that marked the opening years of the Third Republic.

Chapter 6
The Institutionalization
of the Miraculous

P
revious chapters have shown how social and political anxieties
form a background against which miraculous phenomena can
be perceived and interpreted. But it has been evident throughout
that miracles were significant religious events not just because of
their responsiveness to popular needs. The Catholic Church was instrumental in the widespread diffusion of miracle cults, an involvement
that resulted from the Church's perception of itself as the exclusive
mediator of supernatural graces. Miracles not clearly under the control of
the hierarchy were suspect, for they implied that God at times chose to
work outside the Church. The insistence on monopolisitic control over
the miraculous was thus designed to protect the Church's spiritual authority as the One, True, Holy, and Apostolic Church. The Jansenists were
recent examples of how dissidents within the Church could claim supernatural support for their attacks on authority on the basis of supposed
miracles.[1]

Although miracles were a potential threat, the Church was not free to
deny them. The occurrence of miracles in the modern world was a sign of
Christ's continuing presence within the Church, and thus was an important part of the apologetical posture of Catholicism. The subversive
potential of miracles was balanced by their unique ability to verify the
Church's claim to be God's sole representative on earth. The Church
therefore claimed responsibility for investigating the miracles, their context, and the character of those individuals touched by the supernatural. In
such an investigation the ideal, enunciated during the Counterreformation, was to proceed slowly and cautiously.[2] The French Church actively
assumed responsibility for judging the miraculous in the nineteenth cen-

tury, but its deliberations were affected by an environment that made this ideal difficult to apply. The dual objective of this chapter is to trace the pattern of the Church's response to the miraculous and to show how motives and circumstances peculiar to the nineteenth century helped shape national cults that became a predominant feature of French Catholicism.

The Local Response to the Miraculous

The Church became involved with nineteenth-century miracles almost as soon as they occurred, when the witnesses or subjects approached the clergy with their accounts of supernatural intervention. Since the Counterreformation the Church had attempted to convince the laity of its authority over the supernatural. To judge from the events following miraculous apparitions this attempt had succeeded in convincing those chosen as divine messengers that their first duty was to inform the clergy. The local clergy played a critical role in gaining recognition for the miracles, and their enthusiasm gave impetus to cults in their earliest stages.

The most ignorant of the nineteenth-century visionaries, the shepherds of La Salette, are a prime example of the speed with which the clergy became involved in the miraculous. Knowing no doctrine, few prayers, and virtually nothing of the Church, Mélanie and Maximin, acting on the advice of their masters, reported their apparition to the *curé* of La Salette, Abbé Jacques Perrin, the day after it had occurred. Perrin, on the verge of senility, was transferred to another parish within days of the report. But he understood the story told him, believed the children had seen the Virgin Mary, and preached on the apparition at the Sunday Mass on the same day.[3]

Given his condition, Perrin's response might be passed off as insignificant, were it not the case that similar signs of immediate consent and enthusiasm on the part of the local clergy can be found elsewhere. The local *curé* most involved with the La Salette cult's early stages was Abbé Mélin of Corps. Mélin was told of the apparition by the shepherd children the Sunday following the report to Perrin, and although his immediate reaction is unknown, within two weeks he was an active proponent of the cult. Involvement of the clergy in the period when the cult was forming is most apparent at Migné, where the apparition of the cross in the sky took place just as a missionary was concluding his sermon with a reference to the crucifix. During the Restoration local clergy were instrumental in the cult of the thaumaturgic Prince Hohenlohe, serving as intermediaries between their parishioners and the Prince. The cult of Notre-Dame des Victoires and the archconfraternity that was its major institution were the result of supernatural revelations given to Abbé Desgenettes, the *curé* of Notre-Dame des Victoires in Paris. Toward the other end of the century, the apparition at Pontmain enlisted the active participation of the *curé*, who led a congregation of fifty in prayer until Mary disappeared from the view of the visionaries.[4]

In those instances where some of the clergy took a neutral stance others supported the apparitions. At Lourdes, *curé* Peyramale's initial skepticism was tempered by the fact that Abbé Pomian, one of his vicars, supported Bernadette. After being prohibited from returning to the grotto by the civil authorities, Bernadette consulted Pomian, who advised her of her rights to continue to visit the site of her apparitions: "On n'a pas le droit de t'empêcher" ("They don't have the right to stop you").[5] The initial clerical response to the miraculous, then, tended to be enthusiastic and supportive.[6] Despite episcopal efforts to control the incipient cults, this positive attitude continued to dominate clerical behavior in the weeks following the miracle.

In attempting to master the local situation the Church was forced to deal with several concurrent developments, which had the effect of creating a popular cult. These included the support of the laymen of the area, usually as a result of healing miracles, but also because of their realization of the economic advantages that would result from a successful shrine. The continued support, usually tacit, of the local clergy was a further incentive to the cult. The priests were influenced by the belief of their parishioners, and impressed by the pastoral effect of the new devotion. It was sometime early in this period that the local *curé* took the critical step of informing the bishop of the miracles and the cult. This move started the episcopal machinery moving, as the bishop quickly took control of the investigation and attempted to establish authority over the burgeoning movement.

While there are, of course, some differences in the time elapsed and the form of the notification, the first letters written to the episcopal authorities show many similarities. The apparition at Migné, on December 26, 1826, was reported to the bishop in a letter signed by the missionaries, the *curé*, and forty-one other witnesses. The letter was intended to be evidence for the miracle and did, in fact, become a central document in the dossier compiled by the Church to support the apparition.[7] Following the apparition at La Salette, Abbé Mélin of Corps first informed the bishop of Grenoble on October 5, 1846, fifteen days after the miracle. His letter included a report on the vision, information on the already active cult ("La première idée de toute la contrée a été de faire bâtir un oratoire à cet endroit"), and a confession of his own belief.

> Naturally the interpretation of this event by the faithful is that the
> good Mother has come to warn the world before her son lets his
> vengeance fall upon it. My personal interpretation, after all the
> proofs I have gathered, does not differ from that of the faithful, and
> I believe that this warning is a great favor from Heaven.[8]

Letters from the clergy reporting the apparitions at Lourdes and Pontmain follow a similar pattern. Even the circumspect *curé* of Lourdes, Peyramale, betrayed his belief in a letter written just three weeks after the first vision of Bernadette. Peyramale's immediate concern was for a Jubilee which would take advantage of the fervor that prevailed, but he concluded by reporting on a cure which seemed to verify the apparition.

> I entered the home of the child with a vicar. We found him in front
> of an elegant chapel to the Virgin which he made himself, and we
> confirmed the remarkable improvement in his condition. If he is
> radically cured, then we can say with St. Augustine *Causa finita est.*[9]

The local clergy were impressed not only by the direct evidence, such as the testimony of the visionaries and the miraculous cures, but by the impact of the miracles on their communities. As the cults continued to grow, and the bishops began their investigations, pastoral concerns would continue to play a major role in the attitude of the Church toward the miraculous.

The response of the nearby parishes to the new miracle was typically immediate and spontaneous. Pilgrims from throughout the region began to come in increasingly large numbers to the sites of the apparitions at La Salette, Lourdes, and Pontmain. Other miracles, including those ultimately disavowed by the Church, were also able to draw crowds of believers.[10] At the shrines the pilgrims asked for miracles and left ex-voto, including money, in thanksgiving. Even with the early belief of the clergy, the rapid diffusion and success of the new cults cannot be attributed to anything like the clerical conspiracy pictured in anticlerical propaganda. As we have seen in the previous chapters, the miraculous was a familiar, even necessary part of the world view of many Frenchmen throughout the nineteenth century.

The crowds that gathered at the shrines in the early stages of the cult were important for a number of reasons. First, they created a context in which belief was possible on the part of incredulous laymen and the clergy. The crowds, the reports of miracles, and the piety displayed at the shrines made it impossible to ignore the situation. A good example of how the cult was able to convert the doubtful is Jean-Baptiste Estrade, a tax official at Lourdes, who lodged with the police commissioner Jacomet. An early skeptic, Estrade described in his memoirs how the "people" of Lourdes believed in the miracle while the circle of professionals and bureaucrats was divided. After a trip to the grotto as an observer, Estrade came away convinced by the size and spirit of the crowd, and the manner of Bernadette.[11]

The crowds created pressure for belief in a second, more pragmatic sense among the clergy. The pastoral program of the nineteenth century was designed as a response to the new position of the Church in France. The Concordat, while it established a state-supported Church, had eliminated many of the older ties that had held the two institutions together. Sunday Mass, for example, was no longer a legal obligation, and this helps account for the decline in attendance against which pastors struggled throughout the century.[12] The Church's program was built around catechetical instruction for children and missions for adults. The latter were intended to create, through a series of sermons, instructions, and rituals, a fervent atmosphere in which those who practiced their religion would experience an increase in faith, and those who had abandoned the Church would convert. The apparition of the cross at Migné was responsible for the conversion of all but two of those attending the mission, including forty who had been unregenerate up to that point. This kind of impact on their parishioners helps explain why the clergy were active lobbyists for apparitions throughout the century.[13] The Church in France had come to embrace evangelical, emotional appeals, and miracle cults were seen to fit well with this approach to pastoral work.

Some of the clergy did have scruples about the more "superstitious" aspects of the cults, but most were willing to tolerate or even encourage suspicious practices as long as they were also accompanied by orthodox behavior. In fact, there is no reason to believe that any but a few clergy disbelieved in the material efficacy of prayers, pilgrimages; blessed medals, relics, and the other accoutrements of the cults. Such belief is not surprising, for the clergy were recruited for the most part from modest rural families where folkloric practices and superstitions were an integral part of religious life. Nadine-Joseph Chalons' description of the clergy of Rouen can, with some qualification, be applied to France as a whole. "Clerical recruitment based itself in a setting of a traditional society of peasants and rural artisans, respectful of customs and authority."[14] Alfred Loisy, although he became the leading advocate of theological modernism, came from a background typical for the nineteenth-century clergy. Of modest peasant origins, his mother's piety, laced with superstitious beliefs, would likely be viewed with tolerance if not outright sympathy by most of the clergy.

> My mother herself was earnestly devout, but with no special fondness for either theology or mysticism. She was probably just a trifle superstitious. Endowed with an exceptional memory and of an inquisitive disposition, she knew by heart all the old tales that had gone the rounds on winter evenings when she was still young. . . . She could recall, as well, not a few of the formulas of the popular magic; also signs and portents such as constituted the total science of the peasantry in past ages.[15]

Only toward the end of the century, with the stirrings of theological modernism, were miraculous beliefs regarded from a skeptical perspective by some clergy, and modernism, while an important intellectual movement, had little impact on the parochial clergy and their parishioners.[16]

A third source of popular pressure for belief in the early days of the cult was the support provided by those laymen who saw the economic potential of an active shrine in their parish. Local mayors were leaders in the investigation of the apparitions at La Salette and Lourdes, and their involvement was not motivated solely by a concern for the piety of their constituents. At both La Salette and Lourdes work was begun to improve the access to the shrines and the workings of the fountains within a few days of the initial apparitions.[17] At Lourdes the stone workers and carpenters, organized into professional confraternities, volunteered their time in this effort and were also prominent in the religious manifestations at the shrine. As the cults grew, the economic benefits became more and more evident. Innkeepers, merchants, and retailers of devotional objects and literature all prospered.[18] The hope that such prosperity could be made permanent was another motive leading to support of the cult in the local area.

Economic motives were not limited to laymen. The clergy were also sensitive to the possibilities offered by the cult. Specifically, they knew that pilgrims customarily left offerings and that these could, if encouraged, amount to a considerable sum. This is not to accuse the clergy of venality, although this was a common failing of many impoverished *curés* of the last century. But they did respond quickly to the commercial possibilities of the cults. The waters of La Salette and Lourdes were marketed throughout France, and at all the new shrines offerings for masses and novenas became an important part of the ecclesiastical income.[19] A practice developed at La Salette shows how ingenious the clergy could be in encouraging both the religious and economic aspects of the cults. The Perrin brothers who served both the parish and the pilgrimage in its earliest stages instituted a long-distance novena, on the model of those engaged in by Prince Hohenlohe during the Restoration.[20] These priests received letters from many places in France requesting novenas and enclosing a donation, and responded by assigning a specific period during which the parishioners of La Salette would pray for the donor. The income from these novenas was then divided between the clergy and the laymen, and such revenue perhaps made belief in the miracle easier for both groups.[21]

The religious, pastoral, and economic pressures on the Church to accept miracles were cumulative, and built even as the bishops received the initial reports from their local clergy. In considering the episcopal response to the miraculous, the next stage in the development of the cults, these pressures should be kept in mind. For although bishops operated within a larger framework, and were sensitive to influences of a different kind, the continuing support of the cults by the local clergy and laymen was an important factor in the final episcopal decisions.

The Episcopal Investigation

In the period just after the miracles occurred it was the local *curés*, sometimes assisted by civil officials, who took responsibility for questioning the visionaries and *miraculés*. These first interrogations were aimed at establishing the details of the miracles and the credibility of the witnesses. It was believed that any attempt at fraud could be uncovered by close questioning which would force the witnesses into contradictions. The steadfastness of the witnesses, their refusal to alter any detail in their account, even when threatened with punishment for lying, was considered to be evidence in favor of the miracle. In addition to repeated questioning by clergy and civil officials the witnesses also told their story to many visitors who sought a firsthand account of the miracle. Thus before the bishops had the opportunity to become actively involved in the investigation, the miracle had become fixed in the minds of both the *miraculés* and the local populace.[22] Soon after the bishops were informed by the local clergy they began to assert their authority and eventually assigned the investigation to special commissions. The composition, working methods, and objectivity of these groups were controversial in the nineteenth century, for it was correctly perceived by critics that their role was essential in the successful establishment of a cult. The forces with which the commissions had to contend and their own attitudes toward the miraculous reveal a pattern to which all of the major cults conform.

The first miracles that reveal episcopal concern were the cures of Prince Hohenlohe during the early 1820s. These were simpler to deal with than the apparitions that were to occur throughout the century, for there was no question of founding a shrine or organizing a permanent cult dedicated to the German thaumaturge. Nevertheless, bishops from several dioceses had their vicars-general investigate the cures, and allowed publication of the miracles only on their approval. In fact, the investigation consisted mostly of conducting interviews with *miraculés* and immediate witnesses, and obtaining statements from doctors on the nature of the illnesses. The evidence gathered by the vicars-general was then published for the edification of the diocese.[23] The archbishop of Toulouse, for example, approved publication of the statements relating to a cure of Hohenlohe "considering that all of the facts allow us to regard the cure as miraculous; considering, also, that publishing this account cannot but edify and strengthen the faith."[24] The pattern in these cases was elaborated and extended throughout the century, but the basic elements remained constant: clergy handpicked by the bishop were given the responsibility for investigating and reporting on the miracle; an attempt was made to limit publicity on the miraculous to officially sanctioned accounts; medical experts were called on for advice, but real authority remained with the clergy and ultimately the bishop.

Specially appointed episcopal commissions were the chief instruments for the investigation of apparitions. These were dominated by episcopal clergy, with the vicars-general playing a leading role, followed by cathedral canons, seminary professors, and token representation from the parish priests. The commissions submitted reports to their bishops who reviewed their work and, if they approved, published decrees on the miracle. Four such commissions, investigating the apparitions at Migné, La Salette, Lourdes, and Pontmain, produced favorable reports on nineteenth-century miracles. A fifth commission, which investigated the Miraculous Medal apparitions, ruled favorably on some of the healings attributed to the medal, but stopped short of verifying the apparitions themselves. A review of the work of these commissions reveals the social and institutional pressures that led to the Church's approval of the miracles.[25]

There is some evidence of an episcopal inclination to believe in the miracles even before the investigative process had begun. The decree verifying the apparition at Migné is candid in this respect. "As soon as we were told of this surprising apparition, our thoughts were immediately of heaven, and we were unable to prevent ourselves from crying: *The Finger of God* is here. Prudence, however, imposed on us the necessity of suspending our judgment."[26] Similar evidence of a propensity to believe can be found later in the century as well. Within a week of the apparition at Pontmain in 1871, the bishop of Laval had written to a local clergyman of his "growing interest" in the "remarkable report" of the miracle and asked to be kept informed of new developments. On February 13, 1871, before naming the investigative commission, Mgr Wicart wrote to the *curé* of Pontmain in a manner that betrayed his intention to approve of the miracle.

It does not appear to me that the moment has yet come for me to pronounce on the incomparable favor accorded your fortunate parish, but you see that I am preparing myself for this little by little.

Your report of what is happening in your parish adds to my hopes and my joy. Praised, loved, glorified, and blessed a thousand and million times be the Father of infinite mercy and the immaculate Mother of all grace who presents our poor souls with this ineffable indulgence and sovereign goodness. Exhort your good people and these four or five privileged children to remain ever grateful.[27]

The episcopal response to the miracle at La Salette reveals a more hesitant frame of mind and a willingness to let events run their course without official interference. In the weeks following the apparition of September 1846, Mgr Philbert de Bruillard received reports from the superior of his major seminary and several members of the parish clergy. In December, three months after the miracle, he sent the dossier on La Salette to the cathedral canons and the professors of the diocesan major seminary. The professors submitted a cautious report in which they argued that "It is necessary to wait and examine if one desires certitude." The canons were even more wary of making a judgment and restricted themselves to noting the "good effects" of the miracle and advising against any immediate action. "The episcopal authority will always have time to make a pronouncement on the case; there is no danger in delay, and it is prudent to wait."[28]

The advice from the episcopal clergy was taken by Mgr Bruillard; it was only in July 1847, ten months after the miracle, that he appointed Abbés Rousselot and Orcel, both professors at the major seminary, as commissioners to investigate the miraculous healings which had by that time become a prominent part of the new cult. Only in November of 1847 was a commission of sixteen priests named to review the report of Rousselot and Orcel.[29] Other bishops, notably Mgr Laurence of Tarbes, also hesitated before establishing a commission.[30] Eventually, however, the bishops took charge of the investigations leading to an authoritative pronouncement.

The role of the bishops was crucial in the establishment of new cults, and Catholic historians today still argue for the prudence, objectivity, and authority of the commissions and decrees that were their tools.[31] But when the work of the commissions and the bishops is placed in the context of the novel conditions of the nineteenth-century Church their activity seems less an authoritative response to the supernatural than a struggle against forces both outside and inside the ecclesiastical hierarchy that threatened to break away from episcopal control.

The most obvious source of pressure on the bishops and their commissions was the rapidity with which the miracle was communicated not only to the region, but the nation. The publicity given to the miracles prior to and during the work of the commissions significantly influenced the decision-making process. While the commissions delayed final judgment, the press spread news of the miracles and their cults, using them for polemical purposes. The leading local newspapers reported on the miraculous events well before the decision was reached to form an official commission. Local journals would frequently take sides according to their political orientations. The national press became an especially important influence in the cases of La Salette and Lourdes. Newspapers were not the only source of publicity for the new cults. *Colportage* literature on the miracles at La Salette was being sold throughout France within a few months of the initial apparition. Other types of pious materials, including pictures and medals, were also being marketed despite the efforts of the civil and religious authorities to forbid such publicity.[32]

The apparition at Migné, while it did not establish a cult of comparable significance to those which developed around the Marian apparitions, evoked pressures similar to those which would affect later investigations of the miraculous. Immediately after the apparition, and before the episcopal commission had been formed, stories began to circulate, and the miracle was debated in the Parisian press by *L'ami de la religion* and *Le Constitutionnel*. Brochures and five different lithographs were available at Poitiers and Paris, and twenty-five thousand copies of an illustrated pamphlet were sold.[33] In an attempt to gain control over the controversy and establish the facts of the miracle the bishop allowed the commission's report to be published in February of 1827, although the decree officially approving the apparition did not appear until November. The official approval sparked another round in the press debate, and five bishops made public statements in support of the authenticity of the apparition. In 1828 and 1829 Migné was attacked by supporters of *La petite église* and liberals, and defended by the Catholic press. The controversy culminated in the publication of Abbé Vrindts' *La croix de Migné vengée* in 1829. Vrindts' work is a prime example of how a miracle, which seemed at first to belong in the context of local pastoral concerns, could be interpreted as an event of national, even international, significance. *La croix de Migné*, published with the approval of the bishop of Poitiers, began by describing the miracle, and included documents that were used as evidence in the episcopal investigation. But a substantial portion of the work was devoted to the relationship of the apparition to the Church's general position on miracles. Some of Vrindts' chapter headings indicate the level of concern:

That the laws of nature are the continuous and uniform
operation of its author.

That miracles are the extraordinary action of God
different from his sustained and uniform operation.

That miracles are the most energetic language of God, to
intimate his wishes and to teach men his truth.

That faith in miracles that are sufficiently proved is one
of the greatest obligations of a reasonable spirit.

That those who negate miracles are always of bad faith.[34]

The coverage in *L'Univers* given to the apparitions at La Salette and
Lourdes shows a similar tendency to discuss the miracles in a polemical
context. In February of 1847, well before the first episcopal commission
had been named, *Le Siècle* treated the apparition of La Salette sarcastically
and reported an epidemic of apparitions in the Dauphiné.[35] *L'Univers*,
silent until then out of respect for episcopal authority, published a response that stopped well short of sanctioning the miracle but did stress the
conversion of the area and concluded with a warning that showed where
the hopes of the paper lay. "We advise *Le Siècle* not to involve itself in this
matter; what does it matter if the event appears incredible to the paper, if it
is proved that it has taken place? And, if it has taken place, what does it
matter that *Le Siècle* finds it tiresome and an impediment to local
business?"[36] The newspaper debate continued, with *Le Constitutionnel*
joining the opposition to La Salette, and *L'Univers* responding with an
even more positive article that referred to the miraculous cures at the new
shrine.[37]

In the process of engaging in a polemic with the republican press
L'Univers had moved substantially in the direction of committing itself to
the miracle, and it would have been difficult for Louis Veuillot and his staff
to retreat from their position. The influence of the paper with the French
clergy was widely known, and it must have appeared to them that the
Church had something at stake in the question of the miracle. Meanwhile
the bishop of Grenoble was still following his wait-and-see policy.

In October of 1847 the bishop of La Rochelle, Mgr Villecourt, who had
visited La Salette the previous July, refueled the public controversy with
the publication of his *Nouveau récit de l'apparition de la sainte Vierge sur les
montagnes des Alpes*.[38] The manuscript had been submitted to Mgr Philbert
de Bruillard of Grenoble, who made no objection to its appearance.

Veuillot featured a selection from the work in *L'Univers* of October 27, and followed it with an article that showed he considered the case as settled. The combination of public support from Bishop Villecourt and Louis Veuillot's paper was the immediate occasion for the convening of the commission whose decision led ultimately to the final approval of the miracle. But while the bishop of Grenoble belatedly asserted his authority in the case, the national publicity made it appear that a decision in favor of the apparition was inevitable.

Eleven years later, the events leading up to the appointment of a commission to investigate the miracles at Lourdes mirrored those that preceded the La Salette investigation. In May of 1858 *L'Univers* was defending the rights of the bishop to judge the events, while *Le Siècle* favored civil prosecution of the cult and the suppression of the new "superstition."[39] In July Louis Veuillot visited Lourdes and consulted with several bishops of the region, including Mgr Laurence of Tarbes, whose diocese included the new shrine. It was as a result of this meeting that the official commission was named. In a letter to his brother Eugène, Louis Veuillot revealed what was on his mind while at Lourdes. "This fact of Lourdes might well be a second edition of La Salette."[40] Veuillot's use of this publisher's metaphor suggests another aspect of the press coverage given to miracles. As a publicist Veuillot was sensitive to what made good copy, and his experiences with the miracle at La Salette had made him eager to report on a similar apparition. The excitement and controversy surrounding the miraculous as reported in *L'Univers* thus had the effect of making the Church responsive to public opinion that existed outside the control of the hierarchy.

By contrast, the investigation of the Miraculous Medal apparitions in 1836 was not conducted within a polemical context. Nevertheless, the Miraculous Medal investigation confirms the influence of the press and popular belief on episcopal commissions. The archbishop of Paris, Mgr de Quélen, had initially approved the medal's production at the height of the cholera epidemic of 1832. The medal soon acquired a healing reputation, and by 1834 over a hundred thousand had been distributed. Economic and pastoral pressure for clerical approval was compounded by the publication of Père Aladel's *Notice historique sur l'origine et les effets de la nouvelle médaille frappée en l'honneur de la très sainte Vierge* in August of 1834. Within a year Aladel's book had gone through five editions, and there were over one hundred thousand copies of it in circulation. Largely as a result of the publicity given the medal by the *Notice*, the number of medals produced and distributed increased rapidly, reaching one million by the end of 1835.[41] The *Notice* gave extensive coverage to the miraculous origins of the medal in a series of apparitions to Sr. Catherine Labouré, a Daughter of Charity, in 1830 and 1831. As knowledge of the Miraculous Medal spread, it appeared that the approval of the medal in 1832 by Quélen carried with it an implicit sanction of the apparitions. That placed the archbishop in a difficult position, for he had never held formal hearings on the apparitions. The episcopal commission formed in 1836 was designed to correct this irregularity, but its task was complicated by Sr. Catherine's refusal to reveal her identity and testify before its members. Instead, all of the information on the apparitions was funneled to the commission through her confessor, Aladel. Catherine's reticence, and the delay of five years between the apparitions and the investigations, help explain why the episcopal commission in this case refused to verify the apparitions that were the basis of the cult. But the thriving trade in Miraculous Medals and the popularity of the *Notice* made it difficult to disavow the cult, even had the archbishop desired to do so. The investigators spent much of their time determining just how many medals and books had been produced; their findings, along with the evidence that the medal was responsible for numerous cures and conversions, accounts for the episcopal approval of the cult.[42]

The history of the Miraculous Medal suggests that bishops were not simply neutral observers in the period prior to the formation of the commissions. As was seen earlier, there were instances of a favorable attitude toward the miracles even before some of the commissions had been named. Episcopal actions reflected this attitude. While they withheld formal approval until the investigations had been completed, pastoral concerns impelled the bishops to channel and control the popular cults in a manner that implied adherence to them. The distinction between pastoral concern on the one hand and approval of the cult on the other was difficult to maintain, especially in the face of public opposition, which refused to take the distinction seriously.

At La Salette the pattern of episcopal intervention began with Mgr Philbert de Bruillard's decision in December of 1846 to support the shepherd visionaries at a local convent rather than have them returned to their own families.[43] The possibility of losing control over the children, whose ignorance and lack of piety were already a sore point, was too much for the local clergy to contemplate, and they successfully lobbied with the bishop to provide room and board at the convent. The rationalization offered publicly was that such support was normal charity and did not imply approval of the miracle. But clearly Mélanie and Maximin were singled out from other poor shepherds because of their vision, and it is difficult not to see this act as a defensive maneuver on the part of the Church. If the miracle *was* eventually validated, the children would have to be better prepared on questions of the faith and the Church, and this necessitated the intensive course of religious instruction they followed at the convent. But in the act of preparing for this eventuality, the Church at the same time made it more likely. Other signs of support followed, including the approval of a publication on the apparition to compete with Villecourt's work. The fact that the bishop of Bordeaux had published a work in support of the apparition and its cult before the bishop of Grenoble had spoken publicly created pressure in the diocese for some positive action. But the most telling move was the approval of Sunday Mass at the shrine on the first anniversary of the apparition. Abbé Mélin of Corps, who had requested the approval, acknowledged that it did not constitute approval of the cult, but was merely a concession to the numerous pilgrims who would otherwise be deprived of Sunday Mass.[44] But on the anniversary forty thousand pilgrims were present, along with two hundred priests, and masses were said from three A.M. until noon. Those present saw the day as a triumph for the cult, and the presence of the clergy and the celebrations of the masses were properly interpreted as a sign of Church support.[45] After all, if the bishop of Grenoble wanted to maintain absolute neutrality he would not have granted permission for the services, and thus forced the pilgrims to decide between an ordinary Mass at their home parishes or a pilgrimage without Mass at La Salette. This course of action might not have discouraged the pilgrims, but it would have maintained the Church's distance from the cult. The bishop's decision to allow the masses shows him to have been susceptible to the pressures of the local clergy and the populace, whose belief in the cult was already well established. Mgr Philbert de Bruillard was unwilling to deny pilgrims honoring the Virgin Sunday Mass, but the consequence was an even closer identification between the Church and the devotion to Notre-Dame de La Salette.

Other nineteenth-century cults follow a similar pattern whereby a move that was purportedly neutral was generally interpreted as signifying approval of the cult. The *ordonnance* of Mgr Laurence establishing the Lourdes commission withheld judgment on the apparition and the miraculous cures, but the decision to investigate was couched in polemical terms designed to defend the possibility of the miraculous. Laurence forcefully attacked those people who rejected the miracle a priori:

> Their newspapers have first loudly cried, superstition, bad faith; they affirm that the facts of the grotto have a sordid interest as their *raison d'être*, a culpable cupidity; thus they wound the moral sense of our Christian populace. Denying everything and attacking intentions is the easiest way to overcome difficulties, we agree, but besides being disloyal, it is irrational and irritates minds rather than convinces them. To deny supernatural facts is to follow a dated school; it is to abjure Christian religion and to follow in the rut of the incredulous philosophy of the last century.[46]

Laurence's *ordonnance* was an honest document. It did not hide the fact that the polemical issue of the possibility of miracles was involved and that pressures from believers and unbelievers concerning Lourdes were related to this larger question. Laurence's statement was publicized as a defense of the Church's position on the miraculous and, while it only established an investigative commission, its appearance was seen as a victory for the defenders of Lourdes.[47]

The Lourdes commission's early meetings offer further evidence that episcopal investigations were sometimes conducted by men with a bias in favor of the miracles. At the second session on August 3, 1858, for example, the favorable report on the cult written by Jean-Baptiste Estrade was read, and the secretary of the commission, Abbé Fourcade, described the attitude of the members in these terms: "This report bears such sincerity and conviction that it augmented, if possible, the already ardent desire of the commission to achieve, by all possible means, the knowledge of truth."[48] For the commissioners, the quality of belief inspired by the miracles seemed to be as important a factor as the actual occurrence of the miracles. Reports of miraculous cures from Dr. Dozous, who resided at Lourdes and was an active proponent of the new cult, were read at the third and fourth sessions. No member seems to have taken a skeptical point of view, and the evidence presented by Dozous was accepted without question.

The secretary read several depositions from Doctor Dozous. They were about instantaneous cures obtained by the use of water from the Grotto, sometimes after only one use. These depositions had the desirable characteristics of veracity and authenticity; the signatures of the cured were accompanied by a great number of other signatures from doctors or relatives who could perfectly verify the anterior state of the sick and the changes that took place. These signatures were legalized by the municipal authorities.[49]

So eagerly did the commission accept the first information on the cures at Lourdes that it defined its role as one of "verification" rather than investigation.[50] Only after the clergy had collected information on the cures was the dossier handed over to Dr. Vergez for his opinion. Dr. Vergez reviewed the work of the commission, but did not conduct a personal investigation of the *miraculés*. It is also significant that both Dr. Dozous and Dr. Vergez held degrees from the medical faculty at Montpellier, which was known for its advocacy of the importance of spiritual forces in healing.[51] While the final decree approving the apparitions, the cures, and the cult did not appear until January of 1862, the case had been decided well before then. As at La Salette, by the time the bishop's judgment was published the site of the apparition had been purchased and plans for a new shrine begun.[52]

The bishops and their investigators may have been biased as a result of pressure from the press, the clergy, and public opinion, but it is not evident that they acted in bad faith in carrying out their mission. The commissions went about their work conscientiously, collected relevant evidence, and considered alternative explanations for the miracles in the hope of being able to determine whether supernatural intervention had actually occurred. Their conduct of the investigation shows in what areas they were skeptical, and how this skepticism was overcome.

Only the investigation into the apparition at Migné dealt exclusively with testimony relating to the original miracle. This was possible because of the large number of witnesses (two thousand), and necessary because of the absence of a thaumaturgic cult at the site of the miracle. The decree verifying the miracle reflected the commission's efforts to exclude the possibility of a natural explanation for the miracle. Subsequent decrees on other apparitions also took this approach, but the explanations considered by the Migné commission were of a physical and not a psychological nature. The possibility of an unusual cloud in the shape of a cross was raised and dismissed, but the question of hallucination or suggestion was never discussed.[53] Later commissions would continue to study possible alternatives to supernatural causation, but their focus shifted to the psychological and moral state of the *miraculés*. Critics frequently argued that the apparitions were the result of fraud or delusion. The defenses of the witnesses' credibility advanced by the commissions were an attempt to deal with this criticism. The sincerity and candor of the visionaries, and the absence of any mystical pretensions on their part, were personal characteristics which made fraud or delusion unlikely.[54]

With the exception of Migné, the testimony of eyewitnesses was considered insufficient proof that a miracle had occurred. Miracles subsequent to apparitions were thus central to the work of the commissions and figured largely in the investigations and the decisions. Healings were the most important form of confirmation, as Mgr Laurence indicated in his decree on Lourdes.

> There is a strict relationship between the cures and the apparition; the apparition is divine because the cures bear a divine seal. What comes from God is true! Consequently, the Apparition calling itself the Immaculate Conception, which Bernadette has seen and heard, is the Holy Virgin! Thus we cry out: The finger of God is here! *Digitus Dei est hic!* (Exodus 8:9)[55]

After miraculous healings, conversions of individuals and communities were considered the most telling evidence in favor of the apparitions.[56] Cures and conversions were needed because despite attempts to demonstrate the veracity of witnesses, some fear that they could have been deceived by an hallucination or by the devil himself remained. If further miracles more open to investigation and verification, such as cures and conversions, occurred at the site of the apparition, then the evidence of the visionaries gained in force.[57] The commissioners believed that God would not allow an illusion to be confirmed, and that the devil would not work miracles that served to increase piety.

The defense of miracles propounded by the decrees reveals the episcopal clergy's frame of mind. They could conceive of the possibility of mistake or even fraud as an explanation for the miraculous, but only up to a point. That point was reached when miracles began to occur that were obviously beneficial to laymen and clergy alike—cures and conversions. These miracles took place as a result of the new cult's popularity while the episcopal investigation was still being conducted. In fact, the decrees went so far as to admit that the rapid diffusion of the cult was itself reason for approving the founding apparitions. The episcopal statement approving the miracle of La Salette is representative of this position.

> This fact of the apparition acquires a new degree of certitude through the spontaneous and immense gathering of the faithful at the site of the vision, as well as through the many prodigies that have followed the event, and which it is impossible to doubt without violating the rules of human testimony.[58]

Mgr Laurence repeated the point in his statement approving the apparition at Lourdes: "Our conviction is fortified by the immense and spontaneous gathering of the faithful at the grotto, a gathering which has not stopped since the first apparitions, the purpose of which is to ask favors or render thanks for those already obtained."[59]

The Church's interest in the popularity of the new cults is related to its concern over the erosion of religious practice. The crowds that gathered at the shrines must have consoled and encouraged the clergy. In using the popularity of the cults to support their official declarations, the bishops were calling attention to the solid base of faith they believed still existed in France. The cultic literature confirms this point in its emphasis on the devotions' universal appeal.[60] But seeing the appeal of a cult as evidence supporting it also reveals the extent to which popular belief could influence episcopal decisions. What the historian today might label "pressure" was, from the perspective of the nineteenth-century Church, another aspect of the miracle.

Episcopal investigations of miracles were thus forced to work under several constraints. The development of a popular cult might, if not brought under the control of the hierarchy, threaten the Church's spiritual authority. Another source of pressure was the support for the cult by both local and episcopal clergy who perceived how it might assist them in their pastoral work; a third influence was the rapid diffusion of the cult beyond the local area by means of the press and devotional literature. The arguments used in this literature related specific miracles to the larger concerns of the Church. Lourdes was used as evidence to support the papal declaration of the Immaculate Conception, and all the major miracles were used in polemics against critics of the Church.[61] It is ironic that contemporary skepticism about miracles in general led the Church to a more credulous attitude toward particular miracles. In an age when positivism reputedly relied on "facts" in its attacks on the supernatural, miracles presented themselves as empirically verifiable events, which could counter such skepticism.[62] The premise underlying all the investigations was that God "has not withdrawn his arm, and his power is the same today as in past centuries."[63] The Church was responsive to institutional pressures and the weight of public opinion in part because by affirming a specific miracle its position on their possibility in general could be verified. Without such an affirmation the doctrine might have become a dead letter, with the implication that God no longer intervened in the world on behalf of the Church.

Development of the Cults

The decrees inaugurated a new stage in the history of the miracle cults. It was only after official approval that the Church could move freely to disseminate the facts of the miracles along with the orthodox interpretations of the cults. With the exception of the Miraculous Medal, the major Marian cults that originated in the nineteenth century were controlled by bishops. The Miraculous Medal never relied on episcopal support, but was disseminated instead by the Daughters of Charity of St. Vincent de Paul. There are other examples of miracle cults which succeeded through the activity of a religious order and required only the tacit approval of the episcopal authorities.[64] In some cases successful cults were built on the activity of parish *curés*. As will be seen, these cults became a source of conflict between parish clergy and diocesan authorities.[65] Although not all miracle cults were founded by episcopal clergy, there is no case of a cult's surviving episcopal condemnation, and even when bishops chose not to exercise their authority actively, some type of informal approval was still required.[66]

French bishops successfully claimed authority over the miraculous within their dioceses. They were always careful, however, to avoid infringement on the prerogatives of the Holy See, and always stated their willingness to submit to the decisions of Rome. The distinction used by the commissions between moral and juridical certitude was formulated so that bishops could move quickly to approve a miracle which would not share the status of those approved by Rome in cases of beatification and canonization.[67] According to this distinction, absolute certainty was not required for episcopal judgments since these did not involve essential doctrines. Such judgments had nothing in common with ex cathedra declarations on faith or morals, and Catholics were free to disbelieve with impunity. While asserting its autonomous authority, the episcopacy was careful to enlist papal support for the new cults. Roman favors in the form of indulgences and permissions to crown a statue were necessary to legitimize a devotion.[68] These papal privileges were featured in the pious literature, and no cult could have developed a national clientele without them. Rome was thus willing to support the rights of bishops over the miracles that occurred within their dioceses, but its power persisted in the background and required constant deference.

A standard set of institutions was established for episcopal cults and, with some variations, these were also adopted by other cults. Most cults were built around a pilgrimage shrine, a sacred space that commemorated past miracles and held out the promise of others. The shrines of La Salette and Lourdes were so successful that many parishes attempted to create subshrines mirroring the original sites. Miniature "grottos" of Lourdes were and are the most famous instance of this development, and the cult of Notre-Dame de Lourdes at Oostacker in Belgium became the major thaumaturgic shrine in that country during the last third of the nineteenth century.[69]

The shrines approved by episcopal decrees were all eventually staffed by missionary orders. At La Salette a new congregation was founded in 1852, and at Lourdes the order associated with the older diocesan shrine of Notre-Dame de Garaison was transferred to Lourdes and eventually re-named for the new cult. In other cases shrines were either created or revived by orders, with the Oblates of Mary being the most active in this area.[70] As was observed in the first chapter, the use of missionaries at shrines shows to what extent miracle cults, both old and new, were worked into the larger pastoral program of the nineteenth-century Church. Even at parochial shrines the bishops usually agreed to provide additional clergy to serve the pilgrimage, who functioned very much as missionaries in their concern for pilgrims rather than parishioners.[71]

Shrines became centers from which miracle cults were communicated to the region and the nation. A variety of techniques was used, with the most fundamental being the pilgrimage. Individual pilgrimages for spiritual or corporal assistance were deeply ingrained in popular religion, and the new cults encouraged the use of their shrines for these purposes as well. An attempt was made, however, to combine specific requests with the fulfillment of orthodox religious obligations. Attending Mass and receiving Communion, from the cult of Hohenlohe through the cult at Lourdes, were regarded as essential elements in achieving a miraculous cure.[72]

Another traditional practice quickly adapted for the new shrines was the parish pilgrimage in which a commune, led by its *curé*, would participate at certain times, usually on Rogation days. The new shrines became popular among the neighboring parishes and served as centers for the expression of regional solidarity on those days when several communes would gather at the site, each with its distinctive banner.[73] Observers of such scenes never failed to be edified by the pilgrimages, for they presented what was believed to be an ideal image of the operation of religion as part of the fabric of social life. The religiosity of the French peasant and his ties to the village and the Church, as expressed in communal pilgrimages, were thus significant both as a sign of continuity in the religious life of the countryside, and as a symbol of hope for Catholic publicists who were battling disbelief and indifference.[74]

The success of parish pilgrimages was great enough to cause some churchmen to consider a means whereby such events could be expanded to cover a larger area. During the later years of the Second Empire, the development of the national railroad network allowed some shrines to begin drawing groups of pilgrims from further and further away. Lourdes was the major innovator, and others quickly followed suit.[75] The year 1866 was crucial for the expansion of the Lourdes pilgrimage. In that year the trunk line linking Lourdes to the departmental capital of Tarbes was completed, the missionaries of Notre-Dame de Garaison were established at the shrine, and the first Mass was said at the grotto to commemorate the blessing of the new basilica's crypt. In the same year, 3,700 pilgrims visited Lourdes by train, and in 1867 the women of Bayeux arrived at Lourdes on the first train rented especially for a pilgrimage.[76] There were thirty-five other organized pilgrimages that year, bringing twenty-eight thousand visitors. Through 1871 these numbers remained about the same, although in 1869 there was another innovation which was to have major significance for the shrine: collective pilgrimages organized by diocesan authorities.[77]

The triumphant period for Lourdes occurred during the religious revival that followed the Franco–Prussian war. The importance of Lourdes in this period must be in part attributed to the successful institutionalization of the cult, which had already occurred. It was not just the railroad and the missionaries that made the pilgrimage movement possible. New hotels and inns were built in the city, the number of lemonade vendors increased to serve the pilgrims, and merchants of religious objects responded with a complete line of medals, statues, and lithographs.[78] The water from the miraculous fountain had been circulating through France since the early days of the pilgrimage, but the missionaries began marketing their product systematically in the 1860s; at the same time they increased the flow from the fountain and built the famous pools in which pilgrims bathed. By the end of the century over a hundred thousand bottles of Lourdes water were shipped each year to Catholics throughout the world.[79]

The last major innovation in the Lourdes pilgrimage was the immediate result of the revival of 1872–1873. Prior to that period the organization of pilgrimages had never gone beyond the diocesan level. In 1872 a national commission was formed to encourage the pilgrimage movement. The Assumptionists were the major force behind the commission, which was composed of laymen as well as clergy.[80] The major project of the commission was the National Pilgrimage, which became an annual event starting in 1872. Every August trains from throughout France would converge on Lourdes, while Catholics followed the story in the press. At Lourdes, massive processions produced miracles that received extensive coverage in the Catholic press.

The successful nationalization of the Lourdes shrine during the Third Republic is reflected in the distribution of organized pilgrims for the years 1873, 1893, and 1913[81] (see Appendix). In 1873 Lourdes drew more pilgrims than in any other year during the decade of the 1870s. But the figures show the pilgrims came mostly from the south, the southwest, and the massif central, with a scattering of support in the industrial north. By 1913 most of the departments that demonstrated support for Lourdes in 1873 were still sending pilgrims to the shrine in large numbers, but there was a notable increase in the traditionally pious regions of Brittany,

Normandy, and the alpine departments, and some surprising strength east of Paris in an area usually considered religiously indifferent. On the whole, the 1913 figures suggest that Catholic France had committed itself to the shrine at Lourdes.

The chart of the organized pilgrims to Lourdes during the period 1867 to 1908 confirms the growth in the shrine's popularity and suggests some of the forces that help explain the expansion of the pilgrimage.[82] The upward trend in the numbers of pilgrims during this period is clear, but the growth was not always gradual and steady, with peak years in 1872–1873, 1882–1883, and 1908. In 1872–1873, as was seen in chapter 5, pilgrims to Lourdes were responding to the national crisis that followed the defeat in the Franco–Prussian War. The laic legislation of the early 1880s coincides with the next peak, suggesting that bishops sought to mobilize the faithful during a political crisis by means of the Lourdes pilgrimage. Political clashes between Church and State may also explain the peaks in 1901 and 1904, years during which the expulsion of religious orders and the separation of Church and State were being debated in France. But by far the largest number of pilgrims came in 1908, the fiftieth anniversary of the apparitions. If unorganized pilgrims are included, well over a million pilgrims visited Lourdes in that year. Although this evidence does not demonstrate that pilgrims were more motivated by religion than by political concerns, it does suggest that Lourdes cannot be judged solely in political terms. With the encouragement of the Church, pilgrims journeyed to Lourdes to console themselves during a national crisis and to express support for the Church when it was under attack, but also to commemorate the apparitions that had founded the shrine. It is worth noting that if unorganized pilgrims are included Lourdes was averaging over half a million visitors a year during the first decade of the twentieth century. In the same period strike activity in France averaged less than half that number.[83] While it would clearly be an oversimplification to argue from this that the pilgrimage to Lourdes was more significant than labor organization and strikes, this kind of comparison does suggest that the mass movement to Lourdes and other shrines deserves serious attention. By the end of the nineteenth century Lourdes had developed into a center for the mobilization of Catholic France, and thus contributed to the political divisions and the perpetuation of belief in the supernatural in the modern era.

The shrines themselves were another major focus of the episcopal

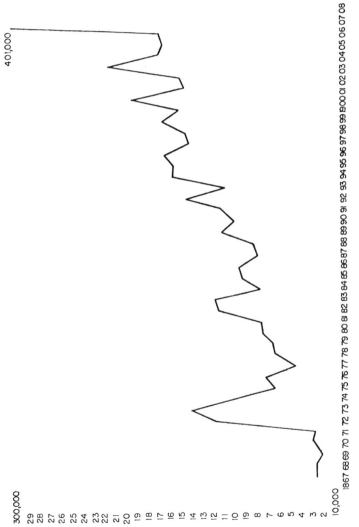

Pilgrims to Lourdes, 1867–1908.

Source: Bertrin, *Histoire critique des événements de Lourdes*.

program to develop a new pilgrimage. The decrees on La Salette, Lourdes, and Pontmain all concluded by announcing major construction programs to be financed by public subscription. The structures produced at these sites have been criticized from an aesthetic point of view, but they are permanent testimony to the willingness of Catholics to support the new cults with significant financial contributions. In the six months following the decree approving the cult at Lourdes, 2,557 subscribers donated 105,712 francs for the shrine to be built over the grotto. Miracle cults were thus of financial as well as spiritual advantage to a diocese.[84]

The development of diocesan and national organizations and the increasing use of the railroad allowed greater access to the major shrines, but pilgrimages did have certain limitations as a method for spreading a miracle cult. The Church was especially concerned with drawing into the cults those individuals who could not or did not visit the shrines. At the same time they needed a method for maintaining contact with those pilgrims who did come. The key institution designed to enlist believers into a permanent organization dedicated to the new cult was the confraternity. Such voluntary associations of the pious have a long history, and Maurice Agulhon has done much to illuminate one particular set of confraternities, the *pénitents blancs* of the ancien régime. Agulhon's work, and other evidence as well, suggests that such parish-based organizations could serve as a basis for lay opposition to a local *curé*, and that their religious character was sometimes secondary to their sociability.[85]

While *pénitents blancs* and similar confraternities occasionally proved troublesome to the Church, another type of voluntary association existed whose focus was more exclusively devotional. During the Counterreformation confraternities devoted to the Rosary and Scapular proliferated under the aegis of the Dominicans and Franciscans as part of the Church's propaganda campaign in support of its doctrine on indulgences.[86] It was this second type of confraternity, whose salvific aims served the goals of the institutional Church, which was a model for the nineteenth-century miracle cults.

The most prominent of the nineteenth-century confraternities, whose spirit and techniques were emulated by the others, was the Archconfraternity of Our Lady of the Immaculate Conception—more commonly known as the Confraternity of Notre-Dame des Victoires, for the parish with which it was associated. Consideration of this association founded by Abbé Desgenettes indicates how the modern movement differed from its predecessors of the ancien régime. The Confraternity of Notre-Dame des Victoires was designed to combat the massive indifference to religion clearly evident in the urban environment of Paris in the 1830s. Appointed *curé* of Notre-Dame des Victoires in 1832, Abbé Desgenettes described his parish to the archbishop of Paris in these terms:

> Since the July Revolution, the sacraments are no longer frequented, the sick die as if there were no future life, the holy table is deserted, the church abandoned; even on the days of our greatest feasts, hardly any faithful assist at the sacred mysteries. . . . The ministers of religion are detested, and while the least of our citizens can walk through our quarter without fear, the priest cannot without first removing the sacred habit which distinguishes him.[87]

In December of 1836, while saying Mass, Abbé Desgenettes heard a voice order him to dedicate his parish to the Immaculate Heart of Mary. Later that month the archbishop of Paris, Mgr de Quélen, approved a parish confraternity, which drew four hundred on the first Sunday night meeting. The *curé* asked for and received supernatural confirmation that his work was approved by God when a free-thinker prayed for by the new association was miraculously converted.[88]

The *curé* of Notre-Dame des Victoires was not content with his local success, and was soon lobbying with the archbishop for an expanded association, an archconfraternity, which could enlist members from throughout France. Mgr de Quélen refused, however, to forward the project to Rome, whose approval was necessary. After a year during which his ambitions were suspended, Abbé Desgenettes succeeded in having a private individual present his idea to Pope Gregory XVI, who approved the Archconfraternity in a papal brief in June 1838.[89] Having won his battle with the episcopacy by appealing directly to Rome, Desgenettes was still faced with the problem of how to disseminate the new cult. Once again divine inspiration came to his aid, and he composed the famous *Manuel* for the association, the success of which the Abbé attributed to Mary's intervention: "The *Manuel* was under Mary's protection. . . . It is Mary who put an end to the anxieties of our mind; it is she who distributed it, and the sovereign of heaven and earth carried it to the extremities of the world."[90]

By 1854, fifteen years after the initial publication, the *Manuel* had gone through fifteen editions totaling seventy thousand copies. In addition, forty dioceses had approved abridged editions, which totaled an additional eighty thousand. The membership in the Archconfraternity reached one million in the early 1860s and during its peak years in the mid 1840s over a hundred thousand members were joining yearly.[91] The success of the Archconfraternity was interpreted by Desgenettes as evidence of God's favor and of a national religious revival. There were, however, other factors at work, an understanding of which is important for the light they shed on all the successful cults of nineteenth-century France.

In the first place, starting in 1839, miraculous healings began to occur as the result of prayers of the Archconfraternity at its regular Sunday night meetings. During the first two years Desgenettes had refused to include requests for healing in the list of "recommendations" read publicly at the service, and had restricted the association to prayers for the conversion of sinners. It was only when one of his parishioners pleaded for prayers for his wife that the *curé* relented; after this initial success such requests became an accepted part of the confraternity's program.[92] The pattern of popular pressure imposing the miraculous on cults whose initial purpose was pastoral is clear for the nineteenth century. During none of the Marian apparitions did Mary ever promise cures; her messages called for penitence (La Salette, Lourdes, Pontmain), and a devotion to her Immaculate Conception (Miraculous Medal, Lourdes, Notre-Dame des Victoires). Yet all of these cults soon developed a thaumaturgic element, which came to be their most important attraction. The example of the parishioner pleading with his *curé* for prayers to heal his sick wife takes on general significance when placed in this context. Abbé Desgenettes could not refuse, and his concession was an important factor in the development of his pastoral work.

A second reason for the success of the Archconfraternity was its suitability, in the eyes of the French clergy, to the problems of the nineteenth century. The Church had defined its major pastoral concern as the conversion of indifferent Catholics, and Desgenettes' *Manuel* was aimed at those Catholics, especially women, whose families included nonpracticing members of the faith. In contrast with the confraternities of the ancien régime, the Archconfraternity of Notre-Dame des Victoires was placed under the strict control of the clergy. In chapter four of the *Manuel*, Desgenettes departs from the sodden piety that characterizes the work to give hard-headed and succinct information to fellow priests on how to establish a chapter in their parishes. After receiving episcopal approval the abbé was instructed, by means of a model letter, to write to Notre-Dame des Victoires requesting affiliation and including a list of the members. The *Manuel* was careful to indicate that the new organization could coexist with the older Scapular and Rosary confraternities. The association was directed at what was commonly perceived as the major pastoral problem, religious indifference and the conversion of sinners, and placed the clergy in a clear position of authority. It was for these reasons that the Sulpicians, the largest single congregation training seminarians in France, soon supported the work of the Archconfraternity.[93]

The healing miracles appealed to the public, and the design and purpose of the confraternity appealed to the clergy. But it is above all in the method by which the cult was propagated and sustained that it distinguished itself as a significant innovator in the pastoral work of the nineteenth century. Other cults, including several originating in the seventeenth century, had published devotional literature featuring the miraculous power they controlled. Some of this literature continued to appear into the nineteenth century, with little revision.[94] Abbé Desgenettes seems to have been the first to conceive of a national organization through which parish chapters would cooperate and communicate, providing each other with mutual support. This concept appears in the *Manuel*, where the founder stresses the necessity for keeping careful membership records. In each succeeding edition, Desgenettes proudly described the expansion of the Archconfraternity into new areas. In the 1840s the central organization began publishing a journal through which chapters around the nation could keep in touch with one another's activities.[95] The *Annales* contained the history of the confraternity, constantly updated by Desgenettes, descriptions of religious feasts in Paris and the provinces, and reports of conversions and miraculous healings. Parish clergy and confraternity members wrote to the *Annales*, reporting the successes of their local chapters, and the graces obtained for themselves and others as a result of the association's prayers. The journal itself became a popular topic, with many letter writers commenting on how much they appreciated and were edified by the news of the religious revival inspired by the Archconfraternity.[96] The tone of the *Annales* suggests that the confraternity successfully communicated to its members an uplifting sense of power as they battled and defeated the forces of unbelief.

Abbé Desgenettes may have been the first churchman to conceive and act on the idea that a national organization existing, to some extent, outside the episcopal hierarchy could be brought into existence by direct contact with the parishes. *L'Univers* was, in the same period, to make a reputation for itself as the newspaper that appealed to the French clergy over the heads of their bishops, and so worked to divide the Church.[97] The possibility of creating a national constituency of Catholics outside the domain of episcopal authority had, in some form or other, occurred to Louis Veuillot. The petition movement in support of "freedom of education" sponsored by *L'Univers* in the 1840s even shows some thought of a national organization. Veuillot's political concerns aroused the opposition of important members of the hierarchy, most notably Mgr Dupanloup. Desgenettes' purposes were pious and pastoral, but his attempt to create an organization that was not directly controlled by the episcopacy was also regarded with some suspicion by Church authorities, as will be seen in the following section. By using the periodical press to help build his archconfraternity, he succeeded in creating a national network of voluntary associations capable of communicating with and supporting each other in the face of the religious indifference that was felt to characterize modern life.

When the success of the Archconfraternity of Notre-Dame des Victoires, built in part on the use of the periodical press, is placed alongside the adaptation of the national railroad network for the Lourdes pilgrimage, it begins to appear that the nineteenth-century Church, for all its antimodernist rhetoric, was able to make use of modern technology for its own purposes. Perhaps the best parallel is the remarkable success contemporary evangelists have had in using radio and television to spread Christian fundamentalism.[98] The creation of a national organization united by means of a periodical publication became a standard element in the nineteenth-century miracle cults; Notre-Dame de La Salette, Notre-Dame de Lourdes, Notre-Dame du Sacré-Coeur, and Notre-Dame de Pontmain all developed similar insitutions. Older cults, such as Notre-Dame de Chartres, also began taking advantage of the publicity available by means of the press. Many of these publications still appear regularly, although the emphasis is no longer placed on miracles. In their nineteenth-century form, the annals of the different cults combined miracle stories with reports of organized pilgrimages to the shrine, and the progress of their archconfraternities.

The use of the press by the miracle cults had important consequences for the cults themselves and for religion generally. Even in the early stages of a cult, miracle stories circulated in *colportage* literature and the Catholic press.[99] Such coverage had a major impact on the formation of attitudes toward the miraculous. Elizabeth Eisenstein has described the ability of print to fix an idea in the mind, to give it a concreteness and reality not otherwise available.[100] Miracle stories and, equally important, pictorial representations of Mary standing before the different visionaries, made it possible to believe in a miraculous event without having to confront the visionary or *miraculé* directly. The literature and images did not strive to introduce the facts of the case for rational scrutiny, but called for a response of faith in which the miracle took on collective significance. The critical sense which would make people skeptical of devotional literature did not necessarily accompany the rapidly expanding literacy of the nineteenth century.[101]

Publications treating the miraculous date, of course, from the origin of the printing press. The innovation of the nineteenth century was the creation of a national cult within which people could find support for their beliefs without having to rely exclusively on family and neighbors. Such an innovation may have been an important means of giving the community of Catholic believers coherence as the wave of indifference mounted. The evidence of Le Bras and others on the decline in religious practice is incontrovertible, but the same results show that a substantial minority of Frenchmen continued to practice and believe despite all the secular influences at work in the century.[102] The clergy and laymen involved in the miracle cults were themselves highly conscious of the declining belief. The goal of the Archconfraternity of Notre-Dame des Victoires was the conversion of sinners, and the other cults stressed similar themes of repentance and conversion. Miracles were judged to be refutations of the materialistic and rationalistic principles fostered by the Revolution, and the successes of the cults, seen in the numbers of medals and manuals sold, the crowds of pilgrims, and the membership rolls of the confraternities, were intended to reassure both the leaders and the members of the general vitality of the faith.[103] In a period of intense political and social crisis, as in the years just after the Franco–Prussian War, this sense of coherence provided by miracle cults took on wider significance and emerged as the pilgrimage movement. The institutionalization of miracle cults over the preceding generation helped make this expression of national mood possible.

Modern miracle cults did experiment with new techniques, but they should not be seen as a radical departure from other aspects of nineteenth-century pastoral work. As was seen in the first chapter, miraculous shrines were frequently integrated into the mission movement by serving as a base of operations from which the diocese or nation could be evangelized. There was also some similarity in the techniques used by the missionary movement and the miracle cults, for both did seek an emotional response on the part of their audiences as a result of impressive ritual displays. There is also, however, an important contrast, for while missions and catechisms stressed the necessity for doctrinal submission and orthodox practice, under pain of damnation, miracles offered stories of saving grace in which God healed and converted, rather than ordered and condemned. Missions, moreover, were restricted in time and place, and there were regions where the movement never penetrated. Miracle cults could rely on an individual reader to discover their message that grace was still at work in the world. The miracle cults can be seen to balance the darker piety of the mission movement in content as well as technique.[104]

Conflicts over Miracle Cults

In presenting the origins and patterns of development characteristic of nineteenth-century miracle cults, it would be misleading to leave the impression that the process of approving the miracles and the derivative institutions was free from serious discussion and conflict. In fact, such conflicts were typically integrated into the mythological account of the cults' foundation. Cultic leaders and publicists argued that in overcoming sometimes powerful opposition, both inside and outside the Church, the miracle and the institutions that propagated it showed themselves to be the work of God.[105] The study of conflicts from a secular perspective reveals not the hand of God but the balance of power in nineteenth-century religious life, and the ways such power was used to advance or, in some cases, to defeat an incipient cult.

At all stages of a cult's development, it was the parish clergy and the episcopal authorities who were most likely to become antagonists. Episcopal authority increased following the Napoleonic Concordat, as bishops gained increased control over their clergy.[106] Although most Church historians have focused on the administrative aspect of episcopal power, the bishops simultaneously were asserting their spiritual prerogatives. Their judgments on the miraculous received widespread support from

French bishops not involved in the investigations, and even those not personally convinced of the miracles made a point of acknowledging their colleagues' authority.[107] In determining where power resided in the nineteenth century, the issue of miracles reveals that authority in spiritual matters complemented the administrative structure.

Parish clergy never claimed the right to pass judgment on miracles, but they did prove truculent at times about who would control shrines and confraternities, along with their revenues, and about their own liberty to disbelieve in a miracle that had episcopal but not papal approval. The context for such animosity dates at least to the eighteenth century, when parish clergy had a relatively greater degree of independence and were jealous of their prerogatives. Their situation was considerably different in the nineteenth century, for the Napoleonic Concordat had given bishops a much greater degree of control. Consequently, a certain tension between bishops and their clergy was endemic, and led at times to outright opposition of episcopal absolutism.[108] This underlying tension fed the specific conflicts that developed over miracle cults.

In the early stages of miracle cults, it was the parish clergy who were active in their behalf and in two cases, Notre-Dame des Victoires and Notre-Dame de Montligéon, the cults never lost their parochial character. The parish *curés* were able to retain control in these instances because neither cult was based on a major apparition that required an authoritative judgment. The cults began as devotional confraternities and requests for special graces—that is, miracles—developed only after the pious organizations had already been established. After the success they experienced in organizing their confraternities, Abbé Desgenettes of Notre-Dame des Victoires and Abbé Paul Buguet of Notre-Dame de Montligéon began to have difficulties with their respective bishops. After the initial episcopal approval, both cults grew rapidly, and became important sources of revenue. The money that flowed into the parishes was part of a huge market in masses, novenas, and other devotional practices that scandalized Church critics in the last half of the century.[109] Notre-Dame des Victoires was especially affluent, and records in the Parisian archepiscopal archives show revenues from masses rising from 86,738 francs in 1861 to 120,577 francs in 1866. By the 1880s it was estimated that over three hundred thousand francs a year were sent to the parish for masses.[110] The council charged with overseeing the finances of the cult donated a portion of this to the diocese, but by the 1870s the archdiocese was attempting to restructure the council and place it more immediately under the control of the archbishop of Paris. This move, which would have led to a loss of control over much of the shrine's revenue, was strongly resisted by Abbé Dumax, Desgenettes' replacement; but the council was eventually reformed. By the early twentieth century, a vicar of Notre-Dame des Victoires was writing to the diocese to request an increase in his salary. In arguing his case, Abbé Émile Cave has left a description of a pilgrimage site far different from the ones that appeared in devotional literature.

> The church of Notre-Dame des Victoires is absolutely unhealthy. The air there is unbreathable, the atmosphere is close and corrupt, because of the smoke and heat which come from the ceaselessly burning candles, and because of the crowds of visitors who fill the church during the parish's offices and the exercises of the arch-confraternity.[111]

Abbé Cave's remarks reveal a somewhat jaded clerical view of the pilgrims and their activities, but it also shows Notre-Dame des Victoires to be a popular shrine early in the twentieth century, a full sixty years after the initial establishment of the confraternity. Despite some internal bickering, the institutionalization of Notre-Dame des Victoires was carried out successfully by the Church.

Problems similar to those of Notre-Dame des Victoires existed with the cult of Notre-Dame de Montligéon. Bishop Trégaro, of the diocese of Orne, did approve five auxiliary chaplains for the cult, but the prefect of the department noted in a report to his superiors that the bishop "has always had a poor opinion of the work of Abbé Buguet, which was founded and developed outside his influence."[112] In the 1890s, within ten years of the foundation of the confraternity, Notre-Dame de Montligéon was bringing in over one million francs annually, and it is likely that, as in the case of Notre-Dame des Victoires, the bishop was jealous of such revenues.

It was not just money, however, that created the conflicts between parish and episcopal clergy. The issue of spiritual authority accompanied the more worldly problem of an equitable division of cultic revenues. At Notre-Dame de La Salette, one of the earliest issues to cause rancor recalls disputes characteristic of the ancien régime.[113] After his first trip to the site of the apparition the archpriest of Corps, Abbé Mélin, carried the rock on which Mary had sat back to his own church. The new *curé* at La Salette objected to this dispossession of what rightfully belonged to his parish, but Mélin refused to part with his new relic, parts of which he began to distribute. Eventually, the bishop intervened and allowed Mélin to retain part of the rock, but most of it was returned to La Salette.

A more serious conflict was to emerge over the apparition and cult of Notre-Dame de La Salette. For a quarter-century the clergy of the diocese of Grenoble were divided and embittered over episcopal actions on behalf of the cult. The dispute began at the time of the episcopal investigation, when a minority of the commission, composed of parish clergy from Grenoble, objected strenuously to the methods and findings of the majority.[114] They refused, in fact, to go along with the results, and appealed the decision to the Metropolitan, Archbishop de Bonald of Lyons, and ultimately to the pope himself. The intricacies of this conflict, though interesting, are too complicated to pursue here, involving accusations of fraud and disloyalty and differing interpretations of canon law.[115] The dispute is significant because opposition to the episcopal initiatives on the miracle led to a more general resentment of the bishop's authority. In condemning a publication of opposition leader Abbé Déléon, Mgr Philbert de Bruillard of Grenoble summarized the dissident position thus:

> The author abuses episcopal authority throughout; he calls it a power of "simple delegation"; quoting the words of St. Paul (Acts 20:28) he says that a bishop is established to "direct" the Church of God, from which it follows that bishops have only the right to direct, and not a veritable authority and jurisdiction. He has even gone so far as to affirm elsewhere that "the Church has placed the sacred deposit of the faith under the safeguard of the faithful and the priests," as if the master of the Episcopacy, and the Episcopacy with him, had need of this safeguard in order to conserve the faith in an inviolable manner.[116]

The bishops of Grenoble were, on the whole, successful in suppressing the opposition to Notre-Dame de la Salette. Abbé Cartellier, *curé* of St. Joseph's parish in Grenoble and a major figure in the opposition, was forbidden to speak or publish about the cult under threat of interdict. Cartellier was effectively silenced despite the fact that belief in La Salette was not required, and was an option which Catholics could in good faith refuse.[117] While this was asserted even by Abbé Rousselot, the most active proponent of the cult, the right to disbelieve ran counter to the lines of spiritual authority in the Church, in which clergy owed obedience to their ecclesiastical superiors. The principle of authority, in this case, was judged more fundamental than the freedom to dissent publicly. The formal submission of Abbé Cartellier did, however, grant him freedom of conscience. Written by Cardinal de Bonald so as to be acceptable to the *curé*, the statement included an abjuration of all his work, an apology for the trouble he had caused, but also an affirmation that his opinion remained the same: "The facts that are found in my *Mémoire* [Cartellier's published attack on the cult] were reported in good faith; but I disavow and condemn all that is false and inexact, while conserving my opinion on La Salette."[118]

The reasons for Cartellier's opposition are detailed in his manuscript history of the cult, now at the Bibliothèque Municipale of Grenoble. Essentially, the *curé* objected to the apparition on aesthetic and theological grounds, and to the subsequent miraculous healings because they were not sufficiently verified. In addition, Cartellier quotes an adage critical of pilgrimages, "One doesn't become holy by traveling," which suggests that he shared an opinion common among parish clergy: that pilgrims could visit a shrine and expect a lenient confessor, thus detracting from the spiritual and moral authority of the parish priest.[119] The opposition of Déléon and Cartellier to the cult of Notre-Dame de La Salette is clear evidence that questions of religious as well as financial prerogatives were at issue in the conflicts between parish and episcopal clergy.

Events at Lourdes reflect similar tensions, but the *curé* of Lourdes, Abbé Peyramale, was a more formidable opponent than the clergy of Grenoble. Peyramale's resentment of episcopal intervention dated from the arrival of the missionaries in 1866, who were given control over the grotto and its development as a national shrine. In order to compete with the diocesan missionaries Peyramale instituted his own building program, and began work on a grandiose reconstruction of the parish church. Unfortunately for the *curé*, he had trouble raising money, ran deeply into debt, and was sued by the contractors. The debt was accumulated against the specific orders of the bishop of Tarbes and Peyramale died under something of a cloud with his project incomplete. Henri Lasserre, the famous chronicler of the cult, also resented the missionaries, who refused to sell his work at the grotto. In 1878, Lasserre was active in organizing a cult to honor the late *curé*, and went so far as to attribute a miracle to Peyramale's intercession. But Lasserre's attempt to defend his friend with the same method used to legitimize the apparition proved unsuccessful in the face of an official prohibition of the new cult.[120] The history of the cults at La Salette and Lourdes reveals the resentment of episcopal power exercised in the development of the shrines; and it also shows that such opposition was effectively checked by the bishops who succeeeded in gaining control of the institutions designed to propagate the cults.

Episcopal authority over miracles and miracle cults was, for the most part, respected and even encouraged by their colleagues. The publication by Mgr Villecourt, the bishop of La Rochelle, of a work on La Salette was a major incentive to the bishop of Grenoble to move in favor of the cult. Villecourt's correspondence with Philbert de Bruillard was incorporated into the decree approving the miracle. At Lourdes, the commission to investigate the miracles was named in large part as a result of pressure from three bishops who occupied dioceses neighboring Tarbes.[121] The decrees approving the apparitions at Migné, La Salette, Lourdes, and Pontmain were followed by numerous letters in support of these judgments from the bishops of France. There was, however, one major instance of episcopal conflict over a miracle and its cult, the results of which confirm the point that bishops succeeded in checking opposition to their cults in the end. The archbishop of Lyons, Cardinal de Bonald, was suspicious of the apparition at La Salette from the outset, because of the "secrets" received by the shepherds, their lack of personal piety, and the language used by Mary in her public message. Much of Bonald's information was received from Abbé Cartellier, who appealed to the archbishop to support the local opposition.[122] Bonald argued for his right to intervene on the basis of the same session of the Council of Trent used by Philbert de Bruillard to support his claims of authority. Session XXV gave bishops the right to judge miracles, but also gave provincial councils authority in those cases where doubts existed. In a letter to the bishop of Grenoble after the decree of September 1851 had approved the apparition, the archbishop of Lyons made his position clear.

> Monseigneur, I recognize assuredly the right you have to examine a supposedly miraculous fact. But when serious doubts still exist on the truth of this fact, when objections which are not without importance are still raised against this fact, has not the Council of Trent attributed to a provincial council the *right* to examine this fact? I think, Monseigneur, that before pronouncing on La Salette, the provincial council should have taken over this affair and examined it. The Council of Trent gave us this right.[123]

In the same letter the archbishop told his colleague that he intended to raise the question on a trip to Rome. This appeal to the pope to back up his claim of authority was, however, unsuccessful. Bonald had demanded a copy of the famous secrets to take to Rome with him, but Philbert de Bruillard circumvented this plan by sending them directly to Rome, where they were read personally by Pius IX.[124] This policy of going over the head of the Metropolitan and appealing directly to Rome continued to be applied successfully. Rome was careful all the while to stop short of affirming the apparition, and even led Bonald and other bishops opposed to the miracle to believe that their position was favored. At the same time, however, Rome agreed that the bishop of Grenoble had the right to publish his decree and granted a variety of indulgences to the new cult.[125]

Cardinal de Bonald's final act in the conflict was to publish a circular addressed to his clergy on August 6, 1852, which, while not making any explicit reference to La Salette, clearly directed itself at the cult.

> We prohibit preaching, without our permission, on any miraculous fact, even when its authenticity is attested by another bishop. This authorization will be given only having consulted the sovereign pontiff, and having received from him a statement guaranteeing the truth of the miracle. In two or three of our parishes, *curés* have believed they could read from the pulpit the decree of a bishop from another diocese on the subject of a miracle, without having consulted us: this is an irregular act.[126]

Despite Bonald's opposition, the decree approving the cult was allowed to stand, and the archbishop never felt his position strong enough to do more than discourage the devotion in his own diocese. Of all the cults established in the nineteenth century, only Notre-Dame de La Salette led to an episcopal conflict. During the 1860s, the bishop of Reims still felt strongly enough about the cult to suggest at a provincial council that disbelief was entirely acceptable. This annoyed some of the diocesan officials of Grenoble, who remained sensitive about the miracle and believed that the controversy had restrained its development.[127]

The parallels between the cults of Notre-Dame de La Salette and Notre-Dame de Lourdes are evident. Both resulted from apparitions to shepherd children by the Virgin, who gave them a public message; both benefited from the miraculous appearance of fountains with thaumaturgic powers; and both were approved and promoted by the episcopal authorities. But for all their similarities, it was Lourdes that came to hold first place in public affection, and by the last third of the century served as an unofficial but widely acknowledged national shrine. To some extent the success of Lourdes was due to fortuitous circumstances. As a market city and then a railroad center, Lourdes had decided advantages over the isolated hamlet in the Alps. Furthermore, the criticisms leveled at La Salette could not, to a large extent, be applied to Lourdes. No one, not even religious skeptics, doubted Bernadette's sincerity and piety, and the Virgin's message to her contained no specific prophecies whose language could be criticized and fulfillment questioned. Finally, the handling of the Lourdes miracles by the episcopal authorities was much more circumspect than of the La Salette ones. At Lourdes, the clergy studiously avoided the grotto until the official investigation had already begun, and no Mass was said there until well after the apparition and cures had been declared genuine miracles. At La Salette, the indiscrete activity of both parish and episcopal clergy raised more questions about the possibility of clerical conspiracy, and this helped compromise the cult. Finally, perhaps in part because of the circumstances just described, Lourdes developed no opposition among the episcopal hierarchy. With hindsight, it appears that La Salette was a first attempt, a test case used by Lourdes to the advantage of the later cult. I do not mean to suggest that a Churchwide conspiracy was formed to create a national Marian cult which, having failed at La Salette, succeeded at Lourdes. But the investigators at Lourdes were highly conscious of the La Salette precedent,[128] and the controversy it sparked had assumed national significance by the 1850s and 1860s. When the histories of the two cults are compared, it appears that the French bishops had learned from the embarrassment that attended the disputes at La Salette, and applied their experience to the cult at Lourdes.

Church–State Conflict

Conflicts over the new miracle cults were not limited to the Church hierarchy. The structure of Church–State relations that bound these institutions together led at times to serious clashes over who had ultimate control over the shrines which were the basis for most cults. During the first half of the century conflicts were rare, but they became a common part of the cults' development under the Second Empire and the Third Republic. In the case of La Salette, the State attempted to control the spread of unauthorized literature, and also expressed concern over the crowds gathering at the shrine. On the whole, however, the cult of La Salette was free to develop in the 1840s, although problems did emerge later.[129] Under certain circumstances the State even supported the miraculous. During the Restoration, a deputy published a letter in support of the apparition at Migné, which was seen by him as a sign of divine support for the Bourbon regime.[130]

More surprisingly, during the Second Republic a subprefect became the most active proponent of the miracles of Rosette Tamisier. M. Grave went so far as to declare that as a representative of the State he had the authority to approve miracles, and came into open conflict with the bishop of Avignon as a result.[131] The bishop acted quickly and effectively to suppress the cult that was forming at the site of Rosette's miracle, which consisted of a picture of Christ that bled following her solitary prayers before it. M. Grave was soon dismissed, and Rosette was convicted of fraud. Although no cult was formed and no major clash between Church and State developed, the incident does demonstrate the potential conflicts of interest over miracles that were to come into play during this period.

The earliest and most famous case of State opposition to a miracle occurred at Lourdes during the first few months of the cult. Within a week of the first apparition Jacomet, the police commissioner of Lourdes, was actively involved in observing Bernadette and the events at the grotto. On February 21, 1858, he interviewed the visionary and forbade her to continue making daily visits to the new shrine. Jacomet's motives, expressed in the numerous reports he filed with the prefect of the Hautes-Pyrénées, were a concern for public order, a belief that the crowds at the grotto constituted a public nuisance, and their use of the fountain a health hazard.[132] The prefect, Baron Massy, also seems to have been interested primarily in maintaining social order and avoiding a public disturbance, even if there was no overt threat of violence or open expression of political discontent.[133] Massy's superiors at the cabinet level shared his concerns, and the Minister of Cults, Gustave Rouland, became involved in the case. The conflict that developed over the new shrine occurred at a time when relations between the prefect and Mgr Laurence, the bishop of Tarbes, were already marred by a dispute over the government's decision to build official stables on a lot next to the diocesan cathedral.[134] The animosity that resulted from this decision carried over into the question of Lourdes, and may have contributed to Massy's intransigence concerning the grotto.

In early May of 1858 the decision was reached, after a visit by Massy to

Paris, to remove all of the religious objects from the grotto. A month later, this measure having failed to stem the crowds of pilgrims who continued to visit the shrine, the mayor of Lourdes, acting on orders from the prefect, attempted to close the grotto.[135] The law which served as the basis for this action stated that government approval was required for all places of public worship. Unfortunately for Massy, the attempt to close the grotto failed to end the cult. People either violated the prohibition and ran the risk of a five-franc fine, or prayed instead at the barrier. In late July, the governess of the imperial prince violated the interdict and visited the shrine. Not long after this the grotto was again opened for public worship following a direct order from the emperor. Not all of the documents necessary to determine just how this decision to end the policy of obstruction was reached are available. It is possible that the piety of Empress Eugénie had something to do with Napolean III's action, and the archbishop of Auch, Mgr de Salinis, has also been considered influential.[136] But a more fundamental reason for the reversal was the combination of continued popular support and the clergy's shift from neutrality to advocacy of the cult. The crowds continued to come despite the interdict, and the prosecution of the local devotees while important visitors such as the prince's governess went free was potentially embarrassing. Furthermore, while the barriers blocking access to the grotto were destroyed at night on several occasions, there was never any overt action against the civil authorities. Only the opposition to the cult created any threat of public disorder. The attitudes of the local clergy had by May already shifted in favor of the cult, and Mgr Laurence felt compelled to write the *curé* of Lourdes on May 9 that he respected the prefect's interpretation concerning the grotto.[137] Just one month later, however, the bishop wrote as follows to his *curé:*

> As far as I am concerned I see nothing dangerous for the public order in the fact that people drink and carry away water from the new fountain of the Grotto. I have had nothing to do with the measures taken, up to the present, relative to the Grotto, and will have nothing to do with those that may yet be announced. The time will come when the ecclesiastical authority will be able to concern itself in this affair.[138]

The administration's intervention at Lourdes was withdrawn because of popular and clerical support of the cult. Where this combination did not exist, the State was more effective in suppressing new cults. The heretical

Eugéne Vintras was successfully prosecuted, as was Rosette Tamisier. In both cases the miracles that were the basis for the cults were used by the State to establish the fact that a fraud had been committed. Despite the combined opposition of Church and State, these cults did have a marginal existence, and the Vintras sect managed to survive until the end of the century.[139] But the State was generally successful in discrediting miracle cults that failed to win the Church's support.

The courts also became involved in the miracles of La Salette and Lourdes, but unlike the prosecutions of Vintras and Tamisier, their work in these cases did not suppress the cults, although they may have done some damage. The most famous trial involved Mlle Lamerlière's suit brought against the clerical opposition to the devotion of La Salette. The clergymen in question, Abbés Déléon and Cartellier, had published an attack on the cult in which they argued that the role of the Virgin had been played by Mlle Lamerlière, a woman from a family of local notables who was noted for her fanatical piety and public proselytism.[140] The suit charged the authors with damage to Mlle Lamerlière's character, and claimed damages of twenty thousand francs. The civil tribunal of Grenoble, in May of 1855, declared that no damages should be rewarded, and their decision was filled with favorable references to the authors, whose only concern was for the "truth."[141] At the time the suit's failure was a clear victory for the opposition, and contributed to the controversy that cut into the cult's popularity.

At Lourdes, the involvement of the court system with the cult was more direct. The public prosecutor stationed at Lourdes, M. Dutour, was ideologically opposed to the wave of superstition he observed, and his reports to the Minister of Justice circulated at the cabinet level and contributed to the decision to close the grotto.[142] In May of 1858, while Baron Massy was attemping to control the pilgrims who came to the shrine, Dutour was responsible for prosecuting those who spread "false rumors" about the cult. A successful prosecution was brought against a book peddler who claimed that the money confiscated by the government was being used to subsidize black masses.[143] But this initial success was followed by an important set of failures. Dutour claimed that three women of Lourdes had circulated rumors that the Emperor had written to Bernadette asking for prayers, and the prosecutor hoped that a conviction would check these and other stories about the cult. The tribunal at Lourdes, however, ruled in favor of two of the defendants. Dutour appealed the acquittals to the court at Pau, which upheld the lower court's verdict and overturned the only conviction.[144] Throughout the summer of 1858 popular support for the cult in Lourdes had continued to manifest itself, as the barriers blocking the path to the grotto were destroyed and the interdict violated. The acquittal of the women accused by Dutour added to the popular enthusiasm, and their return from Pau on July 16 was greeted with a public celebration.[145] The refusal of the judicial system to convict the women who had spread rumors favorable to the cult was a blow to Massy's and Dutour's plans to suppress the devotion. The decision also shows how Lourdes benefited from a disagreement between the executive and judicial branches of the government. The rumors themselves show that popular feelings were not at all directed against the emperor, but in fact looked to Napoleon III to intervene on behalf of the grotto. That Napoleon did make a personal decision to end the policy of administrative opposition can thus be interpreted as both a shrewd public relations move and a surrender in the face of popular and ecclesiastical pressure.

The development of state opposition to miracle cults during the Second Empire was motivated by a combination of ideological and administrative concerns. The court decisions in the cases of Vintras, Rosette Tamisier, and Mlle de Lamerlière advocated a skeptical attitude about miracles and either stated or implied that the supernatural events in question were, in fact, the result of human fraud. The administrative action at Lourdes was also motivated in part by a desire to eliminate "superstition" from true religion. The major concern of the prefect and his subordinates, however, was the maintenance of public order, the prevention of crowds meeting spontaneously at the shrine. When it was sufficiently clear that the crowds posed no threat to authority, and would be supported and to some extent controlled by the Church, the cult was allowed to develop.

During the early years of the Third Republic, when the monarchists controlled the Assembly, there was no sign of State opposition to any of the nineteenth-century cults. Immediately following the republican electoral successes after the *seize mai* of 1877, however, pressures began to be applied to the cults through a series of administrative and legal measures. Administratively, action was taken to restrain communications between Rome and the French bishops regarding the shrines. The Organic Articles attached to the Concordat by Napoleon I required that all communications from Rome be cleared by the Council of State before they could be passed to the episcopacy. During the Second Empire this article had been interpreted as applying only to administrative matters, and not to communications on questions of doctrine or piety. In 1879 the bishop of Grenoble was censured by the Council of State for receiving and publishing the papal permission to crown the statue of Notre-Dame de La Salette. Four years later, a similar measure was taken after a letter from Leo XIII in honor of the silver anniversary of Lourdes was published without prior registration by the Council. The Minister of Cults, in reporting the censure to the prefect of the Hautes-Pyrénées, revealed the government's antipathy toward the Lourdes cult.

> This infraction . . . is of great importance, in that the said document has for its end the confirmation of the existence of a place of cult not authorized by the government; opened contrary to the legal dispositions which regulate the public exercise of the Catholic cult in France, and served by members of a congregation not officially recognized.[146]

Administrative action designed to establish state authority over religious cults was accompanied by the observation of pilgrimages, which were suspected of being political as well as religious manifestations. A file in the Archives Nationales contains several reports from government observers and newspaper clippings on Catholic organizations that made collective pilgrimages, especially in the 1890s.[147] The numbers of pilgrims, their social composition, and any political statements made during the pilgrimage were among the subjects treated in these reports. The suspicion of shrines was part of a more general fear of the religious orders that staffed them; the law of associations in 1902 expelling the religious orders from France initiated a period during which miraculous shrines were seriously threatened by the State. At the time the law was being passed and applied, Jean de Bonnefon, the Parisian editor of *Le Journal* and an intimate of leading republican anticlericals, was a major spokesman advocating a rigorous application of the law in the case of miraculous shrines, especially Lourdes.[148] But despite such public antipathy toward the orders and the pressure for closing the shrines, none of the miracle cults was abolished.

The survival of the miracle cults can be attributed to at least three factors. The first of these was the accommodating attitude taken by the French Church toward the new laws. This spirit of conciliation can be observed in the exchanges between the archbishop of Paris and the Minister of Cults during the first conflict over a shrine in the Third Republic. The bishop of Grenoble insisted on the right of a French bishop to receive communications from the pope without registration by the Council of State, and was intransigent in defending himself concerning the papal brief which approved the crowning of Notre-Dame de La Salette in 1879.[149] Mgr Guibert, the archbishop of Paris at the time, acted to quiet the fears of the government and keep the peace between Church and State. After corresponding with the bishop of Grenoble, Mgr Paulinier, he was able to assure the government that in the future the prelate would comply with the Concordat and that, furthermore, no criticism of the government would be permitted at the crowning. The prefect who was present at the ceremony confirmed that the clergy and pilgrims at La Salette limited themselves to their devotions and did not engage in any political activity.[150]

The conciliatory attitude of the French episcopacy was also evident at the time the laws on associations and the separation of Church and State were passed. Maurice Larkin has shown that most French bishops believed that cooperation with the civil authorities was still possible even after the disestablishment of the Church in 1905.[151] Papal policy made such cooperation difficult, but many bishops did manage to comply peacefully with the abolition of the orders and the inventories of Church property. At La Salette, Lourdes, and Pontmain, diocesan clergy replaced the orders that had formerly served the pilgrims. At Lourdes, the prefect of the Hautes-Pyrénées reported that the bishop had been especially cooperative in eliminating politics from the pilgrimage. Describing the national pilgrimage of 1902, which had in previous years been a showpiece for the Assumptionists, the prefect wrote: "The pilgrimage produced no incident worthy of attention. The pilgrims surrendered themselves to the usual religious manifestations without troubling the public order for a single instant, and without producing the least disorder."[152] In April of 1903 the bishop of Tarbes reported to the Minister of Cults on the status of the missionaries of Notre-Dame de Lourdes. After the dissolution of the order, fifteen of the twenty missionaries continued to serve the shrine as ordinary diocesan clergy. This policy was defended by pointing out that the criticisms most often made of the orders did not apply in this case. The priests at Lourdes were, for the most part, trained at the major seminary of Tarbes and not at Rome, and lived amicably with the parish clergy. Any refusal by the State to allow them to continue to work at the shrine would amount to a suppression of the pilgrimage.[153] In a letter to the prefect Mgr Schoepfer, bishop of Lourdes, emphasized his respect for the government and his intention to comply with the law.[154] This willingness to cooperate with the State continued in the period following the law of separation in 1905. Mgr Schoepfer issued a public protest against the inventory of ecclesiastical property conducted at Lourdes on January 26, 1906; but he allowed two representatives from the diocese to accompany and observe the government agents who were charged with this task and forbade any public demonstration that might have led to violence. The agents themselves were sympathetic and respectful, and even agreed to suspend their work on February 2, the Feast of the Purification.[155] Within five years of the separation all of the property attached to the shrine and confiscated by the State was returned to the bishop of Lourdes. In 1910, after the State ceded to the city of Lourdes most of the land and buildings, including the Basilica and the grotto, the city council immediately resolved to allow the bishop to control the shrine without any interference from the city.[156] The moderate attitude of Bishop Schoepfer helped defuse the anticlerical campaign directed against Lourdes and other shrines. By agreeing to comply peacefully, though under protest, with the laws of association and separation, he worked toward the depoliticization of the pilgrimage. The State, in the face of this effort to obey the law, was willing to tolerate the continued operation of the shrine.

A second factor which accounts for the survival of the shrines was their favorable and sometimes crucial impact on the economy of the area. The Minister of the Interior in 1895 had requested information on the cult of Notre-Dame de Montligéon in the department of Orne, suspecting its founder of political activity. The prefect's response amounted to a vigorous defense of the *curé* in question, Paul Buguet. The main argument in Buguet's favor was his important contribution to the economic development of the region. More than one million francs a year were received at Montligéon as a result of the abbé's concern for the souls in purgatory, and much of this money went toward the construction of a new post office, new waterworks, and a road linking Montligéon to the nearest railroad station at Mauves-Corbon. Future projects included an electric tramway between the two communities. Furthermore, Abbé Buguet had built the most modern printing press in the department. "This factory is provided with the most modern improvements, electric lighting, telephone, etc. . . ." Any action against Buguet would be dangerous, because "he has rendered to this little town and to the region services which cannot be underestimated."[157]

At La Salette, Lourdes, and Pontmain economic arguments were used to oppose abolishing the pilgrimages during the Church–State crisis preceding the 1905 law of separation. Ferri Pisani's pamphlet, *Il ne faut pas fermer Lourdes*, published at Paris in 1906, stressed the dependence of the region on the income generated by the pilgrims. The *syndicat d'hôteliers*, the *cercle de commerce* of Tarbes, and mayors from the villages surrounding Lourdes all testified to their reliance on the tourist trade drawn to the grotto. In 1904 a delegation from the *syndicat d'initiative* founded the year before visited Combes to plead the case of Lourdes, and the Municipal Council of the city passed a resolution in April of 1903 asking that the Basilica not be closed, and pointing out past actions of the State which had helped the pilgrimage. The transfer of the shrine to the bishop by the city council in 1910 was justified by Mayor Lacaze as necessary for the economic interests of Lourdes and the region.[158] Similar evidence of local concern about the economic impact of state suppression exists for Corps, the city that served the shrine at La Salette, and Pontmain.[159] The willingness of the government to tolerate the continued residence of diocesan priests at shrines, even when an argument could be made that they constituted an illegal association, was thus due in part to the knowledge of the economic significance of the pilgrimages.

A third factor in the government's laissez-faire policy on miracle shrines was the continued evidence of popular support for the pilgrimages. Although Pius X and his Assumptionist advisors were mistaken in their belief that the separation law of 1905 would result in massive resistance, several disturbances did occur at the time of the official inventories of Church possessions, causing the government to alter its policy.[160] In several cases manifestations of popular opposition to separation occurred in communities near pilgrimage shrines.[161] In the years following the separation, there was some public pressure to close Lourdes as a health hazard. The fact that crowds continued to visit the shrine and the fear that such action might incite a disturbance helped protect Lourdes. As Ferri Pisani wrote, the government had to take into account the political implications of its policy for religious-minded peasants as well as freethinkers. "As for the so-called reactionary peril for the Republic which results from pilgrimages, take care rather that a clumsy decree does not alienate an entire region from the republican idea."[162]

The separation of Church and State in France was interpreted by many clergymen as a blow to the status of the Church and the religious life of the nation. One consequence of the law, however, was the termination of State concern with shrines and miracle cults. The administration and the courts, which had moved at various times against the cults since the 1850s, now left them alone. It is beyond the scope of this chapter to pursue their history into the twentieth century, and evaluate the impact of the separation on the miracle cults. The institutions constructed by the Church for the new devotions have, however, survived to the present day. Evidence from Lourdes suggests that while Vatican II has had some impact on its style, the pilgrimage still continues to grow in popularity.[163] The issue of whether visitors to Lourdes are "pilgrims" or "tourists" has been raised by Alphonse Dupront but, as he points out, the question can just as easily be asked of those who came to Lourdes in the 1860s and 1870s when the shrine first began to draw a national clientele.[164] The patterns of contemporary Catholic piety can, in many cases, be traced to the nineteenth century, when French miracle cults experienced a period of extraordinary fecundity.

Chapter 7
Miracles and Modernity

N
ear the end of the nineteenth century the Catholic publicist
Arthur Loth published a volume summarizing the numerous
miraculous blessings recently bestowed on France. In the
opening pages of his introduction Loth expressed his antipathy toward the modern world, which he viewed as inherently hostile to
religion.

> The faith in our epoch is experiencing a true crisis; everything
> seems turned against it. The deepest study of nature and its laws,
> the progress of the sciences, new inventions, social organization it-
> self, foreign or hostile to religion, all conspire to destroy the
> faith. . . . The marvels which our century witnesses have been able
> to make men believe that God is useless, and that there are no other
> dogmas than the truth science teaches, no other mysteries than those
> that it discovers, no other miracles than those it works itself![1]

Loth's resentment of the modern world is clearly based on an appreciation
of its intellectual and technological achievements. What angered and
frightened him was the implication that these achievements had made God
"useless." The conviction that social, economic, and intellectual change
undermined religious belief suggested to him a relationship between
modernity and Satan.

> Industry was developing rapidly, with a new ardor for gain, and
> was making society enter into the course of modern civilization.
> Mechanical inventions were beginning to change working con-
> ditions; railroads were going to transform public life. A new world
> of ideas, habits, needs, was forming outside of God. It was the
> work of the Revolution which was going to fulfill itself in the social

order through the invisible action of the devil, the eternal enemy of Jesus Christ.[2]

Loth did not dispute the material success of science and industry, which was evident by the end of the nineteenth century. But because the industrial revolution undermined organized religion he associated it with the Revolution of 1789, the archvillain whose persecution of Christianity was both a symbol and a cause of all subsequent attacks against the Church. Both the original Revolution and its industrial successor were part of a single campaign planned and carried out by Satan in his battle with Christ and the Church. In responding to this attack God's chosen weapons were miracles and prophecies. Miracles were able to counter the achievements of the modern world by forcibly reminding men of God's omnipotence.

> God, however, has not abandoned man to the fascination of science and the sophistication of free-thought. Far from withdrawing from the world, leaving it in the shadows of error, he has on the contrary revealed himself in a tangible manner. . . . In this test of faith God has given extraordinary testimony of his power. He has made himself ever more visible even as science attempted to make him disappear from the sight of men. He has multiplied the supernatural signs. . . . Yes, it has pleased God to manifest himself in a particular manner in these times, in order to equal by the burst of revelation from on high the audacity of the negations of skepticism.[3]

Arthur Loth dealt with his fear that God had been made superfluous in the modern world by an assertion of faith in the authority and power of the Catholic Church. Miracles at Migné, La Salette, Lourdes, Ars, Pontmain, and elsewhere were the clearest evidence he could find in support of his faith. Loth's position can be taken as representative of French Catholicism for, despite some attempts to check abuses, by the end of the nineteenth century a set of new miracle cults had been fully integrated into the life of the Church.

The militant promotion of miracles by the Church in the nineteenth century is part of the long history of the relationship between popular and official Christianity. In the later days of the Roman Empire, when Christianity was first introduced to northern Europe, the cult of the saints propagated by the Church came into conflict with pagan beliefs about healing. Relics distributed by ecclesiastical authorities fixed miraculous power in specific locations that were monitored by the clergy. The Church used relics to encourage a commitment to the saints modeled on the personal relations that bound together the Roman urban aristocracy. But the cult of the saints never entirely effaced the older pagan belief that miraculous healing powers were diffused throughout the environment, and that these could be controlled by magical incantations that did not require a personal relationship with "invisible friends."⁴ The cult of saints became an integral part of the ordinary people's religion, but such bishops as Gregory of Tours battled constantly and not always successfully to insure that an attitude of reverence accompanied the use of relics and shrines.

The tension between popular and official Christianity continued throughout the Middle Ages, but the tales of Boccaccio and Chaucer suggest that members of the clergy at times shared in and cultivated popular credulity about miraculous occurrences.⁵ In the sixteenth century Erasmus criticized "those who think there is nothing they cannot obtain by relying on the magical prayers and charms thought up by some charlatan." The cult of saints was singled out as especially subject to abuse, for it encouraged people to seek material rather than spiritual benefits, and to rely on external ritual rather than internal conversion. The clergy was partly responsible for such practices, because "they know it brings in much profit."⁶

The Council of Trent responded to criticisms like those of Erasmus by coupling a clear affirmation of the power of the saints with a call to suppress those superstitions that detracted from the clerical control of the supernatural.⁷ Some recent scholars have asserted that between the sixteenth and eighteenth centuries the Church played a major role in repressing popular culture and encouraging "the triumph of Lent."⁸ According to this view a spontaneous and independent cultural world that included superstitious beliefs and practices was gradually eliminated and replaced by a homogeneous mass culture controlled by a bourgeois elite that included the clergy. According to Robert Muchembled, in the post-Tridentine era the clergy saw as one of their principle tasks "to prevent their flock from crying miracle too easily."⁹ The success of the repressive activity begun during the Counterreformation can be disputed. The evidence that Church and State cooperated in constructing a harsh system of social control comprises mostly publications and prosecutions directed against superstitions that attest to their survival throughout this period.

But whether or not the battle against superstition was successful, there is little doubt that the Church was anxious to control popular religious attitudes that viewed the world as constantly subjected to supernatural intervention.

In the nineteenth century the Church, while it did not abandon its desire to shape a laity familiar with doctrine and submissive to ecclesiastical authority, showed an increased receptivity to miracles and prophecies. This shift was based on a new sense of what was necessary in order for the Church to fulfill its pastoral mission. Abbé Lecanu, in his introduction to the *Dictionnaire des prophéties et des miracles*, argued that although a few individuals might come to believe in God and the authority of the Church on the basis of rational inquiry, most had to rely on more direct evidence of God's existence and power.

> If man is condemned to discover God only on the strength of his intelligence, who will know Him? Studious men and those with strong intellects; and what will happen to the rest of humanity? No, this cannot be allowed; God has had to manifest Himself, to reveal Himself and God cannot reveal Himself without miracles.[10]

In his book on Purgatory, the prominent Jesuit author Fr. Schouppe published a collection of visions and apparitions, most of which had never been officially verified by the Church. Schouppe defended the publicity he gave to such miracles by pointing out the spiritual benefits they could produce, and he attacked those who sought to apply rigorous critical standards to such tales.

> The theologian who expounds dogmas of faith must be severe in the choice of his proofs; the historian must proceed with rigorous circumspection in the narration of facts, but the ascetic writer, who cites examples to illustrate truths and edify the faithful, is not held to this strict rigour. The best authorised persons in the church . . . when writing their excellent works knew nothing of the fastidious requirements of the present day—requirements that in nowise constitute progress.[11]

Two British ministers who visited France in the nineteenth and early twentieth centuries had vivid experiences of clerical toleration and encouragement of popular religiosity. Thomas William Allies, who traveled in France in 1845, was constantly confronted with evidence of contemporary miracles. After reading at the Calvary of Mont Valérien in Paris an inscription asserting that Mary had the power to work miracles, Allies asked Abbé Ratisbonne for an explanation. "We are children of God," Ratisbonne replied, "we speak to him as children, not as wise men, and ask the indulgence given to children."[12] Clerical approbation of popular belief in miracles was even more apparent to the Reverend Samuel Levermore, who set out to evangelize France in the early twentieth century by handing out tracts and preaching the worship of Christ. Levermore's attacks on the cult of saints won him no converts, however, and his failure was most conspicuous at Lourdes "this seat of Satan . . . this awful orgie of idolatry." Urged on by the clergy a crowd seized Levermore, who reports that he was saved only by the intervention of the Chief of Police, who "told us that it was a miracle we were not killed."[13] This remark may have been either irony or exaggeration, but Levermore's troubles at Lourdes confirm what we have seen throughout this book, that the desire for frequent miraculous intervention was accepted and channeled by the Church in the nineteenth century. Why did the Church modify its position toward popular religiosity, and what were the consequences of this for popular and institutional religion?

Miracles and prophecies were viewed sympathetically because the Church saw them as useful weapons in its attempt to adjust to challenges posed by the modern world. They provided evidence to defend Catholic positions and were the basis of institutions that sought to counter the political, intellectual, and social changes that threatened French attachment to the Church.

The political threat was first posed by the Revolution and haunted the Church for the rest of the century. The State had shown itself prepared to close down churches, expel and even execute clergy, and ban Catholic services. The relief that followed the Napoleonic Concordat of 1801 was qualified by the memory of the Revolution and the increasing intervention of the State in areas of life formerly controlled by the Church. This tendency represents one aspect of the trend toward secularization, which Peter Berger has defined as "the process by which sections of society and culture are removed from the domination of religious institutions and symbols."[14] Leaving symbols aside for the present, the history of education and family law in France presents clear evidence of secularization throughout the century.[15]

In the world of ideas the Church was also on the defensive. As Loth's position makes clear, Catholics feared that the achievements of science would discredit the Church's authority. According to Auguste Comte, theological and metaphysical explanations of the world were characteristic of the early stages of man's history, and were to be replaced by the rigorous application of scientific methodology to all social and intellectual problems. Later positivists such as Paul Bert insisted that everything that happened in the world could be explained by scientific investigations that would yield invariable natural laws. Religious education that stressed man's reliance on God encouraged "inaction, inertia, and superstition."[16] Only an education that cultivated the scientific spirit could lead men to act with confidence in their own power, and achieve personal and social progress. Perhaps even more serious than the attack on the supernatural mounted by positivism were the attempts to understand the Bible as the product of authors not favored with divine revelation. The harsh reaction of the Church to the works of Ernest Renan and Alfred Loisy provides a good example of how apprehensive the Church was of attempts to incorporate the techniques of modern Biblical criticism into Catholic teachings on scripture.[17]

Finally, the social order of France was undergoing major changes in the nineteenth century. Rural migration, industrialization, urbanization, politicization, and the development of mass literacy are among the forces that led to what social scientists have termed "modernization." Different indicators follow different patterns of development, but the demographic, economic, and political evidence gathered by historians makes it clear that the fabric of social life was disrupted in nineteenth-century France. As a result of the changes occurring in France the Church had to develop pastoral methods that could appeal to a more mobile, urban, literate, and politically conscious laity—challenges that it had trouble meeting.[18]

The modernization of France had a major impact on religious behavior. Attendance at Sunday Mass and the reception of Easter Communion fell dramatically, especially in urban areas. Clerical assessments of religious indifference and the corruption of manners were common.[19] There was some counter evidence, however, that suggested a core of religious vitality. In shaping its response to the religious crisis the Church drew on these hopeful signs. Among them were the continued use of religious symbol and ritual to deal with individual and collective crises. The onset of modernity relieved the more extreme problems of economic scarcity, but it has been seen that individual illness, natural disaster, and political disorder could still create severe anxieties amenable to the consolations of religion. Religious ritual and symbol were called on in the case of individual illnesses to create a sense of social solidarity between the sick and their communities. Regardless of how one judges the causes of miraculous healings, they are clear evidence of the ability of religion to mobilize community support for individuals threatened by sickness or death. Similarly, religious ritual was called on in times of natural disaster as a way to deal with threats to collective existence. The popularity of prophecies illustrates another social-psychological function of religion. By placing current events within a framework of traditional Christian eschatology, prophecies were able to explain and justify political and social disorder as a result of moral decadence and religious indifference. After describing the expiatory chastisements, prophecies assured their readers of a future in which France would recover her position as the wealthiest and most powerful state in the world. Miracles and prophecies in modern France were thus essential to the ability of religion to fulfill its basic social functions.

There is, of course, a large body of scholarship that has addressed the question of the way religious movements respond to critical social situations. The study of millennialism by historians of earlier centuries and other cultures is perhaps the leading example of how scholars have dealt with the question of how religion responds to social change.[20] Historians of modern France have generally emphasized the decline in religiosity that accompanied the changes of the past two centuries. Recently Eugen Weber has reminded us that traditional modes of life and thought, including superstitious religious practices, survived to the end of the nineteenth century in France. But even Weber argues that modernization led to the gradual disappearance of traditional religion.[21] It is somewhat puzzling that the forces of "modernization" seen as producing outbursts of religious enthusiasm in other centuries and cultures are generally seen to have no similar consequences for the nineteenth century.[22] The number, significance, and visibility of miracle cults and prophetic movements in France, with Lourdes as the leading example, suggest that our understanding of France's modernization must be revised. The political, intellectual, and social changes of the nineteenth century were accompanied by and related to alterations in religious life that can be observed in the miracles and prophecies of that era.

Popular beliefs and customs survived throughout the nineteenth century, but this was not only because they were part of a traditional world that continued to exist at the periphery of a more modern France. Examples from other cultures illustrate how traditional religious beliefs can be adapted to the modern world. The conviction held by many in contemporary America that the salvation of the world is imminent through the intercession of beings from outer space (what one writer has called "the religion of UFOlogy") combines traditional Christian eschatology with a modern faith in the unlimited possibilities of scientific progress.[23] The modernization of Indonesia in the nineteenth century led to a fundamentalist revival and a resurgence of interest in the pilgrimage to Mecca.[24] In Brazil a miracle cult that began in the late nineteenth century formed the basis for the economic development and political organization of an entire region.[25] The examples suggest that miracles and prophecies might best be viewed not as vestiges of traditional society, but as part of the process through which Frenchmen dealt with modernity.

In the sphere of politics prophecies recalled France's past religious glory as the leader of the Catholic world and looked forward to a millennium in which the Roman pope and French king would cooperate in ruling a world empire. The prophetic movement thus bears comparison with the millennial movements of previous centuries. The future it promised was clearly intended to counter the radical disorder experienced as a result of the political and social upheavals of modern France. The pilgrimage movement and prophetic revival that followed the loss of the Franco–Prussian War are the best examples of a response akin to millennialism in the face of a modern political and social crisis.

The confraternities that were the permanent organizations of many miracle cults offer further evidence of the political potential of traditional religious ideals. Even though confraternities claimed to have no explicit political program they did call on a national audience for support of the Catholic Church in defense of its spiritual and temporal prerogatives. In addition, the miraculous shrines themselves became centers at which political statements could be made. A conscious effort was made at times to avoid the association of the shrines with an overtly partisan position. But even when such efforts were successful, a nationalistic pride, in which Catholicism and France were seen as inextricably entwined, was constantly evoked. Whether or not they were used to promote specific causes such as Bourbon royalism or the restoration of the pope's temporal domain, miracle cults assisted in the development of a mass movement of conservative, religious nationalism. When Ted Margadant writes of modernization as entailing "a basic shift from local to national symbols of group identity" he has in mind the formation of a democratic political ideology, which emerged following the revolution of 1848.[26] But the development of confraternities and shrines shows that conservative political forces, with the help of the Catholic Church, were also capable of creating a constituency in the modern world. The royalism of the 1870s and the anti-Semitism of the late nineteenth century were the most visible manifestations of conservative nationalism. But these climactic expressions were possible in part because nationalism had been a well-established theme in the devotional and prophetic literature that had circulated throughout the century.

From an intellectual perspective belief in miracles became for the Church a crucial test of orthodoxy. The antimodernist oath extracted from the clergy suspected of heterodoxy at the start of the twentieth century included this passage: "I admit and recognize as certain signs of the divine origin of the Christian religion the external arguments of revelation, and principally of miracles and prophecies; I consider them as highly appropriate to the intelligence of men at all times, even of the current period."[27] Miracles were also used to refute those who claimed that science alone could explain all phenomena, making God an unnecessary hypothesis. There is a revealing irony, however, in the way in which miracles were used to verify the claims of the supernatural. At the Lourdes Bureau of Medical Confirmation Catholic doctors made an attempt to be scientific in their collection and evaluation of evidence on miraculous cures. Investigators of miracles at Lourdes and elsewhere sought to exclude the possibility of a natural explanation for miracles, implying that there was a clear distinction in their minds between nature and the supernatural.[28] The state of scientific knowledge determined where the boundary between these two worlds would be drawn. This rational approach to miracles was distinct from the understanding of the supernatural held by the common people. In the world of popular religion the distinction between nature and the supernatural was less distinct, if it existed at all. Miracles and prophecies were the response of God to immediate needs, and not evidence in a polemic between religion and positivism. The position of Catholic intellectuals resembles the reaction of those Moslems described by Clifford Geertz who maintain their faith in the face of modernity's challenges.

What is believed to be true has not changed for these people, or not changed very much. What has changed is the way in which it is believed. Where there once was faith there are now reasons, and not very convincing ones: what once were deliverances are now hypotheses, and rather strained ones.[29]

Miracles were among the important reasons for belief adopted by intellectuals. The need that Catholics like Arthur Loth and Louis Veuillot felt to use miraculous facts to "prove" Catholicism suggests a sense of insecurity about their faith.

Social life is the most complex area in which miracles and prophecies can be seen as a response to the threats posed by the modern world to religion. This is because they were capable of symbolizing an ideal relationship between God and man while also serving as the basis for cults designed to establish that relationship. The survival of belief in miracles in the French countryside was taken as evidence by interested observers among the clergy and laity that the religious faith of traditional France continued into the modern age. The sentimentality of devotional literature reflects a nostalgia for the simple piety of the countryside and a romantic apotheosis of female virtues. One aspect of this sentimentality can be observed in the treatment in devotional literature of the shepherd children who witnessed Marian apparitions. The faith of the shepherds of La Salette and Bernadette of Lourdes, for example, was based on a personal encounter with the supernatural which no amount of argument could disturb. Such a faith was possible because of the innocence of the visionaries, which was due to their ignorance of the modern world. The enormous importance of Mary, whose maternal sweetness and compassion were capable of overcoming man's hardness of heart, reveals another facet of French piety. The romantic ideal of woman as both wife and mother who suffers and forgives characterizes much of the literature of the last century's miracle cults. In propagating miracle cults that idealized the faith of children and the maternity of Mary, the Church sought an escape from a modern urban France in sentimental images of peasant religiosity and the bourgeois family.

Miracles and miracle cults were not, however, just expedient concessions to the traditional religiosity of the countryside and the sentimental relations of modern family life. Church-approved cults were intended to do more than confirm the beliefs and attitudes of the faithful. They were designed to create a national community of Catholics and so to replicate in the modern world the kind of belief thought to have characterized an older, more stable France. Large-scale movements of population, the existence of unbelievers even in small communities, a social structure in which the traditional agricultural sector became less important, and other changes undermined the survival of village life where, it was believed, religion was closely integrated with every other aspect of social life. While miracle cults evoked nostalgic memories of a mythic past of uniform belief, they also offered an alternative to it. The community of belief was no longer to be the neighborhood or the village; it was expanded to include all of France, or at least all those of France who shared similar religious convictions. National confraternities, organized pilgrimages, and the diffusion of mass-produced images and literature were an attempt to use miracles to help create a sense of loyalty to French Catholicism and, beyond that, to the universal Church. The cult of Notre-Dame des Victoires, based in a Parisian parish noted for its religious indifference, was designed to appeal to an urban population. The success of the con-fraternity in attracting members from throughout France has been well documented, suggesting that miracle cults were not anachronistic in the modern world.[30] But in publicizing its own success, as reflected in membership and miracles, the Archconfraternity of Notre-Dame des Victoires also turned itself into a symbol of the Church's ability to meet and conquer modernity at its very center, the city of Paris. The shrine of Notre-Dame de Lourdes is the most important example of how miracle cults worked to create a national Catholic community. By making the pilgrimage to Lourdes Catholics expressed their commitment to the French Church and reassured themselves about the vitality of their religion in an age when it was threatened by hostile relations with the State and skepticism about the supernatural.

The cults of Notre-Dame des Victoires and Notre-Dame de Lourdes, and others like them, were successful in part because of the aggressive organizational work of the Catholic clergy. But in making miracles and prophecies an important feature of devotional life, the Church did not simply impose a set of superstitious beliefs and practices on a credulous public, as critics have sometimes argued. The miracles and prophecies of the nineteenth century were not produced by the Church, but were initially an expression of traditional forms of popular religiosity that met vital social and psychological needs. The prophetic apparitions at La

Salette, Lourdes, and Pontmain and the miraculous healings at shrines throughout France were marketed and promoted by the Church, which sought to use them for its own purposes. The institutionalization of the miraculous resulted in the formation of a "new folklore" which incorporated and contributed to the survival of popular religious traditions. The cults organized by the Church led to a devotional life that was less likely to be rooted in a particular locale and more likely to relate the devotee to the national and international Church.[31] Moreover, miracles and prophecies, as they were absorbed by the Church, were colored by romantic sentiment and associated with the political and doctrinal positions of French Catholicism. But this use of miracles and prophecies did not destroy their popular character, which resided in their ability to deal with the problems of individual illness and social and political disorder. There is nothing inherent in the process of modernization which makes such crises less frightening. Miracles and prophecies persisted in France because they offered meaning and order to people when a secular perspective failed them.

Appendix

Healings and Pilgrims at Lourdes

Department	Healings 1858–1908	Healings 1858–1908 per 100,000	Number of Organized Pilgrims 1873	1893	1913
Ain	12	3.4			1,100
Aisne	24	4.4		1,060	
Allier	4	0.9		40	100
Alpes-Maritimes	3	1.1	400	250	
Ardèche	6	1.6	1,679	1,000	4,150
Ardennes	16	4.9	3,210		
Ariège	3	1.3	1,223	1,900	2,500
Aube	9	3.5			500
Aude	10	3.2	4,395	1,133	1,100
Aveyron	26	6.5		4,100	4,500
Basses-Alpes	1	0.8		350	500
Basses-Pyrénées	26	6.1	5,343	8,552	9,330
Bouches-du-Rhône	22	3.5	3,161	1,650	1,000
Calvados	25	5.8			2,700
Cantal	4	1.7	1,600		1,200
Charente	26	7.2	593	700	1,800
Charente-Inférieure	9	2.0	971		
Cher	23	6.4	400		1,600
Corrèze	2	0.6		1,186	1,000
Côtes-du-Nord	37	6.0		1,000	1,800
Côte d'Or	30	8.0			
Creuse	2	0.7	1,200		
Deux-Sèvres	29	8.2	466		
Dordogne	22	4.6		2,000	2,575
Doubs	20	6.6			1,000
Drôme	2	0.7			1,000
Eure	17	4.9			
Eure-et-Loir	25	8.8			

Department	Healings 1858–1908	Healings 1858–1908 per 100,000	Number of Organized Pilgrims		
			1873	1893	1913
Finistère	23	3.2		2,200	4,800
Gard	21	5.0	3,692	1,850	4,000
Gers	9	3.4	5,814	5,757	5,000
Gironde	33	4.1	5,366	4,100	6,000
Hautes–Alpes	3	2.6			300
Haute-Garonne	27	5.7	16,568	7,852	10,300
Haute-Loire	6	1.9	1,084		
Haute-Marne	13	5.3			
Hautes-Pyrénées	27	12.0	8,566	3,767	3,650
Haute-Saône	5	1.8			
Haute-Savoie	7	2.7			2,800
Haute-Vienne	8	2.1			
Hérault	39	8.5	7,446	2,180	10,000
Ille-et-Vilaine	51	8.1	1,395	1,900	4,300
Indre	9	3.0			
Indre-et-Loire	41	12.2	1,098	600	1,090
Isère	14	2.4			1,230
Jura	17	6.2			1,000
Landes	9	3.0	1,392	2,752	3,600
Loire	58	9.4	315	550	
Loiret	21	5.6			
Loir-et-Cher	18	6.4	431		
Loire-Inférieure	41	6.3	1,213	2,500	4,250
Lot	6	2.4			1,000
Lot-et-Garonne	8	2.7	4,015	4,200	
Lozère	13	9.6	635	1,500	4,500
Maine-et-Loire	46	8.9	2,270	1,350	4,000
Manche	19	3.7		3,000	2,000
Marne	27	6.2			2,400
Mayenne	13	3.9			
Meurthe-et-Moselle	27	6.1			1,200
Meuse	6	2.1			
Morbihan	14	2.6		1,000	
Nièvre	10	2.9			
Nord	132	7.6	620	1,100	10,000
Oise	29	7.2			800
Orne	14	4.0			1,500

Department	Healings 1858–1908	Healings 1858–1908 per 100,000	Number of Organized Pilgrims		
			1873	1893	1913
Pas-de-Calais	69	7.9	620	600	3,350
Puy-de-Dôme	6	1.1	968		
Pyrénées-Orientales	2	0.9	1,123		700
Rhône	158	19.6	315	1,000	6,100
Saône-et-Loire	10	1.6			1,200
Sarthe	13	3.0	1,781		
Savoie	7	2.7			
Seine	308	9.8	20		
Seine-et-Marne	7	2.0			
Seine-et-Oise	20	3.2	688		
Seine-Maritime	56	6.7		1,700	3,000
Somme	14	2.6	466		
Tarn	16	4.6	4,834	1,500	2,150
Tarn-et-Garonne	15	7.3	2,268		4,500
Var	10	3.5	1,922		
Vaucluse	15	6.4	1,179		
Vendée	29	6.5	4,236	2,545	5,000
Vienne	51	14.8	654	1,300	4,300
Vosges	29	7.1	300		
Yonne	7	2.0		900	

Sources: Bertrin, *Histoire critique des événements de Lourdes*, pp. 376–464; *Annales de Notre-Dame de Lourdes*, 1873, 1893, 1913; population data for calculating healings per 100,000 from *Annuaire statistique*, 1891.

Notes

INTRODUCTION

1. The classic account of a medieval miracle cult and its political and social implications is Bloch, *The Royal Touch*, which first appeared in 1924. See also Finucane, *Miracles and Pilgrims*; Sigal, "Maladie, pèlerinage, et guérison au XIIᵉ siècle"; Gauthier and Le Vas, "Analyse socio-économique de quelques recueils de miracles." For the early modern era see B. Robert Kreiser, *Miracles, Convulsions, and Ecclesiastical Politics in Early Eighteenth Century Paris*; Platelle, *Les chrétiens face au miracle*; Cousin, "Deux cents miracles en Provence sous Louis XIV"; Sauzet, "Pèlerinage panique et pèlerinage de dévotion"; and Barbin and Duteil, "Miracle et pèlerinage au XVIIᵉ siècle."

2. Hélias, *The Horse of Pride*, p. 82; Wylie, ed., *Chanzeaux, a Village in Anjou*, p. 245; Laurentin, "The Persistence of Popular Piety."

3. The most prominent novels on Lourdes are Zola, *Lourdes*, and Werfel, *The Song of Bernadette*. Roger Martin du Gard, in the opening pages of *Jean Barois*, used Lourdes as a symbol of traditional religious faith; others to use Lourdes include Huxley, *After Many a Summer Dies the Swan*, and De Vries, *Let Me Count the Ways*. An Academy Award-winning film *The Song of Bernadette*, based on Werfel's novel, appeared in 1944 and contributed to the diffusion and popularity of the Lourdes cult in the United States.

4. The documents on Lourdes, Pontmain, and the Miraculous Medal annotated and edited by René Laurentin are indispensable for any student of French popular religion. But Laurentin's devout Catholicism and his training as a theologian have convinced him that although nonreligious perspectives on the miraculous have some validity, the events he studies must be viewed primarily with what he calls "the light of faith." See Laurentin et al., "Roundtable Discussion on Natural Realities and the Supernatural," p. 150. Two brief treatments of the pilgrimage movement that acknowledge the significance of Lourdes are Dupront, "Tourisme et pèlerinage," and Marrus, "Cultures on the Move."

5. The best introduction to this literature is the series of bibliographical essays published in Mayeur, ed., *L'histoire religieuse de la France*.

6. Wach, *The Sociology of Religion*, pp. 19–34.

7. For some examples of a political perspective on religious history see Maurain, *La politique ecclésiastique du Second Empire*, and Gadille, *La pensée et l'action politique des évêques français*.

8. Langlois and Mayeur, "Sur l'histoire religieuse de l'époque contemporain," p. 440.

9. "Religion is the human enterprise by which a sacred cosmos is established. . . . The sacred cosmos is confronted by man as an immensely powerful reality other than himself. Yet this reality addresses itself to him and locates his life in an ultimately meaningful order" (Berger, *The Sacred Canopy*, pp. 25–26). "Religion is a system of symbols which acts to establish powerful, pervasive, and long-lasting moods in men by formulating conceptions of a general order of existence and clothing these conceptions with such an aura of factuality that the moods and motivations seem uniquely realistic" (Geertz, *The Interpretation of Culture*, p. 90). "Religion is a cultural institution, a complex of symbols, articles of faith, and practices adhered to by a group of believers that are related to, and commonly invoke the aid of, superhuman powers and provide answers to questions of ultimate meaning" (Lewy, *Religion and Revolution*, p. 4). "In speaking of religion . . . I will be using an essentially Tillichian definition—religion is that meaningful structure through which man relates himself to his ultimate concern" (Bellah, *Beyond Belief*, p. 100).

10. For a survey of the field see Claude Savart, "Vie intellectuelle et vie spirituelle," in Mayeur, ed., *L'histoire religieuse de la France*, pp. 97–107. Two recent assessments of French Catholic intellectual history are Paul, "In Quest of Kerygma," and Reardon, *Liberalism and Tradition*.

11. Griffiths, *The Reactionary Revolution*.

12. Paul, *The Edge of Contingency*, p. 16.

13. Le Bras' studies have been collected in *Études de sociologie religieuse*; Boulard, *Premiers itinéraires en sociologie religieuse*; Cholvy, *Géographie religieuse de l'Hérault contemporain*; Pin, *Pratique religieuse et classes sociales*.

14. Rémond, "Recherche d'une methode d'analyse historique"; Cholvy has noted the relative neglect of popular religion by historians of the modern era, and sees a continuing tendency to conform to a scheme of "an irreversible process of dechristianization" ("Réalités de la religion populaire dans la France contemporaine," p. 150).

15. Research of the sociological historians is reviewed in Claude Langlois, "La religion vécue," in Mayeur, ed., *L'histoire religieuse de la France*, pp. 42–49. For an excellent example of the sociological method applied to religious life in America see Lenski, *The Religious Factor*.

16. Marcilharcy, *Le diocèse d'Orléans sous l'épiscopat de Mgr Dupanloup*; Langlois, *Le diocèse de Vannes au XIXe siècle*; Hilaire, *Une chrétienté au XIXe siècle*.

17. James Obelkevich, in his introduction to a recent collection of essays restricted to the years 800–1700, calls attention to the tendency of historians of

popular religion to focus on the medieval and early modern periods of European history: *Religion and the People*, p. 3. For some examples of the study of popular religion in the nineteenth century see Savart, "A la recherche de l'art dit de Saint-Sulpice"; Cholvy, "Expression et évolution du sentiment religieux populaire."

18. According to Obelkevich, *Religion and the People*, p. 5, the relationship of popular to elite religion is at "the heart of the subject [of popular religion]." Alphonse Dupront also emphasizes the importance of this problem in his preface to Froeschlé-Chopard, *La religion populaire en Provence orientale au XVIIIe siècle*, pp. 21–31. Throughout this work my references to the Church are meant to cover the institutional structure of French Catholicism and the clergy who served in it. I realize, however, that some historians and theologians would argue that the Church properly includes all believers, laity as well as clergy. As is generally the case in studies of popular religion, I have adopted a more restricted sense of the word in order to suggest the distance that existed between laity and clergy. I do not mean to imply that all the clergy uniformly agreed with the decisions and actions of the Church, although I do hope to show that there was a substantial consensus in the institution in favor of a receptive attitude toward miracles and prophecies.

19. Guignebert, *Jesus*, p. 191.

20. Bollème, *Les almanachs populaires*; idem, "Représentation religieuse et thèmes d'espérance"; Mandrou, *De la culture populaire au 17e et 18e siècles*; Natalie Davis has criticized the work of Bollème and Mandrou by pointing out that "popular books are not necessarily written by *petites gens*" and that "people do not necessarily agree with the values and ideas in the books they read" (*Society and Culture in Early Modern France*, p. 191).

CHAPTER 1

1. For the historiography of religion during the French Revolution see Plongeron and Godel, "Un quart de siècle d'histoire religieuse"; Plongeron, "A propos des mutations du 'populaire' pendant la révolution et l'empire." The two most important recent accounts of religion during the Revolution are idem, *Conscience religieuse en révolution*, and Vovelle, *Religion et révolution*. Serge Bianchi has written two articles that place the religious history of a local area within a national context; see his "La déchristianization de l'an II," and "Manifestations et formes de la déchristianisation." Richard Cobb established a series of important distinctions for the study of revolutionary dechristianization in *Les armées révolutionnaires*. For brief general surveys see McManners, *The French Revolution and the Church*, and Tackett and Langlois, "A l'épreuve de la révolution."

2. Tackett and Langlois, "Ecclesiastical Structures and Clerical Geography," p. 357. Vovelle, *Religion et révolution*, projects an estimate of twenty thousand

abdications on the basis of his intensive work on the southeastern departments. The figure of thirty thousand *émigrés* and *déportés* is from Latreille, *L'église catholique et la révolution française*, 1:181.

3. For the diocese of Isère see Godel, *La réconstruction concordataire dans le diocèse de Grenoble*, pp. 248–249; data on the *pays creusois* come from Perouas, "L'évolution du clergé." In the diocese of Vannes the number of clergy dropped from 820 in 1791 to 536 in 1805. For these figures, and for Pancemont's concern, see Langlois, *Le diocèse de Vannes au XIX⁰ siècle*, pp. 294–295. Bianchi, "Manifestations et formes de la déchristianisation," reports that the percentage of clergy abdicating throughout France ranged from 14.5 percent (Béarn) to 70 percent (Allier). For the shortage of clergy in the nineteenth century see Hilaire, "La pratique religieuse en France."

4. Cobb, *Les armées révolutionnaires*, 2:641–653; Mitchell, "Resistance to the Revolution in Western France," pp. 250–255.

5. Cobb, *Les armées révolutionnaires*, 2:666–683, describes numerous confrontations between the dechristianizing revolutionary armies recruited in Paris and the Catholics of rural France. See also Palmer, *Twelve Who Ruled*, pp. 142–145, 180–190, 216–218. According to Cobb and Palmer, Robespierre and Saint-Just of the Committee of Public Safety opposed violent dechristianization because of its effect on the peasantry, and suppressed the revolutionary armies in part to prevent the antireligious extremists from further alienating the French countryside.

6. Tilly, *The Vendée*, p. 237.

7. Paillard, "Fanatiques et patriotes dans le Puy-de-Dome," pp. 319–328; Sévestre, *Les problèmes religieux de la Révolution*, 2:555–561. Patrick, "The Vendée revisited"; Lepart, "Les bouleversements de la révolution," pp. 187–189.

8. Godel, *La réconstruction concordataire dans le diocèse de Grenoble*, pp. 101–109; Langlois, *Le diocèse de Vannes au XIX⁰ siècle*, pp. 246–257.

9. The effect of such conflicts on the laity is discussed by Plongeron, *Conscience religieuse en révolution*, pp. 126–127. On sacramental life during the revolution see Longuet, "Les prêtres réfractaires à Caen," and idem, "Une source pour l'étude de l'activité sacerdotale." For the importance of the sacraments in contemporary France see Pannet, *Le catholicisme populaire*, pp. 114–157.

10. Mathiez, *La théophilanthropie et le culte décadaire*, pp. 15–18. For a description of the revolutionary calendar see Palmer, *Twelve Who Ruled*, pp. 111–113. Alexis de Tocqueville also proposed that the French Revolution was comparable to a "religious revival" since it aimed at the "regeneration of the whole human race." But de Tocqueville regarded the revolutionary religion as an "imperfect one, since it was without a God, without a ritual or promise of a future life" (*The Old Regime and the French Revolution*, p. 13). In fact, the Revolution affirmed God and an afterlife, and developed elaborate rituals. See Ozouf, *La fête révolutionnaire*, and Ehrard and Viallaneix, eds., *Les fêtes de la révolution*.

11. Cited in Plongeron, *Conscience religieuse en révolution*, pp. 111–112.

12. Vovelle, *Piété baroque et déchristianisation en Provence*. Vovelle's evidence shows, for example, that requests for a foundation of masses to be said for the repose of one's soul declined in the eighteenth century, with 80 percent of the wills containing such a request in 1720, compared to 40 percent in 1789. Vovelle is careful to point out, however, that *notables* are overrepresented in the sample of wills analyzed, and that in some areas, and for women, the decline in his indices of dechristianization is much less pronounced. Fouché, while a representative on mission in the Nièvre, required that all cemeteries be placarded with signs declaring that "Death is an eternal sleep." It was this kind of antireligiosity that Robespierre and others on the Committee of Public Safety reacted against in establishing the cult of the Supreme Being; see Palmer, *Twelve Who Ruled*, p. 150.

13. The Convention decree is cited in Palmer, *The Age of Democratic Revolution*, 2:127; the *Manuel* is described by Mathiez, *La théophilanthropie et le culte décadaire*, pp. 91–94. For a discussion of the theological tradition within which Robespierre can be placed see Deprun, "Les 'noms divins' dans deux discours de Robespierre." For some enthusiastic responses to the cult of the Supreme Being see Vovelle, *Religion et révolution*, pp. 201–204.

14. McDonald, *Rousseau and the French Revolution*, pp. 155–173; Soboul, "Sentiment religieux et cultes populaires"; Bowman, *Le Christ romantique*, pp. 62–67.

15. Plongeron, "Le fait religieux," p. 108.

16. Gaugain, *Histoire de la révolution dans la Mayenne*, 4:177–179; Angot, *Dictionnaire*, 2:67; Soboul, "Sentiment religieux et cultes populaires," pp. 76–77.

17. Cobb, *Paris and Its Provinces*, pp. 125–126; idem, *Les armées révolutionnaires*, 2:640, n. 7. See also Flament, "Recherches sur le ministère clandestin," pp. 46–47; Henri Forestier, "Le culte laïcal et la crise des effectifs." At the time of the Revolution the clergy did not have a monopoly on religious ritual. In some of the isolated hamlets of the Massif Central lay women known as *béates* continued to preside over religious activities in the absence of priests until late in the nineteenth century. See Rivet, "Des ministères laïques."

18. Tantat, "L'application de la Constitution Civile," pp. 227–232.

19. Cobb, *Les armées révolutionnaires*, 2:669.

20. In the diocese of Blois the statue of Notre-Dame de Nanteuil wept when the pilgrimage was banned in 1793; in 1792 in the diocese of Meaux a tree holding a statue of Mary bled when revolutionaries attempted to chop it down. See Harmon, *Notre-Dame de France*, 1:152, 303. Even more common were miracles in which iconoclasts were killed or maimed by an act of God. See ibid., 2:59, 83, 370; 3:155, 170; 4:30, 502.

21. Plongeron, *Conscience religieuse en révolution*, p. 142.

22. Guillaume de Bertier de Sauvigny, whose work is on the whole sympathetic to the Church, criticizes the "excessive language" and "tactlessness" of the mis-

sionaries, *The Bourbon Restoration*, p. 321. For a thorough treatment of the missionary movement's methods see Sevrin, *Les missions religieuses en France*. For some episcopal opposition to the missionary movement see Vidalenc, *Le département de l'Eure*, p. 549.

23. The distance was perhaps partly the result of the disproportionate numbers of urban clergy in a predominantly rural country. See Tackett, "L'histoire sociale du clergé diocésain," pp. 224–225.

24. Fabre and Lacroix, *La vie quotidienne des paysans*, p. 315; Bouteiller, *Médecine populaire*, pp. 23–25, 51–59, 61–63; Morin, *Le prêtre et le sorcier*, pp. 173–175. Two recent articles that stress the importance of healers in nineteenth-century France are Ramsey, "Medical Power and Popular Medicine," and Léonard, "Les guérisseurs en France."

25. Vincent, *La vie quotidienne des paysans Bourguignons*, pp. 120–125; Arnold Van Gennep, *Manuel de folklore français contemporain*, v. 1, pt. 4, pp. 1963–1965.

26. Thomas distinguishes prayer from magic by pointing out that Christian prayer is "non-coercive." He goes on to say, however, that "this distinction was repeatedly blurred in the popular mind." Thomas, *Religion and the Decline of Magic*, p. 41.

27. Bertrand, *Pèlerinage de Saint Hubert en Ardennes*, pp. 153–154.

28. Sevrin, "Croyances populaires et médecine supranaturelle"; *L'ami du clergé* 14 (1892):107. See also Fournée, *Enquête sur le culte populaire de Saint Martin*, p. 52; Fabre and Lacroix, *La vie quotidienne des paysans*, p. 311.

29. Lecocq, "Recherches sur les enseignes de pèlerinage." A similar description of a *pèlerin marchand* can be found in Vartier, *La vie quotidienne en Lorraine*, pp. 119–139. For the popularity of professional pilgrims in the diocese of Orléans see Marcilharcy, *Le diocèse d'Orléans au milieu du XIXᵉ siècle*, pp. 310–311.

30. Fabre and Lacroix, *La vie quotidienne des paysans*, pp. 118–119.

31. Lecotté, *Recherches sur les cultes populaires*, pp. 262–267.

32. Davis, *Society and Culture in Early Modern France*, p. 222. Bollème, ed., *La Bible bleue*, pp. 344–364, excerpts several prayers and remedies published from the seventeenth to the nineteenth centuries. For the distribution of *colportage* literature see Darmon, *Le colportage de librairie en France*.

33. Nisard, *Histoire des livres populaires*, 2:76.

34. Lecotté, *Recherches sur les cultes populaires*, pp. 262–275, demonstrates the correspondence between the manuscript and the printed prayers. On the impact of printed material on oral culture see Mandrou, *Introduction to Modern France*, p. 64; Eisenstein, *The Printing Press*, 1:80–88.

35. *Le médecin des pauvres* (Rouen, 1851). This edition and the Troyes edition cited below (n. 39) were located at the Bibliothèque Nationale. Lecotté, *Recherches sur les cultes populaires*, p. 262, lists six different versions of this pamphlet available in Seine-et-Marne between 1840 and 1900. See also Bouteiller, *Médecine populaire*, pp. 63–66.

36. *Le médecin des pauvres*, pp. 1–2. For a version of this prayer that was part of the oral tradition of the Burgundian peasantry, see Vincent, *La vie quotidienne des paysans Bourguignons*, p. 165.

37. *Le médecin des pauvres*, p. 5.

38. Ibid., p. 6.

39. *Le médecin des pauvres* (Troyes, 1858). On the attempts of the Second Empire to control *colportage* literature, see Darmon, *Le colportage de librairie en France*.

40. Archives Nationales, F^{19} 5637 contains reports on prosecutions of clergymen from ten different departments for the illegal practice of medicine. On the practice of medicine by the clergy see also Marcilharcy, *Le diocèse d'Orléans sous l'épiscopat de Mgr Dupanloup*, p. 121, n. 2; Léonard, "Les guérisseurs en France," pp. 503–508.

41. Léonard, "Women, Religion, and Medicine," p. 29.

42. Starting with its first issues in 1879, *L'ami du clergé* regularly published medical advice in a section labeled "Courier de l'utile."

43. Henri Bon, *Précis de médecine catholique* (1935), cited in Léonard, "Women, Religion, and Medicine," p. 35.

44. For the cures at the tomb of the deacon Paris following his death in 1727 see Kreiser, *Miracles, Convulsions, and Ecclesiastical Politics*, pp. 91–94. The most prominent priest/thaumaturge in the nineteenth century was the *curé* of Ars, Jean Vianney (see below). For other nineteenth-century examples see Béteille, *La vie quotidienne en Rouergue*, p. 138; Bouteiller, *Médecine populaire*, pp. 45–46; Eugen Weber, *Peasants into Frenchmen*, p. 26; Zeldin, *France, 1848–1945*, 2:402; Marcilharcy, *Le diocèse d'Orléans au milieu du XIXe siècle*, pp. 372–373.

45. Deniel, *Une image de la famille*, pp. 54–55; Eugen Weber, *Peasants into Frenchmen*, p. 27.

46. Varagnac, *Civilisation traditionelle*, pp. 119–120.

47. Collin de Plancy, *Dictionnaire critique des reliques*, 1:368.

48. *L'ami de la religion*, 33 (1823):29–32. See also Grégoire, *Histoire des sectes religieuses*, 5:397–408, and *Dictionnaire de la spiritualité*, 7:586–587.

49. *L'ami de la religion*, 57 (1828):246–247.

50. Lecanu, *Dictionnaire des prophéties*, 825–835; Giray, *Les miracles de La Salette*, 1:422–429.

51. Janvier, *Vie de M. Dupont*, 2:22–40, 193–276.

52. Fourrey, "Un village dont les cinq parties du monde savent le nom"; Boutry, "Un sanctuaire et son saint."

53. Janvier, *Vie de M. Dupont*, 1:145, 230, 374–375; 2:460.

54. Monnin, *Le curé d'Ars*; Fourrey, *Le curé d'Ars authentique*; Boutry, "Un sanctuaire et son saint." Several pamphlets stressed the *curé* of Ars' humility and his concern for pastoral work, especially the hearing of confession. See *Pèlerinage d'Ars et notice sur la vie de J.-M.-B. Vianney*; *Pèlerinage d'Ars: Guide-indicateur pour diriger les pèlerins*.

55. Laurentin and Billet, *Lourdes—documents authentiques*, 1:203, 234, 259–260.

56. Ibid., 1:305.

57. Lasserre, *Notre-Dame de Lourdes*.

58. For Vintras see Garçon, *Vintras—hérésiarque et prophète*, pp. 72–92; Appolis, "Du nouveau sur la secte Vintras"; Marcilharcy, *Le diocèse d'Orléans sous l'épiscopat de Mgr Dupanloup*, pp. 106–110.

59. *L'ami du clergé*, 30(1908):574.

60. Fabre and Lacroix, *La vie quotidienne des paysans*, pp. 106, 208, 349–350; Vincent, *La vie quotidienne des paysans Bourguignons*, pp. 131–135; Béteille, *La vie quotidienne en Rouergue*, pp. 143–147; Brekilien, *La vie quotidienne des paysans*, pp. 251–257; Lecotté, *Recherches sur les cultes populaires*, pp. 254–280; Fournée, *Enquête sur le culte populaire de Saint Martin*, pp. 50–55; Morin, *Le prêtre et le sorcier*, pp. 102–167; Hilaire, *Une chrétienté*, 1:396–398; Chaline, "Pratique et vie religieuse," pp. 88–95; Devos, "Quelques aspects de la vie religieuse," pp. 70–74; Parfait, *Le dossier des pèlerinages*, pp. 138–185.

61. Zeldin, *France, 1848–1945*, 2:401–402; Bouteiller, *Médecine populaire*, pp. 139–142.

62. Nisard, *Histoire des livres populaires*, 2:81; Morin, *Le prêtre et le sorcier*, p. 170.

63. Sébillot, *Le folklore de France*, 2:268; Bouteiller, *Médecine populaire*, pp. 33–36; Lecotté, *Recherches sur les cultes populaires*, p. 254.

64. Fabre, "Le monde du carnaval," presents a table from Claude Gaignebert's recent study *Le carnaval* in which the mythic history of St. Blaise is related to his healing powers. The belief in St. Guinefort's ability to heal children in the Dombes region north of Lyons was based on a story that described his protection of a child against a snake; see Lester Little, "The Greyhound Saint," *New York Review of Books* 28 (April 30, 1981):26–28 for a review of Jean-Claude Schmitt's book on this dog-saint.

65. Sébillot, *Le folklore de France*, 2:270.

66. Lecotté, *Recherches sur les cultes populaires*, p. 284.

67. According to Sébillot, *Le folklore de France*, 2:278: "Of all beliefs related to fountains the most common, the most persistent, and the one most considered as true, is that which attributes to them the power to heal. Innumerable pilgrimages, collective or individual, public or clandestine, attest the vitality of this ancient idea at the dawn of the twentieth century." See also Van Gennep, *Manuel de folklore français contemporain*, 3:527–537, which lists bibliographic references for sacred fountains throughout France.

68. For some examples of nineteenth-century ex-voto depicting cures and acts of protection, see the catalogue of 1950 Parisian exhibit of Marian art, *La Vierge dans l'art français*, nos. 269, 270, 272–278. See also Cuisenier, *French Folk Art*, pl. 145, 149, 150, 156, 163. For an assessment of the impact of the Revolution on ex-voto see Cousin, "L'impact de la révolution française sur l'ex voto peint."

69. Corbin, *Archaïsme et modernité en Limousin*, 1:650; Berenson, "Populist Religion in Rural France."

70. Tackett, *Priest and Parish in Eighteenth-Century France*, p. 214. See also Delumeau, *Le catholicisme entre Luther et Voltaire*, pp. 256–261; Bossy, "The Counter-reformation and the People."

71. *L'ami du clergé* 14 (1892):107; 17 (1895):873.

72. Drochon, *Histoire illustrée des pèlerinages français*; Hilaire, *Une chrétienté*, 1:392–396. Gérard Cholvy also sees a shift from local to clerically approved ultramontane cults occurring during the second half of the nineteenth century: see his "Expression et évolution du sentiment religieux populaire," pp. 300–303. Wilson, "Cults of Saints," pp. 561–562, notes an increase in ex-votos to Mary in Parisian churches during the 1860s.

73. Morin, *Le prêtre et le sorcier*, p. 220; Eugen Weber, *Peasants into Frenchmen*, p. 28, reports that the ringing of bells was a common practice in the French countryside throughout the nineteenth century.

74. Lecotté, *Recherches sur les cultes populaires*, p. 280; Bouteiller, *Médecine populaire*, p. 87.

75. Varagnac, *Civilisation traditionelle*, pp. 46–65; for descriptions of clerical participation in Rogation Day processions see Van Gennep, *Manuel de folklore français*, v. 1, pt. 4, pp. 1637–1649.

76. Van Gennep, *Manuel de folklore français*, v. 1, pt. 4, pp. 1825–1826, reports clerical participation in several areas of France. For the attempt of the Church to suppress the *feux St. Jean* see Delumeau, *Le catholicisme entre Luther et Voltaire*, pp. 259–261. See also Morin, *Le prêtre et le sorcier*, p. 30; Brekilien, *La vie quotidienne des paysans en Bretagne*, p. 198; Cholvy, "Indifference religieuse et anticlericalisme," p. 77. For the support of *feux St. Jean* by the Church in the twentieth century see Varagnac, *Civilisation traditionelle*, p. 49.

77. Cholvy, "Indifference religieuse et anticlericalisme," p. 75; Corbin, *Archaïsme et modernité en Limousin*, 1:622–625.

78. Cited in Drochon, *Histoire illustrée des pèlerinages français*, p. 747; for Notre-Dame de la Seds see Hamon, *Notre-Dame de France*, 7:180–183.

79. Parfait, *Le dossier des pèlerinages*, pp. 141–142.

80. The emphasis on Sunday Mass and Easter Communion as a quantitative index of religiosity was initiated by Gabriel Le Bras, whose essays are collected in *Études de sociologie religieuse*.

81. Chapter 6 discusses in detail why and how diocesan authorities made such decisions.

82. Germain, *Parler du salut*; Sevrin, *Les missions religieuses*.

83. For St. Jean-François Régis see Fabre and Lacroix, *La vie quotidienne des paysans*, pp. 352–357; for St. Anne d'Auray see Langlois, *Le diocèse de Vannes*, pp. 549–552; for St. Martin of Tours see Janvier, *La vie de M. Dupont*, pp. 370–391;

for St. Radegonde see Briand, *Histoire de Sainte Radegonde*. For other local cults that received renewed support from the institutional Church during the nineteenth century see Cholvy, "Un saint populaire"; Soulet, "Aspects du culte de Saint Bernard"; Perouas, "La piété populaire."

84. Hamon, *Notre-Dame de France*, 1:v. For a brief overview of the Marian revival in France see Savart, "Cent ans après."

85. Data on crownings are from Drochon, *Histoire illustrée des pèlerinages français*.

86. Ibid., pp. 398–400; see also Parfait, *Le dossier des pèlerinages*, pp. 76–102.

87. On generalized devotions see Christian, *Person and God in a Spanish Valley*, pp. 46–47, 100–101. Christian draws a sharp distinction between shrines and generalized devotions, however, which I do not believe applies to the French case, where shrines such as Lourdes and La Salette could also become devotions.

88. On medieval pilgrimages see Sumption, *Pilgrimage*; Finucane, *Miracles and Pilgrims*.

89. Eugen Weber, *Peasants into Frenchmen*, p. 350, argues that early in the twentieth century "As a general rule [the priests] accepted current beliefs in healing fountains, stones, and megaliths." But sixteen pages later Weber is able to provide counterexamples that indicate clerical opposition throughout the century to "the whole popular cult of relics, processions, ostentations, rogations, statues, rocks, caves, and healing springs" (pp. 366–367).

CHAPTER 2

1. Bertrin, *Histoire critique*, pp. 438–439. For a chart of the growth of the Lourdes pilgrimage see chapter 6.

2. Morin, *Le prêtre et le sorcier*; Parfait, *Le dossier des pèlerinages*; de Bonnefon, *Lourdes et ses tenanciers*.

3. Zola, *Lourdes*. See also idem, *Mes voyages, Lourdes–Rome*, pp. 11–13.

4. Harrell, *All Things are Possible*; Nolen, *Healing*; Rose, *Faith Healing*; Vecsey, "Mainline Churches Rediscover Healing."

5. Sussman, "The Glut of Doctors," p. 293; Zeldin, *France, 1848–1945*, 1:37.

6. Bouteiller, *Médecine populaire*, p. 19.

7. Fabre and Lacroix, *La vie quotidienne des paysans*, p. 298; Béteille, *La vie quotidienne en Rouergue*, p. 156; Brekilien, *La vie quotidienne des paysans*, p. 251; Corbin, *Archaïsme et modernité en Limousin*, 1:94–96; on the scarcity of money see Eugen Weber, *Peasants into Frenchmen*, pp. 34–40.

8. The case in question occurred in Haute-Savoie in 1882. Abbé Coudevoux was suspended by the Minister of Cults for performing the operation. The bishop, in defending his *curé*, described the condition of an isolated region of France:

"These are the medical conditions of the commune of Abondance. If someone wants to be taken care of by a French doctor he must go to Évion. It takes five hours to descend from Abondance to Évion, and six and one-half hours to climb back up. . . . The fee is 60 frs., not including the cost of the journey. If you go instead to a doctor at Vilain the distance is about the same, but the fee is only 30 frs." (Archives Nationales, F^{19} 5637).

9. Shryock, *The Development of Modern Medicine*, p. 249.

10. Zeldin, *France, 1848–1945*, 1:23. For a radical critique of the medical profession, which attributes advances in public health to nutritional and environmental factors rather than to the corps of doctors, see Ivan Illich, *Medical Nemesis* (New York, 1976), especially pp. 1–27. For a critical assessment of nineteenth-century French medicine see Léonard, "Les guérisseurs en France."

11. *Annales de l'archconfrérie du très saint et immaculé coeur de Marie*, 5 (1845):389.

12. Lebrun, *Les hommes et la mort*, p. 394. For the resources of popular medicine see Bouteiller, *Médecine populaire*, and Vincent, *La vie quotidienne des paysans Bourguignons*, pp. 112–166.

13. Fabre and Lacroix, *La vie quotidienne des paysans*, p. 298; see also Brekilien, *La vie quotidienne des paysans*, pp. 238–239; Beteille, *La vie quotidienne en Rouergue*, pp. 140, 166; Eugen Weber, *Peasants into Frenchmen*, p. 23; Vincent, *La vie quotidienne des paysans Bourguignons*, p. 116; Marcilharcy, *Le diocèse d'Orléans au milieu du XIXe siècle*, pp. 313, 371–373, 390.

14. Lebrun, *Les hommes et la mort*, pp. 392–399.

15. *Manuel de dévotion à Notre-Dame de Fourvières*, p. 142.

16. Macklin, "Belief, Ritual and Healing"; Macklin and Cumrane, "Three North American Folk Saint Movements"; Turner, "A Ndembu Doctor in Practice"; Lévi-Strauss, "The Effectiveness of Symbols."

17. Turner, *Dramas, Fields and Metaphors*, pp. 37–42.

18. *L'ami de la religion*, 40 (1824):88; 43 (1825):102–104.

19. Data for the cures of Prince Hohenlohe are drawn from *L'ami de la religion*, which gave them extensive coverage in the period 1822–1825.

20. Boissarie, *Les grandes guérisons*. Dr. Boissarie was the head of the Bureau of Medical Confirmation at Lourdes. Founded in 1882, the Bureau was given responsibility for verifying scientifically the miracles of Lourdes. See Rose, *Faith Healing*, p. 94; Leuret and Bon, *Modern Miraculous Cures*, pp. 94–121.

21. Aladel, *Notice historique*, pp. 113–114.

22. Laurentin and Billet, *Lourdes—documents authentiques* (hereafter *LDA*), 5:168–169.

23. Ibid., 5:199–200.

24. Ibid., 5:201–202.

25. Bertrin, *Histoire critique*, p. 314.

26. Boissarie, *Les grandes guérisons*, p. 164.

27. Bertrin, *Histoire critique*, p. 101.

28. Data from cures described in *L'ami de la religion*. Since I am concerned here with relations between laity and clergy, I have excluded from these figures members of religious orders healed by Prince Hohenlohe. For other evidence of the involvement of the parish clergy in national miracle cults see *Annales de l'archconfrérie de Notre-Dame des Victoires*, 1:226, 318; 2:157–159, 227–233; 4:320–323; 5:328–329.

29. Janvier, *Vie de M. Dupont*, 2:44; *Vie et miracles de Saint Jean-François Régis*, pp. 88–92, 98–102; Loth, *Le miracle en France*, pp. 87–117.

30. For a cure mediated by the *pénitents blancs* see Mlle des Brulais, *L'écho de la sainte montagne*, p. 207; for cures mediated by other confraternities, including the *enfants de Marie*, see Aladel, *Notice historique*, pp. 170, 240–242.

31. Nourry, *La simulation du merveilleux*, pp. 48–49.

32. Aladel's pamphlet, *Notice historique*, went through eight editions between 1834 and 1842; the first five editions alone came to 109,195 copies; see Laurentin, ed., *Catherine Labouré*, 1:50–152, 217, 245. Abbé Desgenettes' manual for the Archconfraternity of Notre-Dame des Victoires was reprinted at least fifteen times between 1839 and 1867; see *Catalogue général des livres imprimés de la Bibliothèque Nationale*, 39:327.

33. See, for example, the story of the cure of François Macary, as described by Henri Lasserre in *La Croix*, June 24–July 4, 1883. Mlle Moreau of Tartas (Landes) was cured at the grotto after her parents happened to read about the miraculous fountain in the *Messager Catholique* of Bordeaux: *LDA*, 5:194–195.

34. I am suggesting that the transition from sickness to health requires a ritual program similar to those which characterize other transitional moments in the life of an individual. See Van Gennep, *The Rites of Passage*.

35. Turner, *Dramas, Fields and Metaphors*, p. 208.

36. Boisnard, *Les sanctuaires de Marie*, p. 16. See also Brulais, *L'echo de la sainte montagne*, p. 245; *Annales de Notre-Dame de Lourdes*, 1 (1869):9.

37. *L'ami de la religion*, 41 (1824):135–137; 46 (1825):37–40.

38. For a further discussion of the role of the Church in establishing and promoting miracle cults see chapters 1 and 6.

39. Of the thirty statements collected by the episcopal commission charged with the investigation of the first Lourdes miracles, only nine give no indication of family involvement in the social drama leading up to the miraculous cure; *LDA*, 5:371, presents a table of the *miraculés* examined by the commission. See also Platelle, *Les chrétiens face au miracle*.

40. Boissarie, *Les grandes guérisons*, pp. 507–508.

41. In *The Puritan Way of Death*, p. 132, David Stannard has argued that "In traditional, tightly knit societies, where each individual is likely to play an important social role and the problem of dealing with separation through death is a community problem, the reaction to the loss of an individual is generally spread

out among a large group of mourners; in more urban, diversified societies the community is less often so broadly affected by the death of any individual and thus the family becomes the largest unit among whose members the shock of separation must be borne." A similar shift of the psychological burden resulting from illness from community to family may have been occurring in nineteenth-century France. But the effects of this shift may have been mitigated by devotions to shrines like the one at Lourdes, through which the Church organized support for the sick and their families.

42. Boissairie, *Les grandes guérisons*, pp. 502–503.

43. Eliade, *Patterns in Comparative Religion*, p. 200.

44. For the developments in popular religious art in the nineteenth century see Savart, "A la recherche de l'art dit de Saint-Sulpice"; Pirotte, "Les images de dévotion." For an anticlerical point of view on popular religious art see Parfait, *L'arsenal de la dévotion*.

45. Dumax, *Un triple prodige*, pp. 6–7. For the popularity of *Le Pèlerin* see Sorlin, *La Croix et les juifs*, pp. 26–30.

46. Dumax, *Un triple prodige*, p. 12.

47. Ibid., p. 8.

48. Cited in Cros, *Histoire de Notre-Dame de Lourdes*, 3:59.

49. Parfait, *Le dossier des pèlerinages*, p. 110.

50. Ibid., p. 109; on Notre-Dame du Séez see pp. 111–115.

51. *LDA*, 6:245.

52. *LDA*, 1:201, 281.

53. For Pierre de Rudder see Boissairie, *Les grandes guérisons*, p. 94; Nourry, *La simulation du merveilleux*, pp. 328–357; Monden, *Signs and Wonders*, pp. 239–245. For the impact of a miracle on a community see, for example, Aladel, *Notice historique*, pp. 223–224; Brulais, *L'écho de la sainte montagne*, pp. 132–133; *Annales de l'archconfrérie de Notre-Dame des Victoires*, 2 (1843):157–158.

54. *LDA*, 5:156.

55. Macfarlane, *Witchcraft in Tudor and Stuart England*; Thomas, *Religion and the Decline of Magic*, pp. 526–534.

56. Durkheim, *The Elementary Forms of the Religious Life*; idem, *Suicide*.

57. Durkheim, *Suicide*, p. 210.

58. *LDA*, 2:238. Jacomet's enumeration of the crowd at the grotto on April 15, 1858, shows that of a total of 6,457 pilgrims, 5,271 were from the countryside and villages around Lourdes, while 1,186 were from Lourdes itself. Of the same total, 2,361 were men, 3,186 women, and 920 children. One suspects the precision of Jacomet's figures, but as a rough estimate they are probably accurate: *LDA*, 2:195. On another occasion Jacomet noted that public credulity increased as a result of the presence of some local elites, specifically the ex-mayor of a neighboring commune: *LDA*, 1:262–263.

59. *LDA*, 5:194–195. For the appeal of pilgrimages as a response to illness

among middle-class women of the Nord see Smith, *Ladies of the Leisure Class,* pp. 104–105.

60. See map in Boulard, *Premiers itinéraires en sociologie religieuse.*

61. Monnin, *Le curé d'Ars,* 2:22–44; but Boutry, "Un sanctuaire et son saint," pp. 374–375, notes that Ars had a sustained appeal for peasants of the region and for workers from Lyons and Saint-Etienne.

62. Mlle des Brulais, *Suite de l'écho de la sainte montagne,* pp. 13–17.

63. Harrell, *All Things are Possible;* Nolen, *Healing;* Rose, *Faith Healing;* Offner and Van Staelen, *Modern Japanese Religions.*

CHAPTER 3

1. For the prophets of the Cévennes see Schwartz, *The French Prophets;* Le Roy Ladurie, *Les paysans de Languedoc,* 1:607–629; Garrett, *Respectable Folly,* pp. 147–148. On Jansenist prophecy see Kreiser, *Miracles, Convulsions, and Ecclesiastical Politics,* pp. 271–273; Garrett, *Respectable Folly,* pp. 21–24. Prophecies are discussed by Bollème, *Les almanachs populaires,* pp. 17–21, 59–61; Mandrou, *De la culture populaire,* pp. 37, 57–58, 60–63. For a general discussion of the prophetic tradition in the ancien régime see Vuillaud, *La fin du monde,* pp. 128–168; Plongeron, *Théologie et politique,* pp. 25–28. For the medieval origins of the prophetic tradition see Reeves, *Joachim of Fiore;* Cohn, *The Pursuit of the Millennium.* For a review of recent studies of millennial movements see Schwartz, "The End of the Beginning." Prophetic figures are still capable of attracting supporters in parts of France. See Favret-Saada, *Deadly Words,* pp. 234–249, for a description of the career of Robert Brault, a prophet active in western France during the 1960s.

2. Max Weber, *The Sociology of Religion,* p. 46.

3. Bollème, *Les almanachs populaires;* Mandrou, *De la culture populaire;* Darnton, *Mesmerism and the End of the Enlightenment in France.*

4. Mendenhall, *The Tenth Generation;* Cohn, *The Pursuit of the Millennium;* Thomas, *Religion and the Decline of Magic,* pp. 128–146.

5. Lantenari, *The Religions of the Oppressed;* Worsley, *The Trumpet Shall Sound.* For prophetic justifications of some medieval regimes see Reeves, *Joachim of Fiore,* pp. 58–64.

6. *Vie et oeuvres de la bienheureuse Marguerite-Marie Alacoque,* 2:232–234.

7. Max Weber, *Sociology of Religion,* pp. 46–48.

8. Vigier, *La seconde république dans la région alpine,* 2:10–88.

9. Despite its partisan bias, the best general discussion of the apparition at La Salette is Louis Bassette, *Le fait de La Salette.* The message delivered at La Salette was not the only divine communication reported during this period in the Haute-Loire. During the years 1845 to 1851 there was a resurgence of messianism around a septuagenarian who was arrested three times for declaring himself to be God and

predicting the end of the world. Some families continued to believe in this messiah, Jean-Baptiste Diginnet, until the 1930s; see Gadille, "Le Jansenisme populaire." For reports of several apparitions that followed the one at La Salette see Archives Nationales, BB¹⁸ 1454.

10. For a discussion of the text of this prophecy see Bassette, *Le fait de La Salette*, pp. 100–109.

11. Langlois, "La conjoncture miraculeuse," pp. 232–233; Delahaye, "Note sur la légende." For a warning similar to the prophecy of La Salette found in a healer's notebook of the first half of the nineteenth century see Lecotté, *Recherches sur les cultes populaires*, pp. 274–275.

12. The prosecutors' reports on the La Salette pamphlets can be found in Archives Nationales, BB¹⁸ 1452.

13. Note written by the Minister of Justice in response to report from Angers, in ibid.

14. Agulhon, *La république au village*, pp. 49–92, 361–365; Soboul, *Paysans, sans-culottes et Jacobins*, pp. 349–350.

15. *Apparition de la très-sainte Vierge à deux petits bergers*. A sermon delivered by a missionary of La Salette during the anniversary celebration of September 19, 1854, repeated the theme: "My brothers, you complain that commerce stagnates, that the air is unhealthy, the fields infertile. . . . You say the weather is bad, that your miseries are great, that everywhere there is suffering, and you are right. . . . But why do all these calamities weigh on us, if not because we have forgotten the Law of the Lord, and close our ears to the warnings of His Mother and ours who, seeing the arm of her Son raised because of our crimes, descended in tears on this mountain, in the hope of saving her guilty children." Quoted in Mlle des Brulais, *Suite de l'écho de la sainte montagne*, pp. 78–79.

16. Varagnac, *Civilisation traditionelle*; Eugen Weber, *Peasants into Frenchmen*.

17. Bassette, *Le fait de La Salette*, pp. 272–273.

18. Ibid., pp. 184, 190–191.

19. Appolis, "En marge du catholicisme contemporain." For a discussion of the career of Mélanie's secret during the Third Republic see chapter 5, "Prophecy and Ultramontanism."

20. Bollème, *Les almanachs populaires*, pp. 31–32.

21. Garrett, *Respectable Folly*, pp. 19–29; Harrison, *The Second Coming*.

22. Lecanu, *Dictionnaire des prophéties*, 2:55.

23. The prophecy of Jean Prêcheguerre was the most important item in the sixteenth-century *Liber mirabilis*, which experienced a revived popularity during the Restoration. The text of the prophecy was published in Lecanu, *Dictionnaire des prophéties*, 2:55–59. Two other editions of the prophecy can be found at Harvard's Widener library: *Prédiction pour la fin du dix-huitième siècle*; and *Prophétie recueillie et transmise par Jean de Vatiguerro*. See also Vuillaud, *La fin du monde*, pp. 174–176.

24. According to Hyacinthe Olivier-Vitalis, canon of Carpentras and editor of

Prophétie recueillie et transmise par Jean de Vatiguerro, Prêcheguerre's prophecy concluded with a description of "the recall of the Bourbons, the return of the Pope to Rome, and a prediction of a long reign of peace, unity, and happiness whose happy influence we are just beginning to experience." The problem arising from the sixteenth-century dates mentioned in the prophecy was dealt with by the addition of 284 years. This was justified by speculation that Prêcheguerre had dated his account from A.D. 284, the era of the Diocletian persecution; see Lecanu, *Dictionnaire des prophéties*, 2:60.

25. Lecanu, *Dictionnaire des prophéties*, 2:339–340.

26. *La véritable prophétie du vénérable Holzhauser.*

27. Cited in Vuillaud, *La fin du monde*, p. 175.

28. Vuillaud, *La fin du monde*, pp. 176–177; Leroyer, *Vie et révélations*, 1:14–80.

29. Lecanu, *Dictionnaire des prophéties*, 2:597.

30. See the letters of testimony published in Leroyer, *Vie et révélations*, 3:287–306.

31. Lecanu, *Dictionnaire des prophéties*, 1:427–432; La Harpe, *La prophétie de Cazotte*; Viatte, *Les sources occultes*, 1:195–200.

32. Lecanu, *Dictionnaire des prophéties*, 1:354–355. The *Catalogue des imprimés de la Bibliothèque Nationale*, 9:590, lists two editions of Beauregard's sermons published during the Restoration. For other eighteenth-century prophets popular in the nineteenth century see Curicque, *Voix prophétiques*, 1:311–320, 2:232–252.

33. Balzac, *Cousin Pons*, pp. 128–138. François Girault, a close friend of Balzac, published a biography of Mlle Le Normand in 1843; see Marceau, *Balzac et son monde*, pp. 479–480, and Girault, *Mlle Le Normand.*

34. Lecanu, *Dictionnaire des prophéties*, 2:717–720. For other examples of Mlle Le Normand's prophecies see her *Les oracles sibyllins* and *Arrêt suprême des dieux de l'Olympe*. These and the rest of Mlle Le Normand's prophecies were published and sold from her apartment in the faubourg St. Germain.

35. For Martin's career see Lenôtre, *Martin le visionnaire.*

36. Ibid., pp. 67–68, 98–100. Abbé d'Astros, then vicar-general of Paris and later archbishop of Toulouse, also interviewed and believed Martin. For more on the influence of Martin in clerical and Ultra circles see Sevrin, *Mgr Clausel de Montals*, 1:163–171.

37. Sevrin, *Mgr Clausel de Montals*, 2:731–732.

38. Leflon, *Eugene de Mazenod*, 2:349.

39. Webb, *The Occult Underground*, pp. 295–302.

40. Maistre, *Les soirées de Saint-Petersburg*, p. 323. Viatte, *Les sources occultes*, 2:64–95.

41. Maistre, *Les soirées de Saint-Petersburg*, p. 320.

42. Darnton, *Mesmerism.*

43. Sevrin, *Les missions religieuses en France sous la Restauration*; Bertier de Sauvigny, *The Bourbon Restoration*, pp. 302–322.

44. Frayssinous, *Oeuvres complètes*, p. 31.

45. *L'ami de la religion* 54 (1827):145–149. See also Langlois, "La conjoncture miraculeuse."

46. Vrindts, *La croix de Migné*, p. 198.

47. Norman Cohn, "Medieval Millenarianism: Its Bearing on the Comparative Study of Millenarian Movements," in Thrupp, ed., *Millennial Dreams in Action*, p. 3. On the relationship between prophecies and millennialism see Bryan R. Wilson, *Magic and the Millennium*, pp. 272–308.

48. Barkun, *Disaster and the Millennium*, p. 39.

49. See chapter 5, "Religion and Royalism in the 1870s."

50. Price, "Legitimist Opposition." Hilaire, *Une chrétienté*, 1:132, notes the survival of a taste for prophecies in the legitimist press of the 1830s and 1840s in the diocese of Arras.

51. Laurentin, *Catherine Labouré et la Médaille Miraculeuse*, 1:52.

52. Ibid., pp. 42, 50–52.

53. Dujardin, *L'oracle pour 1840*, pp. 157–161; Grand-Carteret, *Les almanachs français*, p. liv.

54. Lecanu, *Dictionnaire des prophéties*, 2:719.

55. Ibid., 2:727–728, prints the bishop of Verdun's official condemnation of the prophecy following an investigation by his vicar-general. The prophecy was condemned in 1849, following a revival of interest resulting from the revolution of 1848.

56. For the attitude of the State toward the prophetic underground see: Lenôtre, *Martin le visionnaire*, pp. 263–265; Webb, *Occult Underground*, pp. 297–298; Garçon, *Vintras*; Appolis, "Du nouveau sur la secte Vintras"; Lecanu, *Dictionnaire des prophéties*, 2:1151–1158.

57. Webb, *Occult Underground*, pp. 304–306.

58. Cited in Fried and Sanders, *Socialist Thought*, pp. 82, 101–102. For an introduction to Saint-Simon see Manuel and Manuel, *Utopian Thought*, pp. 590–614.

59. Manuel and Manuel, *Utopian Thought*, pp. 615–640; Fried and Sanders, *Socialist Thought*, pp. 101–102. The standard work on Saint-Simonism remains Charléty, *Histoire du Saint-simonisme*.

60. Webb, *Occult Underground*, pp. 307–309. See the introduction by Frank Bowman in Constant, *Eliphas Levi*, pp. 5–59.

61. Christopher H. Johnson, *Utopian Communism in France*, pp. 233–235.

62. Newman, "Sounds in the Desert."

63. Sewell, *Work and Revolution in France*, p. 269.

64. Ibid., pp. 157–161, 219–220.

65. Garrett, *Respectable Folly*, p. 225.

66. "Apolcalypse—which represented a scandalous ancestry to socialists who wished to make Marxism compatible with the practice of politicians in a democ-

racy—in reality corresponds perfectly to the general strike which, for revolutionary syndicalists, represents the advent of the new world to come." Georges Sorel, *The Decomposition of Marxism,* cited in Horowitz, *Radicalism and the Revolt Against Reason,* p. 33. See also Humphrey, *Georges Sorel,* pp. 186–203.

67. Garrett, *Respectable Folly,* p. 225.

68. Harrison, *The Second Coming,* p. 224.

69. Talmon, *Political Messianism.*

70. Vincenzo Gioberti, *Del primato morale e civile degli Italiani,* 2 vols. (Milan, 1939) 2:333–335. First published 1843.

71. Salvemini, *Mazzini,* pp. 69–72.

72. Kohn, *Pan-Slavism,* pp. 27–54.

73. Ibid., pp. 125–160.

74. Robert Bellah, *Beyond Belief,* p. 174. See also: Tuveson, *Redeemer Nation;* Hatch, *The Sacred Cause of Liberty.*

CHAPTER 4

1. Delumeau, *Le catholicisme entre Luther et Voltaire,* pp. 62–86.

2. Palmer, *Catholics and Unbelievers,* pp. 53–102; Kreiser, *Miracles, Convulsions, and Ecclesiastical Politics,* pp. 398–400.

3. *Relation des faits miraculeux; Note sur l'existence miraculeuse.*

4. Emmerich, *La douloureuse passion de N.-S. Jésus Christ,* was first translated into French in 1835. By 1850 it had appeared in at least thirty editions. *Vie de la très-sainte vierge* went through at least ten editions during the period 1854–1881: *Catalogue des imprimés de la Bibliothèque Nationale,* 47:328–331.

5. "In every period of human history . . . miraculous communications have been established between heaven and earth. . . . These supernatural manifestations did not occur exclusively in the first centuries of Christianity. History attests that they have been perpetuated from age to age, for the glory of religion and the edification of the faithful" (Episcopal decree approving Lourdes apparitions, Laurentin and Billet, *Lourdes—documents authentiques* [hereafter *LDA*], 6:235). "[We] have insisted on not regarding as impossible an event that the Lord (who would dare deny it?) might allow to occur for his greater glory; because his arm has not been withdrawn, and his power is the same today as in centuries past" (Episcopal decree approving La Salette apparitions, Bassette, *Le fait de La Salette,* p. 233). See also: *Encyclopédie catholique* (Paris, 1847), 14:552–557; Loth, *Le miracle en France,* pp. 7–29. Monden, *Signs and Wonders,* while sensitive to the symbolic significance of miracles, also reiterates the nineteenth-century position that they establish the supernatural credentials of the Catholic Church.

6. Leroyer, *Vie et révélations,* 1:175.

7. Lataste, *Letters and Writings*, 1:14.

8. Congar, *A History of Theology*.

9. Foucher, *La philosophie catholique*, pp. 11–27; Boas, *French Philosophies*, pp. 70–153.

10. Baunard, *Un siècle de l'église de France*, pp. 209–221; Janvier, *Vie de M. Dupont*, 1:277–322; Lestra, *Retourner le monde*; Hédouville, *Monseigneur de Ségur*, pp. 597–605.

11. Lataste, *Letters and Writings*, 3:110–111.

12. Leroyer, *Vie et révélations*, 2:60; Loth, *Le miracle en France*, pp. 321–335, reports several Eucharistic miracles in which hosts were preserved despite the attacks of revolutionaries. It should be recalled that at Lourdes in the late nineteenth century healings were more likely to be produced by the Holy Sacrament than by bathing in the fountain. See chapter 2, "The Social Drama of a Miraculous Cure."

13. The controversial doctrine of indulgences also received support through miraculous visions. See for example Lataste, *Letters and Writings*, 1:304–305; Curicque, *Voix prophétiques*, 2:362–372.

14. Ladoue, "Les écrits de Marie Lataste"; for a list of bishops and vicars-general approving the visions and prophecies of Soeur de la Nativité, see Leroyer, *Vie et révélations*, 3:287–306.

15. The other major dogma identified with the history of the Catholic Church in the nineteenth century, papal infallibility, will be discussed in chapter 5. On the history of the doctrine of the Immaculate Conception, see O'Connor, *The Dogma of the Immaculate Conception*; Warner, *Alone of All Her Sex*, pp. 236–254.

16. Graef, *Mary*, 2:77–78.

17. Pie, *Lettre pastorale*. For a similar reaction to the definition of the dogma, see the article by Dom Guéranger in *L'Univers*, January 14, 1859, p. 1. See also Graef, *Mary*, 2:79–80; *L'Univers*, November–December 1854, passim.

18. Aretin, *The Papacy and the Modern World*, pp. 99–100.

19. Grignon de Montfort, *Oeuvres complètes*, p. viii. Between 1842 and 1895 the *Traité* went through at least fourteen editions; see *Catalogue des imprimés de la Bibliothèque Nationale*, 64:602.

20. Grignon de Montfort, *Oeuvres complètes*, pp. 494, 506.

21. St. Léonard (1676–1751) predicted that a period of universal peace would follow the declaration of the Immaculate Conception. His prediction was cited by Mgr Morlau, bishop of Bruges, in his work, *L'immaculée conception de la bienheureuse vierge Marie* (1857), cited by Curicque, *Voix prophétiques*, 2:135–142; Lataste, *Letters and Writings*, 1:155–158.

22. Aladel, *The Miraculous Medal*, pp. ix–xiv; Graef, *Mary*, 2:86–87; Engelbert, *Catherine Labouré*, pp. 35–38; Guérin, *Abbé Desgenettes*, pp. 2–3.

23. O'Connor, *The Dogma of the Immaculate Conception*, pp. 469–470.

24. For some eschatological references in the Marian literature see Aladel, *The Miraculous Medal*, p. 46; Brulais, *L'écho de la sainte montagne*, pp. 58–66; Saint-John, *L'épopée mariale en France*; Gaume, *Un signe des temps;* Allard, *Paradis terrestre de la fin des siècles*; Guerin, *La vision de la jeune fille de Lourdes*, pp. 53–54. See also Savart, "Cent ans après," pp. 215–216.

25. A selection from *La mère de Dieu* appears in Constant, *Eliphas Levi*, pp. 109–178. See chapter 3, "Prophecy and Politics in the Nineteenth Century."

26. The episcopal decree verifying the apparition made an explicit connection between the miracle and the dogma: "How can we not . . . admire the economy of divine Providence? At the end of 1854 the immortal Pius IX proclaimed the dogma of the Immaculate Conception. . . . And then, only three years later, the Holy Virgin appearing to a child says to her: I am the Immaculate Conception: I want a chapel built here in my honor. Doesn't she seem to want to consecrate with a monument the infallible oracle of the successor of Saint Peter?" *LDA*, 6:242. The early reports of Bernadette's vision based on her own testimony include explicit references to the pose of Mary on the Miraculous Medal. See *LDA*, 1:235; 6:132; Estrade, *The Apparitions of the Blessed Virgin Mary*, p. 129. For other references to the relationship between the Immaculate Conception and contemporary Marian apparitions see Bouix, *Apparitions de Notre-Dame de Lourdes*, pp. 188–193; Mgr Villecourt, in appealing to Pius IX to proclaim the doctrine, argued that the apparition at La Salette was proof of the Immaculate Conception; see Bassette, *Le fait de La Salette*, p. 224, n. 2.

27. Aladel, *The Miraculous Medal*, p. 310; Saint John, *L'épopée mariale en France*, pp. vii–viii; Rousselot, *Manuel du pèlerin*, p. 38.

28. *Le rosier de Marie*, 17 mai 1861; see also ibid., 19 décembre 1858.

29. Cited in Curicque, *Voix prophétiques*, 2:474–475.

30. My understanding of "devotion" is derived from William Christian's usage, in which the word describes "an attitude of reverence toward a sacred figure," and "an ongoing reverence or cult accorded a sacred figure." (*Person and God in a Spanish Valley*, p. 47). For my purposes, a distinction will be drawn between "devotion" and "cult" with the former referring to beliefs and behavior, while the latter relates more specifically to the institutions that support the devotion. The organization and development of cults will be treated in chapter 6; my immediate problem is not the institutional character of devotions, but their psychological and emotional attributes. On nineteenth-century devotions see Pirotte, "Les images de dévotion"; Latreille, "Pratique, piété, et foi populaire"; Cholvy, "Expression et évolution du sentiment religieux populaire."

31. Despite their anticlerical intent, the works of Paul Parfait provide the best introduction to the range of devotions introduced by the Church in nineteenth-century France. See his *L'arsenal de la dévotion* and *La foire aux reliques*.

32. Berger, *The Sacred Canopy*.

33. The standard work on the French mystical writers of the seventeenth century is Brémond, *A Literary History of Religious Thought in France*. See also Graef, *Mary*, 2:31–46.

34. "Anne-Catherine Emmerich," *Dictionnaire de spiritualité*, vol. 4, pt. 2, pp. 622–628. Soeur Emmerich's life of Jesus borrowed from popular tradition in providing details on his childhood and his relationships with his parents (ibid., 624–625). Mgr d'Hulst, the influential educator and publicist, in a lecture at Notre-Dame of Paris, went so far as to compare the human family with the Holy Trinity: "Father, mother, child, this is the human trinity: it is indeed far from resembling the divine trinity. Nevertheless, it retains the imprint of it. The majesty of the celestial father will descend on the head of the domestic society; the beauty of the mother will be enlightened by the Word; love, the work of the spirit, will be exchanged between them and will give birth to the fruit which will complete their union." Such a comparison reveals the intense spiritual intimacy thought to be ideal for family life (*Conférence de Notre-Dame de Paris: la morale de la famille*, Paris, 1894, p. 9).

35. "From the first hour of its publication, *The Life of Jesus* sold like a Waverly novel. Its success was immediate and immense, unprecedented for a scholarly work on a religious subject. . . . New editions of 5,000 copies each were exhausted in eight or ten days. . . . By November [1863], five months after its initial publication, 60,000 copies had been sold" (translator's introduction to Renan, *The Life of Jesus*, p. 16). See also Bierer, "Renan and His Interpreters."

36. Renan, *The Life of Jesus*, pp. 202–203.

37. Shorter, *The Making of the Modern Family*; Robertson, "Home as a Nest."

38. Lataste, *Letters and Writings*, 1:191. For a similar passage see Calvat, *Vie de Mélanie*, p. 185.

39. Parfait, *L'arsenal de la dévotion*, pp. 51–53.

40. Flaubert, *Madame Bovary*, p. 298.

41. Martin, *The Autobiography of St. Thérèse of Lisieux*, pp. 102–103.

42. Mgr Duperray, *Vers un plus grand amour*, cited in Rogé, *Le simple prêtre*, pp. 65–66. According to Père Gouta, an educator of seminarians, "Un culte ardent de la Sainte Vierge s'impose, normalement, pour tout futur prêtre, en raison des rapports si étroits de la Mére de Jesus avec le prêtre autre Jésus et autre saint Jean" (ibid., p. 65). A more erotic view of clerical devotion to Mary can be found in Zola's novel, *La faute de l'Abbé Mouret*, in which Serge Mouret imagines the Virgin putting her arms around his neck and waist. See Moody, *The Church as Enemy*, pp. 167–169. Some of the expressions used by Marie-Joseph Chiron, in a notebook written while attending the major seminary at Viviers during the Restoration, suggest that emotional intimacy with Christ could also be an ideal for religiously minded men. Here are some brief prayers of Chiron: "Who will be able to separate me from my everything? I want only my lover (mon Bien-Aimé). . . . O infinite

226 Notes to Pages 100–103

love! Convert this miserable heart. May I die to everything to live only for you."
Cited in Pognon, *Un prêtre de toujours*, p. 47.

43. Parfait, *L'arsenal de la dévotion*, pp. 320–325, 378–380.

44. "Cantique sur le Memorare," *Le salut facilité aux pécheurs*, p. 136. Marie-Joseph Chiron filled his student notebooks with sentimental appeals to Mary addressed as "Maman." See Pognon, *Un prêtre de toujours*, p. 43.

45. *Neuvaine à Notre-Dame de Lourdes*, p. 8.

46. In both the Miraculous Medal and the La Salette apparitions Mary wore a crown of stars. For examples of visions in which Christ is enthroned as King of Heaven see Lataste, *Letters and Writings*, 1:74; Aladel, *The Miraculous Medal*, p. 11.

47. Beauvoir, *The Second Sex*, p. 206. The characters of Rastignac in Balzac's *Père Goriot*, Julien Sorel in Stendhal's *The Red and the Black*, and Frédéric Moreau in Flaubert's *Sentimental Education* exemplify the secular romantic idolatry of the female. For other examples of the glorification of women see Jules Michelet, *La femme* (Paris, 1860); Jules Simon, "La liberté de la famille," in *La liberté* (Paris, 1859); Ernest Legouvé, *L'histoire morale des femmes* (Paris, 1896). For an excellent treatment of the status and values of middle-class women that pays special attention to the importance of religion see Smith, *Ladies of the Leisure Class*, pp. 93–122.

48. Mathevon, *Les pèlerinages aux XIXᵉ siècle*, pp. 38–39. This kind of sentimentalization of a feminine ideal can be clearly observed in the biographies of nineteenth-century clergy. See, for example, the reactions to their mothers' deaths of Mgr Dupanloup (Lagrange, *Vie de Mgr Dupanloup*, 1:455–459) and Mgr de Ségur (Hédouville, *Mgr de Ségur*, pp. 651–654).

49. Praz, *The Romantic Agony*; Babbit, *Rousseau and Romanticism*, pp. 176–188. See also Beauvoir, *The Second Sex*, p. 193.

50. Janvier, *Vie de M. Dupont*, 1:136–145, 2:1–16; Curicque, *Voix prophétiques*, 2:23–30.

51. Janvier, *Vie de M. Dupont*, 1:146–147; *Dictionnaire de spiritualité*, 2:1831–1833.

52. Janvier, *Vie de M. Dupont*, 2:2.

53. Other devotions specifically designed to make reparation for contemporary sins were the Nocturnal Adoration Society and the Archconfraternity of Our Lady of La Salette, ibid., 1:277–322; Baunard, *Un siècle de l'église de France*, pp. 216–218; Bassette, *Le fait de La Salette*, pp. 155–156; Hostachy, *Histoire séculaire de La Salette*, pp. 236–239.

54. Görres, *La mystique divine*, 2:206–209, 248–253; Imbert-Goubeyre, *Les stigmatisées*; Allies, *Journal in France*, pp. 127–158. In 1846 and 1847 a series of apparitions to a Daughter of Charity at Paris led to the devotion of the Red Scapular designed to augment pious interest in the Passion. The same instruments of the Passion that were on the crucifix worn by Mary at La Salette, a hammer and pincers, were in the vision in which the Red Scapular was revealed: Curicque, *Voix*

prophétiques, 2:17–20. See also Griffiths, *The Reactionary Revolution,* pp. 183–184; Curicque, *Voix prophétiques,* 2:499–515.

55. Bérulle, *Vie et miracles de sainte Philomène,* pp. 12–36.

56. Ibid., pp. 19, 190. For the popularity of the cult of St. Philomena see Nisard, *Histoire des livres populaires,* 2:50–54; Phayer, *Sexual Liberation and Religion,* pp. 129–138; and Boutry, "Un sanctuaire et son saint au XIXe siècle," p. 371.

57. Mario Praz has called attention to G. Lafourcade's association of the popularity of de Sade in literary circles with the "revival of the Christian tradition, with the ensuing stress on martyrdom and the lives of the saints into which sado-masochism strikes its deepest roots" (*The Romantic Agony,* p. 436).

58. Document 17 in the "Collection d'autographes de M. Chaper," manuscript collection R 8668 in the Bibliothèque Municipale of Grenoble.

59. Bloy, *Celle qui pleure,* vol. 5 of *Oeuvres de Léon Bloy; Vie de Mélanie,* intro. by Bloy.

60. Griffiths, *The Reactionary Revolution,* pp. 153–159, stresses the intellectual history of the theme of reparation, but neglects its devotional and popular aspect.

61. Vovelle and Vovelle, *Vision de la mort et de l'au-delà.*

62. For examples of how reparational devotions could affect France, see Desgenettes, *Manuel de l'instruction,* p. 236; Janvier, *Vie de M. Dupont,* 2:5; *Le Mémorial Catholique,* September 1858, cited in *LDA,* 4:271–272; Imbert-Goubeyre, *Les stigmatisées,* 1:181.

63. Plongeron, *Conscience religieuse en révolution,* p. 149, has argued that the publicity given to Benoit Labre (1748–1783) was due to an attempt to create a religious model with mass appeal. Labre's beatification and canonization were completed with the formal declaration of his sanctity on May 20, 1860; see Guillemant, *Pierre-Louis Parisis,* 3:654–669.

64. Leff, *Heresy in the Later Middle Ages,* 1:25–33, 68–83; Little, *Religious Poverty and the Profit Economy.*

65. Gérard Cholvy, "Le catholicisme populaire." On the vogue of literary pastoralism see Williams, *The Country and the City.* The official approval of La Salette and Lourdes amounted to an institutional sanction of the shepherd-heroes of the *colportage* literature of the ancien régime. See Bollème, "Représentation religieuse."

66. Desgenettes, *Manuel de l'instruction,* pp. 130, 251.

67. *LDA,* 1:218.

68. Lasserre, *Notre-Dame de Lourdes,* pp. 18–19.

69. See, for example, Aladel, *The Miraculous Medal,* p. 2; Leroyer, *Vie et révélations,* 1:127; *Letters and Writings of Marie Lataste,* 1:3–4.

70. Duroselle, *Les débuts du catholicisme sociale.* For an excellent discussion of the representative social ideas of Dupanloup see Marcilharcy, *Le diocèse d'Orléans sous l'épiscopat de Mgr Dupanloup,* pp. 37–43.

71. See this chapter, "Miracles and Doctrine."

72. Brulais, *L'écho de la sainte montagne*, pp. 148–149; Mgr Dupanloup, despite his unfavorable opinion of Mélanie and Maximin, wrote after visiting them in 1848: "This respect they have for the things of which they speak is so great that when they give one of their surprising and unexpected answers, which confuse the questioners, cut short all indiscreet questions, and resolve simply and profoundly the gravest difficulties, they don't show any sign of having triumphed over their interrogators." Bassette, *Le fait de La Salette*, p. 160.

73. The introduction to Lataste, *Letters and Writings*, 1:viii, asserts that Marie's visions "could not be the sole unaided work of an illiterate peasant girl." In this case illiteracy was applied loosely, since Marie herself says (1:3–4) that she knew how to read and write. Catherine Labouré could, at the time of the apparition of the Miraculous Medal, "read and write for her own use," but others had trouble interpreting her writing; Engelbert, *Catherine Labouré*, p. 22. Léon Bloy believed that Mélanie's ignorance went so far as to exclude all knowledge of sexual relationships, "ignorance qui était une autre sort de miracle" (*Celle qui pleure*, p. xxiii). The *curé d'Ars* was another religious model whose simplicity was idealized in the pious literature, in which his troubles in school were seen as contributing to his virtue: Monnin, *Le curé d'Ars*, 1:95–96.

74. Thomas, *Religion and the Decline of Magic*, p. 138; Cohn, *The Pursuit of the Millennium*.

75. Leroyer, *Vie et révélations*, 1:114; Aladel, *The Miraculous Medal*, p. 13; Lataste, *Letters and Writings*, 2:269. The importance of spiritual direction from a competent clergyman is stressed by Poulain, *The Graces of Interior Prayer*.

76. Soeur Nativité, Catherine Labouré, Soeur Saint-Pierre, and Soeur Apolline Andiveau (to whom the Red Scapular was revealed) were already in convents when they received their visions. Marie Lataste, Mélanie of La Salette, and Bernadette of Lourdes all entered convents following their visions.

CHAPTER 5

1. Pierre Sorlin has noted that "the important question of pilgrimages at the outset of the Third republic has never been studied" (see *La Croix et les juifs*, p. 246, n. 67). For discussions of the pilgrimage movement see Gadille, *La pensée et l'action politique*, 1:229–237; Chastenet, *Histoire de la troisième république*, 1:149–150; Brogan, *The Development of Modern France*, 1:92; McManners, *Church and State in France*, p. 40; Brugerette, *Le prêtre français*, 3:7–11; Marrus, "Cultures on the Move."

2. Crowds of between thirty and fifty thousand were reported to have attended the pilgrimages to Lourdes (October 6, 1872), Auray (December 8, 1872),

Chartres (May 27, 1873), and Paray-le-Monial (June 20, 1873); see *L'Univers,* December 9, 1872, May 29, 1873, June 22, 1873. Large crowds were also reported at regional shrines; see Drochon, *Histoire illustrée des pèlerinages,* pp. 820–823, 832–835, 1106, 1107.

3. Ricard, *Les pèlerinages de la France,* pp. 165–176; *L'Univers,* October 5–8, 1872, passim; Gadille, *La pensée et l'action politique,* 1:235–236.

4. Laurentin, *Pontmain,* 3:14, 24–25.

5. Ibid., p. 28; for similar letters see pp. 12–13.

6. Ibid., pp. 25, 112.

7. Ibid., pp. 115, 177–178.

8. Drochon, *Histoire illustrée des pèlerinages,* pp. 363–365, 398–400, 1221–1223; Gadille, *La pensée et l'action politique,* 1:229.

9. Laurentin, *Pontmain,* 3:110–111.

10. Curicque, *Voix prophétiques,* 2:241–254. The miracle at Pontmain received national attention when it was reported in *L'Univers,* March 30–31, 1871.

11. Curicque, *Voix prophétiques,* 2:640–654; *L'Univers,* November 17, 1872. The official publication of the diocese of Chartres published a long and favorable account of the apparitions in Alsace; see *La voix de Notre-Dame de Chartres* 23 (1873):58–67. Other diocesan papers reporting favorably on these miracles were *Écho de Fourvières,* diocese of Lyons, February 8, 1873, and the *Semaine Catholique* of Séez, February 6, 1873.

12. Curicque, *Voix prophétiques,* 2:254, 276; Heigel, "Les apparitions de la sainte Vierge." For the religious mood in the east see Lecanuet, *L'église . . . 1870–1878,* pp. 136–140. For an analysis of 1873 apparitions in Hérault see *Notre-Dame du Dimanche.*

13. Curicque, *Voix prophétiques,* 2:266.

14. Ibid., 2:240–282.

15. Lecanuet, *L'église . . . 1870–1878,* p. 202, mentions major pilgrimages to Pontmain, Mont St. Michael, and St. Martin of Tours in addition to those to Auray, La Salette, Lourdes, and Paray-le-Monial.

16. *Le six octobre à Lourdes,* p. 78.

17. M. F. de Champigny, "La question des pèlerinages," *Le Correspondant,* October 25, 1872, pp. 330–331. For a similar reaction to the pilgrimage to Paray-le-Monial see *L'Univers,* June 22, 1873.

18. Marie-Antoine, *Petit trésor,* pp. 88–89.

19. *L'Univers,* October 24, 1872. Mgr de la Bouillerie, coadjutor of Bordeaux, reacting to the religious atmosphere created by the pilgrimages and prophecies, voiced a similar reaction when he declared "Une politique seule peut nous sauver . . . la politique du miracle." *Le Pèlerin,* May 1, 1874, cited in *Notre-Dame du Dimanche,* p. 11.

20. Cited in Gadille, *La pensée et l'action politique,* 1:233.

21. Brugerette, *Le prêtre français*, 2:10–11.

22. Gadille, *La pensée et l'action politique*, 1:294–295; Chastenet, *Histoire de la troisième république* 1:149–151.

23. Rémond, *The Right Wing*, pp. 177–178; Locke, *French Legitimists*, pp. 44–51. For a description of the political and social theories of Mgr Pie and his followers, who constituted a majority of the French episcopate, see Gadille, *La pensée et l'action politique*, 1:46–72. The liberal position adopted by a minority of the bishops led by Mgrs Dupanloup and Maret sought an accommodation between the Church and the modern world. But even liberals believed that the State ought to allow the Church a prominent role in educational and social policy; see ibid., 1:72–105.

24. Brugerette, *Le prêtre français*, 2:123–149. Brown, "Catholic-Legitimist Militancy," and Osgood, *French Royalism Since 1870*, pp. 1–2, both discuss Catholic support of a restoration, but neglect the concurrent religious revival.

25. Rémond, *The Right Wing*, pp. 184–190; see also Mather, *La Croix and the Assumptionist Response to Secularization*.

26. Volumes 7 through 13 of Lorenz's *Catalogue générale de la librairie française* yield the following number of books and pamphlets under the heading of "prophecy": 1840–1849, 8; 1850–1859, 12; 1860–1869, 8; 1870–1879, 43; 1880–1889, 9; 1890–1899, 14; 1900–1909, 24. See also Mayeur, "Mgr Dupanloup." According to Lecanuet, *L'église . . . 1870–1878*, p. 202, n. 2, a pamphlet of the early 1870s entitled *Le grand avènement, précédé du grand Prodige* sold fifty thousand copies within a few weeks.

27. Dupanloup, "Lettre sur les prophéties," p. 1098.

28. Brown, *The Comte de Chambord*, p 3.

29. Chabauty, *Lettres sur les prophéties modernes*, pp. 88–89.

30. Curicque, *Voix prophétiques*, 1:vi–xi. Chabauty and Curicque are cited as the most prominent prophetic authors by Mayeur, "Mgr Dupanloup," pp. 194–196. Chabauty's *Lettres sur les prophéties modernes* went through at least ten editions in 1870 and 1871. Prophecies were defended in *L'Univers*, May 28, 1872. There were also prophecies in favor of "Napoleon IV," some of which tried to enlist Mgr Pie, the legitimist bishop of Poitiers, in their cause. A minor controversy arose when Pie disavowed the movement. See Ernest Merson, *Confidences d'un journaliste* (Paris, 1891), pp. 79–107.

31. Denis, *Les royalistes de la Mayenne*, p. 407.

32. Ibid., pp. 380–406; Locke, *French Legitimists*, p. 48.

33. Lecanuet, *L'église . . . 1870–1878*, p. 203.

34. *L'Univers*, Dec. 9, 1872; Hanotaux, *Contemporary France*, 2:83; Brown, *The Comte de Chambord*, p. 102.

35. Barbier, *Histoire du catholicisme*, 1:164–165. Mgr Pie wrote to Chambord two weeks before the pilgrimage that the ceremonies at Chartres inspired him with

confidence about the future; see Lecanuet, *L'église . . . 1870–1878*, pp. 203–204. Some pilgrims, encouraged by the revival, may have expected divine intervention to bring about a restoration; see Brugerette, *Le prêtre français*, 3:139–140. Even the moderate Catholic journal *Le Correspondant* perceived miraculous potential in the pilgrimage movement. M. F. de Champigny, in an article in *Le Correspondant* of October 25, 1872, p. 326, was inspired by the Lourdes pilgrimage to believe that God might intervene directly to solve the political problems of France and the Church: "Why not recognize that a great fact, a great manifestation has occurred in our midst. . . . We are not able to foresee the future . . . which perhaps contains the seed of our cure. Are we afraid of the supernatural? But after all, whoever believes in God believes in miracles. If there is a God, he is omnipotent; he can go beyond secondary causes, just as he can use them; he can make miracles today, just as he did at the creation."

36. Brown, *The Comte de Chambord*, pp. 102–103; Brogan, *The Development of Modern France*, 1:99; Lecanuet, *L'église . . . 1870–1878*, p. 211.

37. Hanotaux, *Contemporary France*, 2:82–88; Gadille, *La pensée et l'action politique*, 1:230–231; *Journal Officiel de la république française*, July 25, 1873, pp. 5008–5015.

38. This interpretation differs from Brogan, *The Development of Modern France*, 1:98–99, who argues that the debate over the construction of Sacré-Coeur "erected another barrier between the Royalist parties and the hesitant bourgeoisie." Republican propaganda did take advantage of the debate, but at the time of the vote in July it seemed that a restoration was imminent. The success of the right was a significant demonstration of royalist strength in the assembly, a kind of test vote of its support for Chambord. See Chastenet, *Histoire de la troisième république*, 1:153–154, for Catholic reaction to the decision.

39. Brown, *The Comte de Chambord*, p. 112.

40. Locke, *French Legitimists*, pp. 49–50.

41. Brown, *The Comte de Chambord*, p. 132.

42. Cited in Lecanuet, *L'église . . . 1870–1878*, pp. 221–222. The moderate Catholic paper *Le Français* cited prophetic faith in a restoration as one reason why some extremists were willing to ally themselves with the left in opposing the Broglie ministry in 1874; see Mayeur, "Mgr Dupanloup," pp. 199–200. Robert Locke, who kindly responded to an inquiry from me, recalls no evidence in the private archives of the legitimists that shows any direct influence of prophetic literature on political behavior. But he does believe the actions of the extreme right reflect a "prophetic sense."

43. *L'Univers*, January 1, 1874.

44. Chabauty, *Les prophéties modernes vengées*.

45. Cited in Lecanuet, *L'église . . . 1878-1894*, p. 184.

46. *L'Univers*, July 15, 1882.

47. *La Croix*, September 8, 1883.

48. Sedgwick, *The Ralliement in French Politics*, p. 45.

49. Catholic support for Louis Napoleon was based in large part on his decision to use the French expeditionary force at Rome to suppress the Roman Republic rather than mediate between Rome and the pope; see Scott, *The Roman Question*, p. 58; Maurain, *La politique ecclésiastique*, pp. 940–941.

50. Curicque, *Voix prophétiques*, 1:31–44; Loth, *Le miracle en France*, pp. 333–335.

51. Pie, *Discours prononcé*, pp. 16–17.

52. Curicque, *Voix prophétiques*, 2:583–589. See also Rémond, *The Right Wing*, p. 186.

53. Baunard, *Un siècle de l'église*, pp. 255–261. For an example of the successful pressure exerted by Rome in establishing a universal liturgy see Archives Nationales, F^{19} 2531, which documents the conflict between Cardinal de Bonald of Lyons and the Roman Curia over the replacement of the local liturgy.

54. Baunard, *Un siècle de l'église*, pp. 92–110; E. E. Y. Hales, *Pio Nono* (Garden City, N.Y., 1954).

55. Maurain, *La politique ecclésiastique*, p. 397, points out that clerical agitation over the Roman question was not generally shared by Catholics, possibly because the cultic practices central to their religious life were not threatened by an attack on the temporal power of the pope. Clerical support for the pope was universal, however, and there is some evidence of popular support; see ibid., pp. 398–434, 515–532. Michel Denis has characterized the devotion of some Catholics in western France as "papolatrie." See his *Les royalistes de la Mayenne*, pp. 409–411.

56. Curicque, *Voix prophétiques*, 2:34–35.

57. Butler, *The Vatican Council*, pp. 11–43, provides background for these two traditions.

58. Firminhac, "Pie IX, Novembre 1869," in his *Poésies catholiques*, pp. 47–50. On the French devotion to Pius IX see Butler, *The Vatican Council*, pp. 50, 60–61.

59. Langer, *European Alliances*, p. 32.

60. Girard, *Les secrets de la Salette*; Bliard, *Lettres à un ami*.

61. Marie-Antoine, *Petit trésor*, p. 90.

62. Firminhac, "Les grands jours," *Poésies catholiques*, pp. 60–63.

63. Brogan, *The Development of Modern France*, 1:89–91; Chastenet, *Histoire de la troisième république*, 1:155–156, 160. Moderate legitimists like the Duc de Broglie attributed much of the blame for Chambord's failure to recover the throne to the intimate association of royalism, the pope, and the papal territories. According to Broglie, "The cause of religion, that of the temporal power of the pope, and that of the restoration of Henry V were too frequently described . . . as destined to triumph someday by the same means. Nothing was less skillful and nothing gave reason more unfortunately to the ridiculous imputations of the republican press." Cited in Acomb, *The French Laic Laws*, p. 42.

64. Langer, *European Alliances*, p. 38.

65. Larkin, *Church and State*, p. 46.

66. Nicolas, in *Défense et explication du secret*, predicted that "le grand coup" would fall in 1881; Combe, *Le grand coup*; *Considérations sur le projet*; Jean-Marie, *Histoire authentique des secrets*. These attempts to predict apocalyptic events generally coincided with crises in Church-State relations, and based themselves on interpretations of Mélanie's Secret. For the career of this prophecy see Appolis, "En marge du catholicisme contemporain."

67. Chabauty, *Les prophéties modernes vengées*, pp. 1–2.

68. Comte Albert de Mun illustrated this inability to articulate an alternative to the monarchy when, reflecting on the death of Chambord, he wrote: "I no longer have a political faith; I have sought only expedients" (cited in Martin, *Count Albert de Mun*, p. 39). For the divisions in the right see Rémond, *The Right Wing*, pp. 199–204.

69. Cited in Martin, *Count Albert de Mun*, p. 57. For the success of the negative campaign in 1885 see also Goguel, *La politique des partis*, p. 59.

70. Calvat, *L'apparition de la très sainte vierge*, pp. 13–17.

71. *La Croix*, June 6, 1884; cited in Mather, *La Croix and the Assumptionist Response to Secularization*, p. 80.

72. *La Croix*, May 5, 1885; cited in Mather, *La Croix and the Assumptionist Response to Secularization*, p. 81.

73. *L'Univers*, January 2–3, 1883.

74. McIntosh, *Eliphas Levi*, p. 216. On anti-Masonism see also Byrnes, *Anti-Semitism*, 1:304–319; Sorlin, *La Croix et les juifs*, pp. 79–82. For an excellent discussion of Taxil and a presentation of documents see Eugen Weber, *Satan franc-maçon*.

75. Byrnes, *Anti-Semitism*, 1:149–152; Sorlin, *La Croix et les juifs*, pp. 192–193.

76. Drumont, *La France juive*, pp. 167, 196–197; Byrnes, *Anti-Semitism*, 1:144–145. Méry published a series of eight pamphlets on Mlle Couédon in 1896 which related the visionary to the full range of occult concerns of the era, including haunted houses, Marian apparitions, and royalist prophecies.

77. Sorlin, *La Croix et les juifs*, pp. 149–152; on the anti-Semitic riots see Stephen Wilson, "The Anti-Semitic Riots of 1898."

78. Stephen Wilson, "Le monument Henry," p. 280.

79. *La France chrétienne—Revue hebdomadaire, anti-maçonnique et anti-sémitique*, February 3, 1903; September 8, 1904; September 29, 1904; January 26, 1905. These and other articles from the paper have been collected and collated by the Marian Library, University of Dayton. At the time of the Church-State crisis surrounding the separation of 1905 there was some concern among Catholic leaders that a belief in "le grand coup" among the faithful would make them less willing to take up arms and defend their churches against the State. See Sabatier, *A propos de la séparation des éqlises et de l'état*, pp. 208–209.

80. Marrus, *The Politics of Assimilation*, pp. 201–202; Jean-Pierre Peter, "Dimensions de l'affaire Dreyfus," p. 1165.
81. Stephen Wilson, "Le monument Henry," p. 285.

CHAPTER 6

1. Kreiser, *Miracles, Convulsions, and Ecclesiastical Politics*; Shiokawa, *Pascal et les miracles*.
2. Muchembled, *Culture populaire*, pp. 266–267. For the increasing rigor of the Church in investigating miracles used as evidence in favor of beatification and canonization see Delooz, *Conditions sociologiques*, and Kemp, *Canonization and Authority*. In the eighteenth century Cardinal Lambertini, who eventually became Pope Benedict XIV, published a treatise on beatification which established strict standards for the Church in the case of such miracles. A partial translation of this treatise appeared as *Sagesse de l'église dans la béatification et la canonisation des saints* (Brussels, 1852). For the canonical restrictions on the circulation of printed material about miracles see Dupanloup, "Lettre sur les prophéties," pp. 1097–1121.
3. Bassette, *Le fait de La Salette*, p. 67; Hostachy, *Histoire séculaire*, p. 33.
4. Desgenettes, *Manuel de l'instruction*, pp. 82–83; Laurentin, *Pontmain*, 3:21–25. For the involvement of the clergy with Hohenlohe see chapter 2, "The Social Drama of a Miraculous Cure."
5. Laurentin and Billet, *Lourdes—documents authentiques* (hereafter *LDA*), 1:168.
6. This was the case even when the miracles were eventually disavowed by the Church. For examples of favorable clerical responses to miracles later judged fallacious see Garçon, *Rosette Tamisier*, p. 28; Lenôtre, *Martin le visionnaire*, p. 28; Parfait, *Le dossier des pèlerinages*, pp. 33–36. For a nineteenth-century miracle and cult that were never formally approved by the Church, but which were tacitly sanctioned, see *Notre-Dame du Dimanche*. After a period of benevolent neutrality toward a series of apparitions to Estelle Faguet in 1876, the archbishop of Bourges effectively discouraged a cult at Pellevoisin; see Beevers, *The Sun Her Mantle*, pp. 137–140; *Notre-Dame de Pellevoisin*. My primary concern in this chapter is with those cults that were approved and absorbed in some fashion by the institutional Church.
7. Vrindts, *La croix de Migné*, pp. 221–223.
8. Bassette, *La fait de La Salette*, pp. 1–2.
9. *LDA*, 1:248–249. For evidence on the belief of the clergy following the apparition at Pontmain, see chapter 5, "Apparitions, Pilgrimages, and Nationalism."
10. Bassette, *Le fait de La Salette*, p. 19; Hostachy, *Histoire séculaire*, p. 40; *LDA*, 1:157–214; Laurentin, *Pontmain*, 3:41–42; Garçon, *Rosette Tamisier*, pp. 34–40; *Notre-Dame du Dimanche*, pp. 36–37; Parfait, *Le dossier des pèlerinages*, pp. 33–36.

11. Estrade, *The Apparitions*, pp. 78–82.

12. Soboul, *La société française*, pp. 92–93. Le Bras, "L'obligation juridique de pratiquer la religion chrétienne sous l'ancien régime," *Études de sociologie religieuse*, 1:25–26.

13. Vrindts, *La croix de Migné*, p. 24. In 1876 Mgr Pie argued in a commemorative decree that the apparition at Migné was intended to sanction the mission movement. Loth, *Le miracle en France*, pp. 47–50.

14. Chaline, "Le recrutement du clergé," p. 405. See also Huot-Pleuroux, *Le recrutement sacerdotal*, pp. 258–259; Perouas, "L'évolution du clergé," pp. 23–24; Hilaire, *Une chrétienté*, 1:175–180.

15. Loisy, *My Duel with the Vatican*, p. 49.

16. Rodé, *Le miracle dans la controverse moderniste*.

17. Hostachy, *Histoire séculaire*, pp. 179, 230–231; *LDA*, 1:262, 2:27–28, 225.

18. Hostachy, *Histoire séculaire*, 230–231. The imperial prosecutor stationed at Lourdes, M. Dutour, and the prefect of the Hautes-Pyrénées, Baron Massy, both commented on the profits made by local businessmen as a result of the new shrine at the grotto. See *LDA*, 1:255; 2:254–255. For more information on the economic impact of pilgrimages see "Church–State Conflict."

19. On ecclesiastical income from shrines see "Conflicts over Miracle Cults."

20. Hostachy, *Histoire séculaire*, p. 239.

21. Hostachy, *Histoire séculaire*, p. 240. A letter from Abbé Jacques Perrin responding to a request for a parish novena has been preserved at the Bibliothèque Municipale of Grenoble, R 8668, no. 100. Abbé Mélin of Corps reported between forty and fifty requests for fountain water and/or prayers during the early months of the cult at La Salette.

22. For early interrogations of Mélanie and Maximin at La Salette see Bassette, *Le fait de La Salette*, pp. 4–6, 14–17. Bernadette of Lourdes was first questioned by the prosecutor and the police commissioner; see *LDA*, 1:158–167. For her first visit with the local *curé* see ibid., 1:170.

23. See, for example, *L'ami de la religion* 32 (1822):360–361; 34 (1822): 121–122, 216–217.

24. *L'ami de la religion* 34 (1822):122.

25. Only the commission investigating the apparition at Migné had lay participation; see Langlois, "La conjoncture miraculeuse," p. 229.

26. "Mandement de l'évêque de Poitiers à l'occasion de la croix de Migné," *L'ami de la religion* 54 (1827):145.

27. Laurentin, *Pontmain*, 3:24–25.

28. Bassette, *Le fait de La Salette*, pp. 24–25.

29. Ibid., pp. 92–144. Bassette's discussion of the proceedings of the episcopal commission includes lengthy sections of the minutes.

30. *LDA*, 3:30–36.

31. The works of René Laurentin and Louis Bassette are invaluable for their

presentation of essential primary materials, but both are undeniably advocates of the miracles and the commissions that confirmed them.

32. Hostachy, *Histoire séculaire*, pp. 47–48.

33. Langlois, "La conjoncture miraculeuse," p. 231.

34. Vrindts, *La croix de Migné*.

35. *Le Siècle*, February 16, 1847.

36. *L'Univers*, February 17, 1847.

37. Bassette, *Le fait de La Salette*, pp. 32–35, discusses the early controversy over La Salette in the Parisian press.

38. Villecourt, *Nouveau récit*. See Bassette, *La fait de La Salette*, pp. 74–76, for the exchanges between Villecourt and the bishop of Grenoble which preceded the publication of this work.

39. *L'Univers*, May 18, 1858. This first article on Lourdes was a collection of material first published in local journals such as *L'ère imperial* and *L'intérêt public* and the Paris paper *L'Union*: see *LDA*, 2:306.

40. *LDA*, 3:195. For a general discussion of the influence of the press in nineteenth-century France, see Crubellier, *Histoire culturelle*, pp. 169–193.

41. Laurentin, *Catherine Labouré*, 1:42, 50–52.

42. For the minutes of the episcopal inquest on the Miraculous Medal apparitions see ibid., 1:235–249.

43. Hostachy, *Histoire séculaire*, p. 122.

44. Bassette, *Le fait de La Salette*, pp. 77–78.

45. Ibid., pp. 80–81.

46. *LDA*, 3:211.

47. *LDA*, 3:293.

48. *LDA*, 3:253.

49. *LDA*, 3:271–272.

50. *LDA*, 3:253.

51. Zeldin, *France, 1848–1945*, 1:24.

52. Hostachy, *Histoire séculaire*, pp. 229–263; Archives Nationales, F^{19} 2374.

53. *L'ami de la religion* 51 (1827):50–53.

54. Bassette, *Le fait de La Salette*, pp. 113–114. Mgr Dupanloup's favorable report on the shepherd–visionaries of La Salette was frequently cited; see ibid., pp. 156–166. See also *LDA*, 1:251; Laurentin, *Pontmain*, 3:122–123, 126–127.

55. *LDA*, 6:242.

56. Bassette, *Le fait de La Salette*, pp. 139–140; *LDA*, 6:241–242.

57. Bassette, *Le fait de La Salette*, p. 234; *LDA*, 6:241. Laurentin, *Pontmain*, 3:169.

58. Bassette, *Le fait de La Salette*, p. 239.

59. *LDA*, 6:243.

60. For example, see Desgenettes, *Manuel d'instruction*, pp. 68–71; Lasserre, *Notre-Dame de Lourdes*, p. 153; Aladel, *The Miraculous Medal*, pp. 33–71.

61. See chapter 4, "Miracles and Doctrine."

62. According to the Catholic publicist Arthur Loth, miracles were the best argument against naturalism. "The miracle is not a mysterious, occult thing which escapes the investigations of men; it is a visible fact, a fact like all others, able to be easily observed and verified" (*Le miracle en France*, p. 13). The Bureau of Medical Confirmation at Lourdes, opened in 1888, was specifically designed to provide scientific sanction for the miraculous. See Leuret and Bon, *Modern Miraculous Cures*, pp. 94–122.

63. The phrase is drawn from the decree approving the apparition at La Salette; see Bassette, *Le fait de La Salette*, p. 233.

64. The Benedictines promoted the medal of St. Benedict, and the priests of Notre-Dame du Sacré-Coeur successfully marketed a full range of religious objects and literature designed, in part, to obtain special graces from heaven; see Parfait, *Le dossier des pèlerinages*, pp. 73, 86.

65. See chapter 4, "Conflicts over Miracle Cults."

66. At Notre-Dame du Dimanche, although no decree ever approved the shrine and its cult, episcopal permission was granted for the construction of a chapel at the site of the apparition and a vicar-general attended its consecration. See *Notre-Dame du Dimanche*, pp. 73–75.

67. Bassette, *Le fait de La Salette*, p. 119; Laurentin, *Pontmain*, 3:148.

68. Loth, *Le miracle en France*, p. 36; Hostachy, *Histoire séculaire*, p. 175; Parfait, *Le dossier des pèlerinages*, pp. 73–75.

69. *Pèlerinages célèbres* (Lille et Paris, 1901), pp. 193–198.

70. Parfait, *Le dossier des pèlerinages*, p. 367; Lecanuet, *L'église . . . 1870–1878*, p. 299.

71. For the staffing of the parish shrine of Notre-Dame des Victoires see Archevêché de Paris, Archives Historiques, I, P, 33. For Notre-Dame de Montligéon see Archives Nationales, F[19] 5562.

72. See chapters 1 and 2.

73. *LDA*, 7:26, 66–67. Brulais, *L'écho de la sainte montagne*, pp. 209–210.

74. See, for example, Boisnard, *Les sanctuaires de Marie*, pp. 144–174; Fourcade, *L'apparition*, pp. 10–11.

75. Even before the railroad's successful association with the Lourdes pilgrimage, improvements in the roads made travel to shrines easier. The transportation industry was quick to respond to the improvements and the demand for access to shrines. For the rapid development of the travel business feeding Ars, where Jean Vianney was a major cultic figure, see Fourrey, "Un village," pp. 1–10; Boutry, "Un sanctuaire et son saint au XIXe siècle," pp. 56–57. Railroads were used to carry pilgrims to regional as well as national shrines. For example, see Mun, "Pèlerinage à N.D. de Liesse."

76. Billet, "Le fait de Lourdes," p. 235; *LDA*, 7:19–20, 73–75.

77. The history of the expansion of the Lourdes pilgrimage can be most easily

traced in the *Annales de Notre-Dame de Lourdes*, which began publication in 1868 as a quarterly.

78. *LDA*, 7:110–111. The impact of the shrine at La Salette on the city of Corps is discussed by the anonymous author of *L'apparition de La Salette*, a manuscript history written in 1920 and stored at the Bibliothèque Municipale of Grenoble, R 8675. The author reports that Corps came to rely on the pilgrimage for its income, and consequently suffered as it went into decline late in the nineteenth century. The population of Corps fell from 5,346 in 1846 to 3,851 in 1908. For the popularization of the statue of Notre-Dame de Lourdes, see Savart, "A la recherche de l'art dit de Saint Sulpice."

79. Drochon, *Histoire illustrée*, pp. 613–614; *Annales de Notre-Dame de Lourdes* 39 (1906):44.

80. Baudouy, *Le père François Picard*, pp. 176–177.

81. Data for the organized pilgrimages are drawn from the *Annales de Notre-Dame de Lourdes*. For some years, however, the *Annales* reporting of numbers of pilgrims is spotty. The years 1873, 1893, and 1913 were chosen because they were well reported, and because they covered a long enough period within which the diffusion of the Lourdes pilgrimage could be observed. Bertrin, *Histoire critique*, pp. 438–439, reports that an average of 357,000 persons visited Lourdes apart from the organized pilgrims during the period 1899 to 1908. It is impossible to determine, however, the origins of these visitors. Moreover, as an index of devotion to Lourdes organized pilgrims are probably a better measure, since they were more likely to be religiously committed, while individual visitors may have been more tourists than pilgrims. The issue of tourists as pilgrims is discussed in Dupront, "Tourisme et pèlerinage," pp. 97–121.

82. Bertrin, *Histoire critique*, pp. 437–438, provides the data for the pilgrimage to Lourdes. If the unorganized pilgrims are included in the data, the following results are obtained:

Year	Pilgrims to Lourdes	Year	Pilgrims to Lourdes
1899	559,428	1904	652,644
1900	522,244	1905	545,645
1901	629,877	1906	553,896
1902	533,133	1907	540,550
1903	519,544	1908	1,133,990

83. Tilly and Shorter, *Strikes in France*, p. 361.

84. *LDA*, 6:401.

85. Agulhon, *Pénitents et francs-maçons*. For examples of nineteenth-century conflicts between clergy and laity over the control of confraternities see Bée, "La révolte des confréries," p. 89–115; Vidalenc, *Le département de l'Eure*, pp. 568–570.

In 1842 the bishop of Gap abolished a parish confraternity that had engaged in a bitter conflict with its *curé*; see Archives Nationales, F^{19} 5731.

86. Ferté, *La vie religieuse*, p. 360; Vovelle and Vovelle, *Vision de la mort*.

87. Lambert and Buirette, *Histoire de l'église*, p. 281.

88. Ibid., pp. 296–297. See also Desgenettes, *Le salut facilité aux pécheurs* (Angers, 1842), pp. 8–9.

89. Desgenettes, *Le salut facilité*, p. 10.

90. Desgenettes, *Manuel d'instruction*, p. 95.

91. Ibid., p. 101; Savart, "Pour une sociologie," p. 835.

92. Desgenettes, *Manuel d'instruction*, pp. 122–123.

93. Desgenettes, *Le salut facilité*, pp. 38–39; for the support of the Sulpicians see Lambert and Buirette, *Histoire de l'église*, p. 96.

94. For example *Le lys du val*, a devotional work on Notre-Dame de Garaison, appeared in 1630, 1646, 1700, and 1847. See Drochon, *Histoire illustrée*, p. 615. Martin, *Le pèlerinage de Sainte Anne*, although published in 1845, includes only seventeenth-century miracles. See also Nisard, *Histoire des livres populaires*, 2:36–47, 138–145.

95. The *Annales de l'archconfrérie* appeared irregularly from 1842 until 1862, and then became a monthly publication. The earliest bulletins went through several reprintings in the 1840s and 1850s; see Savart, "Pour une sociologie," p. 827.

96. *Annales de l'archconfrérie*, 5th bulletin (1845):362–369. Stories of conversions were especially popular. For example, see bulletin 2 for the famous recital by Alphonse Ratisbonne of his miraculous conversion; see also bulletin 3:221, 224; bulletin 4:295.

97. May, "The Falloux Law," and idem, "The Fourth Estate."

98. Walter Shapiro, "The Liberal Plot to Kill God," *Washington Monthly* 7 (1975):21–30; James Michaels, "Electronic Holy War Brewing," *National Catholic Reporter* 16 (1980):1, 8.

99. See chapter 3, "Prophecy and Economic Crisis."

100. Eisenstein, *The Printing Press*, pp. 311–312, 325–326.

101. Furet and Ozouf, *Lire et écrire*; Jean Hébrard, "École et alphabétisation au XIXe siècle," *Annales-économies, sociétés, civilisations* 35 (1980):66–80.

102. Boulard, *Premiers itinéraires*. For a summary of the findings of Le Bras' followers see Claude Langlois, "La religion vécue," in Mayeur, ed., *L'histoire religieuse*, pp. 42–46.

103. Jourdan, *L'eau de La Salette*. See also references cited in n. 60 of this chapter.

104. On the catechetical movement see Germaine, *Parler du salut*; Sevrin, *Les missions religieuses*.

105. Lasserre, *Notre-Dame de Lourdes*, pp. 68–69; Desgenettes, *Manuel d'instruction*, pp. 89–100.

106. Phillips, *The Church in France, 1848–1907*, pp. 10–12; Langlois, *Le diocèse de Vannes au XIXᵉ siècle*, pp. 178–182; Marcilharcy, *Le diocèse d'Orléans sous l'épiscopat de Mgr Dupanloup*, pp. 63–67.

107. Langlois, "La conjoncture miraculeuse," p. 231; Bassette, *Le fait de La Salette*, pp. 243–289; *LDA*, 4:56–57.

108. Allignol and Allignol, *De l'état actuel du clergé en France*; Phillips, *The Church in France, 1848–1907*, p. 11.

109. Parfait, *Le dossier des pèlerinages*, pp. 66–67, 99–121.

110. Archevêché de Paris, Archives Historiques, I, P, 33. This file contains a great deal of material on the finances of the Archconfraternity.

111. Ibid.

112. Archives Nationales, F¹⁹ 5562. Dossier on Chapel of Notre-Dame de Montligéon, report of prefect of Orne, June 15, 1895.

113. Hostachy, *Histoire séculaire*, pp. 231–232; Geary, *Furta Sacra*.

114. Bassette, *Le fait de La Salette*, pp. 127–128. In 1854 the opposition leaders published a major attack on the cult of La Salette: *La Salette devant le pape, ou rationalisme et hérésie découlant du fait de la Salette, suivie de Mèmoire au pape* (Grenoble, 1854).

115. Bassette, *Le fait de La Salette*, pp. 294–396, presents a thorough review of the conflict.

116. Ibid., p. 337.

117. Ibid., p. 400. Cartellier, *Mémoire sur La Salette*, R 8666 in Bibliothèque Municipale of Grenoble, p. 163. Commenting on the episcopal defense of the miracle cult, Cartellier asked: "Is it possible to be so affirmative about something at least so doubtful? Is it possible to insist on the story of La Salette with the same ardor that one brings to the defense of Jesus Christ?"

118. Bassette, *Le fait de La Salette*, p. 401.

119. Cartellier, *Mémoire sur La Salette*, p. 87.

120. The opposition of Peyramale is discussed in Sempé, *Memoire confidentiel*. Sempé was the superior of the missionaries who staffed the grotto. A printed copy of the Mémoire was found in the Archevêché de Paris, Archives Historiques, 3, G, I, 3. For the defense of Peyramale see Lasserre, *Le miracle du 16 septembre*.

121. Bassette, *Le fait de La Salette*, p. 232; *LDA*, 3:34, 196–197.

122. Letters from Bonald to Cartellier can be found in R 8668, a collection of documents relating to La Salette at the Bibliothèque Municipale of Grenoble, nos. 49, 55.

123. Bassette, *Le fait de La Salette*, p. 243.

124. Ibid., pp. 208–213.

125. Ibid., 230–231.

126. *Deuxième lettre-circulaire de son éminence Mgr le Cardinal de Bonald, archevêque de Lyon et Vienne, addressée au clergé de son diocèse sur ses visites pastorales* (Lyons, 1852), pp. 9–10.

127. Rousselot, *Reims et La Salette.*

128. Bassette, *Le fait de La Salette,* pp. 442–446.

129. A prosecutor from Grenoble did question Mélanie and Maximin, the visionaries of La Salette, but after hearing their testimony decided to leave the issue with the Church; see Hostachy, *Histoire séculaire,* pp. 45–47.

130. Vrindts, *La croix de Migné,* pp. 225–228.

131. Garçon, *Rosette Tamisier,* pp. 39–47. M. Grave published a defense of his action in *L'Univers,* December 30, 1850.

132. *LDA,* 1:182.

133. *LDA,* 1:241–243, 288–289.

134. *LDA,* 3:60–63.

135. *LDA,* 2:252–255, 263–264.

136. *LDA,* 3:40–41, 49–53.

137. *LDA,* 2:262–263.

138. *LDA,* 2:375.

139. Appolis, "Du nouveau sur la secte Vintras"; Marcilharcy, *Le diocèse d'Orléans sous l'épiscopat de Mgr Dupanloup,* pp. 106–110.

140. Déléon, *Lettres à M. Burnoud;* idem, *Lettres à M. Jules Favre.*

141. *Jugement dans l'affaire entre Mlle de Lamerlière.* The decision was upheld by the Imperial Court of Grenoble in 1857; see Bassette, *Le fait de La Salette,* p. 315.

142. *LDA,* 2:207–212, 218–220.

143. *LDA,* 3:127–128.

144. *LDA,* 3:157–177.

145. *LDA,* 3:177, 179–181.

146. Archives Nationales, F^{19} 2374. Minister of Cults to Prefect of Hautes-Pyrénées, January 26, 1883. For the dispute over the crowning of Notre-Dame de La Salette, see Archives Nationales, F^{19} 2373, Letters from Minister of Interior to Prefect of Isère, March 20, July 1, August 4, 1879.

147. Archives Nationales, F^{19} 5562. Special attention was paid to pilgrimages by men to Rome.

148. Larkin, *Church and State,* pp. 168–169; Bonnefon, *Lourdes et ses tenanciers.* Bonnefon was a close friend of Charles Dumay, who served as Minister of Cults from 1896 until the law separating Church from State was passed in 1905.

149. Hostachy, *Histoire séculaire,* pp. 338–356.

150. Archives Nationales, F^{19} 5562.

151. Larkin, *Church and State,* pp. 199–200.

152. Archives Nationales, F^{19} 5562. Report of the Prefect of the Hautes-Pyrénées, August 26, 1902. The prefect noted that twenty thousand pilgrims were present at the grotto for the first national pilgrimage held without the support of the Assumptionist fathers.

153. Archives Nationales, F^{19} 2374.

154. Bernoville, *De Notre-Dame de Garaison,* p. 220.

155. *Annales de Notre-Dame de Lourdes*, 38 (1906):331–336.

156. Ibid., 43 (1910):7–16. It was only during the Vichy régime in 1941 that ownership of the grotto at Lourdes was transferred from the city to the Church; see Robert Paxton, *Vichy France* (New York, 1975), p. 152.

157. Archives Nationales, F¹⁹ 5562. File on Notre-Dame de Montligéon.

158. Pisani, *Il ne faut pas fermer Lourdes*, pp. 13–17; *Annales de Notre-Dame de Lourdes* 43 (1910):14–15.

159. A poster opposing the separation of Church and State is on file in Archives Nationales, F¹⁹ 5637. The poster, which originated in the diocese of Laval where the shrine of Notre-Dame de Pontmain was situated, predicted massive unemployment, especially in the construction industry, and those trades which served religious establishments. Archives Nationales, F¹⁹ 2373, documents 81–89, treat the attempt to close down the shrine at La Salette, and the economic objections raised by Corps. In 1888 the mayor of Puy filed a protest against the prohibition of processions to the shrine of Notre-Dame du Puy because of their contribution "to the development of Puy's commerce and industry." See Drochon, *Histoire illustrée des pèlerinages*, p. 944.

160. Larkin, *Church and State*, p. 194.

161. Mayeur "Géographie de la résistance aux inventaires," p. 1271.

162. Pisani, *Il ne faut pas fermer Lourdes*, p. 5.

163. Laurentin, "The Persistence of Popular Piety"; Marnham, *Lourdes: A Modern Pilgrimage*.

164. Dupront, "Formes de la culture"; idem, "Tourisme et pèlerinage."

CHAPTER 7

1. Loth, *Le miracle en France*, p. 7.

2. Ibid., pp. 133–134.

3. Ibid., p. 8.

4. Brown, *The Cult of the Saints*, pp. 120–124. On the christianization of the cult of fountains in the early Middle Ages, see Audin, "Un exemple de survivance païenne."

5. Giovanni Boccaccio, *The Decameron*, first day, first tale; second day, first tale; third day, eighth tale; Goeffrey Chaucer, *Canterbury Tales*, prologue to the Pardoner's tale.

6. From "The Praise of Folly," in *The Essential Erasmus*, trans. John P. Dolan (New York, 1964), pp. 129–131.

7. Schroeder, *Canons and Decrees*, pp. 215–217.

8. Burke, *Popular Culture*; Muchembled, *Culture populaire*. Some studies that pay more attention to the resiliency of popular culture are Julia, "La réforme

post-tridentine"; Lebrun, "Le 'Traité des superstitions' "; Froeschlé-Chopard, *La religion populaire*; Christian, *Local Religion*. According to Christian (p. 181), during the seventeenth and eighteenth centuries there was "a two-way relation between local and universal religion. While the Catholic Reformation was reaffirming the subordination of the former to the latter, communities continued, as they always had, to adopt and domesticate the symbols and discourse of the Church Universal for local votive use."

9. Muchembled, *Culture populaire*, p. 266.

10. Lecanu, *Dictionnaire des prophéties*, 1:16–18.

11. Schouppe, *The Dogma of Purgatory*, p. xii.

12. Allies, *Journal in France*, p. 83.

13. Levermore, *Miracles in France*, pp. 29–30.

14. Berger, *The Sacred Canopy*, p. 107.

15. Acomb, *The French Laic Laws*; Prost, *Histoire de l'enseignement*; Ozouf, *L'école, l'église et la république*; Claudia S. Kselman, *The Modernization of Family Law: The Politics and Ideology of Family Reform in Third Republic France*," unpublished Ph.D. dissertation, University of Michigan, 1980.

16. Rémond, *L'anticléricalisme*, pp. 191–192.

17. Bierer, "Renan and his Interpreters"; Loisy, *My Duel With the Vatican*.

18. For the problems of the Church in keeping pace with urban development see Daniel, *L'équipement paroissial*. For the disruptions of religious life that resulted from the large numbers of temporary migrants see Chatelain, *Les migrants temporaires*, 2:1073–1079.

19. Claude Langlois, "La religion vécue," Mayeur, ed., *L'histoire religieuse de la France*, pp. 44–45; Latreille, "Pratique, piété, et foi populaire," pp. 283–287.

20. See, for example, Cohn, *The Pursuit of the Millennium*; Thrupp, *Millennial Dreams in Action*; Weinstein, *Savonarola and Florence*; Capp, *The Fifth Monarchy Men*; Worsley, *The Trumpet Shall Sound*. Two recent examples of the study of millennial movements in the French Revolution and the early nineteenth century are Garrett, *Respectable Folly*, and Harrison, *The Second Coming*.

21. Eugen Weber, *Peasants into Frenchmen*, especially pp. 339–356.

22. One notable exception to this is Hobsbawm, *Primitive Rebels: Studies in Archaic Forms of Social Movement in the 19th and 20th Centuries*. But Hobsbawn, as his subtitle indicates, views social movements based on prophetic expectations as intrinsically archaic, even when they are a response to the social changes that accompany modernization. While it is an important contribution to both social and religious history, then, Hobsbawm's study perpetuates the conceptual confusion that results from attempts to view historical change as a linear process in which "modernity" inevitably replaces "traditionalism."

23. Martin Gardner, "The Third Coming," *New York Review of Books* 24 (1978):21–22.

24. Geertz, *Islam Observed*, p. 67.

25. Della Cava, *Miracle at Joseiro*. For the syncretistic cult of Santeria popular among Cubans in the Miami area of the United States during the 1960s and 1970s see Juan J. Sosa, *La Santeria, the Lucumi Traditions of the Afro-Cuban Religions*, unpublished M.A. thesis, St. Vincent De Paul Seminary, Miami, 1972.

26. Ted Margadant, *French Peasants in Revolt: The Insurrection of 1851*. (Princeton: Princeton University Press, 1979), p. 220.

27. Cited in "Miracle," *Dictionnaire théologique*, vol. 10, pt. 2, col. 1799.

28. Boissarie, *Les grandes guérisons*.

29. Geertz, *Islam Observed*, p. 17.

30. Savart, "Pour une sociologie."

31. Philippe Ariès, "Culture orale et culture écrite," Plongeron and Pannet, eds., *Le christianisme populaire*, p. 235. Ariès proposes that the "new folklore" of the nineteenth century was "less pagan, inspired by a Christianity more in conformity with that of the elite." This point of view seems to me to place too great an emphasis on the ability of the elite to control popular religion. A more extreme statement of this position can be found in Crubellier, *Histoire culturelle*. I would argue that religious life in the nineteenth century was shaped as much by popular traditions as it was by Catholic orthodoxy. For the power of popular religion to shape clerical beliefs see the important study of Weinstein, *Savonarola and Florence*.

Bibliography

PRIMARY SOURCES—UNPUBLISHED

Archevêché de Paris, Archives Historiques

3, G, II, 3. File on pilgrimages to Lourdes.
I, P, 33. File on Notre-Dame des Victoires.
4, E, I, 8. Documents on "surnaturel douteux."

Archives Nationales

BB[18] 1452. File on the State's attempt to control publications about Notre-Dame de La Salette.
BB[18] 1454. Material on apparitions in southeast France in 1847.
F[19] 2373. Documents on prosecution of Mgr Fava, bishop of Grenoble, on the issue of crowning Notre-Dame de La Salette.
F[19] 2374. Information on conflict between Church and State regarding the shrine at Lourdes.
F[19] 2531. Dossier on Cardinal de Bonald, including material on his opposition to the cult of Notre-Dame de La Salette.
F[19] 5562. Reports of government officials on pilgrimages, including Notre-Dame de Montligéon, Notre-Dame de Pontmain, Notre-Dame de La Salette, and Notre-Dame de Lourdes.
F[19] 5637. File on illegal secular activities of the clergy, including their practice of medicine.
F[19] 5812. Documents on the division of the clergy of Grenoble over the cult of Notre-Dame de La Salette.

Bibliothèque Municipale de Grenoble

L'Apparition de La Salette. Étude critique sur cet événement commencée en 1905 et achevée en 1920. (R 8675) Anonymous manuscript history of the miracle written from a skeptical perspective.

Cartellier, Jean-Pierre. *Mémoire sur La Salette*. (R 8666) Manuscript history of the cult by one of its antagonists, written in 1850s and 1860s.

"Collection d'autographes de M. Chaper." (R 8668) Letters and documents dealing with the controversy surrounding the cult of Notre-Dame de La Salette.

PRIMARY SOURCES—PUBLISHED

Alacoque, Marguerite-Marie. *Vie et oeuvres de la bienheureuse Marie Alacoque*. 2d ed. 2 vols. Paray-le-Monial: Poussielgue, 1876.

Aladel, J. M. *Notice historique sur l'origine et les effets de la nouvelle médaille frappée en l'honneur de la très sainte Vierge sous le nom de Médaille Miraculeuse*. 5th ed. Paris: Société des Bons Livres, 1835.

————. *The Miraculous Medal: Its Origins, History, Circulation, Results*. Translated from the 8th French ed. Baltimore: Piet, 1880.

Allard, M. *Paradis terrestre de la fin des siècles—apparition de la sainte Vierge à deux bergers de La Salette*. Paris: Lecoffre, 1850.

Allies, Thomas William. *Journal in France in 1845 and 1848*. London: Longman, 1849.

Almanach perpetuel, pronosticatif, proverbial et gaulois. Paris, 1774.

L'ami de la religion.

L'ami du clergé.

Annales de l'archconfrérie du très saint et immaculé coeur de Marie.

Annales de Notre-Dame de Lourdes.

Apparition de la ste. Vierge à deux enfants sur une montagne de La Salette. Paris: Alcan, n.d.

Apparition de la sainte Vierge le 19 septembre sur la montagne de La Salette. Nantes: Charpentier, n.d.

Apparition de la très-sainte Vierge à deux petits bergers. Paris: Bouasse-Lebel, 1847.

Asseline, Louis. *Mary Alacoque and the Worship of the Sacred Heart of Jesus*. Translated by John R. Beard. London: Smart and Allen, n.d.

L'astrologue de la Beauce et du Perche pour 1865. Janville: Decroix, n.d.

Balzac, Honoré de. *Cousin Pons*. Translated by Herbert T. Hunt. Baltimore: Penguin, 1968. First published 1847.

————. *Old Goriot*. Translated by Marion Ayton Crawford. Baltimore: Penguin, 1971. First published 1834.

Barbaste, Dr. *Les miracles de La Salette et de Lourdes*. Paris: Vaton, 1873.

Bertrand, C. J. *Pèlerinage de Saint Hubert en Ardennes*. Namur: Doufils, 1855.

Bertrin, Georges. *Histoire critique des événements de Lourdes.* 8th ed. Paris: Lecoffre, 1906.

———. *Lourdes, a History of Its Apparitions and Cures.* Translated by Mrs. Philip Gibbs. London: Paul, Trench, Trubner, 1908.

Bérulle, J. F. B. *Vie et miracles de sainte Philomène, vierge et martyre, surnommé le thaumaturge du 19ᵉ siècle.* Translated from the 15th Italian ed. Paris: Audin, 1835.

Bez, Nicolas. *Pèlerinage à la Salette, ou examen critique de l'apparition de la sainte Vierge à deux bergers.* Lyons: Guyot, 1847.

Bliard, Félicien. *Lettres à un ami sur le secret de La Salette.* Paris: Palmé, 1873.

Bloy, Léon. *Oeuvres de Léon Bloy.* Vol. 5, *Celle qui pleure.* Paris: Mercure de France, 1970. First published 1908.

Boisnard, Abbé. *Les sanctuaires de Marie.* Paris: Douniol, 1865.

Boissarie, Dr. *Les grandes guérisons de Lourdes.* Paris: Douniol, 1900.

Bonnefon, Jean de. *Lourdes et ses tenanciers.* Paris: Michaud, 1905. This attack on Lourdes was first published as a series of articles in the popular Parisian daily, *La Petite République.*

Bordelebat, P. *Les apparitions de Notre-Dame de Lourdes et la société contemporaine.* Paris: Tequi, 1908.

Bouix, Marcel. *Apparitions de Notre-Dame de Lourdes.* Paris: Lecoffre, 1880.

Briand, Émile. *Histoire de Sainte Radegonde.* Paris: Oudin, 1898.

Brulais, Marie des. *L'écho de la sainte montagne.* Nantes: Charpentier, 1854.

———. *Suite de l'écho de la montagne.* Nantes: Charpentier, 1855.

Bulteau, Abbé. *Manuel des pèlerins à Notre-Dame de Chartres.* Chartres: Noury, 1855.

Calvat, Mélanie. *L'apparition de la très sainte Vierge sur la montagne de La Salette.* Paris and Lyons, 1904.

———. *Vie de Mélanie, berger de La Salette.* Introduction by Léon Bloy. Paris: Mercure de France, 1912.

Casablanca, L. M. *Écrin de Notre-Dame de Lourdes, comprenant les heures pieuses des pèlerins aux pieds de Marie.* Paris: Normand, 1877.

Caston, Alfred de. *Les marchands de miracles: Histoire de la superstition humaine.* Paris: Dentin, 1864.

[Chabauty, Abbé.] *Lettres sur les prophéties modernes.* Poitiers: Oudin, 1871.

———. *Les prophéties modernes vengées.* Paris and Poitiers: Oudin and Palmé, 1874.

Chamard, François. *Le linceul de Christ; étude critique et historique.* Paris: Oudin, 1902.

Chateaubriand, François de. *The Genius of Christianity.* Translated by Charles White. Baltimore: Murphy, 1857. First published 1802.

Chevalier, R. P. *Notre-Dame du Sacré-Coeur.* 2d ed. Paris: Haton, 1881.

Claudel, Paul. *Le symbolisme de La Salette.* Paris: Gallimard, 1952.

Collin de Plancy, Jacques-August-Simon. *Dictionnaire critique des reliques et des images.* 3 vols. Paris: Guien, 1821–1822.

Combe, Émile. *Le grand coup, avec sa date probable—étude sur le secret de La Salette.* Vichy: Vexenat, 1894.

Compierre, Jean de. *Texte authentique et intégral du secret de La Salette.* Paris: Vic et Arnat, 1903.

Constant, Alphonse Louis. *Eliphas Levi, visionnaire romantique.* Edited by Frank-Paul Bowman. Paris: Presses Universitaires de France, 1969.

Corbin, Abbé. *L'apparition de la sainte Vierge à la grotte de Lourdes, près Tarbes, considerée au point de vue de l'art chrétienne.* Bordeaux: Dupuy, 1862.

Le Correspondant.

Credo, Marius. *Les premiers témoins de l'apparition de Notre-Dame de La Salette. Extraits des auteurs contemporains.* Ribemont-sur-l'Ancre (Somme): Douchet, 1904.

———. *Considérations sur le project de la loi et de la séparation de l'église et l'état.* Méricourt: Henri Douchet, 1905.

La Croix.

Croix miraculeuse apparue à Migné, près Poitiers, le 17 décembre 1826. Paris: La Bibliothèque Catholique, 1827.

Curicque, Abbé. *Voix prophétiques.* 5th ed. 2 vols. Paris: Palmé, 1872.

Daudel, Jules. *Satan et deux bergers des Alpes.* Paris: Richard, 1847.

Déléon, Joseph. *Lettres à M. Jules Favre.* Grenoble: E. Blanc, 1857.

Déléon, Joseph, and Jacques Cartellier. *La Salette devant le pape, ou rationalisme et hérésie découlant au fait de La Salette, suivie de Mémoire au pape, par plusieurs membres du clergé diocésain.* Grenoble: Redon, 1854.

Desgenettes, Charles Dufriche. *Manuel de l'instruction et de prière à l'usage de l'archconfrérie du très-saint et immaculé coeur de Marie.* 20th ed. Paris: Bray, 1867.

De Vries, Peter. *Let Me Count the Ways.* Boston: Little, Brown, 1965.

Dozous, Dr. *La grotte de Lourdes, sa fontaine, ses guérisons.* Paris: Chance, 1874.

Drochon, Jean-Emmanuel. *Histoire illustrée des pèlerinages français de la très sainte Vierge.* Paris: Plon, 1890.

Drumont, Édouard. *La France juive.* 2 vols. Paris: Flammarion, 1887.

Duchaine, Abbé. *Nouvelle relation de l'apparition miraculeuse de la sainte Vierge.* Paris: Dopter, n.d.

Dujardin, Henri. *L'oracle pour 1840 et les années suivantes.* Paris: Belacour, 1840.

Dumax, Victor. *Un triple prodige du à l'intervention de la très-saint et immaculé coeur de Marie.* Paris: Haton, 1883.

Dupanloup, Felix. "Lettre sur les prophéties publiées dans ces derniers temps." *Le Correspondant,* March 25, 1874, pp. 1097–1121.

Emmerich, Anne-Catherine. *La douloureuse passion de N.-S. Jésus Christ, d'après les méditations d'Anne-Catherine Emmerich.* Paris: Debécourt, 1835.

———. *Vie de la très-sainte Vierge.* Translated by E. de Cazalles. Paris: Sagnier et Bray, 1854.

Estrade, Jean-Baptiste. *The Apparitions of the Blessed Virgin Mary at the Grotto of Lourdes: An Eyewitness Account.* Translated by J. H. Girdlestone. Westminster: Art and Book, 1912.

Firminhac, Jean-Jacques. *Poésies catholiques.* Bordeaux: Chayne, 1873.

Flaubert, Gustave. *Madame Bovary.* Paris: Conrad, 1921. First published 1857.

———. *The Sentimental Education.* Translated by Perdita Burlingame. New York: Signet, 1972. First published, 1869.

Fourcade, Abbé. *L'apparition à la grotte de Lourdes.* Tarbes: Fouga, 1862.

La France Chrétienne. Bound set of clippings from 1903–1905 at Marian Library, University of Dayton.

Frayssinous, Denis. *Oeuvres complètes de Denis Frayssinous, évêque d'Hermopolis.* Paris: Migne, 1856.

Gallet, Amédée. *Pèlerinages à Tours et à Poitiers. Lettres à un vicaire Vendéen.* Nantes: Forest et Grimaud, 1865.

Gaume, Jean-Joseph. *L'eau bénite au dix-neuvième siècle.* 3rd ed. Paris: Gaume et Duprey, 1866.

———. *Un signe des temps, ou quatre-vingts miracles de Lourdes.* Paris: Gaume, 1878.

Girard, C. R. *Les secrets de La Salette.* Grenoble: Allier, 1871.

———. *Complément du livre: les secrets de La Salette.* Grenoble: Allier, 1872.

———. *Vérité et réalisation des prédictions et des secrets de La Salette.* Grenoble: Allier, 1872.

Girard, Jules. *Les mystères de Lourdes: Miracles dévoilés.* 2d ed. Bordeaux: Lacornée, 1874.

Girault, François. *Mlle Le Normand, sa biographie, ses prédictions.* Paris: Breateau et Pichery, 1843.

Görres, Joseph von. *La mystique divine, naturelle, et diabolique.* 3 vols. Translated by Charles Sainte-Foi. Paris: Poussielgue, 1854.

Grignon de Montfort, Louis Marie de. *Oeuvres complètes.* Paris: Editions du Seuil, 1966.

Guérin, Louis. *La vision de la jeune fille de Lourdes.* Paris: Poullet, 1858.

Hamon, André. *Notre-Dame de France.* 7 vols. Paris: Plon, 1861–1866.

Histoire et miracles de Notre Dame de Lourdes. Toulouse: St.-Cyprien, 1877.

Holzhauser, Abbé. *La véritable prophétie du vénérable Holzahuser.* Abbé Viguier, ed. Paris. Crapart, 1816.

Huxley, Aldous. *After Many a Summer Dies the Swan*. London: Chatto and Windus 1939.

Huysmans, Joris Karl. *Les foules de Lourdes*. Paris: Plon, 1958. First published 1906.

Imbert-Goubeyre, Antoine. *Les stigmatisées*. 2d ed. 2 vols. Paris: Palmé, 1873.

Jean-Marie. *Histoire authentique des secrets de La Salette*. Gros-Theuil (Eure): Chabousset, 1905.

Jourdan, Dr. *L'eau de La Salette et le rationalisme*. Paris: Castermann, 1858.

Journal Officiel de la République Française. 25 juillet 1873: 5008–5015. Final debate and vote on the construction of Sacré-Coeur.

Jugement dans l'affaire entre Mlle de Lamerlière d'une part, MM. les abbés Déléon et Cartellier, et M. Redon, imprimeur, d'autre part. Grenoble: Redon, 1855.

La Harpe, Jean François de. *La prophétie de Cazotte*. Paris: Gavone, 1927. First published during the Restoration.

Lambert, Abbé. *Puissance de la croix: Discours prononcé à Migné le jour anniversaire de l'apparition de la Croix*. Poitiers: Barbier, 1827.

Lasserre, Henri. *Notre-Dame de Lourdes*. Paris: Palmé, 1877. First published 1869. This was the most popular account of Lourdes, going through 150 editions by 1908.

———. *Le miracle du 16 septembre 1877*. Paris: Société générale de librarie catholique, 1878.

Lataste, Marie. *Letters and Writings of Marie Lataste*. 2d ed. 3 vols. London: Burns and Oates, 1893.

Laurentin, René, ed. *Pontmain—histoire authentique*. 3 vols. Paris: Lethielleux, 1970. Vol. 3: *Documents*.

———, ed. *Catherine Labouré et la Médaille Miraculeuse*. 2 vols. Paris: Lethielleux, 1976–1979.

Laurentin, René, and Bernard Billet, eds. *Lourdes—documents authentiques*. 7 vols. Paris: Lethielleux, 1957–1962.

Lecanu, Auguste François. *Dictionnaire des prophéties et des miracles*. 2 vols. Paris: Migne, 1852–1854.

Le Normand, Mlle. *Les oracles sibyllins*. Paris: chez l'auteur, 1817.

———. *Arrêt suprême des dieux de l'Olympe*. Paris: chez l'auteur, 1833.

Leroyer, Jeanne (Soeur de la Nativité). *Vie et révélations de la Soeur de la Nativité*. 3d ed. 4 vols. Paris: Périsse, 1849.

Lettre pastorale de Mgr l'évêque de Tarbes sur la clôture de cinquantenaire des apparitions de la Vierge Immaculée de Lourdes. Lourdes: Imprimerie de la Grotte, 1909.

Levermore, Samuel. *Miracles in France*. New York: Charles Cook, 1916.

Loisy, Alfred. *My Duel With the Vatican: The Autobiography of a Catholic Mod-*

ernist. Translated by Richard Boynton, New York: Dutton, 1924; repr. ed., New York: Greenwood, 1968.

Loth, Arthur. *Le miracle en France au XIXe siècle*. Lille: Desclée, 1898.

Madrolle, Antoine. *Le grand prophète et le grand roi*. Paris: Garnier, 1851.

Maistre, Joseph Marie de. *Les soirées du Saint-Petersburg*. Paris: La Colombe, 1960. First published 1821.

Manuel de dévotion à Notre Dame de Fourvières. Lyons: Lambert-Gentot, 1855.

Marie-Antoine, R. P. *Petit trésor du pèlerin à Notre-Dame de Lourdes*. Toulouse and Paris: Privat and Palmé, 1873.

Martin, Arthur. *Le pèlerinage de Sainte Anne d'Auray*. Vannes: J. M. Galles, 1845.

Martin, Marie-Françoise-Thérèse. *The Autobiography of St. Thérèse of Lisieux*. Translated by John Beevers. New York: Image Books, 1957. First published, 1898.

Martin du Gard, Roger. *Jean Barois*. Translated by Stuart Gilbert. New York: Viking Press, 1949. First published 1913.

Mathevon, Gustave. *Les pèlerinages au XIXe siècle*. Paris: Noubel, 1873.

Médaille authentique de Notre-Dame de Lourdes, patronée et approuvée par l'évêque de Tarbes et par les RR. PP. missionnaires de Lourdes. Paris: Conin, 1870.

Le médecin des pauvres. Rouen: Surville, 1851.

Le médecin des pauvres. Troyes: Audot, 1858.

Le médecin des pauvres. Orléans: Morand, [1896].

Le mois de Notre-Dame de Lourdes. Toulouse: St. Cyprien, n.d.

Morin, A. S. *Le prêtre et le sorcier*. Paris: Armand le Chevalier, 1872.

Mun, Adrien Albert Marie. *Discours du comte Albert de Mun*. 7 vols. Paris: Poussielgue, 1888–1904.

Neuvaine à Notre-Dame de Lourdes. Toulouse: St. Cyprien, n.d.

Nicolas, Amédée. *Défense et explication du secret*. Nimes: Peladonc, 1881.

Nicolas, Auguste. *La vierge Marie et le plan divin*. Paris: Vaton, 1856.

Nortert, Abbé. *Les fêtes du couronnement de Notre-Dame de La Salette*. Grenoble: Allier, 1879.

Note sur l'existence miraculeuse de la révérende mère Emmerich. Lyons, 1820.

Notre-Dame de La Salette, relation très circonstanciée de l'apparition de la très-sainte Vierge à deux bergers sur la montagne de La Salette près Corps (Isère) le 19 septembre 1846. Grenoble: Prudhomme, n.d.

Notre-Dame de Pellevoisin. Paris: Bouasse, 1895.

Notre-Dame et deux bergers des Alpes. Paris: H. Vrayet de Surcy, n.d.

Nourry, Émile [P. Saintyves]. *Le discernement du miracle*. Paris: Nourry, 1909.

———. *La simulation du merveilleux*. Paris: Flammarion, 1912.

Office et prières de l'association établie en l'église de Notre-Dame des Victoires, en l'honneur du saint et immaculé coeur de Marie, pour la conversion des pécheurs. Paris: Bailly, 1837.

Pacifique, F. *La Salette et ses prophéties.* Bussières (Yonne): chez le curé, 1902.

Parfait, Paul. *L'arsenal de la dévotion, notes pour servir à l'histoire des superstitions.* Paris: Decaux, 1876.

————. *Le dossier des pèlerinages.* 2d ed. Paris: Alcan-Lévy, 1877.

————. *La foire aux reliques.* Paris: Dreyfus, 1879.

Pèlerinage à Fourvières et dans les sanctuaires de Marie. Lyons: Perachon, n.d.

Pèlerinage à Notre-Dame de Bon-Secours. Motifs de dévotion à Notre-Dame de Bon-Secours. Nancy: Wagner, [1862].

Pèlerinage d'Ars: Guide-indicateur pour diriger les pèlerins dans la visite. Lyons: Josserand, 1874.

Pèlerinage d'Ars et notice sur la vie de J.-M.-B. Vianney, curé d'Ars. Lyons: Mathon, 1845.

Le pèlerinage de Sainte-Anne d'Auray. 3d ed. Vannes: Galles, 1845.

Pie, Louis-Eugène. *Discours prononcé dans la solennité du six centième anniversaire de la consécration de l'église de Notre-Dame de Chartres.* Chartres: Garner, 1860.

————. *Lettre pastorale . . . à l'occasion du XXVe anniversaire de la proclamation du dogme de l'Immaculée Conception.* Poitiers, 1879.

Pisani, Ferri. *Il ne faut pas fermer Lourdes: Réponse à M. Jean de Bonnefon.* Paris: Édition de "La Défense Sociale," 1906.

Pius XII (Pope). *The Lourdes pilgrimage: Encyclical of His Holiness Pope Pius XII issued in the centenary of the apparition of the Blessed Virgin at Lourdes.* Washington, D.C.: National Catholic Welfare Conference, [1958].

Pontmain—guide du pèlerin. Laval: Goupil, n.d.

Poulain, Augustin François. *The Graces of Interior Prayer: A Treatise on Mystical Theology.* Translated from 6th French ed. by J. V. Bainvel. St. Louis: Herder, 1950. First published 1901.

Poulinier, P. A. J. *Apparition de Notre-Dame de La Salette.* Paris: Palmé, 1872.

Pratiques de piété en l'honneur de l'Immaculée Conception. Toulouse: St. Cyprien, n.d.

Prédiction pour la fin du dix-huitième siècle, tirée du Mirabilis Liber. Paris: Marielle and Lebreton, 1797.

Prophétie écrite en 540, par César, évêque d'Arles. Paris: Chaumont, 1815.

Prophétie recueillie et transmise par Jean de Vatiguerro: extraite du Liber Mirabilis. Hyacinthe Olivier-Vitalis, ed. Carpentras: Devillario-Quenin, 1814.

Proyart, Liévin Bonaventure. *Louis XVI détrôné avant d'être roi.* London, 1800.

Rapports et mandements sur la Croix apparue à Migné, près Poitiers, le 17 décembre 1826. New ed. Poitiers: Barbier, 1829.

Relation des faits miraculeux concernant la révérende mère Emmerich. Paris, 1820.

Relation très détaillée de la très-sainte Vierge à deux bergers sur la montagne de La Salette près Corps. 10th ed. Grenoble: Prudhomme, 1849.

Renan, Ernest. *The Life of Jesus.* Translated. New York: Random House, 1927. First published 1863.

———. *Souvenirs d'enfance et de jeunesse.* Paris: Nelson, 1932. First published 1883.

Retz, Pierre. *Petit manuel des pèlerins. Notre-Dame des Ermites.* Montbéliard: Hoffmann, 1889.

Ricard, Antoine. *Les pèlerinages de la France à Notre-Dame de Lourdes en 1872.* Paris: Régis-Ruffet, 1873.

Le rosier de Marie.

Rosnay, Felix de. *Petite histoire de Paray-le-Monial.* Paris: Retaux, 1900.

Roussel, Napoléon. *Les mystères de La Salette.* Paris: Marc Declaux, n.d.

Rousselot, Pierre-Joseph. *Manuel du pèlerin à Notre-Dame de La Salette.* Grenoble: Baratier, 1848.

———. *Reims et La Salette.* Namur: Doufils, 1859.

Sabatier, Paul. *À propos de la séparation des églises et de l'état.* Paris: Fischbacher, 1906.

Saint-John, Bernard. *L'épopée mariale en France au XIXᵉ siècle.* Paris: Beauchesne, 1905.

Le salut facilité aux pécheurs, par la dévotion au très-saint et immaculé coeur de Marie, dans l'Archconfrérie de Notre-Dame des Victoires. 4th ed. Angers: Launay-Gagnot, 1843.

Schouppe, F. X. *The Dogma of Purgatory Illustrated by the Lives and Legends of the Saints.* Translated from the French. Rockford, Ill.: Tan, 1973. First published in 1893.

Sempé, Père. *Mémoire confidentiel communiqué à nos seigneurs les évêques de France.* 1877.

Le six octobre à Lourdes, lettres publiées dans L'Univers. Paris: Bureau du Bulletin Catholique, 1872.

L'Univers.

Veuillot, Louis. *Oeuvres complètes.* 26 vols. Paris: Lethielleux, 1924–1932. Vol. 8: *Ça et là.* Includes Veuillot's position on miracles. Vol. 7: *Rome pendant le concile.*

Vie et miracles de Saint Jean-François Régis. Limoges: Martian Ardant, 1854.

Villecourt, Clement. *Nouveau récit de l'apparition de la sainte Vierge sur les montagnes des Alpes.* Lyons: Mathon, 1847.

La vision de la jeune fille de Lourdes, avec l'ordonnance de Mgr l'évêque de Tarbes sur le sujet. Paris: Poullet, 1858.

Vivent, Abbé. *Petit manuel du pèlerinage de Lourdes.* Paris: Chance, 1874.

La voix de Notre-Dame de Chartres.

Vrindts, Abbé. *La croix de Migné vengée de l'incrédulité et de l'apathie du siècle.* Paris: Rusand, 1829.

Vues sur le second avènement de Jésus-Christ, ou analyse de l'ouvrage de Lacunza sur cette importante matière. Paris: Eberhardt, 1818.

Werfel, Franz. *The Song of Bernadette.* Translated by Ludwig Lewisohn. New York: Viking, 1942.

Wicart, Casimir-Alexis-Joseph. *Jugement sur l'apparition qui a eu lieu à Pontmain le 17 janvier 1871.* Laval, 1872.

Zola, Émile. *Lourdes.* New York, 1897. First published 1894.

———. *The Abbé Mouret's Sin.* Translated by Alec Brown. London: Elek, 1957.

———. *Mes voyages, Lourdes—Rome.* Edited by René Ternois. Paris: Fasquelle, 1958.

SECONDARY SOURCES

Acomb, Evelyn. *The French Laic Laws, 1879–1889.* London: King, 1941.

Agulhon, Maurice. *Pénitents et franc-maçons de l'ancienne Provence: Essai sur la sociabilité méridionale.* Paris: Fayard, 1968.

———. *La république au village.* Paris: Plon, 1970.

Angot, Alphonse. *Dictonnaire historique, topographique, et biographique de la Mayenne.* Mayenne: Floch, 1962.

Appolis, Émile. "Du nouveau sur la secte Vintras: La doctrine, les adeptes." *L'éventail de l'histoire vivante: Hommage à Lucien Febvre.* Vol. 1, pp. 233–240. Paris: Colin, 1953.

———. "En marge du catholicisme contemporain: Millénaristes, cordiphores et naundoriffistes autour du 'Secret' de La Salette." *Archives de sociologie des religions* 14 (1962):101–121.

Aretin, Karl Ottmar von. *The Papacy and the Modern World.* Translated by Roland Hill. New York: McGraw-Hill, 1970.

Ariès, Philippe. *Centuries of Childhood: A Social History of Family Life.* Translated by Robert Baldick. New York: Vintage, 1962.

———. "Le XIXe siècle et la révolution des moeurs familiales." Robert Prigent, ed., *Renouveau des idées sur la famille*, pp. 111–118. Paris: Presses Universitaires de France, 1954.

Aubert, Roger. *Le Pontificat de Pie IX.* 2d ed. Paris: Bloud et Gay, 1962.

Babbit, Irving. *Rousseau and Romanticism.* New York: Meridian, 1957. First published 1919.

Barbier, Emmanuel. *Histoire du catholicisme libéral et du catholicisme social en France.* 5 vols. Bordeaux: Cadoret, 1923–1924.

Barbin, H., and J. P. Duteil. "Miracle et pèlerinage au XVIIᵉ siècle." *Revue d'histoire de l'église de France* 61 (1975):246–250.

Barkun, Michael. *Disaster and the Millennium.* New Haven, Conn.: Yale University Press, 1974.

Bassette, Louis. "Le chanoine Pierre-Joseph Rousselot et les origines du culte de Notre-Dame de La Salette." *Bulletin de l'académie Delphinale*, 6th ser. 15–17 (1944–1946):cxxii–cxxiii.

———. "Notre Dame de la Salette." *Sanctuaires et pèlerinages* 30 (1963):1–14.

———. *Le fait de La Salette.* Paris: Cerf, 1965.

Baudouy, Ernest [E. Lacoste]. *Le père François Picard, second supérieur général de la congrégation des Augustins de l'Assumption (1831–1903).* Paris: Maison de la Bonne Presse, 1932.

Baunard, Louis. *Histoire de Madame Barat, fondatrice de la Société du Sacré-Coeur de Jésus.* 2 vols. Paris: Poussielgue, 1876.

———. *Histoire du Cardinal Pie, évêque de Poitiers.* 2 vols. Poitiers: Oudin, 1886.

———. *Le général de Sonis.* 3d ed. Paris: Poussielgue, 1891.

———. *Un siècle de l'église de France: 1800–1900.* 3d ed. Paris: Poussielgue, 1902.

Beach, Vincent W. *Charles X of France: His Life and Times.* Boulder, Col.: Pruett, 1971.

Beauvoir, Simone de. *The Second Sex.* Translated by H. M. Parshley. New York: Vintage, 1953.

Bée, Michel. "La révolte des confréries de charité de l'Eure en 1842–1843." *Annales de Normandie* 24 (1974):89–115.

Beevers, John. *The Sun Her Mantle.* Westminster, Md.: Newman Press, 1953.

Bellah, Robert. *Beyond Belief: Essays on Religion in a Post-Traditional World.* New York: Harper and Row, 1976.

Belot, Victor. *Coutumes et folklores en Yvelines.* Paris: Guenegaud, 1977.

Berenson, Edward. "Populist Religion in Rural France, 1830–1848." Paper presented at a meeting of the Society for French Historical Studies, Bloomington, Ind., 1981.

Berger, Peter. *The Sacred Canopy: Elements of a Sociological Theory of Religion.* Garden City, N.Y.: Doubleday, 1969.

Bernoville, Gaetan. *Un promoteur de la renaissance catholique au XIXᵉ siècle: Emmanuel d'Alzon, 1807–1880.* Paris: Grasset, 1957.

———. *De Notre-Dame de Garaison à Notre-Dame de Lourdes, Jean-Louis Peydessus, 1807–1892.* Paris: Grasset, 1958.

Bertier de Sauvigny, Guillaume de. *The Bourbon Restoration.* Translated by Lynn Case. Philadelphia: University of Pennsylvania Press, 1966.

Béteille, Roger. *La vie quotidienne en Rouergue avant 1914.* Paris: Hachette, 1973.

Bianchi, Serge. "La déchristianisation de l'an II." *Annales historiques de la révolution française* 50 (1978):341–371.

———. "Manifestations et formes de la déchristianisation dans le district de Corbeil." *Revue d'histoire moderne et contemporaine* 26 (1979):256–281.

Le Bienheureux Pierre-Julien Eymard, 1811–1868, d'après les pièces du procès de béatification. 2 vols., Paris: St. Paul, 1928.

Bierer, Dora. "Renan and His Interpreters: A Study in French Intellectual Warfare." *Journal of Modern History* 25 (1953):375–389.

Billet, Bernard. "Le fait de Lourdes." Jean Laffon, ed., *Histoire du diocèse de Tarbes et Lourdes*, pp. 231–252. Paris: Letouzey and Ané, 1971.

Bloch, Marc. *The Royal Touch: Sacred Monarchy and Scrofula in England and France.* Translated by J. E. Anderson. London: Routledge and Kegan Paul, 1973.

Boas, George. *French Philosophies of the Romantic Period.* New York: Russell and Russell, 1964. First published 1925.

Bois, Jules. *Les petites religions de Paris.* Paris: Flammarion, 1894.

Bolle, Kees W. "Secularization as a Problem for the History of Religion." *Comparative Studies in Society and History* 12 (1970):242–257.

Bollème, Geneviève, ed. *Livre et société dans la France du XVIIIe siècle.* Paris: Mouton, 1965.

———. *Les almanachs populaires aux 17e et 18e siècles: Essai d'histoire sociale.* Paris: Mouton, 1969.

———. "Représentation religieuse et thèmes d'espérance dans la Bibliothèque Bleue." *La Società religiosa nell'età moderna*, pp. 219–244. Naples: Guida Editori, 1973.

———, ed. *La Bible bleue: anthologie d'une littérature populaire en France du XVIIIe au XIXe siècle.* Paris: Julliard, 1975.

Bossy, John. "The Counter-reformation and the People." *Past and Present* 47 (1970):51–70.

Boulard, Fernand. *Premiers itinéraires en sociologie religieuse.* Paris: Éditions Ouvrières, 1956.

———. *Premiers itinéraires en sociologie religieuse.* New ed. Paris: Éditions Ouvrières, 1966.

Bouteiller, Marcelle. *Médicine populaire d'hier et d'aujourd'hui.* Paris: Maisoneuve, 1966.

———. "Le pèlerinage de Notre-Dame de Bellevau (Charente)." *Arts et Traditions Populaires* 16 (1969):135–150.

Bouton, André. *Le Maine: Histoire économique et sociale au XIXe siècle.* Le Mans: André Bouton, 1974.

Boutry, Philippe. "Un sanctuaire et son saint au XIXe siècle—Jean-Marie-Baptiste Vianney, curé d'Ars." *Annales—économies, sociétés, civilisations* 35 (1980):353–379.

Bowman, Frank-Paul. *Le Christ romantique*. Geneva: Droz, 1973.

Brekilien, Yann. *La vie quotidienne des paysans du Bretagne au XIXe siècle*. Paris: Hachette, 1966.

Brémond, Henri. *A Literary History of Religious Thought in France from the Wars of Religion down to Our Own Times*. 3 vols. London: S.P.C.K., 1928.

Bressolette, Claude. *L'abbé Maret: Le combat d'un théologien pour une démocratie chrétienne, 1830–1851*. Paris: Beauchesne, 1977.

Brogan, D. W. *The Development of Modern France*. 2 vols. New York: Harper and Row, 1966.

Brown, Marvin L. *The Comte de Chambord: The Third Republic's Uncompromising King*. Durham, N.C.: Duke University Press, 1967.

———. "Catholic-Legitimist Militancy in the Early Years of the French Third Republic." *Catholic Historical Review* 60 (1974):233–254.

———. *Louis Veuillot: French Ultramontane Catholic Journalist and Layman, 1813–1883*. Durham, N.C.: Moore, 1977.

Brown, Peter. *The Cult of the Saints: Its Rise and Function in Latin Christianity*. Chicago: University of Chicago Press, 1981.

Brugerette, Abbé Joseph. *Le prêtre français et la société contemporaine*. 3 vols. Paris: Lethielleux, 1933–1935.

Brux, Alan. "Les pèlerinages à Bénoite-Vaux au XVIIe siècle." *Le pays Lorrain* 51 (1974):115–126.

Burke, Peter. *Popular Culture in Early Modern Europe*. New York: Harper and Row, 1978.

Butler, Edward Cuthbert. *The Vatican Council, 1869–1870*. London: Collins and Harvill, 1962. First published 1930.

Byrnes, Robert F. *Anti-Semitism in Modern France*. Vol. 1. New Brunswick, N.J.: Rutgers University Press, 1950.

Chaline, Nadine-Josette. "Le recrutement du clergé dans le diocèse de Rouen au XIXe siècle." *Revue d'histoire économique et sociale* 49 (1971):385–405.

———. "Pratique et vie religieuse au XIXe siècle." *Cahier des Annales de Normandie* 8 (1976):35–116.

Charléty, Sébastien. *Histoire du Saint-Simonisme (1825–1864)*, Paris: Hartmann, 1931.

Charlton, Donald Geoffrey. *Secular Religions in France, 1815–1870*. London: Oxford University Press, 1963.

Chastenet, Jacques. *Histoire de la troisième république*. 7 vols. Paris: Hachette, 1952–1960.

Chatelain, Abel. *Les migrants temporaires en France de 1800 à 1914*. 2 vols. Lille: Presses Universitaires de Lille, 1977.

Chaussy, Yves, ed. *L'abbaye d'Almeneches Argentan et Sainte Opportune—sa vie et son culte*. Paris: Lethielleux, 1970.

Chevullon, André. *L'enchantement Breton*. Paris: Plon, 1925.

Cholvy, Gérard. *Géographie religieuse de l'Hérault contemporain.* Paris: Presses Universitaires de France, 1968.

————. "Un saint populaire? La lente renaissance du culte de Saint Roch dans le diocèse de Montpellier durant la première moitié du XIXe siècle." *Béziers et le Biterrois,* pp. 359–367. Montpellier: Fédération historique du Languedoc et du Rousillon, 1971.

————. "Indifférence religieuse et anticléricalisme à Narbonne et en Narbonnais au XIXe siècle." *Narbonne du XVIIe au XXe siècle,* pp. 73–93. Montpellier: Fédération historique du Languedoc et du Rousillon, 1973.

————. "Le catholicisme en Rouergue aux XIXe siècles: première approche." *Études sur le Rouergue,* pp. 249–281. Fédération historique du Languedoc, Méditerranéen et du Rousillon et Fédération des sociétés académiques et savantes Languedoc, Pyrénées, Gascogne, 1974.

————. "Le catholicisme populaire en France au XIXe siecle." Bernard Plongeron and Robert Pannet, eds., *Le christianisme populaire,* pp. 199–223. Paris: Éditions du Centurion, 1976.

————. "Expression et évolution du sentiment religieux populaire dans la France au temps de la Restauration catholique (1801–1860). *La piété populaire de 1610 à nos jours: Actes du 99e congrès national des sociétés savantes, Besançon, 1974,* 1:289–320. 2 vols. Paris: Bibliothèque Nationale, 1976.

————. "Réalités de la religion populaire dans la France contemporaine." Bernard Plongeron, ed., *La religion populaire dans l'occident chrétien,* pp. 149–170. Paris: Beauchesne, 1976.

Christian, William, Jr. *Person and God in a Spanish Valley.* New York: Seminar Press, 1972.

————. "Holy People in Peasant Europe." *Comparative Studies in Society and History* 15 (1973):106–114.

————. *Local Religion in Sixteenth-Century Spain.* Princeton: Princeton University Press, 1981.

————. *Apparitions in Late Medieval and Renaissance Spain.* Princeton: Princeton University Press, 1981.

Cobb, Richard. *Les armées révolutionnaires.* 2 vols. Paris: Mouton, 1963.

————. *Paris and Its Provinces 1792–1802.* London: Oxford University Press, 1975.

Cohn, Norman. *The Pursuit of the Millennium.* 2d ed. New York: Harper and Row, 1961.

Congar, Yves. *A History of Theology.* New York: Doubleday, 1968.

Corbin, Alain. *Archaïsme et modernité en Limousin au XIXe siècle.* 2 vols. Paris: Marcel Rivière, 1975.

Cordier, Eugène. *Les légendes des Hautes-Pyrénées, suivies des lettres de deux abbés contre l'auteur et sa réplique.* 2d ed. Bagnères: Cazenave, 1878.

Cousin, Bernard. "Deux cents miracles en Provence sous Louis XIV." *Revue d'histoire de la spiritualité* 52 (1976):225–244.

———. "L'impact de la révolution française sur l'ex-voto peint." *Annales historiques de la révolution française* 52 (1980):280–293.

Cros, L.-J.-M. *Histoire de Notre-Dame de Lourdes.* 2d ed. 3 vols. Paris: Beauchesne, 1925–1926.

Crubellier, Maurice. *Histoire culturelle de la France: XIXe–XXe siècle.* Paris: Armand Colin. 1974.

Cuisenier, Jean. *French Folk Art.* New York: Kodanska, 1977.

Cuming, G. J., and Derek Baker, eds. *Popular Belief and Practice.* Cambridge: Cambridge University Press, 1972. Vol. 8: *Studies in Church History.*

Daniel, Yvan. *L'équipement paroissial d'un diocèse urbain—Paris (1802–1956).* Paris: Éditions Ouvrières, 1956.

Dansette, Adrien. *Histoire religieuse de la France contemporaine.* 2d ed. Paris: Flammarion, 1965.

Danviray, Louis-Marie. "Dupont, Léon." *Dictionnaire de spiritualité* 3:1831–1833.

Darmon, Jean-Jacques. *Le colportage de librairie en France sous le second empire.* Paris: Plon, 1972.

Darnton, Robert. *Mesmerism and the End of the Enlightenment in France.* New York: Schocken, 1970.

———. "The High Enlightenment and the Low Life of Literature in Pre-Revolutionary France." *Past and Present* 51 (1971):81–115.

Davis, Natalie. "Some Tasks and Themes in the Study of Popular Religion." Charles Trinkaus and Heiko Oberman, eds., *The Pursuit of Holiness in Late Medieval and Renaissance Europe,* pp. 307–336. Leiden: Brill, 1974.

———. *Society and Culture in Early Modern France.* Stanford: Stanford University Press, 1975.

Delahaye, Hippolyte. "Note sur la légende de la lettre du Christ tombée du ciel." *Bulletin de la classe des lettres et des sciences morales et politiques— Académie Royale de Belgique* (1899):171–213.

Della Cava, Ralph. *Miracle at Joseiro.* New York: Columbia University Press, 1970.

Delooz, Pierre. *Conditions sociologiques de la sainteté canonisée.* 2 vols. Liège: Université de Liège, 1960.

Delumeau, Jean. *Le catholicisme entre Luther et Voltaire.* Paris: Presses Universitaires de France, 1971.

———. "Ignorance religieuse et mentalité magique sous l'ancien régime." Paper presented to the annual meeting of the Society for French Historical Studies. Ottawa, March, 1972.

Deniel, Raymond. *Une image de la famille et de la société sous la Restauration.* Paris: Éditions Ouvrières, 1965.

Denis, Michel. *L'église et la république en Mayenne (1896–1906)*. Paris: Klinck-sieck, 1967.

————. *Les royalistes de la Mayenne et le monde moderne (XIXe–XXe siècles)*. Paris: Klincksieck, 1977.

Deprun, J. "Les 'noms divins' dans deux discours de Robespierre." *Annales historiques de la révolution française* 44 (1972):162–180.

Devos, Roger. "Quelques aspects de la vie religieuse dans le diocèse d'Annecy au milieu du XIXe siècle." *Cahiers d'histoire* 11 (1966):49–83.

Douglas, Mary. *Purity and Danger*. Baltimore: Johns Hopkins University Press, 1961.

Duboscq, Guy, Bernard Plongeron, and Daniel Robert, eds. *La religion populaire*. Paris: Éditions du Centre National de la Recherche Scientifique, 1979.

Dupeaux, Georges. *Aspects de l'histoire sociale et politique du Loir-et-Cher*. Paris: Mouton, 1962.

Dupront, Alphonse. "Formes de la culture des masses: de la doléance politique au pèlerinage panique (xviiie–xxe siècles)." *Niveaux de culture et groupes sociaux*, pp. 149–168. Paris: Mouton, 1966.

————. "Tourisme et pèlerinage: Réflexions de psychologie collective." *Communications, École Pratique des Hautes Études, Centre d'Études des Communications de Masse* (1967):97–121.

Durkheim, Emile. *The Elementary Forms of the Religious Life*. Translated by Joseph Ward Swain. New York: Free Press, 1965.

————. *Suicide: A Study in Sociology*. Translated by John A. Spaulding and George Simpson. New York: Free Press, 1966.

Duroselle, Jean-Baptiste. *Les débuts du catholicisme sociale en France (1822–1870)*. Paris: Presses Universitaires de France, 1951.

Ehrard, Jean, and Paul Viallaneix, eds. *Les fêtes de la révolution, Colloque de Clermont-Ferrand (juin 1974)*. Paris: Société des Études Robespierristes, 1977.

Eisenstein, Elizabeth. *The Printing Press as an Agent of Change*. 2 vols. Cambridge: Cambridge University Press, 1980.

Eliade, Mircea. *Patterns in Comparative Religion*. New York: Meridian, 1963.

Engelbert, Omer. *Catherine Labouré and the Modern Apparitions of Our Lady*. Translated by Alastair Guinan. New York: Kennedy, 1959.

Everdell, William R. "The *Rosières* Movement, 1766–1789: A Clerical Precursor of the Revolutionary Cults." *French Historical Studies* 10 (1978): 23–36.

Fabre, Daniel. "Le monde du carnaval." *Annales—économies, sociétés, civilisations* 31 (1976):394–395.

Fabre, Daniel, and Jacques Lacroix. *La vie quotidienne des paysans du Languedoc au XIXe siècle*. Paris: Hachette, 1973.

Favret-Saada, Jeanne. *Deadly Words: Witchcraft in the Bocage.* Translated by
Catherine Cullen. Cambridge: Cambridge University Press, 1980.

Ferté, Jeanne. *La vie religieuse dans les campagnes parisiennes (1622–1695).* Paris:
Vrin, 1962.

Finucane, Ronald C. *Miracles and Pilgrims: Popular Beliefs in Medieval England.*
London: Dent, 1977.

Flament, P. "Recherches sur le ministère clandestin dans le département de
l'Orne pendant la révolution." *Société historique et archéologique de l'Orne*
(1972):45–74.

Forestier, Henri. "Le culte laïcal et la crise des effectifs dans le clergé diocésain
(1801–1821)." *Annales de Bourgogne* 24 (1952):105–107; 175–177.

Foucher, Louis. *La philosophie catholique au XIXe siècle.* Paris: Vrin, 1955.

Fournée, Jean. *Enquête sur le culte populaire de Saint Martin en Normandie.*
Nogent-sur-Marne: S.P.H.A.N., 1963.

Fourrey, René. "Un village dont les cinq parties du monde savent le nom,
Ars." *Sanctuaires et Pèlerinages* 5 (1956):1–10.

———. *Le curé d'Ars authentique.* Paris: Fayard, 1964.

———. *Le curé d'Ars tel qu'il fut. L'homme et son entourage.* Paris: Fayard, 1971.

Frank, Jerome. *Persuasion and Healing: A Comparative Study of Psychotherapy.*
New York: Schocken, 1963.

Fried, Albert, and Ronald Saunders, eds. *Socialist Thought: A Documentary History.* Garden City, N.Y.: Doubleday, 1964.

Froeschlé-Chopard, M.-H. "Univers sacré et iconographie au XVIIIe siècle:
Églises et chapelles des diocèses de Vence et de Grasse." *Annales—économies, sociétés, civilisations* 31 (1976):489–519.

——— *La religion populaire en Provence orientale au XVIIIe siècle.* Preface by
Alphonse Dupront. Paris: Beauchesne, 1980.

Furet, François, and Jacques Ozouf. *Lire et écrire: l'alphabétisation des Français de
Calvin à Jules Ferry.* 2 vols. Paris: Éditions de Minuit, 1977.

Gadille, Jacques. *La pensée et l'action politique des évêques français au début de la
IIIe république.* 2 vols. Paris: Hachette, 1967.

———. "Le Jansenisme populaire. Ses prolongements au XIXe siècle: le cas du
Forez." *Aspects de la vie religieuse en Forez.* Études Foreziennes, no. 7.
St. Etienne, 1975.

Garçon, Maurice. *Vintras—hérésiarque et prophète.* Paris: Émile Nourry, 1928.

———. *Rosette Tamisier ou la miraculeuse aventure.* Paris: Cahiers de la Quinzaine, 1929.

Garrett, Clarke. *Respectable Folly: Millenarianism and the French Revolution in
France and England.* Baltimore: Johns Hopkins University Press, 1975.

Gaugain, Ferdinand. *Histoire de la révolution dans la Mayenne.* Vol. 4. Laval:
Chuillard, 1917.

Gauthier, Dominique, and Clair Le Vas. "Analyse socio-économique de quel-

ques recueils de miracles dans la Normandie du XIe au XIIe siècles."
Annales de Normandie 24 (1974):3–36.

Geary, Patrick. *Furta Sacra: Thefts of Relics in the Central Middle Ages.* Princeton: Princeton University Press, 1978.

Geertz, Clifford. *Islam Observed: Religious Development in Morocco and Indonesia.* Chicago: University of Chicago Press, 1971.

———. *The Interpretation of Cultures.* New York: Basic Books, 1973.

Germain, Elisabeth. *Parler du salut? Aux origines d'une mentalité religieuse.* Paris: Beauchesne, 1967.

Giray, Joseph. *Les miracles de La Salette: Étude historique et critique.* 2 vols. Grenoble: St. Bruno, 1921.

Godel, Jean. *La réconstruction concordataire dans le diocèse de Grenoble après la révolution, 1802–1809.* Grenoble: chez l'auteur, 1968.

Goguel, François. *La politique des partis sous la troisième république.* Paris: Seuil, 1946.

Gosselin, Louis Léon Théodore [Lenôtre, Georges]. *Martin le visionnaire, 1816–1834.* Paris: Perrin, 1925.

Graef, Hilda. *Mary, A History of Doctrine and Devotion.* 2 vols. New York: Sheed and Ward, 1965.

Grand-Carteret, John. *Les almanachs français: Bibliographie, iconographie.* Paris: Alisié, 1896.

Greeley, Andrew M. *The Persistence of Religion.* London: S.C.M., 1973.

Grégoire, Henri. *Histoire des sectes religieuses.* 5 vols. Paris: Boudouin, 1829.

Griffiths, Richard. *The Reactionary Revolution: The Catholic Revival in French Literature.* New York: Ungar, 1965.

Guérin, Louis. *Abbé Desgenettes.* Paris: Vrayet de Surcy, 1860.

Guignebert, Charles. *Jesus.* Translated by S. H. Booke. New York: University Books, 1956.

Guillemant, Charles. *Pierre-Louis Parisis.* 3 vols. Pas-de-Calais: Brunet, 1916–1925.

Hanotaux, Gabriel. *Contemporary France.* 4 vols. London: Constable, 1903–1905.

Hare, Augustus John Cuthbert. *Biographical sketches.* New York: Dodd, Mead, 1895.

Harrell, David Edwin, Jr. *All Things are Possible: The Healing and Charismatic Revivals of Modern America.* Bloomington, Ind.: Indiana University Press, 1975.

Harrison, J. F. C. *The Second Coming: Popular Millenarianism, 1780–1850.* New Brunswick, N.J.: Rutgers University Press, 1979.

Hatch, Nathan O. *The Sacred Cause of Liberty: Republican Thought and the Millennium in Revolutionary New England.* New Haven, Conn.: Yale University Press, 1977.

Hédouville, Marthe de. *Monseigneur de Ségur: Sa vie, son action, 1820–1881.* Paris: Nouvelles éditions latines, 1957.

Heigel, Henry. "Les apparitions de la sainte Vierge en Lorraine de langue allemande en 1800 et 1873." *Cahiers Lorraine* (1957), no. 4:68–74.

Hélias, Pierre-Jakez. *The Horse of Pride: Life in a Breton Village.* Translated by Jean Guicharnaud. New Haven, Conn.: Yale University Press, 1978.

Hilaire, Yves Marie. "La pratique religieuse en France de 1815 à 1878." *L'information historique* 25 (1963):57–69.

———. *Une chrétienté au XIXe siècle. La vie religieuse des populations du diocèse d'Arras (1840–1914).* 2 vols. Villeneuve d'Ascq: Université de Lille, 1977.

Hill, Michael. *The Religious Order: A Study of Virtuosi Religion and Its Legitimation in the Nineteenth-Century Church of England.* London: Heinemann, 1973.

Hobsbawm, Eric J. *Primitive Rebels: Studies in Archaic Forms of Social Movement in the Nineteenth and Twentieth Centuries.* New York: Norton, 1959.

Horowitz, Irving L. *Radicalism and the Revolt Against Reason: The Social Theories of Georges Sorel.* New York: Humanities Press, 1961.

Hostachy, Victor. *Histoire séculaire de La Salette.* Grenoble: Editions de la Revue "Les Alpes," 1946.

———. "Le pèlerinage dauphinois de La Salette dans les lettres français." *Bulletin de l'Académie Delphinale,* 6th ser. 15–17 (1944–1946):213–235.

Humphrey, Richard. *Georges Sorel: Prophet Without Honor.* Cambridge: Harvard University Press, 1951.

Janvier, Pierre Désiré. *Vie de M. Dupont.* 3rd ed. 2 vols. Tours: Alfred Mame, 1886.

Johnson, Christopher H. *Utopian Communism in France: Cabet and the Icarians, 1839–1851.* Ithaca, N.Y.: Cornell University Press, 1974.

Johnson, Paul E. *Psychology of Religion.* New York and Nashville: Abingdon Press, 1965.

Julia, Dominique. "La réforme post-tridentine en France d'après les procès-verbaux de visites pastorales: Ordre et résistance." *La Società religiosa nell'età moderna.* Naples: Guida Editori, 1973.

Keller, Emile. *Les congrégations religieuses en France: Leurs oeuvres et leurs services.* Paris: Poussielgue, 1880.

Kemp, Erich Waldram. *Canonization and Authority in the Western Church.* Oxford: Oxford University Press, 1948.

Knox, Ronald A. *Enthusiasm: A Chapter in the History of Religion.* New York: Oxford University Press, 1950.

Kohn, Hans. *Pan-Slavism, Its History and Ideology.* 2d ed. New York: Vintage, 1960.

Kreiser, B. Robert. "Religious Enthusiasm in Early Eighteenth-Century Paris." *Catholic Historical Review* 61 (1975):353–385.

———. *Miracles, Convulsions, and Ecclesiastical Politics in Early Eighteenth-Century Paris.* Princeton: Princeton University Press, 1978.

Ladoue, C. de. "Les écrits de Marie Lataste." *Revue de Gascogne* 19 (January 1924):69–78.

Lagrange, Abbé. *Vie de Mgr Dupanloup.* 5th ed. 3 vols. Paris: Poussielgue, 1886.

Lambert, Edmond, and Aimé Buirette. *Histoire de l'église de Notre-Dame des Victoires.* Paris: Curot, 1872.

Langer, William. *European Alliances and Alignments, 1870–1890.* 2d ed. New York: Knopf, 1966.

Langlois, Claude. "Les effectifs des congrégations féminins au XIXe siècle. De l'enquête statistique à l'histoire quantitative." *Revue d'histoire de l'église de France* 60 (1972):40–64.

———. "La conjoncture miraculeuse à la fin de la restauration: Migné, miracle oublié." *Revue d'histoire de la spiritualité* 49 (1973):227–242.

———. *Le diocèse de Vannes au XIXe siècle (1800–1830).* Rennes: Université de Haute-Bretagne, 1974.

Langlois, Claude, and Jean-Marie Mayeur. "Sur l'histoire religieuse de l'époque contemporaine." *Revue historique* 252 (1974):433–444.

Lantenari, Vittorio. *The Religions of the Oppressed.* Translated by Lisa Sergio. New York: Mentor, 1963.

Larkin, Maurice. "The Church and the French Concordat, 1891 to 1902." *English Historical Review* 81 (1966):717–739.

———. *Church and State after the Dreyfus Affair.* London: Macmillan, 1974.

Latreille, André. *L'église catholique et la révolution française.* 2 vols. Paris: Hachette, 1946.

———. *Histoire du catholicisme en France.* 3 vols. Paris: Spes, 1963. Vol. 3: *La période contemporaine.*

———. "La déchristianisation en France à l'époque moderne." *Cahiers d'histoire* 1 (1969):13–35.

———. "Pratique, piété, et foi populaire dans la France moderne au XIXe siècle." G. J. Cuming and Derek Baker, eds., *Popular Belief and Practice,* pp. 277–290. Cambridge: Cambridge University Press, 1972.

Laurentin, René. *Pontmain, histoire authentique,* 3 vols. Paris: Lethielleux, 1970. Vol. 1: *Un signe dans le ciel.*

———. "The Persistence of Popular Piety." *Concilium* 81 (1973):144–156.

Laurentin, René, Thomas Kselman, and Theodore Koehler. "Roundtable Discussion on Natural Realities and the Supernatural." *Marian Library Studies* 10 (1978):147–158.

Le Bras, Gabriel. *Études de sociologie religieuse.* 2 vols. Paris: Presses Universitaires de France, 1955–1956.

Lebrun, François. *Les hommes et la mort en Anjou aux 17ᵉ et 18ᵉ siècles.* Paris: Mouton, 1971.

———. "Le 'Traité des superstitions' de Jean-Baptise Thiers: Contribution à l'éthnographie de la France du XVIIIᵉ siècle." *Annales de Bretagne* 83 (1976):443–466.

———, ed. *Histoire des catholiques en France du XVᵉ siècle à nos jours.* Paris: Privat, 1980.

Lecanuet, Édouard. *L'église de France sous la troisième république, 1870–1878.* Paris: Poussielgue, 1910.

———. *L'église de France sous la troisième république, 1878–1894.* Paris: Alcan, 1931.

Lecocq, Ad. "Recherches sur les enseignes de pèlerinage et les chemisettes de Notre-Dame de Chartres." *Mémoires de la Société Archéologique d'Eure-et-Loir* 6 (1876):200–201.

Lecotté, Roger. *Recherches sur les cultes populaires dans l'actuel diocèse de Meaux.* Paris: La Fédération Folklorique de l'Ile-de-France, 1953.

Leff, Gordon. *Heresy in the Later Middle Ages.* 2 vols. New York: Barnes and Noble, 1967.

Leflon, Jean. *Eugene de Mazenod, Bishop of Marseille, Founder of the Oblates of Mary Immaculate.* 4 vols. Translated by Francis Flanagan. New York: Fordham Press, 1966.

Lenski, Gerhard. *The Religious Factor: A Sociological Study of Religion's Impact on Politics, Economics, and Family Life.* Rev. ed. Garden City, N.Y.: Doubleday, 1963.

Léonard, Jacques. "Women, Religion, and Medicine." Robert Forster and Orest Ranum, eds., *Medicine and Society in France,* pp. 24–47. Vol. 6, selections from the *Annales—économies, sociétés, civilisations.* Baltimore: Johns Hopkins University Press, 1980.

———. "Les guérisseurs en France au XIXᵉ siècle." *Revue d'histoire moderne et contemporaine* 27 (1980):501–516.

Lepart, Jean. "Les bouleversements de la révolution." Guy-Marie Oury, ed., *Histoire religieuse du Maine,* pp. 175–205. n.p.: Normand, 1978.

Le Roy Ladurie, Emmanuel. *Les paysans de Languedoc.* 2 vols. Paris: Mouton, 1966.

Lestra, Antoine. *Retourner le monde: Les origines des congrès eucharistiques.* Paris: Vitte, 1959.

Leuillot, Paul. *L'Alsace au début du XIXᵉ siècle.* 3 vols. Paris: S.E.V.P.E.N., 1960. Vol. 3: *Religions et culture.*

Leuret, François, and Henri Bon. *Modern Miraculous Cures*. New York: Farrar, Straus, 1957.

Lévi-Strauss, Claude. "The Effectiveness of Symbols." *Structural Anthropology*, pp. 181–201. Garden City, N.Y.: Doubleday, 1967.

Lewy, Guenter. *Religion and Revolution*. New York: Oxford University Press, 1974.

Limouzin-Lamothe, Roger. *Mgr de Quélen, archevêque de Paris*. 2 vols. Paris: Vrin, 1957.

Limouzin-Lamothe, Roger, and Jean Leflon. *Mgr Denys-August Affre, archevêque de Paris (1793–1848)*. Paris: Vrin, 1971.

Little, Lester. *Religious Poverty and the Profit Economy in Medieval Europe*. Ithaca, N.Y.: Cornell University Press, 1978.

Locke, Robert. *French Legitimists*. Princeton: Princeton University Press, 1974.

Longuet, Paul. "Une source pour l'étude de l'activité sacerdotale des prêtres réfractaires dans le Calvados: Les actes des baptêmes et des mariages clandestins." *Annales historiques de la rèvolution française* 42 (1970): 329–345.

———. "Les prêtres réfractaires à Caen pendant la révolution." *Cahier des Annales de Normandie* 3 (1976):203–232.

McDonald, Joan. *Rousseau and the French Revolution, 1762–1791*. London: Athlone Press, 1965.

Macfarlane, A. D. J. *Witchcraft in Tudor and Stuart England*. New York: Harper and Row, 1970.

McIntosh, Christopher. *Eliphas Levi and the French Occult Revival*. London: Rider, 1972.

Macklin, June. "Belief, Ritual and Healing: New England Spiritualism and Mexican-American Spiritualism Compared." Irving Zaretsky and Mark Levin, eds., *Religious Movements in Contemporary America*, pp. 383–417. Princeton: Princeton University Press, 1974.

Macklin, June, and N. Ross Cumrane. "Three American Folk Saint Movements." *Comparative Studies in Society and History* 15 (January 1973): 89–105.

McManners, John. *The French Revolution and the Church*. London: S.P.C.K., 1969.

———. *Church and State in France, 1870–1914*. New York: Harper and Row, 1973.

Mandrou, Robert. *De la culture populaire au 17ᵉ et 18ᵉ siècles*. Paris: Stock, 1968.

———. *Introduction to Modern France, 1500–1640*. Translated by R. E. Hallmark. New York: Harper and Row, 1977.

Manuel, Frank E., and Fritzie P. Manuel. *Utopian Thought in the Western World*. Cambridge: Cambridge University Press, 1979.

Marceau, Félicien. *Balzac et son monde*. Paris: Gallimard, 1971.

Marcilharcy, Christianne. *Le diocèse d'Orléans sous l'épiscopat de Mgr Dupanloup, 1849–1878: Sociologie religieuse et mentalités collectifs*. Paris: Plon, 1962.

———. *Le diocèse d'Orléans au milieu du XIXᵉ siècle*. Paris: Sirey, 1964.

Marnham, Patrick. *Lourdes: A Modern Pilgrimage*. New York: Coward, McCann, and Geoghegan, 1981.

Marquiset, Alfred. *La célèbre Mlle Lenormand*. Paris: Champion, 1911.

Marrus, Michael. *The Politics of Assimilation*. Oxford: Oxford University Press, 1971.

———. "Cultures on the Move: Pilgrims and Pilgrimages in Nineteenth-Century France." *Stanford French Review* 1 (1977):205–220.

Martin, Benjamin F. *Count Albert de Mun, Paladin of the Third Republic*. Chapel Hill, N.C.: University of North Carolina Press, 1978.

Mather, Judson Irving. *La Croix and the Assumptionist Response to Secularization in France*. Ph.D. dissertation, University of Michigan, 1971.

Mathiez, Albert. *Contributions à l'histoire religeuse de la révolution française*. Paris: Alcan, 1907.

———. *La théophilanthropie et le culte décadaire*. Geneva: Slatkine-Megariotis Reprints, 1975. First published 1903.

Maurain, Jean. *La politique ecclésiastique du second empire*. Paris: Alcan, 1930.

May, Anita Rasi. "The Falloux Law, the Catholic Press, and the Bishops: Crisis of Authority in the French Church." *French Historical Studies* 8 (1973):77–94.

———. "The Fourth Estate Within the First Estate." *Societas* 4 (1974): 303–325.

Mayeur, Jean-Marie. "Géographie de la résistance aux inventaires (février–mars 1906)." *Annales—économies, sociétés, civilisations* 21 (1966): 1259–1272.

———. *La séparation de l'église et de l'état (1905)*. Paris: Julliard, 1966.

———. "Mgr Dupanloup et Louis Veuillot devant les prophéties contemporaines en 1874." *Revue d'histoire de la spiritualité* 48 (1972):193–204.

———, ed. *L'histoire religieuse de la France, 19ᵉ–20ᵉ siècle: Problèmes et méthodes*. Paris: Beauchesne, 1975.

Mellot, Jean. "Le culte de Saint Vincent en Berry depuis la fin de la période révolutionnaire," *Actes du 94ᵉ congrès national des sociétés savantes, Paris, 1960*. Paris: Bibliothèque Nationale, 1971.

Mendenhall, George. *The Tenth Generation: The Origins of the Biblical Tradition*. Baltimore: Johns Hopkins University Press, 1973.

Mentalités religieuses dans la France de l'ouest aux XIXᵉ et XXᵉ siècles. Cahier des *Annales de Normandie*, no. 8. Caen, 1976.

Mitchell, Harvey. "Resistance to the Revolution in Western France." Douglas

Johnson, ed., *French Society and the Revolution*, pp. 248–285. Cambridge: Cambridge University Press, 1976.

Monden, Louis. *Signs and Wonders: A Study of the Miraculous Element in Religion*. New York: Desclee, 1966.

Monnin, Alfred. *Le curé d'Ars*. 15th ed. 2 vols. Paris: Douniol, 1905.

Moody, Joseph. *The Church as Enemy: Anticlericalism in Nineteenth-Century French Literature*. Washington, D.C.: Corpus Books, 1968.

Muchembled, Robert. *Culture populaire et culture des élites dans la France moderne (XVᵉ–XVIIIᵉ siècles)*. Paris: Flammarion, 1978.

Neame, Alan. *The Happening at Lourdes*. New York: Simon and Schuster, 1968.

Newman, Edgar Leon. "Sounds in the Desert: The Socialist Worker Poets of the Bourgeois Monarchy, 1830–1848." *Proceedings of the Third Annual Meeting of the Western Society for French History* 3 (1975):269–299.

Nisard, Charles. *Histoire des livres populaires*. 2 vols. Paris: Dentin, 1864.

Nolen, William. *Healing: A Doctor in Search of a Miracle*. New York: Random, 1976.

Notre-Dame du Dimanche—les apparitions à Saint Bauzille-de-la-Sylve. Paris: Beauchesne, 1973.

Obelkevich, James, ed. *Religion and the People, 800–1700*. Chapel Hill, N.C.: University of North Carolina Press, 1979.

O'Connor, Edwin. *The Dogma of the Immaculate Conception: Its History and Significance*. South Bend, Ind.: University of Notre Dame Press, 1958.

Offner, Clark, and Henry Van Staelen. *Modern Japanese Religions with Special Emphasis on Their Doctrine of Healing*. Leiden: Brill, 1963.

Osgood, Samuel. *French Royalism Since 1870*. 2d ed. The Hague: Martinus Nijhoff, 1970.

Ozouf, Mona. *L'école, l'église et la république (1871–1914)*. Paris: Colin, 1963.

————. *La fête révolutionnaire, 1789–1799*. Paris: Gallimard, 1976.

Paillard, Yvan-Georges. "Fanatiques et patriotes dans le Puy-de-Dome: Histoire religieuse d'un département de 1792 à Thermidor." *Annales historiques de la révolution française* 42 (1970):294–328.

Palmer, Robert R. *Catholics and Unbelievers in Eighteenth-Century France*. Princeton: Princeton University Press, 1939.

————. *The Age of Democratic Revolution*. 2 vols. Princeton: Princeton University Press, 1958, 1964.

————. *Twelve Who Ruled*. Princeton: Princeton University Press, 1970.

Pannet, Robert. *Le catholicisme populaire*. 3rd ed. Paris: Centurion, 1974.

Partin, Malcolm. *Waldeck-Rousseau, Combes, and the Church: The Politics of Anticlericalism*. Durham, N.C.: University of North Carolina Press, 1969.

Patrick, Alison. "The Vendée Revisited: New Evidence on the Civil War." Paper presented at meeting of Society for French Historical Studies, Pittsburgh, Pennsylvania, 1979.

Paul, Harry W. "In Quest of Kerygma: Catholic Intellectual Life in Nineteenth-Century France." *American Historical Review* 125 (1969): 387–423.

———. *The Edge of Contingency.* Gainesville, Fla.: University of Florida Press, 1979.

Perouas, Louis. "La piété populaire au travail sur la mémoire d'un saint, Grignon de Montfort." *La piété populaire de 1610 à nos jours: Actes du 99ᵉ congrès national des sociétés savantes, Besançon 1974,* 1:259–272. 2 vols. Paris: Bibliothèque Nationale, 1976.

———. "L'évolution du clergé dans le pays creusois depuis 450 ans." *Revue d'histoire de l'église de France* 64 (1978):5–26.

Peter, Jean-Pierre. "Dimensions de l'affaire Dreyfus." *Annales—économies, sociétés, civilisations* 16 (1961):1141–1167.

Phayer, Michael. *Sexual Liberation and Religion in Nineteenth-Century Europe.* London: Croom Helm, 1977.

———. "Politics and Popular Religion: The Cult of the Cross in France, 1815–1840." *Journal of Social History* 11 (1978):346–365.

Phillips, Charles Stanley. *The Church in France, 1789–1848.* London: Mowbray, 1929.

———. *The Church in France, 1848–1907.* New York: Russell and Russell, 1967. First published 1936.

Pin, Émile. *Pratique religieuse et classes sociales dans une pariosse urbaine, Saint-Pothin à Lyon.* Paris: Éditions Spes, 1956.

Pirotte, Jacques. "Les images de dévotion, témoins de la mentalité d'une époque (1840–1965)." *Revue d'histoire de la spiritualité* 50 (1974):479–505.

Platelle, Henri. *Les chrétiens face au miracle: Lille au XVIIᵉ siècle.* Paris: Éditions du Cerf, 1968.

Plongeron, Bernard. *Conscience religieuse en révolution: Regards sur l'historiographie religieuse de la révolution.* Paris: Ricard, 1969.

———. *Théologie et politique au siècle des lumières (1770–1820).* Paris: Droz, 1973.

———. "Le fait religieux dans l'histoire de la révolution française." *Annales historiques de la révolution française* 47 (1975):95–133.

———. "A propos des mutations du 'populaire' pendant la révolution et l'empire." *La religion populaire dans l'occident chrétien,* pp. 129–147. Paris: Beauchesne, 1976.

Plongeron, Bernard, and Jean Godel. "Un quart de siècle d'histoire religieuse, 1945–1970." *Annales historiques de la révolution française* 44 (1972):181–203, 352–389.

Plongeron, Bernard, and Robert Pannet, eds. *Le christianisme populaire: Les dossiers de l'histoire*. Paris: Centurion, 1976.

Pognon, Edmond. *Un prêtre de toujours: Marie-Joseph Chiron (1797–1852), fondateur de Sainte-Marie de l'Assomption*. Paris: Vrin, 1969.

Poulat, Émile. "Une enquête anticléricale de pratique religieuse en Seine-et-Marne (1903)." *Archives de sociologie des religions* 3 (1968):127–148.

Poulet, Charles. *La sainteté française contemporaine*. 2 vols. Paris: Beauchesne, 1946–1952.

Praz, Mario. *The Romantic Agony*. Translated by Angus Davidson. New York: Meridian, 1965. First published 1933.

Price, Roger. "Legitimist Opposition to the Revolution of 1830 in the French Provinces." *Historical Journal* 17 (1974):755–778.

Prost, Antoine. *Histoire de l'enseignement en France, 1800–1967*. Paris: Colin, 1968.

Ramsey, Matthew. "Medical Power and Popular Medicine: Illegal Healers in Nineteenth-Century France." *Journal of Social History* 10 (1977): 560–587.

Reardon, Bernard. *Liberalism and Tradition: Aspects of Catholic Thought in Nineteenth-Century France*. Cambridge: Cambridge University Press, 1975.

Rearick, Charles. *Beyond the Enlightenment: Historians and Folklore in Nineteenth-Century France*. Bloomington, Ind.: Indiana University Press, 1974.

Reeves, Marjorie. *Joachim of Fiore and the Prophetic Future*. New York: Harper and Row, 1977.

Regnier, Henri François Joseph de. *Paray-le-Monial*. Paris: Émile-Paul, 1926.

Rémond, René. "Recherche d'une méthode d'analyse historique de la déchristianisation depuis le milieu du XIXe siècle." *Colloque d'histoire religieuse (Lyon, October, 1963)*, pp. 123–154. Grenoble: Allier, 1963.

———. *The Right Wing in France from 1815 to de Gaulle*. Translated by James M. Laux. Philadelphia: University of Pennsylvania Press, 1966.

———. *L'anticléricalisme en France de 1815 à nos jours*. Paris: Fayard, 1976.

Rivet, Auguste. "Les inventaires en Haute-Loire," *Cahiers d'histoire* 11 (1966):285–307.

———. "Des ministères laïques au XIXe siècle? Les Béates de la Haute-Loire." *Revue d'histoire de l'église de France* 64 (1978):27–38.

Robertson, Priscilla. "Home as a Nest: Middle Class Childhood in Nineteenth-Century Europe." Lloyd de Mause, ed., *The History of Childhood*, pp. 407–431. New York: Harper and Row, 1975.

Rodé, François. *Le miracle dans la controverse moderniste*. Paris: Beauchesne, 1965.

Rogé, Joseph. *Le simple prêtre*. Paris: Casterman, 1965.

Romano, Octavio Ignacio. "Charismatic Medicine, Folk Healing, and Folk Sainthood." *American Anthropologist* 67 (1965):1151–1173.

Rosa, Gabriele da. *Vescovi, popolo e magia nel sud: Ricerche di storia socio-religiosa dal XVII al XIX secolo*. Naples: Guido, 1971.

Rose, Louis. *Faith Healing*. Harmondsworth, England: Penguin, 1971.

Rumeau, Guy le. *Apocalypse Mariale: La Salette, Fatima, Kerizinen, Garabandal, San Damiano*. Paris: chez l'auteur, 1970.

Salvemini, Gaetano. *Mazzini*. Translated by I. M. Rawson. New York: Collier, 1960.

Sanson, R. "La fête de Jeanne d'Arc en 1894. Controverse et célébration." *Revue d'histoire moderne et contemporaine* 20 (1973):444–463.

Sauzet, Robert. "Pèlerinage panique et pèlerinage de dévotion: Notre-Dame de Rochefort en XVIIᵉ siècle." *Annales du Midi* 77 (1965):375–398.

Savart, Claude. "Pour une sociologie de la ferveur religieuse: L'Archconfrérie de Notre-Dame des Victoires." *Revue d'histoire ecclésiastique* 59 (1964):823–844.

———. "Cent ans après: Les apparitions mariales en France au XIXᵉ siècle—un ensemble?" *Revue d'histoire de la spiritualité* 48 (1972):205–220.

———. "À la recherche de l'art dit de Saint-Sulpice au XIXᵉ siècle." *Revue d'histoire de la spiritualité* 52 (1977):265–282.

Schmitt, Thérèse-Jean. *L'organisation ecclésiastique et la pratique religieuse dans l'archdiaconé d'Autun de 1650 à 1750*. Paris: Picard, 1957.

Schroeder, H. J. *Canons and Decrees of the Council of Trent*. St. Louis: Herder, 1941.

Schwartz, Hillel. "The End of the Beginning: Millenarian Studies, 1969–1975." *Religious Studies Review* 2 (1976):1–14.

———. *The French Prophets: The History of a Millenarian Group in Eighteenth-Century England*. Berkeley: University of California Press, 1980.

Scott, Ivan. *The Roman Question and the European Powers*. The Hague: Martinus Nijhoff, 1969.

Sébillot, Paul. *Le folklore de France*. 4 vols. Paris: Maisoneuve et Larose, 1968. First published 1907.

Sedgwick, Alexander. *The Ralliement in French Politics, 1890–1898*. Cambridge: Harvard University Press, 1965.

Sévestre, Émile. *Les problèmes religieux de la révolution et de l'empire en Normandie*. 2 vols. Paris: Picard, 1924.

Sevrin, Ernest. "La pratique des sacrements et des observances au diocèse de Chartres sous l'épiscopat de Mgr Clausel de Montals." *Revue d'histoire de l'église de France* 25 (1939):316–344.

———. "Croyances populaires et médicine supranaturelle en Eure-et-Loir au XIXᵉ siècle." *Revue d'histoire de l'eglise de France* 32 (1946):263–314.

————. Un évêque militant et gallican au XIXe siècle: Mgr Clausel de Montals, évêque de Chartres, 1769–1857. 2 vols. Paris: Vrin, 1955.

————. Les missions religieuses en France sous la restauration. 2 vols. Vol. 1, Saint Mandé: chez l'auteur, 1948. Vol. 2, Paris: Vrin, 1959.

Sewell, William H., Jr. Work and Revolution in France: The Language of Labor From the Old Regime to 1848. Cambridge: Cambridge University Press, 1980.

Shiokawa, Tetsuya. Pascal et les miracles. Paris: Nizet, 1977.

Shorter, Edward. The Making of the Modern Family. New York: Basic Books, 1975.

Shryock, Richard H. The Development of Modern Medicine. New York: Knopf, 1947.

Sigal, P. A. "Maladie, pèlerinage, et guérison au XIIe siècle—les miracles de Saint Gibrien à Reims." Annales—économies, sociétés, civilizations 24 (1969):1522–1539.

Smith, Bonnie. Ladies of the Leisure Class: The Bourgeoises of Northern France in the Nineteenth Century. Princeton: Princeton University Press, 1981.

Soboul, Albert. "Sentiment religieux et cultes populaires pendant la révolution: Saintes, patriotes et martyrs de la liberté." Archives de sociologie des religions 1 (1956):73–87.

————. Paysans, sans-culottes et Jacobins. Paris: Clavreuil, 1966.

————. La société française dans la second moitié du XVIIIe siècle. Paris: Cours à la Sorbonne, 1969.

Sorlin, Pierre. La Croix et les juifs (1880–1889), contribution à l'histoire de l'antisémitisme contemporain. Paris: Grasset, 1967.

Soulet, Jean-François. Traditions et réformes religieuses dans les Pyrénées centrales au XVIIe siècle. Paris: Marrimpouey Jeune, 1974.

————. "Aspects du culte de Saint Bernard dans les Pyrénées au XIXe siècle." Revue des Comminges Pyrénées Centrales 41 (1978):263–270.

Spencer, Philip. Politics of Belief in Nineteenth-Century France: Lacordaire, Michon, Veuillot. London: Faber and Faber, 1954.

Stannard, David. The Puritan Way of Death. New York: Oxford University Press, 1977.

Sumption, Jonathan. Pilgrimage: An Image of Medieval Religion. London: Faber and Faber, 1975.

Sussman, George. "The Glut of Doctors in Mid-nineteenth Century France." Comparative Studies in Society and History 19 (1977):287–305.

Tackett, Timothy. Priest and Parish in Eighteenth-Century France—A Social and Political Study of the Curés in a Diocese of Dauphiné. Princeton: Princeton University Press, 1977.

———. "L'histoire sociale du clergé diocésain dans la France du XVIIIᵉ siècle." *Revue d'histoire moderne et contemporaine* 26 (1979):198–234.

Tackett, Timothy, and Claude Langlois. "Ecclesiastical Structures and Clerical Geography on the Eve of the French Revolution." *French Historical Studies* 11 (1980):352–370.

———. "A l'épreuve de la révolution (1770–1830)." François Lebrun, ed., *Histoire des catholiques en France*, pp. 215–289. Paris: Privat, 1980.

Talmon, Jacob L. *Political Messianism: The Romantic Phase.* New York: Praeger, 1960.

Tantat, Pierre. "L'application de la Constitution Civile au clergé à Avallon." *Annales historiques de la révolution française* 22 (1950):221–246.

Thomas, Keith. *Religion and the Decline of Magic.* New York: Scribners, 1971.

Thrupp, Sylvia, ed. *Millennial Dreams in Action.* New York: Schocken, 1970.

Tilly, Charles. *The Vendée.* New York: Wiley, 1967.

Tilly, Charles, and Edward Shorter. *Strikes in France, 1830–1968.* Cambridge: Cambridge University Press, 1974.

Tocqueville, Alexis de. *The Old Regime and the French Revolution.* Translated by Stuart Gilbert. Garden City, N.Y.: Doubleday, 1955.

Trénard, Louis. "Aux origines de la déchristianisation: Le diocèse de Cambrai de 1830 à 1848." *Revue du Nord* (1965):399–459.

Turner, Victor. "A Ndembu Doctor in Practice." Ari Kiev, ed., *Magic, Faith, and Healing.* New York: Free Press. 1964.

———. *The Ritual Process: Structure and Anti-structure.* Chicago: Aldine, 1969.

———. *Dramas, Fields and Metaphors: Symbolic Action in Human Society.* Ithaca: Cornell University Press, 1974.

———. *Image and Pilgrimage in Christian Culture: Anthropological Perspectives.* New York: Columbia University Press, 1978.

Tuveson, Ernest. *Redeemer Nation: The Idea of America's Millennial Role.* Chicago: University of Chicago Press, 1968.

Valvekens, Jean-Baptiste. "Emmerich, Anne-Catherine." *Dictionnaire de spiritualité.* Vol. 4, pt. 2, cols. 622–628.

Van Gennep, Arnold. *Manuel de folklore français contemporain.* 4 vols. Paris: Picard, 1937–1958.

———. *The Rites of Passage.* Translated by M. B. Vizedom and G. L. Caffee. Chicago: University of Chicago Press, 1960. First published 1909.

Varagnac, André. *Civilisation traditionelle et genres de vie.* Paris: Albin Michel, 1948.

Vartier, Jean. *Sabbats, juges, et sorciers: Quatre siècles de superstition dans la France d'l'est.* Paris: Hachette, 1968.

———. *La vie quotidienne en Lorraine au XIXᵉ siècle.* Paris: Hachette, 1973.

Vecsey, George. "Mainline Churches Rediscover Healing." *New York Times,* March 21, 1979. Pp. C1, 10.

Veuillot, Eugène, and François Veuillot. *Louis Veuillot.* 4 vols. Paris: Lethielleux, 1901–1913.

Viatte, Auguste. *Les sources occultes du romantisme: Illuminisme, théosophie.* 2 vols. Paris: Champion, 1965. First published 1928.

Vidalenc, Jean. *Le départment de l'Eure sous la monarchie constitutionelle.* Paris: Marcel Rivière, 1952.

La Vierge dans l'art français. Paris, 1950.

Vigier, Philippe. *La second république dans la région alpine,* 2 vols. Paris: Presses Universitaires de France, 1963.

Vincent, Henri. *La vie quotidienne des paysans Bourguignons au temps de Lamartine.* Paris: Hachette, 1976.

Vovelle, Gaby, and Michel Vovelle. *Vision de la mort et de l'au-delà en Provence, d'après les autels des âmes du purgatoire, XVe–XXe siècles.* Paris: Colin, 1970.

Vovelle, Michel. *Piété baroque et déchristianisation en Provence au XVIIIe siècle.* Paris: Seuil, 1978.

———. *Mourir autrefois: Attitudes collectives devant la mort aux XVIIe et XVIIIe siècles.* Paris: Gallimard, 1974.

———. *Religion et révolution: La déchristianisation de l'an II.* Paris: Hachette, 1976.

Vuillaud, Paul. *La fin du monde.* Paris: Payot, 1952.

Wach, Joachim. *The Sociology of Religion.* Chicago: University of Chicago Press, 1962.

Wallace, Anthony F. C. "Revitalization Movements." *American Anthropologist* 58 (1956):264–281.

Warner, Maria. *Alone of All Her Sex: The Myth and Cult of the Virgin Mary.* New York: Wallaby, 1978.

Webb, James. *The Occult Underground.* LaSalle, Illinois: Open Court Press, 1974.

Weber, Eugen. *Satan franc-maçon.* Paris: Gallimard, 1964.

———. *Peasants into Frenchmen: The Modernization of Rural France.* Stanford: Stanford University Press, 1976.

Weber, Max. *The Sociology of Religion.* Translated by Ephraim Fischoff. Boston: Beacon Press, 1964.

Weinstein, Donald. *Savonarola and Florence: Prophecy and Patriotism in the Renaissance.* Princeton: Princeton University Press, 1970.

Williams, Raymond. *The Country and the City.* London: Chatto and Windus, 1973.

Wilson, Bryan R. "Millennialism in Comparative Perspective." *Comparative Studies in Society and History* 6 (1963):93–114.

————. *Magic and the Millennium: A Sociological Study of Religious Movements of Protest Among Tribal and Third World People.* London: Heinemann, 1973.

Wilson, Stephen. "The Anti-Semitic Riots of 1898 in France." *Historical Journal* 16 (1973):789–806.

————. "Le Monument Henry: La structure de l'antisémitisme en France, 1898–1899." *Annales—économies, sociétés, civilisations* 32 (1977):265–291.

————. "The Cult of Saints in the Churches of Central Paris. *Comparative Studies in Society and History* 22 (1980):548–575.

Worsley, Peter. *The Trumpet Shall Sound: A Study of "Cargo" Cults in Melanesia.* 2d ed. New York: Schocken, 1968.

Zeldin, Theodore, ed. *Conflicts in French Society: Anticlericalism, Education, and Morals in the Nineteenth Century.* London: Allen and Unwin, 1970.

————. *France, 1848–1945.* 2 vols. Oxford: Clarendon, 1973–1977.

Index

Agulhon, Maurice, 166
Alacoque, Margaret Mary, 62. *See also* Sacré-Coeur
Aladel, Père, 93, 153–154
Allies, Thomas William, 192–193
Almanacs, 60–61
Ami de la religion, L', 23
Ami du clergé, L', 18, 25, 28
Antichrist, 61, 70–71. *See also* Satan
Anticlericalism, 27. *See also* Church, relations with State
Anti-Masonism, 137–140
Anti-Semitism, 137–140
Apolline, Saint, 20–21, 26
Apparitions: and Franco-Prussian War, 114–118; investigation of, 142–160; of Notre-Dame de La Salette, 62–68; of Notre-Dame de Lourdes, 3, 92–93, 143–145; of Notre-Dame de Pontmain, 114–116
Archconfraternity of Our Lady of the Immaculate Conception. *See* Notre-Dame des Victoires, confraternity of
Associations, law of, 185–186
Assumptionists, 50, 121–122, 163

Balzac, Honoré de, 72, 101, 107
Barkun, Michael, 77
Beauregard, Père, 72
Beauvoir, Simone de, 100–101
Bellah, Robert, 82, 206 n. 9
Berger, Peter, 193, 206 n. 9
Bernadette Soubirous, Saint. *See* Soubirous, Bernadette
Bert, Paul, 194
Bertrin, Georges, 44, 58
Bible, 96–97, 194
Bishops, 147–160, 179–186
Bismarck, Otto von, 134
Bloy, Léon, 105
Boissarie, Dr. Prosper-Gustave, 42, 48, 58
Bollème, Geneviève, 9
Bonald, Cardinal Louis-Jacques-Maurice de, 175–178
Bonnefon, Jean de, 184
Bourbons, 62, 68–75, 121–130
Bourg, Mère du, 123
Brentano, Clemens, 85, 96
Brugerette, Abbé Joseph, 120
Brulais, Marie des, 59
Buising, apparitions at, 117
Bureau of Medical Confirmation (Lourdes), 49, 58, 197

Cabet, Étienne, 80
Calvat, Mélanie (visionary of La Salette), 63, 104, 109, 136
Cartellier, Abbé Jean-Pierre, 175–176
Catherine Labouré, Saint. *See* Labouré, Catherine
Catholic Church. *See* Church
Cazotte, Jacques, prophecy of, 71
César, Saint: prophecy of, 69
Chabauty, Abbé, 123, 128–129, 138
Chambord, Comte Henri de, 121–130
Champigny, M. F. de, 119
Charette, General Athanase, 116
Charles X, 73–74
Chesnelong, Charles, 126–127
Chevau-légers, 127, 129
Chiron, Abbé Marie-Joseph, 225 n. 42
Church: definition of, 207 n. 18; internal developments in, 67, 132; and miracle cults, 84–85, 109–110, 159–160, 172–179; and modern society, 90, 105–106, 109, 137–138, 170, 189–200; and prophecies, 61–62, 76, 121–122; relations with State, 4–5, 121, 130–140. *See also* Clergy
Clergy: as healers, 22–24, 38, 214 n. 8; and miracle cults, 44, 142–147, 160–172, 190–193; recruitment of, 146; and Revolution of 1789, 12–13. *See also* Assumptionists; Missionaries
Cobb, Richard, 16
Colportage literature, 20–22, 65–66, 151. *See also* Popular literature
Committee of Public Safety, 15
Commune of Paris, 113
Comte, Auguste, 194
Concordat of 1801, 17, 132, 173, 183–184

Confraternities, 45, 166–170, 196–197. *See also* Notre-Dame des Victoires, confraternity of
Conservatives, 135. *See also* Royalism
Constant, Alphonse, (Eliphas Levi), 80, 92
Couédon, Mlle, 138
Council of Trent, 85, 191
Counterreformation, 142, 166, 191
Cousin Pons, 72
Croix, La, 129, 136–139
Curé of Ars. *See* Vianney, Jean
Curicque, Abbé, 116, 123–124, 132

Daughters of Charity, 42, 78
Decazes, Elie, 73
Dechristianization, 6, 13
Déléon, Abbé Claude-Joseph, 175
Desgenettes, Abbé, 107, 166–170. *See also* Notre-Dame des Victoires
Dictionnaire des prophéties et miracles, 68, 192
Doctors, 38–39, 41–42, 58, 157, 197
Dozous, Dr., 157
Dreyfus Affair, 139
Drochon, Abbé Jean-Emmanuel, 28
Drumont, Édouard, 138
Dugué, Perrine, cult of, 16
Dujardin, Henri, 78
Dumax, Abbé Victor, 50, 174
Dupanloup, Mgr Felix, 122–123, 228 n. 72
Duperray, Mgr, 99
Dupont, Léon, 24, 102–103
Durkheim, Émile, 57
Dutour, M. 182–183

Eisenstein, Elizabeth, 171
Emmerich, Anne-Catherine, 85, 96, 103
Enfantin, Barthélemy-Prosper, 80
England, 55, 81, 109

Erasmus, 191
Estrade, Jean-Baptiste, 145, 156
Eucharist, 47–49, 87–88, 130
Ex-voto, 26–27, 52–53, 144

Family: and devotional life, 96–102;
  and healings, 55–56, 216 n. 41
Faute de l'Abbé Mouret, La, 225 n. 42
Feux St. Jean, 29
Firminhac, Abbé Jean-Jacques, 133,
  134
Flaubert, Gustave, 98, 101
Fountains, 26, 48–49, 146, 163
France chrétienne, La, 139
Franco-Prussian War, 113–119
Frayssinous, Mgr Denis, 73, 75
Freemasons, 134, 137–138

Ganneau, Jean-Simon, 79
Garrett, Clarke, 81
Geertz, Clifford, 197–198, 206 n. 9
Genet, Abbé, 70
Gioberti, Vincenzo, 82
Giraud, Maximin (visionary of La
  Salette), 63, 109, 142, 155
Griffiths, Richard, 5
Grignon de Montfort, Saint. *See*
  Montfort, Grignon de
Guérin, Abbé Michel, 114
Guibert, Cardinal Joseph Hippolyte,
  120, 185
Guignebert, Charles, 8

Hamon, Abbé André, 33
Harrison, J.F.C., 81
Healers, 18–19, 22–25
Healings, 40–54, 156–157, 168, 195.
  See also Doctors; Illness
Hélias, Pierre-Jakez, 3
Hilaire, Yves, 7, 28
Hobsbawm, Eric, 243 n. 22

Hohenlohe, Prince de, 23–24, 41–42,
  56–57, 143, 147
Holy Face, devotion to, 102–103
Holzhauser, Abbé, prophecy of, 70
Hulst, Mgr Maurice d', 225 n. 34
Huysmans, Joris-Karl, 105

Illness, 38–40, 44, 54–56
Immaculate Conception, 89–94, 159
Israel, 61, 71–72
Italy, 81–82

Jacomet (police commissioner of
  Lourdes), 57, 180
Jansenism, 60–61, 106, 141
Jean Vianney, Saint. *See* Vianney,
  Jean
Jesus: biographies of, 96–97; devo-
  tion to, 97–99, 102–103; Sacred
  Heart of, 62; visions of, 62, 85–88.
  See also Eucharist
Joseph, Saint, 100
July Monarchy, 28, 77–79, 180

Labouré, Catherine, 78, 91–92, 154
Labre, Saint Benoit, 106
Ladoue, Mgr, 88
La Harpe, Jean-François de, 71
Lamerlière, Mlle de, 182
Langalen, Mgr de, 118–119
Larkin, Maurice, 185
Lasserre, Henri, 107, 176
Lataste, Marie, 86–88, 91, 97–98, 110
Laurence, Mgr, 150, 153, 180–181
Le Bras, Gabriel, 6
Lebrun, François, 39
Lecanu, Abbé Auguste François, 68,
  192
Le Normand, Mlle, 72–73
Leo XIII (pope), 134–135
Leroyer, Jeanne (Soeur Nativité), 70–
  71, 86–88

Levermore, Reverend Samuel, 193
Levi, Eliphas. *See* Constant,
   Alphonse
Loisy, Alfred, 146, 194
Loth, Arthur, 189–190, 198
Louis Philippe, 77
Louis XIV, 62
Louis XVII, 73–74, 79
Louis XVIII, 73
Lourdes. *See* Notre-Dame de
   Lourdes

Macchi, Mgr, 123
Madame Bovary, 98
Maistre, Comte Joseph de, 74–75, 87
Malachie, Saint: prophecy of, 132
Mandrou, Robert, 9
Margadant, Ted, 197
Martin Thérèse, 98–99
Martin, Thomas (prophet of Gallar-
   don), 73–74
Mary: apparitions of, 3, 63–65, 78,
   80, 91–92, 114–118, 142–143, 167;
   Immaculate Conception of, 89–90,
   159; prophecies about, 90–94. *See
   also individual cults under* Notre-
   Dame
Massy, Baron, 180–181
Mathevon, Gustave, 101
Mathiez, Albert, 14
Mazenod, Mgr Eugène, 74
Mazzini, Giuseppe, 82
Médecin des pauvres, Le, 20–22
Mélin, Abbé Pierre, 142, 144
Mentalités, history of, 7, 9
Méry, Gaston, 138
Mesmerism, 75
Migné: apparition of cross at, 76; in-
   vestigation of, 142–144, 149, 151–
   152, 157–158
Millennialism, 62, 77, 81, 90–92,
   121–123, 196

Ministry of Cults, 73, 180
Ministry of Justice, 65–66, 182–183
Miraculés, 54–58
Miraculous Medal, 42, 78, 91–92,
   102, 153–154
Missionaries, 17, 32, 161
Missions, 16–17, 75–76, 145, 172
Modernism, 146, 197
Modernization, 197
Montfort, Grignon de, 90–91
Moreau, Mlle, 57
Morel, Abbé, 130
Muchembled, Robert, 191

Nancy, miraculous statue in, 117
Napoleon I, 68, 72–73, 82
Napoleon III, 131, 181–183
National Assembly (Third Republic),
   114
Nationalism, 81–83, 93, 100, 197. *See
   also* Anti-Masonism; Anti-Semitism
Nativité, Soeur, 70–71, 86–88
Naundorff, 79
Neubois, Marian apparitions in, 117
Newspapers, 150–153. *See also La
   Croix; L'Univers*
Nisard, Charles, 20
Nostradamus, 60, 70
Notre-Dame d'Avenières, shrine of,
   115
Notre-Dame de Chartres, 125, 131,
   170
Notre-Dame du Chêne, shrine of,
   52
Notre-Dame de Délivrance, shrine
   of, 116
Notre-Dame de Fourvières, shrine
   of, 40
Notre-Dame de La Salette: apparition
   of, 62–68; clerical conflict over,
   175–179; devotion to; 104–105,
   144; investigation of, 150, 152–155;

missionaries of, 161; opposition to, 65, 184

Notre-Dame de Lourdes: apparitions of, 3–4, 92–93; Church-State conflict over, 180–187; contributions to, 52–53, 166; and French nationalism, 100, 118–120; healings at, 42–44, 47–49, 51–54; and the Immaculate Conception, 92–93; influence of, 3–4, 199; investigation of, 143–144, 153, 156–159; and Notre-Dame de La Salette, 178–179; pilgrimage to, 37, 118–120, 162–165; and ultra-montanism, 134

Notre-Dame de Montligéon, 173, 186–187

Notre-Dame de Paris, 72, 75

Notre-Dame de Pellevoisin, 234 n. 6

Notre-Dame de Pitié, shrine of, 116

Notre-Dame de Pontmain: apparition of, 114–116; investigation of, 149–150; and royalism, 124

Notre-Dame du Sacré-Coeur, 33–34

Notre-Dame du Salut, 45

Notre-Dame du Séez, shrine of, 52

Notre-Dame de Verdelais, shrine of, 46

Notre-Dame des Victoires: confraternity of, 102, 166–170, 173–174, 199; devotion to, 100, 107; healings at, 50–51, 168

Novenas, 45–46

Oblates of Mary, 33, 161

Olivarius, prophecy of, 72–73

Oracle pour 1840, L', 78

Pancemont, Mgr, 13

Papacy: authority of, 89, 92–93, 132, 160–161; prophecies about, 69, 132–135

Papal territories, 121, 130–132

Paray-le-Monial, 125–126

Paris, Comte de, 127, 129

Pâris, François de, 22

Paul, Harry, 5

Paulinier, Mgr, 185

Pélerin, Le, 50

Pénitents blancs, 45, 166

Periodical literature, 169–171. *See also L'ami de la religion; L'ami du clergé*

Peyramale, Abbé, 143–144, 176–177

Philbert de Bruillard, Mgr, 150–152, 154–155, 175–178

Philomena, Saint: devotion to, 103–104

Philosophes, 70–71, 85

Pie, Mgr Louis François, 28, 89–90, 125–126, 130–131

Pilgrimages: and healings, 18–19, 26–28, 46–49; during Third Republic, 118–120, 162–165. *See also* Shrines

Pius VII (pope), 22–23, 130

Pius IX (pope), 89, 108, 132–134

Plongeron, Bernard, 15–16

Poland, 82

Pomian, Abbé, 143

Popular literature, 9–10, 19–22, 45, 65–66, 122–123, 167–171. *See also Colportage* literature; Newspapers

Porsat, Madeline, 94

Port-Maurice, Saint Léonard de: prophecy of, 91

Positivism, 160, 194

Prêcheguerre, Jean, prophecy of, 69–70

Processions, 29–30, 48–49, 118–119, 162

Prophecies: in ancien régime, 60–62; and anti-Semitism, 138–140; during July Monarchy, 77–80; about Mary, 90–94; and millennialism, 77, 92–94, 196; and nationalism,

Prophecies (*continued*)
81–83; of Notre-Dame de La Salette, 63–69, 136, 139; during Restoration, 68–75; and royalism, 68–
75, 122–123, 127–130; during
Third Republic, 116, 122–123,
136–137
Protestants, 60–61, 89

Quélen, Mgr de, 153–154, 167

Railroads, 162–163, 170, 237 n. 75
Ralliement, 129
Ratisbonne, Alphonse, 92
Real presence, 48–49, 87–88. *See also*
Eucharist
Religion, definitions of, 4–5, 206 n. 9
Rémond, René, 6, 121–122
Remy de Simony, Henri, 129
Renan, Ernest, 96–97, 194
Restoration, 68–77
Revolution: of 1789, 12–17, 68; of
1830, 73–74, 77–78; of 1848, 66–
67, 80
Romanticism, 10, 83, 98, 101–102,
107, 112, 198, 226 n. 47, 227 n. 57
Roman Question, 121, 130–135
Rosier de Marie, Le, 93–94
Rouland, Gustave, 180
Rousselot, Abbé, 150, 175
Royalism, 121–130
Rudder, Pierre de, 53
Russia, 82

Sacraments, 6, 14, 32, 62
Sacré-Coeur: church of, 128–127; de-
votion to, 62, 125–126
St. Anne d'Auray, shrine of, 33, 52
St. Hubert, shrine of, 18
St. Jean-François Régis, shrine of, 33
St. Martin of Tours, shrine of, 33

St. Radegonde, shrine of, 33
Saints, cult of, 25–26, 191, 224 n. 30.
See also Mary; Pilgrimages; Shrines
Saivet, Mgr, 128
Satan, 135–140
Savonarola, 69, 244 n. 31
Schoepfer, Mgr, 185–186
Schouppe, Fr., 192
Second Empire, 21–22, 28, 113, 130–
131
Secret, prophecy of Notre-Dame de
La Salette, 67–68, 136, 178
Secularization, 193
Seine-et-Marne, 26, 29
Separation of Church and State, law
of, 186–188
Shrines: clerical involvement with,
27–36, 164–165, 199–200; eco-
nomic significance of, 146–147,
186–187; as healing centers, 26–27;
state suspicion of, 183–188. *See also*
Pilgrimages; *individual shrines listed
under* Notre-Dame *and* Saint
Siècle, Le, 52
Socialism, 79–81, 92
Soirées de Saint-Petersburg, Les, 74–75
Sorcery, 18, 26, 39
Sorel, Georges, 81
Soubirous, Bernadette, 3–4, 24–25,
92–93, 108, 111, 143, 180, 198
Stigmata, 103
Superstitions, 18–19, 39, 191
Syllabus of Errors, 90

Tackett, Timothy, 28
Tamisier, Rosette, 180
Taxil, Leo, 137–138
Theophilanthropy, cult of, 15
Thérèse of Lisieux, Saint. *See* Martin,
Thérèse
Thiers, Adolphe, 125

Thomas, Keith, 18, 22, 55
Trégaro, Mgr, 174
Trinity, doctrine of the, 86–87, 225
 n. 34
Turner, Victor, 40–41, 46

Ultramontanism, 130–135
Ultras, 73
Union des Droites, 135
United States, 82–83
Univers, L', 89, 120, 128–129, 130,
 137, 152–153, 170

Vatican Council: First, 133; Second,
 188
Vergez, Dr., 157
Veuillot, Eugène, 137
Veuillot, Louis, 152–153, 170, 198
Vianney, Jean, 24, 50–51, 237 n. 75

Viguier, Abbé, 70
Villecourt, Mgr, 152–153
Vintras, Eugène, 25, 79, 182
Vovelle, Michel, 15
Vrai christianisme, Le, 80
Vrigné-aux-Bois, miraculous host of,
 130
Vrindts, Abbé, 76, 151–152

Wach, Joachim, 4
Wallace, Anthony, 77
Webb, James, 74, 79
Weber, Eugen, 195, 214 n. 89
Wicart, Mgr, 115–116, 149–150
Wilson, Stephen, 55–56
Witchcraft, 55–56

Zola, Émile, 36, 225 n. 42